The Archaeology Education Handbook

SOCIETY FOR AMERICAN ARCHAEOLOGY

The Society for American Archaeology (SAA) is an international organization dedicated to the research, interpretation, and protection of the archaeological heritage of the Americas. With more than 6,600 members, the society represents professional, student, and avocational archaeologists working in a variety of settings including government agencies, colleges and universities, museums, and the private sector. Since its inception in 1934, SAA has endeavored to stimulate interest and research in American archaeology; advocated and aided in the conservation of archaeological resources; encouraged public access to and appreciation of archaeology; opposed all looting of sites and the purchase and sale of looted archaeological materials; and served as a bond for those interested in the archaeology of the Americas.

Society for American Archaeology
900 Second Street NE #12
Washington, DC 20002-3557
http://www.saa.org

Society for American Archaeology books copublished with AltaMira Press:

The Archaeology Education Handbook: Sharing the Past with Kids, edited by Karolyn Smardz and Shelley J. Smith, 2000, ISBN 0–7425–0252–X (cloth), 0–7425–0253–8 (paper)

The American Archaeologist: A Profile, by Melinda A. Zeder, 1997, ISBN 0–7619–9192–1 (cloth), 0–7619–9194–8 (paper)

Native Americans and Archaeologists: Stepping Stones to Common Ground, edited by Nina Swidler, Kurt E. Dongoske, Roger Anyon, and Alan S. Downer, 1997, ISBN 0–7619–8900–5 (cloth), 0–7619–8901–3 (paper)

The Archaeology Education Handbook

Sharing the Past with Kids

■

Karolyn Smardz
Shelley J. Smith
editors

A Division of Rowman & Littlefield Publishers, Inc.
Walnut Creek ■ Lanham ■ New York ■ Oxford

Published in cooperation with the
SOCIETY FOR AMERICAN ARCHAEOLOGY

ALTAMIRA PRESS
A Division of Rowman & Littlefield Publishers, Inc.

Published in the United States of America
by AltaMira Press
A Division of Rowman & Littlefield Publishers, Inc.
1630 North Main Street, No. 367
Walnut Creek, California 94596
http://www.altamirapress.com

Rowman & Littlefield Publishers, Inc.
4720 Boston Way
Lanham, Maryland 20706

12 Hid's Copse Road
Cumnor Hill
Oxford OX2 9JJ, England

British Cataloguing in Publication Data available

Library of Congress Cataloging-in-Publication Data

The archaeology education handbook: sharing the past with kids / Karolyn Smardz, Shelley J. Smith, editors.
    p. cm.
    Includes bibliographical references and index.
    ISBN 0–7425–0252–X (cloth; alk. paper)—ISBN 0–7425–0253–8 (paperback; alk. paper)
    1. Archaeology—Study and teaching (Elementary)—United States. 2. Archaeology—Study and teaching (Secondary)—United States. I. Smardz, Karolyn. II. Smith, Shelley J. III. Title.

CC95 .A77 2000
930.1'071'273—dc21

00–021240

Printed in the United States of America

∞ ™ The paper used in this publication meets the minimum requirements of American National Standards for Information Sciences—Permanence of Paper for Printed Library Materials, ANSI Z.39.48–1984

Editorial Production: Carole M. Bernard
Cover Design: Margery Cantor

Contents

Acknowledgments

This all started with a challenge. During lunch at the 1996 Society for American Archaeology meetings in New Orleans, Louisiana, Brian Fagan and Karolyn Smardz were lamenting that practitioners of archaeology education were without guidance to help them provide quality programs and avoid making the same mistakes that pioneers in the field had. They attributed a large portion of the problem to the dearth of literature in the field. Fagan laid down the gauntlet: "Well, write a book! Don't complain about a problem if you're not going to step up and try to fix it." Smardz accepted the challenge, enlisted Shelley J. Smith, and, on Brian Fagan's recommendation, began discussing the concept of an introductory text on archaeology education with Mitch Allen of AltaMira Press. So, first we thank Brian Fagan for prompting this opportunity and for his ongoing encouragement while we pursued it.

Mitch Allen, our publisher, was remarkably patient and trusting, giving us full license to craft this book as we saw fit. We thank him for all of his support and understanding as this effort stretched well beyond the time we had predicted for its completion. We are grateful for his interest in archaeology education and for his enthusiasm, excellent guidance, and unfailing generosity in entertaining new ideas from a pair of neophyte editors.

Tobi Brimsek, executive director of the SAA, and the SAA Board of Directors were very supportive and demonstrated no small measure of faith in us by permitting the use of public education funds to underwrite the costs associated with producing this volume. We appreciate their confidence and assistance.

Ed Friedman, "Public Ed," deserves special thanks for all he has done for us personally and professionally. As chair of the SAA's Public Education Committee, he forged a family of public educators out of a very enthusiastic bunch of individuals.

Really, he gave us our start by nurturing the young field of archaeology education and by creating conditions under which it could thrive. While we were preparing this book, Ed gave inspiration and advice and just the right amount of chiding.

George Smith, National Park Service and former member of the SAA Board of Directors, assisted by garnering support for this effort. He has championed public archaeology at every opportunity. His efforts, along with those of Ed Friedman, deserve much of the credit for making archaeology education within the SAA the vibrant enterprise it is today.

An edited book is the creation of numerous individuals, and this particular volume has even more contributors than is typical for a book of this nature. We cannot say enough about our thirty-four colleagues, who generously contributed chapters and even more generously entrusted us to edit their work so that it fit our vision of what this text should be. To a person, the contributors were diligent in writing and revising chapters and cheerful in attending to details. Their knowledge and professionalism in discussing points raised along the way, and their enthusiasm for what we were creating together kept us both motivated and delighted to be in their company. We learned a lot from them, and are honored and grateful to have had the chance to work with them.

We are especially grateful to Anne Rogers, of Western Carolina University, Cullowhee, and to Elaine Davis, of Crow Canyon Archaeological Center, Cortez, Colorado. Both of these very busy women generously gave us immediate and extensive assistance when we needed their expertise to complement a few chapters. Rogers worked on our request while conducting a field trip and even contacted us from a phone booth at the beach rather than have us wait another two days until she returned to her office. Davis somehow carved time out of her jam-packed field season to help.

KC Smith of the Florida State Museum, Tallahassee, shared her gift of clear expression with us and edited the sections of this book that we wrote ourselves. After many revisions, we were no longer able to tell if what we had written even made sense. KC Smith, in her tactful and immensely efficient way, sifted through our convoluted writing, and overnight gave us back a text that was much more clear and straightforward. John Jameson was also helpful in evaluating the overall impact of the manuscript, and we thank him for his kind help and encouragment. Of course, we are fully responsible for any errors or omissions that may remain in the volume.

Working on this book has been a high point in our professional lives. We both were very fortunate to have had several people helping us make the time and space to produce it:

Karolyn: Public archaeology, by its very nature, involves enlisting the aid of an enormous number of people, so I hardly know where to begin with my personal note of thanks. But I cannot express enough gratitude to my co-editor and friend, Shelley J. Smith, who worked through holidays, the flu, conferences, and social events; shared her home and her friendship with me; and always, always, believed in this book. I thank my friend Martha Williams, who inspired me through her work with the SHA public education committee, and Brian Fagan, who encouraged, cajoled, and scolded me all through the process of producing this volume. I also want to thank my former staff of the Archaeological Resource Centre in Toronto—Peter Hamalainen, Ellen Blaubergs, Carole Stimmel, Michelle Tremblay, Rod Crocker, Greg Purmal, and the late Duncan Scherberger—from whom I learned everything that I know about public archaeology. My mother, Laura Smardz, who always *knew* that there wasn't anything that I couldn't do, helped make this book a reality. And finally, I thank Norm Frost, who somehow juggled four kids, rural living, a teaching career, a ton of community service work, my repeated absences, and taking care of a frazzled me to help make sure this book got written.

Shelley: First of all, I thank my friend Karolyn Smardz for getting me into this in the first place; I'm truly honored by her confidence in inviting me to work with her on this project. Karolyn's energy and conviction in this book never lagged, and I am deeply grateful to have shared this challenging and intellectually stimulating experience with her. I am continually grateful to my parents, Bob and Dorothy Smith, for their unwavering support for my various endeavors and for the peace and peace of mind their many days of grandchild-tending gave me. Stephen Poreda likewise assisted with extra-duty childcare. Dave McFerren offered time, wonderful meals, and encouragement and tolerated countless hours of me being effectively absent. I thank him for his patience, confidence, and caring. Alexander Poreda, my first-grader, doesn't care much about any of this, but he's my inspiration. The wonder of watching him grow and expand his awareness of the world is my primary catalyst for wanting to bring the benefits of archaeology education to his generation.

Finally, Shelley and Karolyn thank the readers of this book, because it is you who are taking the time to work with the public, and to share the past with the young people who will be its guardians in the future.

Karolyn Smardz
Singhamton, Ontario
November 1999

Shelley J. Smith
Bel Air, Maryland
November 1999

Preface

As you read this volume, you will note that one of the threads that runs through it is the role of the Society for American Archaeology's Public Education Committee (PEC). Of the thirty-four authors, twenty are, or have been, members of the PEC.

The Society for American Archaeology (SAA) is an international organization dedicated to the research, interpretation, and protection of the archaeological heritage of the Americas. With more than 6,100 members, the society represents professional, student, and avocational archaeologists working in a variety of settings including government agencies, colleges and universities, museums, and the private sector.

Since its inception in 1934, the SAA has endeavored to stimulate interest and research in American archaeology; advocated and aided in the conservation of archaeological resources; encouraged public access to and appreciation of archaeology; opposed all looting of sites and the purchase and sale of looted archaeological materials; and served as a bond among those interested in the archaeology of the Americas. (SAA Web site http://www.saa.org)

I have been asked to relate briefly the story of the formation of the PEC, describe some of its outstanding work, and outline its plans for the future. My qualifications for this task are that I was a participant in the PEC's formulation and then its chair for eight years. I am also a friend of the editors and most of the authors.

The following chapters make it clear that numerous individuals, working in relative isolation, were involved in teaching and using archaeology in the K–12 setting for many years. It was not until 1989 and the SAA's working conference, "Save the Past for the Future," that these individuals really understood that they were not alone.

The goal of the conference was to develop a strategy to combat the rampant vandalism that was destroying the nation's archaeological resources. The participants were divided into three work groups with the following foci: Identifying the Problem, Combating the Problem, and Preventing the Problem. The Preventing the Problem work group focused on the idea that educating the public was the only viable solution to the problem of site vandalism. This work group achieved three major objectives: (1) It developed a substantial list of actions items to be applied to the problem of site vandalism; (2) It unanimously decided to band together to ensure that its recommended action items were implemented by the SAA; and, probably most important (3) those individuals who had been laboring in isolation discovered they really did have colleagues and were not working alone.

That same year, a follow-up meeting to the conference was held in Minneapolis. The participants of this meeting undertook the effort of reducing the more than 100 action items from the Save the Past conference into a workable action plan to be submitted to the SAA Board of Directors. At the top of the list was the creation of a standing committee within the SAA to address public education.

The PEC was launched officially at the SAA's annual meeting in Las Vegas in 1990. The Action Plan that was approved by the board became our marching orders. About twenty people were in attendance; some had been at the Save the Past conference, others at the Minneapolis meeting. These individuals were in on the ground floor. As a group of dedicated and involved people who like to share their enthusiasm for archaeology and working with the public, meetings and face-to-face discussions were and are a very important component of this group's success.

The members of the PEC embrace introspection and evaluation of where they are and where they need to go. The PEC's first attempt at self-evaluation took place at Greeley, Colorado, in 1992. We felt it was time to look at the Action Plan of 1989 and see what was successful and should be continued, what was unsuccessful and should be eliminated, and what should be added to the Strategic Plan. It was a very important meeting, not only for the strategic planning that was accomplished, but also because it was the PEC's first experience at admitting new people to the group. We didn't do this very well, and we learned that we needed to share the excitement of what we were doing with new people. The lesson was learned well!

The SAA organized a sequel to the Save the Past conference, Save the Past II, held in Breckenridge, Colorado, in 1994. Again there were three work groups. The Public Education group focused on K–12 education and related matters. The goal of this conference was to refine the 1994 Strategic Plan without expanding its scope. The nonexpansion goal was not achieved, which resulted in the PEC having two guiding documents—the 1992 Strategic Plan and the Breckenridge Report.

The "final plan," at least for the next five years, was a revised Strategic Plan, including elements of the Breckenridge Report. This version of the Strategic Plan may be found at the SAA Web site: http://www.saa.org/Education/pecstratplan.html

What has all this energy and talent accomplished?

Numbers don't always count for much, but it is worth noting that the PEC has grown from twenty members to over seventy-five today. More than 120 SAA members have served on the PEC in the past nine years. And the PEC just keeps getting better. The energy level is amazing. Another gratifying facet of the PEC's past membership is that several of its members have resigned from the committee to run and be elected to the SAA Board of Directors, thus further serving the society and the goals of public education.

Archaeology and Public Education, the newsletter of the PEC, attained a readership of over 10,000. The last printed issue of the newsletter was produced in late 1998. Two new formats now replace the newsletter for getting the message across to our colleagues, educators and archaeologists alike. The SAA Web site's education section reports on current events, publications, opportunities in public education, and the like. A theme-based publication series presents archaeology education modules.

The PEC and its members have sponsored workshops and symposia at the SAA annual meetings for the last ten years. The concept of inviting the public into the meeting for a session specifically designed for them has been a part of SAA for nine years and has included speakers such as Brian Fagan, Jean Auel, David Hurst Thomas, and, most recently, Clive Cussler.

A major accomplishment is the partnership that is being forged between the Native American educator community and the PEC. PEC members have offered workshops at Haskell Indian University and at Western Carolina University. These workshops have been well received and more are in the offing. The idea is not to teach educators to be archaeologists, but to be comfortable enough to use archaeology as a means of teaching skills to others.

A spin-off from the PEC is the SAA Task Force on Curriculum. The task force was established as a recommendation from the workshop's Teaching Archaeology in the 21st Century. The workshop, held in Wakulla Springs, Florida, in 1998, considered reform of the archaeology curriculum taught in the college and university setting (Bender and Smith 1998). The need for the workshop was first identified by the Public Education Workgroup, Public Involvement subgroup, at the Save the Past for the Future II conference in Breckenridge, Colorado. The growing role of public education in the profession of archaeology was one of the driving forces for organizing the Wakulla Springs workshop.

Another accomplishment of the PEC was the creation of the position of Manager of Public Education in the SAA office. While this position now is funded on "soft money," a situation that we have all experienced at some time during our career, the PEC is working to have the SAA include this position as part of its annual budget.

The accomplishments listed above just scratch the surface of the work carried out by the PEC, and I am sure there is much more in store. In this volume, you will read about the work of archaeology educators and the idea of a new subfield of archaeology, "archaeology education." Nine years ago, when the PEC was founded, these terms were not even considered. Today they herald a new dimension of the archaeological profession.

The nine years during which I was directly associated with the PEC were some of most enriching ones of my career. To have had the opportunity to work with these talented, creative, energetic, and dedicated individuals was a rare treat, and I thank them all for letting me come along for the ride. I urge each of you to get involved in archaeology education, whether by joining the PEC, giving public talks, working intensively with a K–12 educator, or contributing to the SAA's Public Education Fund. Whatever level you choose, it will make a difference.

FRANCIS P. MCMANAMON ■

Foreword

Public Education
A Part of Archaeological Professionalism

That public education is an important part of American archaeology is not a new idea. More than ninety years ago, the Antiquities Act was enacted to regulate how archaeological sites were to be treated on public lands. This statute emphasized expert, systematic, careful excavation and recording as part of any archaeological investigation on public lands. In order for a permit to be issued, the applicant had to ensure that any material excavated or collected would be placed in a "public museum" and that the finds should be "accessible to the public" (43 CFR 3.17). From the very beginning of governmental efforts to protect American archaeological resources, therefore, the importance of public education and the accessibility of archaeological information was recognized as an important part of any investigation (Lee 1970; McManamon 1996). The focus on public education has not been limited to the United States. In Canada (Smardz 1997) and other parts of the world, similar linkages between archaeology and public education have been recognized (Stone and MacKenzie 1990; Stone and Molyneaux 1994; Stone 1997).

More recently, public education has been emphasized strongly, especially by public agency archaeologists and archaeological organizations like the Society for American Archaeology, the Archaeological Institute of America, the Society for Historical Archaeology, and the Archaeological Conservancy (Archaeology 1991; B. D. Smith 1993; Messenger 1994, 1995; Few et al. 1995; Society for American Archaeology 1995a; O'Brien and Cullen 1995). These efforts have focused on three general areas: (1) what we have learned about ancient and historic times using archaeological investigations; (2) the methodology and techniques of archaeology; and (3) the importance of proper stewardship of archaeological resources to ensure their preservation and appropriate uses. Contributing to public education and outreach should be standard parts of the professional activities of every archaeologist (McManamon 1998).

A great deal has been accomplished, especially during the last decade, yet much remains to be done, and most of what is underway requires continued efforts (see the articles in this volume; McManamon 1991, 1994; Jameson 1997; Lerner and Hoffman 2000). We must develop effective means of spreading accurate interpretations of the past and contemporary human behavior based on scientific archaeology. We must more persuasively show the benefits of these insights and this perspective. Education and outreach activities need to be diverse to accommodate the range of public interests and levels of knowledge about archaeology. These efforts need to be undertaken nationally, regionally, statewide, and locally.

A generation after the United States Antiquities Act was passed, Jesse L. Nusbaum, the first departmental consulting archaeologist, reported to the secretary of the interior about the challenges of preserving archaeological remains on the public domain. He included as a crucial factor improving public appreciation and understanding of archaeology.

Because of the tremendous area involved, the problem of protecting archaeological remains in the public domain is primarily that of educating the public to appreciate properly the value of scientific investigation by qualified scientific and educational institutions as contrasted with the destructive work of pothunters, curio-seekers, and vandals. In the former case, the information and the materials gained are accessible to the public through published reports and public museums, while in the latter, all benefit to the public is lost (Nusbaum 1929).

Nearly a century after the Antiquities Act was passed and seventy years after Nusbaum's report, the importance of public education and outreach has not diminished. In both the United States and abroad, the growth of population and increase in settlement density threatens many sites. In some countries, such as the United States, private ownership of land and archaeological sites along with the general lack of knowledge about archaeology and ancient history, make the need to focus substantial professional activity on public education and outreach even greater. Professional archaeologists in all domains of the discipline must ensure through their actions that the progress in outreach that has occurred during the past decade is not lost. We need to make education and outreach programs and support for them part of the regular business of professional archaeology.

A consistent and complementary set of public education and outreach programs, each aimed at different audiences throughout the country, is needed. Activities are needed nationally, as well as at the regional, state, and local levels. The topics for continued activity and attention can be generalized as: formal education, supplementary education, public access to archaeological information, and professional and graduate education for archaeologists.

This volume brings together as editors and authors some of the most committed and knowledgeable archaeologists who have been involved in efforts to include archaeological topics in the formal educational programs in elementary and high schools. The articles and commentary in this volume distill the expertise, insights, and recommendations of expert archaeological educators.

Programs involving the formal educational system have been a focus of archaeological attention during the last decade. Activity on this front has occurred nationally, in states, and locally. Nationally, efforts have been aimed at how to coordinate educational activities so that information can be efficiently shared among archaeologists and educators. At the state and local levels, activities have concentrated on developing teaching tools, such as lesson plans and material to use with particular lessons. Important efforts at the state level also have included working with state departments of education to have archaeological information incorporated formally into statewide standards for learning. At both of these levels, the focus has been on working with teachers to develop ways of including archaeological concepts and information derived from archaeological investigations in established school curricula. History and other social studies subjects have been one focus of these efforts, but math and science courses also provide opportunities for incorporating archaeological examples or information. There are some examples as well of individual precollegiate courses in archaeology offered as electives.

Why Is Public Education Important for Archaeology?

Providing a tangible, accessible return for public support of archaeology and maintaining or building public support are often put forward as the justifications for public education in archaeology. Yet, other important reasons justify these efforts. Fundamentally, the interpretation of the archaeological record for general audiences, as well as its protection, is simply too important to leave exclusively to others. The interests of some others (for example, looters and treasure hunters), after all, are completely counter to the interests of archaeologists, involving as they do the commercial exploitation of the archaeological record or its wanton destruction by other means (Herscher and McManamon 1995; Lynott and Wylie 1995). Others with interests counter to scientific archaeology include religious fundamentalists (for example, Deloria 1995), for whom knowledge of the past is provided fully by traditional beliefs uninformed by scientific study of the past. These individuals are uninterested in learning about the past using archaeological investigation, even when this is linked to the historical exploration of traditional history as recommended by Echo-Hawk (1993, 1997).

F. Sherwood Rowland, past president of the American Association for the Advancement of Science, noted the general problem of public understanding, or misunderstanding of science. "[T]he scientific community . . . [has] lost control of what gets described as science. The designation 'scientific' often is applied as a kind of public relations cover for projects whose true origin is in economic activity unable to prosper on its own merits" (1993:1575).

The results of poor understanding range from simple cases of inconsequential ignorance or misinformation to large and costly errors of judgment to widespread misunderstanding or deceit. Specific archaeological examples fitting this range of misunderstandings are easily recalled. Archaeology, in fact, may be more susceptible to public misunderstanding and misinterpretation, as examples from the Moundbuilder myth to Indiana Jones testify. These public misconceptions are sometimes harmless—the common misunderstanding that prehistoric humans and dinosaurs coexisted, for example. With some forethought and skill, the interest that nonarchaeologists have about archaeology can be used to turn such misunderstandings to good purpose, enhancing the interest and correcting the misconceptions.

More serious and potentially damaging are pseudo-archaeologists, or individuals perceived as archaeologists by an underinformed public. Eric Von Daniken, Barry Fell, and Mel Fisher come to mind in this context. Feder (1990, 1999) and S. Williams (1988, 1991) have described in detail many historic and current examples of these dangerous charlatans and their interpretations.

Also problematic is the startling lack of overt support for scientific investigations of archaeological records in recent years. This has been most noticeable in the face of claims by some Native Americans or treasure hunters for control over all or parts of archaeological sites. Contrast this with the political initiative and support for archaeology in the United States during the 1970s and 1980s, for example. Then, detailed and substantial legal protection for archaeological resources and the need for archaeological investigations as part of public undertakings were regarded as important. Legislation was sponsored and supported by representatives and senators from many parts of the country. Moss, Bennett, Domenici, Bingaman, and Udall were the most active and prominent supporters, but many others voted for archaeological preservation and protection laws. Of course, the threats to the archaeological record then were from wanton destruction in the face of federal construction projects and from rapacious looters.

The implicit or explicit political power of interpretations of the past, including those based on archaeological information, establish an importance in public interpretation beyond funding and support. Advocates of this perspective emphasize that archaeologists must explain how archaeological interpretations are constructed as much as explaining the interpretations themselves so that the informed public understand not only the past, but also its use in the present (see, for example, Leone, Potter, and Shackel 1987; Leone and Preucel 1992; Potter 1994).

Another major justification for public education programs is that actions by individuals often determine whether individual archaeological sites are preserved or destroyed. Law-abiding and conscientious citizens will not vandalize or loot sites if they can be convinced that these actions: (1) often are illegal and (2) diminish the cultural heritage left to all people. Through their own public efforts, archaeologists must be among those spreading these messages. Some people are even willing to work actively to promote site protection and preservation by helping to monitor the existing condition of archaeological sites through regular observation and reporting to preservation authorities about site condition (Davis 1990; Hoffman 1991).

Archaeological sites must be protected from other dangers. Individuals and groups of concerned citizens are among the most effective means of working to protect sites in local development schemes and land use plans. Individuals in the general public can serve as the eyes and ears of local, state, or even national officials who are responsible for archaeological preservation. Certainly, there are not enough officials or even trained archaeologists in most countries, including the United States, to serve such a widespread monitoring function, nor will there ever be. An active, informed public, supportive of archaeology and archaeological preservation, can be an invaluable source of political, volunteer, and economic backing. If archaeological sites are to be preserved for the very long term, and if archaeological administration, planning, investigations, reporting, and curation are to be supported for the long term, more and better public education must become an actively pursued and highly regarded part of the discipline of archaeology.

Archaeological Public Education in Formal Education Programs

Educators, and by extension their students, have discovered that archaeology can provide a stimulating subject matter for teaching a wide range of subjects (Rogge and Bell 1989; Selig 1989; Selig and London 1998; articles in Smith and McManamon 1991). In turn, primary and secondary school teachers have become the focus of attention for archaeologists seeking to inculcate their subject matter into formal classroom curricula and presentations. By reaching teachers, hundreds, even thousands of students can be brought into contact with archaeological information and topics (Selig 1991). Fay Metcalf, a distinguished American educator experienced and familiar with issues at the local, state, and national levels, recognizes the excitement and intrigue that archaeological approaches and information can bring to formal education. Using material culture, its spatial context, and archaeological methodology promotes complex thinking skills involving the evaluation of data, the construction of inferences, and the flexibility of interpretations (Metcalf 1992).

Specialized newsletters have created a focus on teaching archaeology and anthropology in elementary and secondary schools. Among the most useful of these publications are *Anthro Notes*, published by the Department of Anthropology, National Museum of Natural History, Smithsonian Institution. Selig and London (1998) recently collected some of the articles from this newsletter into a useful volume. Until last year, *Archaeology and Public Education*, was published by the Public Education Committee of the Society for American Archaeology (see KC Smith 1998). Many public agencies at all levels of government also have recognized the utility of this approach and have active programs with formal educational systems (see articles in Charles and Walden 1989; J. A. Williams 1989; Ellick 1991; Hawkins 1991, 1998; Butler 1992; S. J. Smith et al. 1996; Chiarulli and Hawkins 1998).

In the United States, for example, archaeology has obvious connections with history, geography, and social studies generally (Metcalf 1992; MacDonald 1995; KC Smith 1995; Lavin 1996). All American schoolchildren learn U.S. history, state history, and ancient history at least twice during a normal twelve-year exposure to elementary and secondary education. Information from archaeological investigations can address U.S. prehistory, early contact between Native Americans and European colonists, and later periods of U.S. history (MacDonald 1995).

Along with classic texts and ancient writings, archaeology is a basic source of information about ancient civilizations. Many teachers have found that incorporating archaeological information and discussions of how the investigation of material remains can illuminate aspects of history stimulates student interest. Archaeological examples also can provide intriguing introductions to topics in biology, chemistry, and physics. For example, radiocarbon dating is a natural entrée to a discussion of general atomic structure; two- and three-dimension coordinate geometry can be explored using standard archaeological horizontal and vertical recording of artifacts and features.

In other countries, archaeologists and educators have also linked their knowledge and skills for mutual benefit. Articles focusing on public education have been assembled from many archaeological and educational symposia held at national and international conferences (Stone and MacKenzie 1990; Stone and Molyneaux 1994; Jameson 1997, 2000; McManamon and Hatton 1999; Moe 1999).

The Archaeological Message in Education

There is no single archaeological message for archaeologists to aim at the public. Archaeologists should explore and discover what the public knows, thinks about, or uses from the past as part of the effort to construct interesting, useful messages (Society for American Archaeology 1999). From the perspective of critical analysis, such outreach and reflection on the modern context in which archaeology is being done is essential. Certainly, from a practical perspective in public education this also is good advice and, again, it is emphasized by others in their own work and experience from working with local media (Peters, Comer, and Kelly 1987; DeCicco 1988; Fagan 1991:19).

One of the archaeological messages in any public education effort must be of at least local interest and enticing to individuals without special archaeological training or knowledge. Local interest helps individuals draw connections between themselves and the archaeological record of their own place. Such stories might relate how people lived in an area at some point in the past, an unexpected event or an unusual kind feature, or artifact found locally. Local, community-specific topics are essential to successful public education. Yet, communication with the public also should directly or indirectly make general points related to the value of archaeological resources, the care that must be used when studying these resources, the necessary effort to curate artifacts and records following excavations, and the nonrenewable, often fragile, nature of archaeological remains (see, Stuart and McManamon 1996). General points such as these were identified as important messages to be used in educational, volunteer, and other public outreach programs designed to work over the long term on preventing archaeological looting and vandalism (Lerner 1991:103).

There are a few basic messages about archaeology for incorporation in educational programs. These might be passed along in relation to specific local resources or interpretations, or they might be included as general points. One part of the message is that interesting and useful knowledge can be learned from archaeological remains if they are studied properly. We should communicate that the proper study of archaeological remains is careful, painstaking work that includes fieldwork, lab work, report preparation and distribution, and that ultimately, it involves the curation of collections and records. We should make it clear that archaeological remains are often fragile, always nonrenewable, and ought not to be destroyed wantonly. Much of archaeological research involves consumption and destruction of the in situ archaeological record. So, messages about archaeology and archaeological interpretations need to discourage individual excursions into archaeological fieldwork by enthusiasts.

We might consider successful transmission of these general messages as the ultimate goal of public education. A public that appreciates and understands archaeology and archaeological resources would be a public that abhorred site destruction and supported archaeological activities and preservation. Only a small percentage of the public explicitly holds these beliefs at present, yet working to increase that percentage is both an important and a worthwhile goal (McManamon 1991, 1994).

These specific and general messages need effective messengers. Archaeologists and educators ought not to be alone in communicating these messages. Reporters, filmmakers, and a host of others already are enlisted in these efforts. However, archaeologists should have some role in public education, even if only as cheerleaders and supporters for those who actively take on this challenge. So says Principle No. 4: Public Education and Outreach in the "Principles of Archaeological Ethics" of the Society for American Archaeology:

> Archaeologists should reach out to, and participate in cooperative efforts with, others interested in the archaeological record with the aim of improving the preservation, protection, and interpretation of the record. In particular, archaeologists should undertake to: (1) enlist public support for the stewardship of the archaeological record; (2) explain and promote the use of archaeological methods and techniques in understanding human behavior and culture; and (3)

communicate archaeological interpretations of the past. Many publics exist for archaeology including students and teachers; Native Americans and other ethnic, religious, and cultural groups who find in the archaeological record important aspects of their cultural heritage; lawmakers and government officials; reporters, journalists, and others involved in the media; and, the general public. Archaeologists who are unable to undertake public education and outreach directly should encourage and support the efforts of others in these activities. [Society for American Archaeology 1996:452]

Public education and outreach have become a focus of professional archaeological activity during the past decade. There is a risk that these efforts might falter if the perception becomes prevalent that this heightened activity had served to overcome a "crisis" in archaeological public education and outreach. On the contrary, continued consistent and complementary public education and outreach programs are needed as an ongoing element of modern archaeological practice. Activities are needed at all organizational levels—national, state, and local. The integration of archaeological information and information about archaeological methods and techniques in formal educational settings are important parts of the overall public education and outreach effort. All archaeologists have a stake in its successful execution.

Professional archaeologists cannot afford to be uninterested in public education and outreach. They must be willing to devote their own professional activity to it or to set higher priority for it among the activities of the institutions where they work. Brian Fagan (1993) justifiably lashed out at "arrogant archaeologists" who ignore or denigrate such publicly oriented activities and their tragically myopic inattention. All those concerned must lament the contemporary mistreatment of archaeological sites and the distortion of archaeological interpretation by looters, misdirected hobbyists, some developers, and other charlatans. Yet, lamentation alone is insufficient; action is needed.

SHELLEY J. SMITH ■
KAROLYN SMARDZ

Introduction

The Archaeology Education Handbook
Sharing the Past with Kids

The last decade has seen a rapid florescence of public-oriented archaeology education in North America. Indeed, the very contours of the archaeological profession are being redefined by this movement. Increasingly, public education is part of the work that archaeologists do.

There are many reasons for the growth of archaeology education, but foremost is an acknowledgment of the crucial role that the public can play in helping to discover and conserve our fragile legacies from the past. Encouraging positive public involvement and support requires deliberate outreach efforts by professional archaeologists and others committed to the movement, and that's where educational archaeology enters the picture. This outreach mission has developed in ways that are predicated on teachers' participation in the process. The underlying assumptions are that precollegiate students are an appropriate audience for the transmission of heritage education standards and ethics, and that teachers wish to incorporate archaeology into their demanding classroom schedules and curricula.

The archaeological profession in general has been remarkably silent about how teachers are to gain access to archaeological curriculum materials. This is particularly true of materials appropriate to the age, ability, and cultural and ethnic compositions of the exceedingly varied classrooms in U.S. and Canadian educational milieus at the end of the twentieth century. On the other hand, efforts by the Society for American Archaeology, Society for Historical Archaeology, Archaeological Institute of America, and other professional organizations to provide curriculum materials aimed at educators through various media have made great strides. Some government agencies also have targeted teachers as an audience for classroom materials, workshops, teaching guides, and fieldwork opportunities. In addition, individual archaeologists have taken it upon themselves to improve access to the discipline for educators and the public at large.

Despite these efforts, a significant gap remains in the resources for designing, implementing, evaluating, and sustaining archaeology education programs for audiences from kindergarten to grade twelve (K–12). Teachers provide the primary interface with precollegiate students; to be effective, an archaeology education program must meet their pedagogical and practical needs. But to date, no scholarly source of information exists about the theoretical underpinnings, experiences, experiments, or outcomes of practicing the integration of archaeology and education. This book seeks to fill that gap.

The book was written for archaeologists preparing to engage in archaeology education and for veterans of outreach efforts who want to broaden their understanding of the profession of education and its application to archaeology education. We also hope that it will be useful to classroom teachers who wish to teach with archaeology; museum educators who want more closely to align their programs with archaeology education, land managers who are charged with conserving and interpreting cultural remains; and professors who must ensure that the next generation of heritage specialists consider outreach and education as professional responsibilities.

The book gives pragmatic guidance about the realities of successfully bringing archaeology into the classroom. It contains the basic information that archaeologists need before starting to talk to teachers and students, as well as advice about how to develop, implement, and assess effective teaching programs for various school-age audiences. In the following pages, readers will discover how teachers teach, how kids learn, what challenges exist in our modern classrooms and how to overcome them, and some of the forms that archaeology education can take.

The Archaeology Education Handbook: Sharing the Past with Kids contains the comments and observations of thirty-four veteran archaeology educators, chosen for their expertise in aspects of this instructional medium. The five parts of the book provide readers with an overview of factors affecting archaeology education in modern schools, and ways and means for approaching program development and implementation. First and foremost, public archaeology is a means for transmitting the stewardship message to the largest possible public audience, and by the most effective, accurate, and engaging means. We have assembled this book to help you to contribute in your own way to making archaeological conservation a familiar concept to the thousands of school-age children whom you likely will encounter in the course of your career.

Why Do Archaeology Education?

Virtually all professional archaeology in North America is public archaeology, funded directly or indirectly with public monies and mandated by popularly supported legislation. Archaeology has a mysterious hold on people, conjuring up notions of intrigue, romance, excitement, and discovery. Never mind that these are seldom experienced in quotidian practice; most of the public ranks archaeology as an adventurous form of recreation. This is good, in that taxpayers who support archaeological research have a keen, if occasionally misguided, interest in it. The down side is that false perceptions about the goals and contributions of archaeology may result in a reluctance to fund more mundane but necessary aspects of the work, or to weigh the costs and benefits equitably with other competing public interests. This situation is reason enough to quicken concern among archaeologists for what the public believes is valuable about the profession. In other words, we have some public education work to do.

Another compelling reason for archaeology education is that the database of cultural resources is finite and shrinking. In addition to losses from natural processes, increased recreation on public lands, development, and continued looting and illegal collecting all contribute to the attrition of the archaeological record. A conservation ethic has guided the discipline for more than two decades (Lipe 1974), and national laws and regulations (e.g., the National Historic Preservation Act in the U.S.) are designed to require careful consideration by decision makers before authorizing excavations or data recovery. The expense of fieldwork, analysis, report preparation, and curation of artifacts and records has a braking effect on the rate of legal site consumption. Consider the irony that archaeologists are among the last to see North America's cultural sites as they disappear in the face of bulldozers, off-road recreational vehicles, and looters' probes. Many people in our society clearly do not understand the necessity of conserving sites, and sites are therefore extremely vulnerable. The only hope for their preservation is a populace that is educated about the value of the archaeological record and that has an ethic of site conservation.

The adult public needs a basic comprehension of the nature of archaeological data and research contributions so that they can take thoughtful actions regarding the archaeological record. These actions include voting on zoning and municipal laws that protect archaeological sites; sitting on juries that hear prosecutions of statute violations; making charitable contributions; supporting museum curation and exhibits; encountering sites or looters unexpectedly; and accessing knowledge about people of the past who resided in the very places that we live today. The lay public does not, however, need to be expert in archaeology to achieve this level of ethical understanding, just as they do not need in-depth expertise in ecology to fathom the effects of overgrazing or toxic waste in waterways. The task of archaeologists is both simple and daunting. Every educated adult needs to assimilate only a dozen or so concepts about archaeological data, methods, and the contributions that heritage conservation makes to society (this is the simple part). The challenge for the archaeology educator is providing people with the requisite opportunities to gain such understanding.

Which brings us to the major audience for archaeology education: schoolchildren. Every future adult in North America will be a student first, in public, private, or home school settings. To be blunt, the K–12 audience is virtually captive. For thirteen years, young people are learning how to think, solve problems, and understand the workings of their world. In addition, their values are forming, as each student develops the character that he or she will carry through life. Children also have a remarkable way of influencing the attitudes of adults in their lives. A concerted effort to assure that youths learn essential points about archaeology is perhaps our greatest opportunity for conserving the archaeological record and for having a future adult generation that understands and values the discipline.

What's in It for Educators?

Teachers have more than enough to do without having to learn a new field of specialty, even one as intriguing as archaeology. To take a leaf out of the book of professional salespeople, it's hard to sell something to people that they don't believe they need. Therefore, we archaeology educators need to provide teachers with clear and cogent reasons for teaching archaeology before we can expect already overburdened classsroom teachers to make room for new topics in their busy classroom schedules.

Fortunately, archaeology is a superb teaching subject—it's interdisciplinary, participatory, and perfect for developing both cognitive and affective skills in children. It also can be presented in such a way as to help teachers meet educational objectives that are set before them by various levels of government. Broadly speaking, teachers must meet the requirements of national and local curriculum standards; assure that students achieve "benchmarks" of concept and skills attainment; and develop cooperative learning, problem-solving, and citizenship skills in ways that are appropriate to the age and abilities of their highly diverse classes. For teachers to be successful, kids must be curious, intellectually stimulated, and engaged. Teachers have a daunting mission without seeking even more to do.

Can the objectives of educators and archaeologists be made to mesh effectively? Can the goals of instilling students with an ethic of stewardship for the archaeological record and an appreciation for other cultures find space in the classroom? As experience and this book show, the answer is an emphatic "yes." The interdisciplinary nature of archaeology is one of its strengths, but the greatest attraction for teachers is the inherent fascination that kids seemingly have for the past. An archaeological investigation is a real-life detective story that uses the scientific method and multiple modes of inquiry. Moreover, the profession has demonstrated accessibility and achievement for both genders, although greater involvement by minorities still is needed.

Teachers can be drawn to classroom archaeology because it can help them to accomplish their regular requirements in real-world, fun, and exciting ways. Because most teachers don't realize what archaeology has to offer, part of our task is to market our product. We first have to sell the discipline and its teaching resources to educators, then close the deal by providing products that are user friendly, well designed, relevant, and accessible so that teachers will return to them again and again. The easier a curriculum package is to use and the better it fits educational requirements, the more likely it is to be used, and reused time after time, in North American classrooms.

Archaeology Education, a Hybrid Discipline

Archaeology always has been an eclectic discipline. It borrows from myriad fields to acquire theories and techniques to apply to research. Educational archaeology requires the same kind of open-minded borrowing, but from a new perspective: education. As a formal field, professional education has been practiced since the time of the ancient Greeks, and probably earlier. Archaeology, on the other hand, is only about 150 years old. We have a lot to learn from a profession that specializes in conveying new concepts and values to a highly diverse audience.

Archaeology educators need an understanding of pedagogical precepts. Sometimes, archaeologists are not the best teachers of their own concepts and methods because they don't have formal training in teaching. Learning the basics of how teachers teach and how various audiences learn is crucial to becoming effective transmitters of information about the past. It is a humbling thought, but an experienced teacher may be better equipped to teach archaeology to a group of sixth-graders than seasoned professionals with years of fieldwork behind them. Professional conceit has no place here. It is time to sit at the feet of the masters to learn how best to engage school children in the excitement of learning about archaeology. The very continuance of our discipline as a vital enterprise may depend on it.

Archaeology education is a newly forged specialty, and this hybridization of two disciplines should be familiar to those who have studied the history of archaeology in North America (see Willey and Sabloff 1980). Archaeology intersects with countless other disciplines—biology, geology, botany, political science, art history, philosophy, medicine, computer science, physics, and astronomy to name a few—and few archaeologists acquire doctoral-level expertise in a related field. We are not suggesting that archaeologists also seek degrees in education or immerse themselves in pedagogical theory, although those intending to practice archaeology education extensively or exclusively will profit from doing so. Rather, archaeologists need a working familiarity with the central tenets of educational theory and a cognitive map of how the educational system is organized and authorized. Indeed, some archaeologists will specialize in archaeology education; most others will encounter it periodically over the course of their careers, as the inclusion of the public increasingly becomes a component of field and laboratory research. Moreover, government contracts often specify a public education product as one of the contract's deliverables.

For myriad reasons, then, public involvement is and will remain a fixture of North American archaeology. Professional ethics require that archaeologists take this charge seriously and accept the responsibility of providing meaningful opportunities to the public. In terms of the K–12 audience, the onus on archaeologists is to create educational opportunities. We must learn what teachers need and what they can use as teaching methods and materials. We need to accommodate their objectives so that they will help to accommodate ours.

Themes and Threads that Run Through This Volume

While archaeology education is a nascent field, several tenets already have emerged from its short-lived practice (and others probably could be identified). These tenets are explored, elaborated, and interwoven in this volume, but they deserve explicit discussion here. As archaeology educators, we need to:

- know our audience;
- be aware of our own biases;
- acknowledge the special responsibilities attendant with teaching about heritage;
- understand the challenges of choosing our messages carefully and conveying them clearly; and
- be committed to program-specific and overarching evaluations of the results of archaeology education itself.

The Audience

The diversity in modern classrooms means that archaeology educators must be prepared to address various student needs and abilities. There are tested and well-documented pedagogical methods appropriate for teaching students with special needs, students who speak little or no English, or students who have short attention spans because they are young or challenged by special learning conditions.

In addition, students often have little understanding of the cultural milieus from which you, the archaeology educator, may assume they come. In other words, children may not share a common starting point for North American education because of poverty, ethnic background, religious strictures, or economic and environmental differences between rural and urban populations. Lots of inner-city kids, for example, have never seen a real live deer, let alone a deer bone. A basic principle of education is that "you work from what they know to what they don't know." Finding out what they know is part of the preparation good archaeology education demands.

It is essential that we "know our audience," student or adult, before we try to teach. To create effective lessons, we also need to understand how people learn. These cautions apply to museum professionals, adult education specialists, university professors, and cultural resource interpreters as well as archaeology educators. People assimilate information in different ways—some by listening, others by seeing, and still others by reading or doing. Since we want to distribute our message as widely as possible, we must present it in ways that ensure that large numbers of people learn what we are saying. In addition, because the ability of children to learn and apply skills evolves as they age, understanding the development and rate of that ability is an essential component of good program design.

Bias

North American archaeologists most often are trained as anthropologists, but they rarely consider what they do as archaeology educators to be an anthropological exercise. However, in doing educational archaeology, we are entering a new world— that of the professional educator—and we need to apply anthropological principles to this endeavor. This includes understanding our own starting points. Most archaeologists come from white middle-class suburban backgrounds. To share the discipline effectively with the broadest possible audience, archaeologists need to recognize their own biases; we tend to teach things in the same way that we learned them. This may be utterly inappropriate for the student audience that we are trying to reach. This cautionary note is especially germane if the ethnic or religious values of a particular group of student conflicts with world views and ideas that archaeologists believe to be true about cultures and peoples of the past. Sensitivity about cultural and belief systems manifest in a student audience can help archaeology educators to avoid statements and assumptions that are hurtful at best and confrontational at worst.

Special Responsibilities

In classrooms as diverse as those in many North American schools, it is critical that archaeology educators acknowledge the sensitive nature of what they are setting out to do. We actually tell people what they should believe about the past and their heritage. It would be reprehensible to denigrate, intentionally or not, the cultural heritage of any person whom we encounter in the course of our careers. An archaeology educator must "teach consciously," which means recognizing that information presented may affect how a child perceives his or her cultural background, as well as how other children will view that individual henceforth.

It is important, then, that archaeology educators begin their careers with a clear sense of the professional responsibility that they have. It is their task to interpret the heritage remains of past cultures to modern people. In so doing, children and their parents are sent a message about themselves as the heirs and cultural descendants of those cultures. Archaeological interpretations may challenge students' beliefs about their own and others' nations, ethnicity, religious and mythological background, and technological accomplishments. If archaeology educators have an obligation to present information accurately, we have an equal charge to understand our audiences and to compose archaeology education programs sensitively.

The Message

An archaeology educator must have a clearly defined set of goals and objectives for every program and every lesson. Knowing what you are trying to teach and how to teach it most effectively to a given audience are keys to ensuring that the message is actually transmitted. Most people try to convey more information than their audience can assimilate at one time.

With this in mind, we need to ask ourselves several questions: What do educated Americans need to know about archaeology? What is the best way to ensure that they will know it? How does an archaeology educator distill years of information acquired through school and research into a fundamental catechism? What is the students' level of understanding? Various chapters in this volume discuss the messages that we do and ought to present, but each archaeologist must examine both explicit and implicit communications. We need to be sure that we are choosing the most important messages and that we are transmitting them successfully.

A serious aspect of public archaeology is the potential to be misunderstood: That is, the message that you're trying to teach is not the one that your audience is receiving. This may seem somewhat silly; we all speak the same language, don't we? But in today's diverse global village, the answer is "no," we don't. Ensuring congruity between the message, the medium, and the audience's perception of each requires deliberate attention and feedback. For example, there is considerable debate about the implicit message sent by student excavation experiences (this discussion is elaborated in Part III). Most people think of archaeology as a dig, so students expect to "get down and dirty" when they are told that they are going to learn about archaeology. The potential for creating a generation of pothunters by unwittingly transmitting the archaeology-is-fun-let's-all-set-up-a-dig-in-our-backyard idea to teachers and students cannot be overemphasized. Yet, experiential learning is emphasized throughout this book, and it is a basic tenet of modern educational theory. Resolving the conflict between what archaeologists want to teach about archaeology and what teachers want their students to learn requires that great care be taken in crafting our messages.

Once again, other disciplines can assist. Communication skills drawn from the business world—specifically, marketing and advertising—greatly can enhance an archaeology educator's ability to transmit effective and accurate information. Knowing how to write a press release and give an effective interview can help to prevent nightmare headlines such as "Schoolchildren Dig for Buried Treasure Downtown" or "Archaeologists Suggest Dinosaurs Roamed Manhattan." Research into how concepts are perceived and the emotional responses prompted by the use of certain words will help the archaeology educator to keep the audience enthralled and enchanted.

Archaeology has a direct and real impact in the modern world. Thus, teaching archaeology to the public is an intentionally political act. Of course, we need to encourage the interest of politicians and government officials in our work, which helps us to get permits, support, equipment, and funding. Working with the press is similar; the press encourages political interest in a project, which, in turn, engenders support. Yet archaeology education itself is political; after all, we are trying to teach children what we want them to know. We have our own propaganda message that we are working hard to transmit.

This opens another aspect of archaeology-as-politics that is vexing and potentially dangerous. Archaeological information has been used by purveyors of governmental, cultural, or religious concepts to bolster acceptance of their belief systems. Cases in point include the Nazi use of archaeology to prove original Aryan ownership of Poland and the suppression of archaeological evidence of an entire wealth of African accomplishments by British, French, and Portuguese colonials. Archaeology educators must ensure that information people learn about archaeology is as factual and complete as possible.

Evaluation

A sobering fact about the current state of archaeology education is that we really don't know the long-term behavioral effects of what we are doing. Archaeology education is being done largely on faith. Obviously, many of us believe deeply that our efforts are effecting positive attitudinal change in young people. We can and do measure the immediate results of our educational programs on knowledge comprehension and opinion. And we can estimate the past price of not doing archaeology education: reduced government funding for heritage discovery and conservation efforts, vandalism, looting, the illegal antiquities market, perhaps intolerance for other and earlier ethnic groups, perhaps lessened citizenship skills. Still, in darker moments, archaeology educators may wonder at the real value of their often intangible work.

Rather than being cause for discouragement, the lack of knowledge about the effects of our educational efforts is really a call for explicit evaluation and thoughtful reflection as part of any archaeology education program. It is also a consequence of archaeology education's infancy. Until quite recently, not enough concerted archaeology education had been done, or done for long enough, to register lasting results. It is a sign of a field's maturation when inward-looking evaluation becomes a concern.

About This Book

Archaeology education is vitally important to the profession and to the public. As we have shown, it is an essential means for increasing public awareness, enhancing site stewardship, and engendering respect and support for heritage conservation among our various audiences. Indeed, all the major North American professional archaeological organizations have active education committees and outreach materials. Education is becoming an accepted, if not yet quite mainstream, aspect of our profession. Most archaeologists these days have some direct involvement with the lay public in a professional context. Every indication is that public interest in archaeology is infectious and that people increasingly will expect involvement with and access to what we do. Further, our own professional concerns require that we interact with the public.

There are many forms of public and educational archaeology. Working with teachers and students is one of the most effective and efficient means for transmitting our messages. By focusing on K–12 education, archaeology education is forwarded by the classroom teacher to hundreds of school children over the course of his or her career. Moreover, when you reach a child in the formal education environment, you have a means for reaching an entire family.

This book is a text designed for archaeologists working with K–12 teachers and students. It offers practical advice on how to incorporate archaeology education into a curriculum and how to get teachers interested in archaeology in the first place. It will help you to talk to a group of third graders, create lesson plans for secondary-school science students, offer teacher workshops, infiltrate the upper levels of a school district bureaucracy, write a curriculum that someone other than you actually can follow, found a regional public research center, and establish a system for assessment. It also should help you to steer clear of trouble spots.

This is not a case-study book. Several very useful volumes describing public archaeology projects already exist (see Stone and MacKenzie 1990; Smith and Ehrenhard 1991; Jameson 1997). It also is not a teaching guide or a book of lesson plans; many of these also already exist and are referenced here. Rather than centering on what to teach or where it has been taught, this book focuses on how archaeology can be presented practically and effectively to a K–12 audience.

Most current archaeology educators learned their skills and techniques by working with education professionals, taking courses, making mistakes, and developing ever-increasing personal tool kits as they progressed from program to program. In other words, most of us spent years making it up as we went along. We developed public archaeology initiatives while working for federal, state, provincial, municipal, or community-based agencies or museums or as teachers and administrators in school districts. Public interpretation either was part of our mandate or part of what we wanted to do with our interest and training in archaeology. We did it by hook or by crook, often with limited institutional support, and sometimes in the face of active hostility from our less publicly inclined colleagues. There's no particular virtue in this; we simply had little to go by. After a while, it became clear that we could help each other to avoid mistakes that we had made and to benefit from our successes. This book, then, also is an attempt to rectify this unavailability of information.

Until quite recently, archeologists wanting to do outreach and education were pretty much left to their own devices. Despite this, we have come to remarkably similar conclusions about the nature of effective education programs. Having collectively invented and reinvented the wheel, we often have converged on like programs and methodologies. Apparently, sound pedagogy combined with the objective of teaching sound archaeology dictates that certain types of programs will be the most effective.

About the Editors

The editors of this book reflect this coincidence in microcosm. Both are long-time members of the SAA Public Education Committee. Smardz, originally trained as a European classicist, worked on sites ranging from North American prehistoric through French medieval. She returned to her hometown of Toronto convinced that, for archaeology to have a direct benefit to the people paying for it—the taxpayers—and whose heritage it was—again, the taxpayers—a new approach to public education and communication had to be developed. She founded the first public archaeology facility in any metropolitan school board in the world, a center that specialized in conducting urban excavations with literally thousands of school children each year. Many of her charges were recent immigrants; sites chosen for excavation were the homes and businesses of Toronto's nineteenth-century immigrant population, something to which every nascent excavator in her programs could relate. The educational goals thus were explicitly political and conveyed: a deepening cultural pride through enhanced knowledge of heritage resources; antiracist education through increased interethnic understanding; heightened awareness of the need for heritage preservation; and an appreciation for archaeological sites as a way to connect with other immigrants' experiences and contributions.

Smith's career almost exclusively has been as an archaeologist in the western United States, working for a public land-managing agency in field specialist and senior policy and program management capacities. Vast acreage in remote areas, numerous prehistoric archaeological sites, and a thriving illegal antiquities market made stemming vandalism and looting the thrust of her archaeology education efforts. Smith directed the development of the *Intrigue of the Past* archaeology education program, which today is implemented in twelve states as *Project Archaeology*. *Intrigue* focuses on building a stewardship ethic in school children, and its form and content were geared for wide dissemination in a school setting. Successful environmental education programs with similar stewardship goals were a significant influence on its design. They helped to shape *Intrigue*'s strategy of building an individual's knowledge of and appreciation for heritage resources to engender thoughtful and responsible action toward the fragile remnants of the past being lost so rapidly to looting and vandalism.

Similarities in the editors' philosophies and practical approaches to archaeology education have been astonishing at times—which is not to say that we haven't had some lively debates! A contributing factor to our congruent approaches, and to those of many of our colleagues, may be the immeasurable assistance provided by our early association and collaboration with professional educators.

Given archaeology education's decade of experience, we came to the conclusion that it was time to record what has been achieved, and to provide some guidance for archaeologists who want to begin working with K–12 students. As archaeology educators we still have much to learn, but it seems appropriate to start signing the way and sharing what knowledge we already have gained. We don't expect that this book offers the definitive answers on how best to do archaeology education henceforth, but we are confident that it suggests sound approaches to interfacing archaeology with the current educational scene in North America.

Book Organization

The Archaeology Education Handbook: Sharing the Past with Kids is organized into five parts that build sequentially on each other. Part I, "The Culture of Teaching: The Educational System and Educational Theory," introduces readers to the culture of the education profession. Since archaeologists already have an understanding of their own discipline's culture—its language, goals, professional organizations, journals, ethics, and instructional sequence—Part I provides a parity for the education profession. How educational systems in North America formally are organized and funded, subjects that government standards and assessments require teachers to cover, the sequence of children's cognitive development, learning styles, and special needs all are discussed.

Part II, "The Interface: Archaeologists Working with Educators," centers on the meeting of the two professions of archaeology and education. It explores ways and means through which archaeologists and teachers meet and collaborate. Most teachers know next to nothing about archaeology and don't necessarily want to. The word "stewardship" may have no meaning for them at all, for instance. The onus on archaeologists is to reach out to teachers and find ways through which professionals in both arenas can help each other reach their particular goals. Part II offers guidance about how to reach teachers; locate existing educational resources, including electronic media; make the most of the typical short-term contact with a K–12 audience; and evaluate an archaeology education program. This latter topic cannot by overemphasized. A program's success is not based solely on feedback that "teachers love it" or the fact that archaeologists have repeat business. Evaluation finds out whether the teaching objectives of the archaeologist and the educator were achieved.

Part III, "The Danger Zones: Issues in Teaching Archaeology," describes trouble spots and offers suggestions for working through and around them. Part III also presents the debate among archaeology educators on the value of excavation experiences, real or simulated, for the K–12 audience. The interface between archaeology and education contains pitfalls; we know that because we've fallen into most of them. There are sensitivities and flash points in teaching archaeology that are difficult to anticipate, as well as many that are predictable but puzzling to address. Trying to shape student attitudes and behavior often treads on thin ice, but archaeology education is not alone in this. The changing of values, beliefs, and attitudes can be contentious, and it is notoriously hard to measure. But that usually doesn't stop school systems from teaching about safe sex, environmental education, the dangers of smoking and drug use, antilittering, and conservation ethics.

Part IV, "The Provenience: Archaeology Education in the Real World," brings together the concepts, principles, and approaches presented throughout the book and realizes them in actual settings. Museums, archaeological parks, regional public research centers, urban sites, and even university anthropology departments all are venues where archaeology education is taking place, and they all have unique characteristics to consider. There are, of course, many other locations that are not addressed here such as home schools, youth camps, and organizations. The methods and approaches described in this book can be applied to any public archaeology situation and audience, as can the underlying information about learning styles, educational theory, audience diversity, sensitive issues, and teaching resources. Adults also have learning styles; they visit archaeological parks; and they love to discover the distant past. And, remember, every kid has parents and other adults in their lives who can become educated about archaeology.

The Archaeology Education Handbook: Sharing the Past with Kids closes with "Conclusions and Perspectives." Here we discuss the mutual effects of the meeting of the two disciplines and ponder the future of archaeology education. Two perspectives offer guideposts to this exercise. Environmental educator Norm Frost outlines the genesis and growth of environmental education and describes lessons learned that can be applied to its younger sibling, archaeology education. This history and analysis of environmental education, a field closely aligned with our interests, can illuminate our way as we engineer the future of archaeology education. Veteran archaeology educator Martha Williams then shares her personal retrospective on the movement. Martha was there at the beginning, twenty-five years ago. Her experiences with the birthing of this new subdiscipline are inspiring and instructive.

We have spent many pages discussing why it is a "Good Thing" for the archaeological profession to embrace archaeology education. However, there is a larger reason that transcends all others: the overriding social values that archaeology education can bring to school children. These include good citizenship; a sense of the greater human whole to which each person owes allegiance and responsibility; and the belief that each culture, past or present, has something to teach us. Different cultures do the same things in various ways that are fascinating and valuable and that contribute to their society's ability to survive in a given place and time. That cultural diversity makes the world interesting. Knowledge about each nation's past has worth, and it belongs to every person who lives in that nation, regardless of his or her ethnicity, class, or religion. These are values that children can absorb through archaeology education. This is the most compelling argument for archaeology to be included in school curricula today, and for you, as an archaeology educator, to learn how to offer effective archaeology education programs and materials.

PART I

The Culture of Teaching
The Educational System and Educational Theory

The first section of this book sets the stage for everything that follows. It introduces archaeologists to the world of precollegiate education, a new world with its own set of rules, values, and priorities. For many archaeologists, the discipline of education is a foreign culture.

What is insidious about this feeling is its familiarity. You understand (or so you believe) the meaning of the words being spoken, and people are doing things that you would expect in this context. But there seems to be a different set of rules at play, a different vocabulary, motivations, tools, procedures, and expectations. Why, even the tiny furniture is disarming! Welcome to the world of formal education.

You have encountered a field with roots as old as humanity. Western education today is a highly diverse and evolved profession. Because its practitioners are entrusted with nurturing to fruition so many hopes that society has for tomorrow's citizens, they often are at the center of larger debates on the future of our society. As an anthropologist, you know that you have to prepare for your foray into this other culture by consulting knowledgeable sources, in this case about formal education. Part I relates the work of several expert sources and is intended as an ethnographic primer to the education profession.

Archaeologists are motivated to work with teachers and children for various reasons, including concern for site preservation, the pleasure of working with kids, improving multicultural understanding and relations, enhancing quality learning opportunities, and repaying public investment in archaeologists' work. But even the most altruistic, dedicated, and brilliant archaeologist can't work effectively with teachers and students without knowing about child development and the educational system. Expertise in a discipline does not correlate necessarily with being an effective teacher of that discipline, just as a teacher's acquired knowledge of archaeology does not ensure capability to practice it. The competent archaeology educator must become, to use Ruth Selig's term (this volume), a "cultural broker" between the two fields of archaeology and education. The following chapters allow archaeology educators to glean a basic understanding of the education system's structure and functioning. As archaeologists, we already have some understanding of our profession's culture. Part I provides corresponding information about the education profession, so that archaeologists can begin the task of "brokering" between the two cultures.

The basic framework for education in North America is institutional. How are educational systems arranged? How do outsiders access the system? Cross-cultural interactions with educators must be approached with an understanding of the system within which they work. Cathy MacDonald and Paula Burtness, educators from Canada and the United States, respectively, describe how public education is organized, funded, and administered in those nations. From national to state or provincial to local government, the authors present what an archaeology educator needs to know to access the education system in ways that minimize frustration and maximize effectiveness.

With the organization of the educational system as a framework, archaeologists embarking on instructional programs next need to know that North American education is regulated by government standards and assessments. These broadly define what students should know after completing a course of study at a given grade level and which skills they should have acquired along the way. Not surprisingly, the development of such standards has been controversial and political, and Elaine Davis's chapter recounts this development. She offers insight into the appropriate fit of archaeological concepts with government standards and proposes ways to work within and around educational bureaucracies. As experienced archaeology educators reiterate throughout this book, archaeologists who craft programs to meet formal education standards most likely will produce materials that actually are used in the classroom.

Educational systems and governmental standards are broad contexts framing modern education; they are the sideboards within which formal education occurs in North America. Even educational alternatives such as private and home schools are responsive to this framework. The next step is to turn to what archaeology educators need to know about the learners themselves: How do children learn and develop, cognitively and morally? The developmental characteristics of kids constitute another broad context that archaeology educators must understand before they can convey values and ethics of heritage preservation to young audiences effectively.

Compared with classroom teachers, archaeology educators operate at a disadvantage. Because they seldom have long-term or in-depth relationships with students, they don't know an audience's unique characteristics in terms of background, interests, or levels of ability. To counterbalance the truncated relationship and maximize the effectiveness of their offerings, it is imperative that they design educational materials and programs that are developmentally appropriate. Kids of different ages process, store, and retrieve information differently, and their capacities for moral reasoning develop as they mature. For programs to be effective, they need to be synchronized with a learner's developmental stage. Further, archaeology education often is undertaken with the goal of instilling audiences with a stewardship ethic toward archaeological resources. Emily Johnson's chapter provides a general description of children at various cognitive stages and the implications for archaeology education. Johnson also discusses how children's moral reasoning capacities develop information that is essential to building stewardship-focused learning activities.

Even within cognitive development stages, there is variety in the ways that people receive and process information. This differential has become known as "learning styles." In the next chapter, Vic Geraci outlines the historical development of learning style theory and the "seven basic intelligences" that describe how people most easily take in new concepts and acquire new skills. He also makes the important point that being aware of one's own learning and, hence, teaching style enables an educator deliberately to include a variety of learning opportunities in the teaching repertoire. Thus, a more diverse curriculum can result, one that includes an array of activities and that is inclusive of the entire audience. Geraci gives examples of ways to structure learning activities so that various learning styles are accommodated.

The modern North American classroom is seldom homogeneous; students vary significantly in capabilities, primary languages, backgrounds, or ethnic origins. Today's heterogeneous, multicultural classrooms demand a diverse and flexible approach to teaching. Archaeology education will exclude many students if it focuses solely on kids with "normal" development and on those from homes where English is the primary means of communication. In her chapter, Renata Wolynec outlines the characteristics of and considerations for working with exceptional students with learning, social, or physical disabilities; with children whose first language is not English; or with children who are recent immigrants. She offers suggestions for practical modifications of teaching materials and activities so that archaeology education is as inclusive as possible.

A classroom is the confluence of the educational system structure, governmental standards, students' developmental characteristics and learning styles, and heterogeneous classroom composition. The classroom is the place where the above-described forces converge and are actualized. Pam Wheat's chapter personalizes the teacher's world. She describes the typical demands and responsibilities of teachers, and deriving from this reality, what constitutes "teacher-friendly" materials and programs. She also suggests how to include archaeology in school curricula in ways that are beneficial to both educators and archaeologists.

CATHY MACDONALD
PAULA BURTNESS

Chapter One

Accessing Educational Systems in Canada and the United States

Teachers of elementary and secondary school students are generally more than receptive to the educational potential of archaeology. Many of them actually seek to utilize archaeological concepts and methods, as well as archaeologically derived data, in their classrooms. A lack of available, pedagogically sound curriculum materials has long frustrated certain members of the educational community, to the point where teachers have produced their own lesson plans and instructional media to use in introducing archaeology into their classroom programs.

The archaeology educator seeking to enter the world of the professional educator performs a great service to both education and to archaeology. The first step in this process, however, is knowing what teachers need and what they are permitted and encouraged to use within the constraints of academic standards imposed by both their discipline in general, and departments of education in particular. A clear understanding of the workings of the modern school system, coupled with a knowledge of where archaeology most appropriately fits into the curriculum, goes a long way toward ensuring the formation of productive partnerships between teachers and archaeologists.

Education systems differ from community to community. For the archaeologist seeking to work effectively with students and teachers, it is essential to invest the time to develop a working partnership with the local educational community and to understand how it is organized and administered.

The information contained in this chapter will help the archaeology educator access the right individuals and groups within the educational system, both locally and nationally. At the same time, needless bureaucratic entanglements can be avoided if an informed approach is taken. The first section of this chapter reviews the organizational structure of educational systems in the United States and Canada. The second part addresses funding for educational programs in the schools, and the kind of assistance or cooperation one might expect from the educational system. The third section discusses diversity and the special needs of students within the school system.

Organizational Structure of Educational Systems

Great excitement can be created when one makes contact with the appropriate decision makers in an educational community; great frustration can result when one does not. Archaeology educators need to be knowledgeable and informed about how educational systems are organized. Long and disappointing search processes can be avoided by locating and getting to know the relevant people. It is important for someone interested in accessing the educational system to understand that the classroom teacher is rarely an independent agent; he or she is accountable both to the educational hierarchy and to the public in the political and polemic social atmosphere that surrounds North American education.

In Canada and the United States, provincial and state governments play a large role in education. The federal governments focus on providing funding for research and job training, although these responsibilities may also spill over into state or local government levels as well. If an archaeology program involves internships and job training, it would be advisable to explore the possibility of partnerships within one of the federal programs. However, local boards and departments of education are at the center of what happens educationally within a community, and direct funding may well be available there too.

Each provincial or state government has a Ministry or Department of Education responsible for designing curriculum and setting standards at the elementary and secondary-school levels. More generally, nationally approved guidelines also apply in each discipline; U.S. state and local curricula are internally designed under such rubrics. At the local level, a school board is comprised of elected officials headed by a chairperson. The board controls the overall budget and is charged with the task of implementing policies from the Ministry or Department of Education.

Accessing the System: American Education

In the United States, each state has its own Department of Education. A gubernatorially appointed commissioner of education heads the department. Carrying out education-related laws, initiatives, and policies set by the State Board of Education is the responsibility of the Department of Education. For this reason, departments of education can be a helpful source of information about curriculum standards at the elementary and secondary school levels. Staff can describe current state educational initiatives and funding, as well.

A state is comprised of independent school districts, each having its own board of education and superintendent of schools. The superintendent is responsible for day-to-day operations of the school district. The elected school board officials and the superintendent work together to provide leadership and to be a decision-making body for the school district. The superintendent is ultimately responsible for state and federal education policies, the budget, curriculum, standards, licensed and nonlicensed personnel, and the physical plant. The size of the school district determines the number of additional administrators.

In larger school districts, the curriculum director is in charge of the overall kindergarten through grade 12 curriculum, implementation of state and federally mandated standards, and district and state testing. This individual also oversees various district-level committees and is responsible for teacher in-service programming within the district. The curriculum director is directly responsible to the superintendent. Like curriculum consultants in Canada, individuals in this position are interested in learning about new programs that can benefit students within the school district and in meeting rigorous educational standards and criteria. They are essential points of contact for archaeology educators seeking to introduce programming on a district-by-district basis.

Principals of elementary, middle, and secondary schools are responsible for staff, curriculum implementation, and policies at the building level. They are involved with the ongoing daily as well as long-term operations of a school staff and structure. Depending on the size of the school district, a principal can be an excellent contact person for the archaeology educator who wishes to explore the implementation of a heritage education program. The principal will know his or her staff's interests and capabilities, as well as the curriculum requirements and priorities at each grade level. Thus, a school principal is likely to be able to suggest how archaeology education programming could be most effectively and appropriately adopted into a particular grade level's curriculum.

Many school districts also have site management teams. The team is comprised of teachers, parents, and usually one administrator. Shared decision making at the individual school level is the team's primary purpose. This group may have responsibility to decide curriculum-related issues or how best to manage a school's budget; a site management team could be an excellent place to generate interest and enthusiasm for an archaeology education program. In addition, the site management team would be knowledgeable about local district resources, procedures, and interested participants.

Department heads are another relevant group for the introduction of new curricular resources to a school. These discipline-based leaders are familiar with curriculum methods, procedures and most important, content, while having personal knowledge of both standards and staff within their departments. They can help direct the discussion on how best to integrate an archaeology curriculum into secondary school programming. They are knowledgeable about the potential for other departments to engage in experimental programs on the multidisciplinary basis so appropriate to archaeology education.

The elementary-grade level leader can provide assistance similar to that given by secondary-school department heads. An elementary-grade level leader would be able to provide a point of contact and communication with all teachers, districtwide, at a particular grade level. These individuals can assist in networking with other educators in building support for, and participation in, a program.

Accessing the System: Canadian Education

In Canada, a staff of senior teachers acting in the roles of director and superintendents work in conjunction with the school board. Each superintendent is responsible for a district within the board area. The director bears the overall responsibility for the entire school district, curriculum, standards, budgeting, teaching personnel, and the physical plant. Everyone ultimately has to answer to this individual, who then is directly responsible for his or her staff's activities to the board of trustees and thence, directly to the electorate.

Working also at the board level are elementary- and secondary-school curriculum consultants. These highly experienced former classroom teachers assist educators in a variety of ways to implement ministry guidelines and new initiatives. At the elementary level, the consultants are responsible for all subjects; primary for kindergarten to grade three, junior for grades four to six, and intermediate for grades seven and eight. At the secondary level, the curriculum consultants are usually in charge of a subject area (mathematics, science, history, etc.).

Consultants can be invaluable to an archaeology education program for a variety of reasons. First of all, part of their mandate is to attend workshops and seminars on current educational matters, programs, and practices and, in turn, to train teachers within their own board. They also assist teachers in their classrooms with implementing new ideas. Their role is to provide input, fresh ideas, and suggestions, so they are interested in learning of programs that help them apply ministry guidelines in new and creative ways.

As previously noted, education is very politicized in North American society. Hence, curriculum emphases and priorities change with newly elected governments, as well as when alternate social trends and issues arise that impact on the classroom. This offers a wonderful opportunity for the archaeology educator. New and changing trends and priorities in education allow the archaeology educator an opportunity to tailor curriculum suggestions and resource submissions to meet directly the needs of the busy and overburdened classroom teacher. This is an excellent means for ensuring that the archaeology education materials will be greeted with enthusiasm by consultants and teachers alike.

An archaeological education program intended for an entire school board is best initiated through the superintendents and curriculum consultants. Superintendents have responsibility for overseeing school curriculum, principals, and teachers in a particular area of the board. Principals must answer to superintendents for budgetary expenditures. These senior officials have authority to direct schools to implement and emphasize certain curriculum initiatives.

Curriculum consultants are great networkers. They are regularly in touch with Ministry of Education staff to learn of the latest directives. Most provinces have a consultants' association, useful in distributing materials on that level. Consultants know which schools and teachers on the board would be most receptive to participating in pilot projects and most consultants are more than willing to help facilitate such initiatives.

Consultants can also design archaeology education program to fit the needs of their schools. They are experts in applying ministry guidelines and can help convey ministry requirements. Thus, it is essential that the archaeology educator work closely with the relevant consultant(s) in the target board before initiating any program or creating any material. As well, teachers will need to provide an educational rationale for participating in any new programs or field trips, something the consultant can facilitate. With every dollar counting, it is vital that a new program demonstrate its direct relevance to curriculum priorities, while offering a high-quality educational experience for students.

Familiarity with curriculum guidelines enables an archaeology program to be offered as an interdisciplinary adventure, whereby students are allowed to develop their cognitive skills in a variety of subject areas. Evaluation criteria, methods, and standards that classroom teachers must implement and meet are parts of the guidelines. The more applicable programs and materials are to a variety of subject areas, the more likely they will be used in the classroom.

Moving to the individual school level, the key people are the principals, curriculum chairs, department heads, or subject deans at the secondary level, and lead or senior teachers at the elementary level. Department heads or curriculum chairs are responsible for overseeing the programming and the implementation of ministry guidelines at the secondary-school level. They would be the best initial contact for the archaeology educator, as they are knowledgeable about the entire program, set program priorities, and serve as gatekeepers to the appropriate teacher or teachers within the school system. Because archaeology is a multidisciplinary subject, the head could also help draw other departments into a network, as they have direct relationships with department heads in other subject areas and are more likely to perceive intercurricular links and possibilities more readily than the subject-specific classroom teachers. This is especially valuable for an archaeology program that takes a holistic, cross-subject approach—something that incidentally meets one of the most important current trends in precollegiate education across the continent.

At the elementary level, the lead teacher or division leader would perform the same function, being able to see how an archaeology education program could, for example, fit into the grade six program during the second term. These school curriculum leaders can help market as well as pilot programs.

Special Considerations

There are many factors about which school board officials and teachers have to be aware that are not immediately obvious to archaeologists engaging in school program development for the first time. These include insurance and liability issues, safety and security of students, considerations relating to publicity and public relations, physical plant requirements such as separate bathrooms for boys and girls, and various regulations that apply to publicly funded organizations in general and schools in particular. It is extremely important that the archaeology educator become thoroughly familiar with state and provincial regulations and issues in such matters prior to the implementation of any program that will impact on students.

These factors are so numerous and vary so widely between school districts that they cannot be detailed in this paper. But it is important to emphasize that no archaeology program should endanger the safety or security of children. For instance, publicity and public relations efforts should include permission forms for each child whose image or name may appear in slides, television, or print media accounts of the program or in any display materials. Children under agency protection from violent family situations can and have been endangered by their pictures appearing in the media. This does not immediately spring to mind as the delighted archaeology educator enters a grade-school classroom or greets the press at the gateway to the site on a busy day. Insurance is another matter; whenever planning for and working with students, keep in mind responsibility and liability. Liability can be a major issue if a student becomes hurt or injured while participating in an archaeology education program. Liability coverage should be an important issue for an archaeology educator; insurance must take into account that the public, and especially schoolchildren, will be participating or visiting the dig site or working with archaeological materials.

Funding

Cutbacks are an unpleasant reality in education today. The positive side is that the economic situation has forced educators to be creative and to maximize each dollar.

Funds are available for creative education; the challenge is to design archaeological programs and materials that match educational objectives as closely as possible so that archaeological education is perceived as an asset in achieving those goals. In most provinces and states, funding comes from local property taxes. Advance planning can help the archaeology educator achieve funding goals for the implementation of a new program.

It is important to note that educational funding operates quite differently between Canadian and U.S. school boards; in Canada, school funding is fairly equitably distributed on a per capita basis throughout each province although some significant differences may be apparent between rural and urban areas and between provinces or territories. This is less true in the United States, where great variation can occur, even within the same city or county.

On the other hand, because of political priorities and sensitivities, it is often difficult for Canadian educators to access additional sources of funding for developing new curricula; fundraising from private and corporate sources for use in schools may be unacceptable. American educators have long been able to encourage private support for acquiring educational materials and testing new programs. Public sector grants in Canada are few and difficult to acquire when compared with the U.S. educational situation; American educators have a plethora of private and public sector foundation monies that can be applied to educational purposes.

America's Education Dollar

State Level

The State Department of Education can be an excellent resource for learning about the availability of grants for archaeology education curriculum development and implementation. There will always be a need for outstanding curriculum specifically designed to meet state and national standards. Enlisting the support of school board members could prove critical for implementing an archaeology education program, or influencing the direction of budget cuts or changes.

As school district financial resources continue to be scarce, the importance of community partnerships has never been greater. They provide an invaluable link back into the community, while ensuring local leadership, resources, and funding for a proposed program. Local historical and preservation societies are a natural community partnership for archaeology education. Likewise, libraries, city and county boards, business groups, nonprofit organizations of various types, clubs, religious groups, and groups of innovative community leaders can all provide invaluable aid in having a new archaeology education program accepted and valued within the local district.

School Level

Individual schools usually do not receive direct tax-based funding for curricular or program development; that is done at the district level. Parent advisory councils are an important funding source at this level, however. These groups meet on a monthly basis during the school year. Fund raisers are held to support special programs, field trips, and events for the school. The parent council may decide to underwrite a program they feel would be particularly important to the students in their school.

In all outside fundraising efforts, including the acquisition of grants from public and private foundations, corporations, organizations and so on, it is essential that permissions be acquired from both the school district and from school board authorities before submitting grant proposals to any agency or group. Conflict with other funding priorities, educational philosophies and the like can all be avoided in this way. Likewise, the application for archaeology education funding will be immeasurably strengthened if accompanied by the written endorsement of the Parent Advisory Council for the school or group of schools in conjunction with any grant application. Hence, the partnership at this level is essential to the success of any archaeology education program fundraising efforts.

Canada's Education Dollar

Provincial Level

Recent political changes in school funding in Canada have resulted in varying authority levels across the country for both allocation of educational budgets and application of curriculum standards. In some provinces, general funding is decided at the provincial level and then directly applied under the supervision of school boards at city or county levels. In others, funding is developed from the local tax base and allocated according to the will of the local board under more general guidance from provincial education ministries.

Many subject areas at the secondary level have provincewide associations, such as the Ontario History and Social Science Teachers Association (OHASSTA). These groups have an executive body dealing with matters relating to their subject area, and to lobby for changes in curriculum requirements and standards at the Ministry of Education level. They also keep abreast of the latest pedagogical methods, host annual conferences for the dissemination of information, and hold workshops where publishers have the chance to display their latest wares. While the subject associations cannot usually fund program initiatives, conducting a workshop for teachers or having a display booth at an annual conference is an excellent platform for marketing materials and programs.

Board Level

On a day-to-day basis, it is the local board of education that governs operations within school districts in both Canada and the United States. In most instances, school board trustees pass annual budgets allocating resources based on the recommendations of superintendents and principals. As the ultimate approval for spending on programs and materials comes from these elected officials and trustees, educating them as to the value and benefit of a particular program or material is sound advice, because to the uninitiated, archaeology may sound more recreational than educational. The direct applicability of archaeology programming to meeting interdisciplinary curriculum development requirements may also be less than obvious. At the very least, trustees can draw attention to a program within the board and suggest where other sources of funds may be available.

Curriculum consultants also have budgets from which they can allocate funds to purchase resources for the board as a whole. They prefer to purchase kits and class sets of materials which can then be rotated throughout the system. Consultants' budgets are seldom large. Nevertheless, a consultant can suggest the advantages of a special program or materials to all schools in the board, and can often supply money for program and curriculum development on a more limited level. *Be aware that any curriculum materials and programs developed with board money are legally the property of the school board.*

Department heads at the secondary-school level typically meet as subject councils. They arrange for the purchase of shared resources. Attending a council meeting is a good way to bring programs to the attention of these important educational leaders, offering a chance for the archaeology educator to acquire at least some limited financial backing for program development or testing.

School Level

It is unusual for program development funds to be allocated at the individual school level. However, school principals, both elementary and secondary, receive a portion of their annual budgets for subsidizing student field excursions and programs that are brought into the school, such as visiting experts for talks, dance and theatre groups, and so on. Another potential funding source at this level comes from the parent councils, which are usually quite open to presentations by individuals with curriculum suggestions and which often purchase materials for schools or subsidize school trips and programs.

School librarians or learning resource teachers spend a significant amount resourcing their schools. Meeting them individually or at their council meetings to promote materials would be advised. Likewise, department heads at the secondary-school level are responsible for purchasing teaching resources and materials for their own subject areas. This should be kept in mind when the archaeology educator is developing resources for subjects that pertain to the high-school curriculum. It is recommended that department heads be involved in developing and field testing all materials archaeologists and other specialists seek to introduce into schools.

Reduced school budgets affect educators at all levels, from board to school to classroom. All is not lost, though; if an archaeology education program is demonstrably applicable to existing and upcoming curricular and skills development priorities, and if it can be shown that the program helps students enjoy learning those things that they have been mandated to learn, some financial support from different levels of the educational system is then a reasonable expectation.

Diversity and Change in North American Schools

In Canada and the United States, there are many alternatives to the public education system. Most provinces and states have parochial and private education systems, while home schooling is a trend of some significance across the continent. Each alternative offers a similar curriculum to what might be found in a public school, but they operate more autonomously. The complex bureaucracy of public schools does not bind parochial and private schools. Such schools are not responsible for adhering to the same education-related rules and mandates, although they are still often governed by the general provincial, state and federal government standards.

At the same time, there may be a much higher degree of involvement by parents' and other groups in the actual design and implementation of curriculum, especially in respect to focus and content. The archaeology educator must be very aware of the particular perspective of a parochial or private school when presenting curriculum and educational material for use in the classroom; underlying religious, political, and philosophical policies may influence the kinds of learning materials that would be welcomed in a given educational environment.

School cultures also vary widely between urban, suburban, and rural settings. The trend in many urban areas is declining enrollment among school-aged students coupled with an appreciable increase in the adult learner population. Suburban schools tend to be larger, often with close to 2,000 students in each school. Rural areas are characterized by regional schools in which up to 90% of the students rely on long-distance busing.

Schools today are highly inclusive environments. Most schools admit and program for students of all ability and disability levels. In addition, many schools are dealing with high immigrant populations whose first language is not English. Public schools are required by law to offer equal educational opportunities to all students. Accommodations for students' disabilities must be incorporated into any of the educational opportunities that a school offers. The goal of Special Education or Program Support, as it is now called in Canada, is to offer all students opportunities to participate in each phase of the educational program without being limited by linguistic, physical, or learning challenges.

Archaeology educators who offer program suggestions and materials without taking into account the variously challenged children of today's integrated classroom risk the rejection of both their curriculum and, indeed, their discipline, as inappropriate for school use. Further, acquiring funds for program development is usually dependent on meeting inclusion standards, so it is necessary that archaeology educators understand these criteria in order to gain financial as well as pedagogical support for their programs.

Finally, be sensitive to the fact that integrated classrooms contain children of all ability levels, ethnic and religious backgrounds, and philosophical persuasions. It is essential that archaeology education programs—which, after all, deal with human cultures and societies—not in any way jeopardize the happiness and well-being of any student or group of students. Gender and racial neutral language, sensitivities to children who are variously challenged, and unbiased and nonjudgmental language used in all descriptions of cultural attributes, past and present, will go a long way toward ensuring that your program is both useful and appreciated by everyone affected by it (see Wolynec and Connolly, this volume).

When planning an archaeology education program, inclusive educational environments should be viewed as an asset, not a detriment. Look on this criterion for educational program design as an opportunity to highlight the unique qualities that an archaeology education program has to offer for *all* students. An archaeology program in the public school system would need to include and incorporate necessary accommodations for physical, behavioral, or intellectual challenges some students may face. Be open to the participation of these populations in a program, and consider new and innovative ways to bring the students with special educational needs into an archaeology education program (see Wolynec, this volume). Your contacts within the school system can provide advice and assistance in this sensitive area.

One of the most important trends in recent years and one that is having an impact on curriculum and more general education spending is a focus on better preparing students for the world of work. Especially at the secondary level, cooperative education and apprenticeship programs are receiving tremendous financial incentives from various government areas. If an archaeology education program can mesh with this priority, it can increase its viability in the educational market place. An archaeology education program can be an excellent vehicle for learning, offering opportunities for critical thinking, problem solving, and cooperative learning; it can offer the skills that students will need to bring to the world of work.

Conclusion

It is critical for archaeology educators to realize that their programs must fit into existing curriculum needs and requirements for such programs to be accepted and used by professional educators. Funding, too, is directly dependent on the archaeology educator's clear understanding of how and why new programs are financed, managed, and approved at the federal, provincial or state, and local levels.

Hence, flexible, cross-curricular approaches will garner more success within today's school systems. Connecting with the right people and groups can make all the difference in building a strong program, and ensuring it reaches the intended audience. Whether conducting feasibility studies before implementing program design or marketing, or evaluating a program, knowledge of the educational system and its funding mechanisms is crucial to your success in bringing archaeology into our modern school classrooms.

M. ELAINE DAVIS ■

Chapter Two

Governmental Education Standards and K–12 Archaeology Programs

The setting is a fifth-grade classroom. A twelve-foot timeline is on display with each foot representing 1,000 years of human occupation in the Americas. Students are generating a list of historical events and locating each of these on the timeline. After a dozen or so have been placed, a clear pattern has emerged. Other than one lone point representing the crossing of the Bering land bridge about 12,000 years ago, the events all rest on the last six inches of the timeline—the time since Columbus. Students explain this pattern by saying that there was no change in those earlier years, that we do not know anything about those years, or that nothing happened.

Education is profoundly political. Decisions regarding the kinds of knowledge and information that will be conveyed to the next generation are never reached without struggle. The scene described above is a reflection of the sanctioned historical knowledge taught in most American schools. Precollege archaeology programs operate within the broader context of public education and are, thus, impacted by political decisions as well as by the evolution of educational theory and practice. An important aspect of education in the 1990s has been the development and implementation of government-initiated education standards. The long-range significance of the standards movement remains to be seen; however, without a clear understanding of the requirements and structure under which classroom teachers operate, archaeology educators run the risk of producing and disseminating materials that will never be put to use.

Many agendas enter into the making of public school curricula, and change is often painfully slow. Social reform efforts, such as those of the 1960s, have had an amazingly minor impact on what children learn in the classroom thirty years later. A case in point would be the role of women in North American history. The women's rights movement became a prominent political voice in the mid-1960s, yet in one of the most used American history texts, *A History of the United States* (Boorstin, Kelly, and Boorstein 1992), less than 3% of the content is about women (Sadker and Sadker 1994). Would the fifth graders involved in the timeline activity assume that this means we do not know what women did or, perhaps, that they did nothing? Values and issues of power form the foundation upon which educational curricula are built, and the environment it is constructed within is often fraught with controversy and conflicting views. It is appropriate that a discussion of governmental education standards begins with this point, because it is an essential understanding for anyone who wishes to affect what youngsters will study in school. Certain disciplines undoubtedly carry greater potential for igniting conflict than others and the focus of this volume—the teaching of heritage, culture, and the human past—is among those topics that have the power to generate an impassioned response. Just as education is political, so too is curriculum development. In this chapter, I hope to clarify some of the politics of instituting curricular change, provide information that places governmental standards in the appropriate context to the teaching of archaeology, and propose some strategies for working both within and around educational bureaucracies.

Understanding Standards

Improving educational quality became a global concern during the 1980s. For many countries, this commitment found expression in the form of national education standards. Simply put, standards are statements of what we believe is important. The standards movement, however, has been anything but simple. In some countries—such as Japan, France, and Great Britain—the call for academic standards has led to the development of a national curriculum that precisely defines both instructional method and content for core curricular areas. The British National Curriculum, for example, outlines standards for eleven school subjects. British teachers and schools are given the latitude to select materials and design their own lesson plans, but they are held accountable for student performance in these core areas.

Reaching agreement on "what we believe is important" is a complex task; where the population is larger and more diverse, such as in the United States and Canada, the push for educational standards is generally slow and arduous. Education in the United States has always been a local affair. With over 15,000 local schools districts and fifty state boards of education (Ravitch 1995:1), in addition to the federal Department of Education, reform at the national level is a highly involved undertaking. In Canada, the provincial ministries of education have a fairly high degree of influence on local curriculum offerings, but regional differences make one vision extremely difficult to achieve. When the voices of textbook publishers, schools of education, teachers' unions, interest groups, and the media are added to this list of agencies, the difficulty of instituting change becomes apparent. Some researchers who study the process of educational reform contend that actual reform in American education may be an unattainable goal. They argue that opposing perspectives on the nature of knowledge have an endlessly dichotomizing effect on the system and that while these positions may generate temporary shifts in policy and practice, over the long term they work to maintain the system and subvert educational reform (Noblit and Dempsey 1996). Even those who are more hopeful regarding the possibility of educational change have cautioned that, where standards are concerned, "Whether change or inertia prevails probably will not be known for fifteen to twenty years" (Ravitch 1995:175).

Beyond the convoluted political nature of educational standards and the ambiguity of meaning from one country to another, is confusion over the types of standards that have been developed. At the most basic level are content standards and performance standards; these exist in virtually every country that has entered into the standards writing process. Content standards broadly identify what students should know, understand, and be able to do in a specific discipline at a particular grade level. It is recognized, however, that simply identifying what children should learn is not a reliable method for bringing change to educational practice. Thus, wherever content standards have been developed, clear and consistent methods for assessing mastery of subject matter—performance standards—have been created as well.

Until recently, assessment has played a minor role in the standards movement. The process of defining standards for curricular content proved to be such a drawn-out and difficult struggle in many countries that accountability became a rather hazy issue. Until agreement can be reached on what students should know, defining how they should exhibit that knowledge seems a moot point. How this is resolved will ultimately vary from nation to nation and state to state. A system of school inspection and public reporting has been instituted in England that will, among other things, look at how standards for achievement are being implemented in schools. In the United States, performance instruments are being developed that are aligned with content standards. Whether these will be used, however, will be determined at the state and local levels.

In addition to content and performance standards, a number of organizations have developed guidelines for every aspect of the educational continuum. The *National Science Education Standards* (National Research Council 1995), for example, include standards for science teaching, professional development, science education programs, and science education systems.

Whether standards make a difference for education, whether the movement is a swing of the pendulum or a successful route to reform is not the primary concern for archaeology education. Rather, the point is to be an informed "insider" regarding policy and trends in education. At present, this means, among other things, understanding the discourse on educational standards. Interpreting the language of standards goes far deeper, however, than clarifying the associated terms. Knowledge of governmental education standards requires an examination of the imbedded issues that spark opinion and lead to debate. The following discussion highlights the major arguments that have emerged in the struggle for educational standards in the United States.

Governments and the Control of Ideology

In the United States, the discussion of national education standards began in the late 1980s during the Bush administration. In 1989, President Bush made an agreement with the nation's governors to set national education goals. According to many who have tracked the standards movement, the Bush administration was opposed to standards legislation because such policy was in opposition to state and local control of schools (Ravitch 1995:28). Instead, the point was to inspire new ideas in education so that the United States might maintain its leadership position in the global economy (G. B. Nash et al. 1997:150). This opens up a fundamental issue in American education. From its inception, public schooling in the United States has been the domain of state and local governments. A centralized system of education controlled by the federal government has been fiercely opposed throughout much of the nation's history. Federal legislation of education is limited almost exclusively to special needs and issues of equity. The primary responsibility for education rests with state and local governments, which pay more than 90% of the cost of education.

Arguments opposing education standards in the United States have been varied, the most fundamental one being resistance to a national ideology. This has historically been the stance of conservatives, but those with more liberal perspectives have also voiced concern that the setting of standards would place the federal government in the position of defining official knowledge (Arons 1995). Other criticisms include the belief that standards would not raise the quality of schooling, but would instead lower expectations and result in mediocrity. Some have asked how standards would address issues of educational equity, suggesting that they may actually intensify the disparity in academic achievement between groups (Cross and Joftus 1997). Obviously, many counter arguments exist that promote standards and, as the movement has made steady progress in the United States, these are the positions that have prevailed.

The idea of standards gained momentum in the early nineties with the election of President Clinton, who was a strong proponent of excellence in education. Early in his administration, federal legislation, referred to as "Goals 2000," was enacted into law. One of the goals called for standards to be set in five curricular areas. After protest from the disciplines not represented, three additional areas were included. Professional organizations representing the excluded disciplines felt that being left out of the standards legislation was a statement regarding the relevancy of their subject areas and that the omission could conceivably, over time, lead to their disappearance as school subjects. Among those on the final list were history, English, science, mathematics, civics, and geography. Some organizations representing those subjects not included, such as the National Council for Social Studies, voluntarily chose to construct their own academic standards. At present, standards have been completed, or are in draft, for mathematics, science, geography, history, physical education, foreign language, English/language arts, reading, economics, civics, and art. These documents are not a national curricula, but are to be used as guides by states and local school systems in the development of their own curriculum frameworks.

Waging War Over History

To understand fully the extent to which national standards can be controversial and evoke passionate public response, it is important to take a brief look at the battle fought over history standards in the United States. The standards were developed under the administration of the National Center for History in the Schools at the University of California, Los Angeles, and funded by the National Endowment for the Humanities (National Center for History in Schools 1996). The four-year project, co-directed by Gary Nash and Charlotte Crabtree, involved thousands, including thirty-three national education organizations, parents, historians, teachers, and many others who teach history in schools. When the standards were originally released in late 1994, criticism was immediate and harsh. Particularly significant was an opinion piece in the *Wall Street Journal* written by Lynne Cheney, former head of the National Endowment for the Humanities, which had provided funding for the project.

Cheney's remarks centered around the revisionist nature of the teaching examples that accompanied each of the standards. According to Cheney, women and minority groups figured too prominently in the standards, and traditional historic figures such as George Washington and the Wright brothers were invisible. Additionally, she criticized the world history standards for not emphasizing Western civilization as the organizing principle of the last 500 years. Bob Dole and many members of the newly elected Republican Congress echoed these sentiments, adding that the standards painted a gloomy picture of America's past by focusing on topics like the rise of McCarthyism and the Ku Klux Klan. The Senate rebuked the standards in a ninety-nine to one nonbinding resolution. Following much publicity and debate, a panel organized by the Council for Basic Education was set up to suggest revisions, sending Nash, Crabtree, and their committees back to the drawing board. A new edition was released in April 1996 that contained all the standards from the original version but eliminated the teaching examples that had raised so much ire. Other changes included increased focus on science and technology. Appeasing all who were so critical of the first version would have been impossible but, all things considered, the revised standards experienced a far more positive reception.

The history wars are not over: In fact, many say they are just beginning to heat up because history itself is currently "hot" (R. J. Nash 1997). An increase in the number of people involved in the dialogue increases the number of perspectives that are brought to the table. Archaeology is a discipline distinct from that of history; however, the aspects of history that fueled the war over standards are also common to archaeology. Both disciplines seek to understand and interpret the human past. For this reason, it is important that those involved in archaeology education consider carefully the drama that unfolded in the struggle to develop national history standards. There are lessons to be learned here, the primary ones being: the arena of public education is open territory; people feel very strongly about what is taught in schools, especially about heritage and culture; and educational program design in this area requires both cultural sensitivity and awareness of contemporary educational issues on the part of the archaeology educator.

Interpreting Curriculum Standards for Archaeology Education

If curriculum standards are such a "hotbed" for conflict, why even consider where archaeology education would fit into them? The answer lies in the area of assessment. As previously stated, most countries involved in the development of content standards have now moved into designing ways to evaluate student learning related to these standards. As contrary to logic as it may seem, assessment tends to drive instruction in public schools. To make a sweeping generalization, the pressure of accountability has frequently "placed the cart before the horse in education." Teachers often feel that the academic achievement of their students is the only thing standing between themselves and the unemployment line. Such tension leads to an undue emphasis on the tests themselves; they come to define the curriculum rather than reflect it.

It is easy to be critical of this kind of instruction; "teaching to the test" is a reductive approach to education. Nevertheless, assessment is a powerful force around the globe. Where measures of student achievement are linked to standards, teachers will most assuredly be giving serious attention to those standards as they select materials and set their curricula.

To return to the question, "Why consider the standards," it seems obvious that we can't afford not to. To my knowledge, archaeology is not a clear part of the curriculum for any of the countries where standards have been developed. If teachers are feeling compelled to tailor their instruction to these documents, and if we want to bring archaeology to K–12 students, then it is essential to become knowledgeable regarding education standards and interpret where they correlate with the content and process of archaeology.

Although archaeology does not have its own niche in the various education standards, it is uniquely suited to the teaching of a number of disciplines for which education standards have been written. In the United States and the parts of Canada for which provincial standards apply, the most obvious would be history, science, social studies, and geography. Not as closely related, but with potential for the inclusion of archaeology, are mathematics and art. Before discussing where correlations exist between archaeology and each of these disciplines, a comment on educational ideology and the nature of these standards is in order.

The National Content Standards developed in the United States were designed in various manners, most of them through a professional organization closely associated with the discipline. Given that so many voices entered into the creation of these documents, it seems amazing that they would have any similarities. They do, however, seem to have a kind of cohesiveness that centers around three areas:

1. content depth and breadth,
2. the context of learning, and
3. critical thinking.

With the first of these, the actual scope of content, the standards developers have almost overwhelmingly favored a curriculum that emphasizes *in-depth study* rather than superficial contact with large bodies of information. For example, in science, a fifth-grade student might spend days or weeks understanding the process of erosion through both text and hands-on experimentation rather than read a few brief paragraphs about erosion one day and move on to reading about the water cycle the next. The same is true for history. A seventh-grade class might spend an extended period of time learning about the various motivations for, and perspectives of, slavery and the plantation system rather than race through the Civil War chapter in the attempt to reach the end of the textbook before June.

The second point of intersection for the content standards, *the context of learning*, is perhaps the most substantive move made in the development of these standards, for it helps to answer the age-old question of youngsters, "Why should I learn this; how is this useful?" By situating learning in the context of real problems, teachers do not have to answer this question because the applicability of the content and skills is apparent. Project-based learning is one method for achieving this goal. For example, rather than learning math skills in isolation or in the context of contrived "word problems," students use mathematics as a tool for solving problems that have meaning, such as in the analysis of real data generated in scientific research.

Critical thinking, the third element that runs through the standards, is not such a newcomer to education. For at least twenty years, proponents have been making the argument that without critical thinking skills, students are unable to make use of the fact-based knowledge they possess. In the mid-1980s, the American Federation of

Teachers supported research in the teaching of critical thinking and sponsored staff development for the enhancement of critical thinking. While such efforts impacted instruction to a certain extent, critical thinking was often tacked on rather than woven through curricula. The prominence of critical thinking in the National Standards has given it a legitimacy that did not exist before.

In sum, these three strands come together to make a statement about education in the United States that is exciting and that should not be missed. All three relate in some way to the same philosophical perspective on the nature of knowledge. Critical, in-depth study within the context of meaningful problems runs counter to the belief that content and process should be separated in education. To put this into historical context, this is the pendulum swinging back to the earlier part of the century and the beliefs of John Dewey and the progressive movement. Regardless of whether, or when, the United States swings back toward a more industrial model for education, the current focus provides a path for teaching archaeology in a more holistic project-based fashion rather than fragmenting it into process and content. This approach is addressed more specifically in the next section of this chapter, but first a closer look at the particulars of some of the standards and how they relate to archaeology is warranted.

It would be impossible, in the scope of this chapter, to give great detail concerning the specific ways archaeology intersects in each of the disciplines mentioned. (Appendix I provides an example of the ways archaeology can fit with the National Content Standards; it shows a correlation of archaeology and the standards for science and for math.) However, the broad categories within each discipline where space for teaching archaeology might be found will be identified (Appendix II). The standards developed for geography are easily the closest fit for archaeology. The six broad areas for which standards have been written in geography are: Seeing the World in Spatial Terms, Places and Regions, Physical Systems, Human Systems, Environment and Society, and Applying Geography. Embedded in these broad areas are numerous concepts and processes that are also part of archaeological investigation, such as using maps, understanding the processes, patterns and functions of human settlement, and learning how physical systems affect human systems (Geography Education Standards Project 1994).

The social studies standards also provide a comfortable space for teaching archaeology. Ten thematic strands define learning in the social studies, and the first three of these, Culture; Time, Continuity, and Change; and People, Places, and Environments are central to the field of archaeology. In a description of the first strand, Culture, the document reads, "In schools, this theme typically appears in units and courses dealing with geography, history and anthropology, as well as multicultural topics across the curriculum" (National Council for the Social Studies 1994). The fact that the three strands most connected to archaeology are the first three in the list of ten is important to note. This prominence provides a solid foundation in which to ground the teaching of archaeology in precollege classrooms.

The history standards, as volatile as they might seem, are important for archaeology educators to consider because history, like archaeology, is devoted to the study of past peoples. It is also probable that history represents a larger slice of the curricula in most schools than does either social studies or geography. The history standards are a bit more complex to interpret for they are divided into separate standards for grades K–4 and grades 5–12. In addition, there are two subdivisions —standards for historical thinking and historical content were developed for all grades, and the 5–12 curriculum is further divided into United States history and world history. And five standards were developed for historical thinking: chronological thinking, historical comprehension, historical analysis and interpretation, historical research capabilities, and historical issues analysis and decision making (National Center for History in the Schools 1996).

If we take the broader definition of history, that it is a study of all of the human past, rather than the discipline-based definition, then it is easy to see how each of these standards might also relate to archaeology. The Standards for Historical Content are separated into eras for both United States and world history. Certain of these eras are more suited for the teaching of archaeology than others. In era one, for United States history, the standards actually require students to draw on data provided by archaeologists to explain migration into the Americas. It could be argued, however, that archaeology has a place in the content standards because many of the concepts students are asked to explore in history are central to archaeological investigation as well. Among these would be social organization, the relationship between geography and settlement patterns, and the spread of agrarian societies.

It is interesting that, particularly for the elementary and middle-school grades, archaeology is frequently taught in the context of science. This should not be surprising; archaeological investigation is scientific in nature and a number of scientific disciplines, such as geology and botany, inform archaeological research. However, it would be difficult to build a rationale for teaching archaeology in the science classroom based on a point by point review of the National Science Education Standards. In all the content standards, only Standard A, Science as Inquiry, directly relates to the work of archaeologists. There have been problems with teaching archaeology in the science class and these same problems can arise if the National Science Standards are considered in an isolated fashion separate from other disciplines. The difficulty lies in the teaching of process without a discussion of culture. In this model, the interpretive part of the archaeological process becomes impoverished—the teaching of method alone is not a responsible way to teach archaeology. The argument could probably be made for the reverse as well, that if archaeology is taught within the context of history, students never come to understand how archaeologists "know what they know."

The scientific process is an integral piece of archaeology, but so are the concepts regarding culture that are taught in geography, social studies, and history.

Archaeology is an interdisciplinary field of study and, as such, may be located in the context of a variety of subject areas. Correlating archaeology with curriculum standards is an important and necessary endeavor, but we must not allow standards to fragment artificially the nature of the discipline. If the precollege teaching of archaeology must be confined to a particular subject area, then social studies and geography, which are also interdisciplinary, would be appropriate choices.

There are two other points to consider before leaving this discussion of standards. The first of these is a reminder that National Curriculum Standards mean different things in different countries. As discussed earlier in this chapter, some countries have developed a national curriculum; the United States with its commitment to local control of education and its diverse range of cultural and political perspectives has not. The National Curriculum Standards discussed here have been used as guides by state and local school systems in the development of their own curriculum frameworks. As archaeological educators, it is our responsibility to become informed regarding the specific sets of educational standards that relate to our work. If we are developing curricula for a state park, then we need to be knowledgeable about the curriculum framework for that particular state. If the lessons or activities we prepare are intended for use in a more local area, then we need to consult local curriculum standards or guidelines.

Accessing such documents is not as difficult, or confusing, as it was a few years ago. While a phone call or letter to the appropriate agency would likely provide the needed information, the quickest route to education standards is through the Internet. Most school systems now have their own home page and many of these have links to their curriculum standards; such Web sites have been developed for state education also. A highly comprehensive Internet "super-site," called Developing Educational Standard, provides entrée into virtually every standards site in existence. The site, developed by Charles Hill at the Putnam Valley, New York, schools, is an annotated list of Internet sites with K–12 educational standards and curriculum frameworks documents. It is described as "a repository for as much information about educational standards and curriculum frameworks from all sources (national, state, local, and other) as can be found on the Internet." The Web address for the site is: http://putwest.boces.org/standards.html#section.

The second point I want to make about standards and educational practice relates to the idea of teachers as "gatekeepers." This term is used to emphasize the powerful role the individual teacher plays in deciding what students will be taught. Regardless of educational policy and curriculum standards, it is teachers who decide what happens once the classroom door closes. We should never assume we understand what students are being taught simply because we have read the curriculum framework, or that the lessons we prepare will be used just because they correlate with the curriculum framework. The gatekeepers are important people, but they are too often left out of decision making in education and have, traditionally, become the curriculum deliverers but not the developers. When we develop curricula for teaching archaeology, it is essential that we work in a fully collaborative manner with teachers.

Teaching Archaeology: Possibilities and Potentials

A number of the points that have been made throughout this chapter will be synthesized in this closing section into an approach for developing archaeology curricula and programs. A holistic approach to archaeology education was alluded to earlier; this section will clarify the meaning of this term and discuss how we might achieve it.

Archaeology is an interdisciplinary field; to initiate curriculum development with the idea of meeting particular education standards is a sure design for fragmentation. This is the same slippery slope education down which the Western world has been heading for decades. The result has been compartmentalization of knowledge to the extent that students often see no relationship between one field and another. The separation of disciplines has been so thorough in most North American schools that mathematics has become a subject rather than a tool, and science is a collection of facts rather than a process for investigation and understanding. The developers of the various National Education Standards have designed their documents to counter this type of fractured learning. Many of them advocate the teaching of their particular discipline within the context of meaningful problems or projects. Their intent is for students to develop conceptual understandings rather than to memorize data. Considering this, the starting place for curriculum development in archaeology education is with the goals and objectives of the archaeology program. Once these become clear, we can then identify specific education standards that the program or lessons address. A holistic approach to archaeology education is one that sets out to teach both the content and the process of the discipline.

What *do* governmental education standards mean for archaeology education? If we align our programs and curricula with the standards, will archaeology become a legitimized part of precollegiate education? Will alignment serve to sustain archaeology education programs? The answers are yes and no. Governments around the world have expressed a belief that standards should guide education. This may be a long-term commitment, or it may be a commitment for now. The greater the extent to which we, as archaeology educators, concern ourselves with the broader picture in education, the more likely we are to develop curricula that is current, appropriate and accepted. Education, however, is an open system and change will certainly happen.

In his book, *The End of Education,* Neil Postman suggested that everything students are taught at the K–12 level could be taught through three disciplines, archaeology, anthropology, and astronomy (Postman 1995). Furthermore, he said that students would find meaning in their studies and that they would be excited by learning. Archaeology is broader than any particular set of standards; it reaches across many disciplines, is infinitely fascinating, intellectually engaging, and intrinsically meaningful. This is a powerful rationale for teaching precollege archaeology.

RECOMMENDED READINGS
Standards Documents

Geography Education Standards Project
　　1994　*Geography for Life: National Geography Standards.* National Geographic
　　　　Research and Exploration, Washington, D.C.
　　The geography standards address how physical and human phenomena are spatially distributed over the earth's surface. The standards provide direction for helping students become geographically informed; see meaning in the arrangement of things in space; recognize relationships between people, places and environments; use geographic skills; and apply spatial and ecological perspectives to life situations.

National Center for History in the Schools
　　1996　*National Standards for History.* National Center for History in the
　　　　Schools, Los Angeles.
　　This guide to the National History Standards is divided into two parts: Part 1 covers National Standards for History grades K–4, and Part 2 includes National Standards for United States and World History for grades 5–12. Both sections include thoughtful essays on the development of standards and standards for historical thinking. Part 1 is organized by topic, such as regional history; Part 2 is organized by era.

National Council for the Social Studies
　　1994　*Expectations of Excellence: Curriculum Structure for Social Studies.*
　　　　National Council for the Social Studies, Washington, D.C.
　　This volume, developed by NCSS, addresses the purpose for standards in the Social Studies, provides clear guidelines for using the standards, and discusses the relationship of social studies to other standards in the field. The core—the actual standards—are organized according to ten thematic strands, the first three are particularly relevant to archaeology: Culture; Time, Continuity, and Change; and People, Places, and Environments.

National Research Council
　　1995　*National Science Education Standards.* National Academy Press,
　　　　Washington, D.C.
　　Standards are given for teaching science, professional development in the area of science, assessment in science education, science content, science education programs, and science education systems. The science content section is further broken into levels K–4, 5–8, and 9–12.

OTHER READINGS

Nash, Gary B., Charlotte Crabtree, and Ross E. Dunn.
   1997   *History On Trial: Culture Wars and the Teaching of the Past*. Knopf, New
      York.
   The authors of this book were project directors for the development of the National
History Standards. In this work they provide a revealing look at the politically charged
atmosphere that surrounded the development of the standards and provide insightful discussion
regarding the controversial nature of teaching history and culture.

Scheurman, Geoffrey, and Michael M. Yell, eds.
   1998   *Social Education: Constructing Knowledge in Social Studies* 62:1.
      National Council for the Social Studies, Washington, D.C.
   Constructivist theory has been a part of the dialogue in science education for a number
of years. This issue of the National Council for the Social Studies journal, *Social Education*,
focuses on how the same theoretical model is relevant to learning in the social studies.
Background information regarding constructivism is helpful for those who are not familiar with
this theoretical position.

APPENDIX I
Correlation for Archaeology and National Science
Content Standards: Grades K–12

CODES: D = Direct correlation, ID = Indirect correlation, P = Partial correlation, X = No correlation

National Science Content Standards	Correlation with Archaeology Education	Comments
K–4		
A. Science as Inquiry		
Abilities necessary to do scientific inquiry	D	
Understanding about scientific inquiry	D	
B. Physical Science		
Properties of objects and materials	D	
Position and motion of objects	ID	
Light, heat, electricity, and magnetism	X	
C. Life Science		
The characteristic of organisms	D	
Life cycles of organisms	D	
Organisms and environments	D	
D. Earth and Space Science		
Properties of earth materials	D	
Objects in the sky	X	
Changes in earth and sky	D	
E. Science and Technology		
Abilities of technological design	ID	
Understanding about science and technology	D	
Abilities to distinguish between natural objects and objects made by humans	D	
F. Science in Personal and Social Perspectives		
Personal health	ID	
Characteristics and changes in populations	D	
Types of resources	D	
Changes in environment	D	
Science and technology in local challenges	D	
5–8		
A. Science as Inquiry		
Abilities necessary to do scientific inquiry	D	
Understanding about scientific inquiry	D	
B. Physical Science		
Properties and changes of properties in matter	D	

| Motions and forces | X |
| Transfer of energy | X |

C. Life Science
Structure and function of living systems	ID
Reproduction and heredity	X
Regulation and behavior	D
Populations and ecosystems	ID
Diversity and adaptations of organisms	ID

D. Earth and Space Science
Structure of the earth system	P
Earth's history	ID
Earth in the solar system	X

E. Science and Technology
| Abilities of technological design | ID |
| Understanding about science and technology | D |

F. Science in Personal and Social Perspectives
Personal health	P
Populations, resources, and environments	D
Natural hazards	D
Risks and benefits	D
Science and technology in science	D

G. History and Nature of Science
Science as a human endeavor	D
Nature of science	D
History of science	D

9–12

A. Science as Inquiry
| Abilities necessary to do scientific inquiry | D |
| Understanding about scientific inquiry | D |

B. Physical Science
The structure of atoms	X
Structure and properties of matter	D
Chemical reactions	D
Motions and forces	X
Conservations of energy and increase in disorder	X
Interactions of energy and matter	X

C. Life Science
The cell	X
Molecular basis of heredity	X
Biological evolution	P
Interdependence of organisms	ID

Matter, energy, and organization in living systems	P
Behavior of organisms	D
D. Earth and Space Science	
Energy in the earth system	X
Geochemical cycles	X
Origin and evolution of the earth system	X
Origin and evolution of the universe	X

E. Science and Technology
Abilities of technological design	ID	*this section is more concerned with the dis-
Understandings about science and technology*	D	ciplinary aspect of archaeology

F. Science in Personal and Social Perspectives
Personal and community health	ID
Population growth	D
Natural resources	D
Environmental quality	ID
Natural and human-induced hazards	D
Science and technology in local, national, and global challenges	D

G. History and Nature of Science
Science as human endeavor*	D	*this section is more concerned with the dis-
Nature of scientific knowledge*	D	ciplinary aspect of
Historical perspectives	D	archaeology

SOURCE: Public Education Committee, Society for American Archaeology.

APPENDIX II
*Correlation for Archaeology and National Math
Content Standards: Grades K–12*

CODES: D = Direct correlation, ID = Indirect correlation, P = Partial correlation, X = No correlation

National Mathematics Content Standards	Correlation with Archaeology Education
K–4	
A. Mathematics as Problem Solving	D
B. Mathematics as Communication	P
C. Mathematics as Reasoning	D
D. Mathematical Connections	P
E. Estimation	D
F. Number Sense and Numeration	D
G. Concepts of Whole Number Operations	D
H. Whole Number Computation	D
I. Geometry and Spatial Sense	D
J. Measurement	D
K. Statistics and Probability	D
L. Fractions and Decimals	D
M. Patterns and Relationships	D
5–8	
A. Mathematics as Problem Solving	D
B. Mathematics as Communication	ID
C. Mathematics as Reasoning	D
D. Mathematical Connections	D
E. Number and Number Relationships	D
F. Number Systems and Number Theory	P
G. Computation and Estimation	D
H. Patterns and Functions	D
I. Algebra	D
J. Statistics	D
K. Probability	ID
L. Geometry	D
M. Measurement	D
9–12	
A. Mathematics as Problem Solving	D
B. Mathematics as Communication	ID
C. Mathematics as Reasoning	D
D. Mathematical Connections	D
E. Algebra	D
F. Functions	D
G. Geometry from a Synthetic Perspective	ID
H. Geometry from an Algebraic Perspective	P
I. Trigonometry	P
J. Statistics	D
K. Probability	DD

L.	Discrete Mathematics	D/ID
M.	Conceptual Underpinnings of Calculus	D/ID
N.	Mathematical Structure	X

SOURCE: Public Education Committee, Society for American Archaeology.

Chapter Three

Cognitive and Moral Development of Children
Implications for Archaeology Education

Archaeologists are often at a distinct disadvantage when asked to provide an appropriate archaeology lesson for children. Many archaeology educators serve as resource people who are invited into a classroom as special "speakers" once or twice a year and relatively infrequently during a child's K–12 educational career. Thus, archaeology educators rarely have the opportunity to truly get to "know" their precollegiate audience in terms of ability levels, interest areas, family, ethnic and cultural heritage, and so on. Classroom teachers who see students on a regular basis can come to know their students and use this knowledge to plan appropriate, relevant educational experiences. Of course, these regular teachers must also know and utilize knowledge of human development to guide their pedagogy. Given the archaeology educators' lack of specific knowledge about their audiences, a sound understanding of children's cognitive development can increase the likelihood of successful teaching and satisfied audiences.

All educators, regardless of their discipline or the age of their students, can benefit from understanding normal human development. In particular, an understanding of cognitive developmental levels and of how children of varying ages process information can lead to developmentally appropriate practices in educational settings and preparation of well-honed educational materials. In this chapter, a broad overview of three theoretical perspectives on cognitive development will be discussed. This will be followed by a brief discussion of moral development in children. The three theoretical perspectives include those of Jean Piaget, Lev Vygotsky, and an Information Processing approach.

Swiss theorist, Jean Piaget, has perhaps been one of the most influential individuals of the twentieth century with regard to human cognition. Piaget also offered one of the first theories of moral development, upon which other theorists such as Lawrence Kohlberg derived later moral reasoning theories. Lev Vygotsky, a contemporary of Piaget's but whose sociocultural theory reached American shores only within the past three decades or so, provides an important social dimension to understanding cognitive development. The information processing view emerged, in part, from dissatisfaction with Piaget's theory and, in part, from new research methodologies that allowed researchers a better means of examining how children attend to, store, and retrieve information or, in general, make meaning out of the information they receive. Following the discussion of the different theoretical perspectives I provide a general description of children at three different cognitive stages, drawing implications from each that can inform educational practice and help archaeology educators design appropriate experiences and lessons for their audiences.

Cognitive-Developmental Theories

Piaget: Active Learners in Their Environment

Piaget's theory of cognitive development holds that children are intrinsically motivated learners who actively construct their own knowledge through experiences they have with the physical environment (Berk 1997). His stage theory of cognitive development and view of human cognition as an "integrated set of reasoning abilities that develop together and can be applied to any task" (Berk 1997:211) has been instrumental in changing our view of children as learners. Prior to Piaget's theory, children tended to be viewed as relatively passive, empty vessels waiting to be filled with knowledge. Under such a view, lecturing to children and reinforcing them for correct or near correct responses were viewed as sufficient teaching strategies.

Rather than seeing children as passive recipients of knowledge, Piaget argued that they make their own meaning, and that to know something, one must act on it (Piaget 1964). Thus, children need to have hands-on experiences with their physical world to advance cognitively. Piaget also argued that just as the physical body matures, so, too, does the mind, and it is the combination of the biologically maturing mind and relevant experiences that propel an individual toward more complex reasoning abilities or the next stage of cognitive development (Thomas 1996:5, 8). Piaget proposed four invariant, universal stages of cognitive development (all ages are approximate):

1. sensorimotor (the first two years of life)
2. preoperational (ages two–seven)
3. concrete operations (ages seven–eleven)
4. formal operations (eleven–twenty years).

Within each stage, a particular set of schemes prevails. That is, at each stage children apply the same general set of reasoning abilities to solve a wide variety of problems or to adapt to the demands of their world. For example, children in the sensorimotor stage learn about and know their world largely through their senses in combination with motor acts, while the preoperational child is able to know his or her world symbolically through words, make-believe play, and pictorial representations.

Piaget argued that children are constantly adapting to their environment. They are continually building schemes through interaction with their environment using the processes of assimilation and accommodation. During assimilation, children interpret their world through already existing schemes. For example, the young child who has played a great deal in her sandbox, digging with her shovel and filling her bucket with sand, will approach another sandy area such as the beach or desert or even a sandy archaeology site with the idea that this place is meant for digging, and she will search for tools that represent the shovel and bucket so that she can begin her "work." Accommodation occurs when an old scheme doesn't seem to fit the new information. Sometimes external forces (for example, an adult saying "no, no") provide the stimulus that tells the child that the existing scheme doesn't fit, and the child must begin to modify her schemes or build new ones. For example, the child about to dig in a simulated archaeology site might be told "no" by an adult and be handed a brush to brush away the sand. This child must develop a new scheme about what to do with sand and perhaps develop a new scheme for the use of brushes that, previous to this time, were used only for painting.

A great deal of research carried out since Piaget's theory was first introduced has cast doubt on how well his theory accurately describes children's reasoning abilities within each stage and on the entire notion of invariant, universal stages. Perhaps one of the most significant pedagogical outcomes from Piaget's theory is the concept of children as active learners who construct their own knowledge. Thus, developmentally appropriate curricula must allow children opportunities to manipulate objects, experiment with materials, and in other ways actively explore their world in order to develop knowledge and increase their cognitive abilities. For the archaeology educator working within a K–12 education setting, an understanding of children as active learners as well as descriptions of the cognitive abilities of children at each developmental level can enhance the teaching and learning experience for all.

Lev Vygotsky's Sociocultural Theory

Similar to Piaget, Vygotsky saw the individual as active in his or her own learning. But rather than focus, as Piaget did, on interactions with the physical environment for increasing cognitive complexity, Vygotsky argued that it is through social interaction with others that children come to know and understand their world. Piaget saw the child as the most important source of cognitive change (Berk 1997). In many respects, he viewed children as little scientists—"busy, self-motivated explorer[s]" who form their own ideas and theories about the world and go about testing them without need of external pressure (Berk 1997:247). Vygotsky believed that the child and the social environment work together to influence the conceptual reasoning of children, that cognitive development is part of a social system shared among people (Sroufe, Cooper, and DeHart 1996).

Vygotsky (1978) emphasized the role of language as a transmitter of culture and means for increasing a child's cognitive complexity. As children participate in culturally meaningful activities, they often engage in cooperative dialogues with more knowledgeable members of a society (most often these are adults, but social interaction with more knowledgeable peers can also lead to increased skills). It is through these cooperative dialogues that children acquire the ways of thinking and behaving that constitute each child's culture. The language used in the cooperative dialogues becomes part of that child's thinking. Later, the child will internalize essential aspects of this dialogue and use it to guide his or her independent work. For example, if we listen carefully to young children attempting to put a puzzle together by themselves, we are likely to hear them guiding their own behavior by using some of the same language that they heard when they worked with their teacher to complete the puzzle. Thus, unlike the independent little scientist that Piaget described, Vygotsky suggests that children need to engage in assisted discovery or guided participation (Rogoff 1993) in order to increase their cognitive skills.

In addition, Vygotsky argued that this assisted discovery needs to occur within the child's "zone of proximal development." The zone of proximal development is the distance between what the child can do independently and what that child might be able to accomplish with guidance from an adult or more knowledgeable peer (Vygotsky 1978). Effective interaction and instruction, therefore, should be aimed toward what is beyond the child's independent ability, but which he or she clearly can accomplish with assistance. A dynamic interplay occurs as children gain more skill; the amount and type of assistance changes to allow the child more opportunity for independent work. Thus, the child gradually moves from other regulation to self-regulated activity (Vygotsky 1978). An important role for the teacher is therefore that of "scaffold builder"—or one who carefully structures the task and gradually changes the amount and kind of support such that the child can successfully move toward independent work, self-regulation, and increasing mastery of complex tasks and understandings. This requires careful observation of children's independent functioning and knowledge of differing levels of support. Examples of decreasing levels of support include (1) partially completing a task for a child to (2) modeling an action to (3) giving verbal directions to (4) asking questions that guide the activity.

One additional aspect of the zone of proximal development that allows learning to occur is a concept referred to as intersubjectivity, or shared understanding (Miller 1993). For learning to take place, the child and partner must have a common focus of attention and shared goal. In day-to-day interaction this may often occur as a parent or teacher reminds a child of past events that are similar to the task at hand, saying something like "Remember when we . . . ; this is just like that, only this time. . . ." In a typical classroom setting where teacher and students know each other well, a shared understanding of expectations and tasks have developed over time, readily allowing for appropriate interaction within the zone of proximal development to occur. However, archaeology educators often face a first-time meeting with K–12 students where no opportunity for shared understanding has taken place. It therefore becomes essential that the educator learn as much as possible about the student's previous work related to archaeology and that the educator begin with examples or activities that are familiar to the audience.

Information-Processing Approach to Cognitive Development

The information-processing approach to cognitive development offers the clarity and precision in understanding mental processes that Piaget's theory did not (Berk 1997). This approach seeks to understand how we encode, decode, store, and retrieve information. Many theorists within this perspective view the mind like a computer or a symbol-manipulating system and attempt to describe what happens as we receive input from the environment through our senses and provide output in the form of a response (Thomas 1996; Berk 1997). Focusing on such mental components as attention and memory, investigators within this perspective have helped us better understand why younger children often struggle with certain problem-solving tasks while older children can often complete them almost effortlessly.

Unlike Piaget's explanation of qualitative differences in the cognitive structure of each stage, information-processing theorists argue that children use essentially the same processes as adults when encountering new information, tasks, or problems. However, because of their immature neurological system and limited experience and knowledge, the memory or problem-solving strategies used by children are often inefficient for handling novel or complex tasks. As children's neurological systems mature and as they gain more experience, practice, and knowledge their attentional, memory and problem-solving strategies become more efficient. In fact, from this perspective, practice and repeated exposure to information facilitates greater mental efficiency. Information that is heard repeatedly or skills that are frequently practiced become automatic (this does not mean that these repeated practices need to be done in the same way over and over, or that they need to be boring—indeed, they should not).

In information-processing terms, this automaticity frees up "working memory" to allow an individual to concentrate on more complex problems or issues. Working memory refers to that aspect of mind where we can consciously manipulate information, but which has limited attention resources allotted to it (Baddley 1992 as cited in Whitney 1998; Berk 1997). For example, a child in kindergarten who is first introduced to the word "archaeology" and "archaeologist," and who is asked to compare the work of an archaeologist with that of a paleontologist may never come to understand this distinction. This child's working memory may be taken up with the fascination of these new sounding words and with learning how to pronounce "archaeologist" and "paleontologist." However, once a child has heard these words frequently, the pronunciation of these words becomes automatic and working memory is now "free" to consider the distinction between these two fields of study.

This holds true of any individual when confronted with new and complex information. If an individual's working memory is occupied with the basic under-standing of new skills or information, he or she will not immediately be able to process the more abstract or complex aspects of the task. The more familiar and practiced we are with concepts and skills, the more readily we can engage and succeed in more complex tasks.

In addition to the familiarity of concepts is the degree to which ideas are similar and mentally connected with one another. For any given problem that requires knowledge or skills from several domains, the more connections between concepts or the more similarity among the concepts, the more efficiently we will be able to reason logically and solve the problem (Sroufe et al. 1996). Although Piaget argued that the cognitive skills and abilities characteristic of each stage of develop-ment would be applied to all problems in all situations and domains, information-processing theorists have found that cognitive skills and knowledge seem to be quite domain specific and not readily transferable to other domains (Siegler 1991). Thus, a sixth-grade student who has done very well in her or his basic science course may not utilize the same skills or problem-solving strategies when encountering a new area of study, such as archaeology. The teacher may need to initially help students make these connections from the known to the unknown or help students find the similarities between one area of study and another. The teacher may also need to help students recognize the generalizability of some problem-solving strategies across different domains.

Information-processing theorists are interested in how individuals remember information, that is, how information is encoded and retrieved. Although there are many components to understanding memory, one important concept that is relevant here is the notion of "scripts." Children's vast general knowledge systems must grow out of their own personal experiences (Berk 1997). One way that even very young children appear to organize and remember these events is to build "stories" or sequences of events called scripts. With repeated exposure to similar experiences and events, new experiences get fused into the same script. These scripts can then be used to "remember" an event or to predict what might happen in a similar situation in the future. For example, children who are exposed to several interesting and "hands-on" archaeology lessons may develop a basic script about archaeology as a science that tries to discover information about people who lived long ago.

With each exposure to archaeology, the new information gets fused with this first basic script and, simultaneously, the script may become a more realistic representation of the field.

One additional aspect of information processing relevant to pedagogical practice is a child's development of metacognitive skills. As early as four years of age, children begin to understand that humans have a mental life that is not readily observable by others (Berk 1997). But it is not until the middle to late elementary school years that children begin to view the mind as constantly active and start to think about thinking, becoming aware of what they know or do not know and thinking about the problem-solving skills or steps that are necessary to solve a given problem. Furthermore, metacognition involves the ability to monitor one's activities and progress on a task and engage in self-regulation. Increased metacognitive skills enable children to monitor their own work more carefully, to reflect on the applicability of problem-solving strategies across different domains, and to see relationships between diverse fields of study. Metacognition also appears to be important for children to engage in scientific reasoning, test theories and evaluate the evidence that may or may not support a given theory (Kuhn 1992). Although metacognitive skills become more apparent during the elementary school years, it is often not until adolescence that children begin to use them spontaneously and in more day-to-day activities.

Moral Development of Children

Part of the objective of archaeology education is to instill in school children an ethic of stewardship toward the archaeological record and an appreciation for the many other cultures that have come before us. As future taxpayers, jury members, outdoor recreators, land owners, consumers, and philanthropists, today's students need a firm grounding in the issues confronting the discipline of archaeology, so that they can act responsibly and thoughtfully toward it. Archaeology educators need to be mindful of the stages of moral development in children as they prepare educational practices that enable students to develop their archaeological ethics.

Children's development of moral reasoning and moral behavior is closely related to other cognitive abilities. As other aspects of their cognitive abilities become more complex, so, too, do their understanding and definition of fairness and justice and of right and wrong. Research findings, however, suggest that moral reasoning lags behind other aspects of cognitive functioning (Thomas 1996). Thus, while children in late elementary school or early middle school may begin to grapple with abstract concepts related to academic subjects, their reasoning about moral issues may still be based in concrete and egocentric terms. This has direct relevance for archaeology education, especially in view of the controversies surrounding "character" or "values education," as discussed by Moe (Part III, this volume).

Jean Piaget's and Lawrence Kohlberg's theories on moral reasoning provide the basis for much of our current knowledge and research in this area and offer a basic guide to sequences in children's moral reasoning (Cole and Cole 1996; Berk 1997). According to Piaget's theory of moral development (Piaget 1964), children initially view rules as absolute and as handed down from higher authority figures. Furthermore, young preschool-age children tend to have a belief in imminent justice and do not always consider the intentions of an individual as they evaluate the "rightness" or "wrongness" of an act. Imminent justice is a belief in immediate punishment, even if no one observed the wrong-doing taking place. Later, during the middle to later elementary school years, children begin to understand that rules are made by people and that rules can change.

Kohlberg (1976, 1984) based much of his theory on Piaget's theory of cognitive development and thus the moral development stages he proposed coincide with the cognitive stages within Piaget's theory. According to Kohlberg, and similar to Piaget, morality is initially externally controlled via children's concept of authority figures. Elementary school-aged children base their moral judgments on rules handed down from authority figures and egocentric concerns such as whether they will get punished or if there is some tangible reward for acting in a particular way. These children find it difficult to consider a situation from another's perspective but gradually move toward a sense of reciprocity that acknowledges different viewpoints, but is still based on self-interests, a "tit for tat" philosophy (Berk 1996, 1997).

The older elementary school-aged child and early adolescent gradually move from a base of self-interest to an understanding of the necessity of rules for social harmony and maintenance of positive human relationships. This stage is characterized by a desire to "be good," to do what will please the important people in their lives and to live by the "golden rule" (Cole and Cole 1996). Not until late adolescence or early adulthood do individuals begin to base moral reasoning on a larger scale and the more abstract perspective of "societal good." Rules are viewed as necessary to promote the well-being of a society, and all individuals are expected to adhere to these laws or rules at all times to insure social order (Berk 1997). Moral judgments at this level are generally viewed in absolute black and white terms, as before, but now with the broader perspective of the well-being of society. Only later, and seemingly for relatively few individuals, does moral reasoning become based on abstract principles and ethical values that apply in all situations and for all individuals, principles and values that can call into question the laws and rules of a society. At this last level of moral development, individual conscience and self-chosen ethical principles may supersede societal laws if necessary to universally protect and respect human worth and dignity.

Although the basic sequences of Piaget's and Kohlberg's theories have been borne out in research, the research methodology used by each may have led to an underestimation of moral development in children. Several studies suggest that children as young as three and four years of age begin to distinguish between social conventions or those arbitrary rules that govern such things as table manners and dress, and moral rules that refer to such things as honesty and the protection of the rights and welfare of others (Smetana 1981, 1985). Young children judge transgressions of moral rules as more serious, and they judge moral transgressions as still wrong even if an adult did not see them or no overt rules existed to prohibit them (Berk 1997). In addition, young children can judge an act as morally wrong even if the act were committed by an adult (Astor 1994). More recent research suggests that both Piaget and Kohlberg may have placed too much emphasis on fear of punishment and respect for authority figures as the basis for young children's moral reasoning (Eisenberg 1982; Damon 1988). Children begin very early to extrapolate "rules" about appropriate conduct from their own experiences and the experiences of others. They note adult responses to different types of transgressions and begin categorizing these into distinct moral and social conventions (Smetana 1989; Turiel, Smetana, and Killen 1991).

Although cognitive development may play a significant role in determining one's level of moral reasoning, other factors are also necessary. Kohlberg emphasized the importance of perspective taking, which, in itself, is related to cognitive level. Perspective taking refers to an individual's ability to imagine what another person may be thinking or feeling (Berk 1997). More advanced forms of moral reasoning are found among individuals who are capable of third-party or societal perspective taking. Robert Selman's (1976, cited in Berk 1997) theory on perspective taking posits that only gradually can children move from a very egocentric single-minded perspective of a situation to one that acknowledges multiple viewpoints. A recent study by Flanagan (1995, cited in Cole and Cole 1996) suggests that when considering social issues such as homelessness or poverty, younger adolescents tended to answer as if there were only one legitimate solution. Older adolescents were more likely to look at several dimensions of the problem and consider the issues from multiple perspectives. During late childhood and early adolescence, children become capable of viewing a situation from an objective third-party perspective and consider multiple perspectives simultaneously. By mid- to late adolescence or early adulthood, individuals are able to consider societal values along with third-party perspectives. These perspective-taking skills, in turn, allow older children and adolescents to begin to understand moral issues from multiple perspectives, but these may not be sufficient for the most advanced form of moral reasoning that Kohlberg argued was based on universal ethical principles.

In addition to cognitive-level and perspective-taking skills, moral reasoning and moral behavior seems to be related to years of schooling, personal experiences, child rearing practices, and one's culture (Berk 1997) as well as empathy, motivation, and other emotions (Hoffman 1988). Peer interaction, especially in situations where peers must confront and cooperatively resolve problems, also seems to be related to more advanced moral reasoning (Kruger 1992). Such advances appear to be more likely when young people are faced with problems that challenge their current belief systems and encourage them to think about moral issues in more complex ways (Berk 1997).

Because an important goal for many archaeology educators is helping their audiences understand and adhere to the preservation concept, knowledge of moral reasoning can help them approach this topic in developmentally appropriate ways. Although young children in kindergarten or the early primary grades will not be able to understand fully the concept of preservation or why it is important, or perhaps not be able to see it as an ethical or moral issue, they can be introduced to this idea through their own experiences. For example, children can be asked about their own past and how photographs of their grandparents or other relatives may have helped them know about their past. They can be asked to think of things that grandparents may have used in their homes that are no longer used—and how photographs and, preferably, the real objects help us understand what life may have been like many years ago. Also, because moral development involves empathy and other emotions, children can be asked about their own treasures and how they would feel if someone destroyed them and how best to keep them safe. These types of early lessons can then build a foundation for later ones on what preservation means and why it is vitally important. As children and adolescents gain more cognitive and perspective-taking skills and more experience, preservation can be introduced in a more realistic archaeological fashion, although ties to children's (or to any audience's) own experiences will allow for a better understanding. Older adolescents can also engage in debates about site preservation and role-play various parties that may view this ethic differently, thereby further enhancing their understanding of the issue.

Overview of the Child at Three Stages of Development

Below, I describe the cognitive abilities of children at three stages of development, utilizing Piaget's three latter stages, Preoperational, Concrete Operational, and Formal Operational. Although I use these terms, the descriptions below are a blend of concepts from the three theoretical perspectives described above. Vygotsky's theory permeates all three stages in stressing the importance of social interaction, scaffolding, intersubjectivity, and teaching within the zone of proximal development. Implications for archaeology education are included within each stage description. It is important to keep in mind that considerable cognitive variability will exist within all grade levels due to a combination of innate abilities, interests, learning styles, experiences, and other background factors. Ages associated with each stage are only approximations. Sample archaeology lessons for all developmental stages are shown in Box 3.1. Some basic strategies for working with all developmental stages are listed in Box 3.2.

BOX 3. 1
Sample Archaeology Lessons:

Archaeologists study what people left behind and create a story about past people. The suggestions below provide a broad overview for approaching the above archaeology concepts with children of different ages. More than one session is necessary to accomplish the various goals.

GOAL GRADES K–2: The goal here is to help children develop a basic understanding of the kind of work and the kind of thinking that archaeologists do. At this level children will not fully grasp the field of archaeology, but begin to understand concepts of the past and artifacts and how artifacts tell us something about the people who used them. Children can also be introduced to a comparison between archaeologists and paleontologists because so many children at this level are interested in dinosaurs. Hands-on experiences are a must.

Strategy: Focus on children's own lives, including perhaps their lives as infants and information about their grandparents. Children can be asked to mention things that they used as babies versus things that they use now and how an archaeologist might be able to tell something about their age and what they did based on these "artifacts." In advance of a lesson, children can be asked to bring in objects that represent their babyhood and objects that they "borrow" from a grandparent that tells something of their past. Educators should also bring in possible household and farming items that came from the early or mid-1900s that can represent a grandparent or great-grandparent generation and objects that represent more modern life. Children can classify these by category (household vs. outdoor/ gardening/farming) and suggest ideas about how these "artifacts" might have been used and by whom. Children can be asked to think about their own grandparents, and how these objects help us know something about how they lived. Children can also classify object as current and "long ago"—that is, select objects that are in use today from those that were more likely used in past generations. In learning to distinguish between the work of an archaeologist and a paleontologist, children can categorize pictures or items that represent both fields, and perhaps identify some areas where the two fields of study overlap.

GOAL GRADES 2–6: A wide range of abilities is represented in this "concrete operational" period. While the goals remain similar to those above, children should be able to more readily and realistically understand archaeology as a separate field of study. At the younger ages, lessons similar to that described above are suitable, perhaps with more challenges in terms of objects and the kind of classification system used. The older the child, the more sophisticated the lesson can be, but it must still be couched initially in the familiar. Hands-on experiences remain important and cooperative group work should be encouraged.

Strategy: Lesson could again start with questions/discussion about their own pasts. Most children at this level can readily read and write, so they can write down things that they use now and things that they used as babies or write short stories about what life may have been like for their grandparents. They, too, especially in the younger grades, can be asked in advance of a lesson to bring in objects that represent their own past and their grandparent's lives. They should also be able to use artifacts that are less familiar (or fragments of objects) that the educator provides and make more inferences about the people who might have used them. Children in the older grades will be more able to categorize using a matrix (cross-classification system) and make inferences about the people and the past based on this information. Children in the older grades should be better able to find relations among objects that give a more realistic picture of past life. Because children are more familiar with their communities, any pictures or artifacts from their own area can be used to have them generate ideas about what their communities may have been like in the past. Children in the older grades are also more familiar with distant regions and can make comparisons across various communities or even across various time periods within the same communities. Children can also generate ideas about what objects in use today would tell future generations about our lives. Children could create a time capsule. They can work in groups to create a story of the people who may have used the artifacts.

GOAL GRADES 6–12: As children move into formal operational thought, more abstract ideas and hypothetical deductive reasoning is possible. The middle school preadolescents will need more help engaging in scientific and abstract reasoning than will high-school–age adolescents. Although the basic goals remain the same, the depth of understanding should increase and comparisons across fields of study become more apparent and understandable. Methodology and tool use across areas of study can be made and children can embark on more scientific thinking about people of the past. Beginning with the familiar, hands-on experiences and continued group work is important.

Strategy: Lessons here can again begin with a discussion of the students' own past and present and comparisons of objects (artifacts) that indicate the changes in their lives and changes in the community. Because these students have more familiarity (automaticity) with history, geography, science, mathematics, etc., and because adolescents can be multidimensional thinkers, many of these areas can be brought into a study of past people and discussions can pertain to nonlocal discoveries. At the upper middle school and high school level, adolescents may deal with inferences regarding climate and land forms that inform about life in the past. Less familiar artifacts or sherds can be used to generate hypotheses about the past and students can hypothesize about relations between artifacts that might provide a more complete picture (theory) of past life. Adolescents can engage in sophisticated role play and be introduced to ethnography or other methods archaeologists use to both study and understand people of the past. Students may still need support and guidance in making connections between different aspects of archaeology and different pieces of evidence. Tremendous variability may be seen within each grade level and between the youngest and oldest grades in terms of background knowledge, experience, ability to reason scientifically, etc. Group work with a mixture of ability levels can help accommodate this variability as long as all individuals can request assistance of the educator.

Box 3.2

Survival Strategies for Archaeology Educators

Below is a quick list of some basic strategies for successful developmentally appropriate practice when working with K–12 students:

- Have realistic goals; students do not and cannot learn all or even the most important aspects of archaeology in just one or two lessons.
- Know your audience developmentally, educationally, regionally, and locally.
- The younger the students, the more likely their knowledge and experience is limited, and the more basic the lesson needs to be.
- The younger the students, the more likely they view things from a single perspective (egocentric).
- Variability in interest and abilities is to be expected within any grade level and across different settings.
- Develop activities that quickly assess children's familiarity with and understanding of archaeology; come prepared for several different lessons if your audiences knows a lot more or a lot less than expected.
- It is just as important to connect archaeology with adolescents' own lives as it is to do this with younger children.
- Do not assume that adolescents will be able to reason scientifically without support or that they can engage in highly abstract reasoning, especially if information is novel or complex.
- Incorporate experiences of students into archaeology lessons.
- Work from the familiar to the unfamiliar.
- Use hands-on activities whenever possible at all age levels.
- Remain flexible, creative, and imaginative.
- Cooperative group work helps develop ideas and concepts, and is often more enjoyable.
- Avoid long periods of "telling" (lecture); the younger the children, the shorter the period of telling, but even adults get tired and become unfocused with long periods of being talked at.
- Develop a "bag of tricks" or activities that can be used in a variety of ways with a variety of age levels and which can easily be substituted when even the best-prepared lessons go awry.
- Show enthusiasm for the subject and the audience.

The Preoperational Child (Early Childhood: Grades K–2, Ages Five–Seven)

Although these young children will not understand much of what archaeologists feel is vital and important to their field, it is at this level that archaeology educators can begin introducing the very basic concepts and lay the ground work for later "lessons" and greater understanding. When lessons are presented in simplistic ways and connected to their common experiences, young children can begin to understand the importance of archaeology. Children at this level tend to be extremely curious and energetic, quickly soaking up and organizing new experiences to better comprehend their world. These children appear at times quite mature and logical, and, at other times, illogical and full of limited and magical explanations (Berk 1996).

Although Piaget described these children as prelogical representational thinkers and tended to emphasize what they cannot do, subsequent research suggests that they can reason logically if the problems or questions asked of them are simplified and based on familiar events, objects, or experiences. For example, many children between four and seven are intrigued by and become miniature "experts" on dinosaurs. In one classroom, I observed a five-year-old boy busily naming many of the dinosaurs when his teacher, jokingly, showed him a picture of a fish and asked what that dinosaur was called. Promptly and matter-of-factly, the boy replied, "Fishasaurus," a very logical and rational response. Young children gradually gain more sophisticated ways of representing reality in the form of language, play, and writings and drawings and gradually replace their magical beliefs about the cause of events into more plausible explanations (Berk 1997). By the primary grades, most children are nearing the end of the preoperational period and are more consistently applying simple logic and more realistic thinking in understanding the world. Recent research suggests a cognitive shift at about age four when children first show evidence of a "theory of mind" as discussed earlier. Use of appropriate "scaffolding" within a zone of proximate development allows these children more opportunity for successful work with relatively complex tasks than what might otherwise occur without this support structure.

When young children are faced with unfamiliar topics, they may often use illogical, coincidental happenings to explain cause and effect. For example, if an archaeology educator visited a first-grade classroom bringing artifacts (such as a projectile point and pieces of pottery) that had been recovered from a nearby archaeological site, preoperational children may draw an erroneous conclusion that archaeologists always carry with them and collect arrowheads and pottery. The next time these young children meet with an archaeology educator, even in a different setting, they may ask "Where is your arrowhead? or "How many arrowheads do you have now?" Furthermore, children's ability to reason is hampered by knowledge and attention limitations and ineffective memory strategies.

While it is probably accurate to say that young children have short attention spans, it is also true that they do not always attend to the appropriate aspects of a task and can quite easily have their attention diverted by irrelevant or coincidental information. In addition, these children are not always aware of what they know or don't know nor do they automatically employ appropriate memory strategies, such as rehearsal, even if they are aware of such strategies (Sroufe et al. 1996). These metacognitive limitations and lack of automaticity in many tasks often lead to "working memory overload" in young children when they are confronted with novel information. Working memory bottlenecks may also explain why young children are often taken in by appearances. Children initially will focus attention and hold in memory only one or two dimensions of a situation or problem, which in turn, leads to erroneous or illogical conclusions.

Kindergarten and primary grade children, by age alone, have limited experiences and most of these are within the confines of their home, neighborhood, and community. For impoverished families, the experiences are often even more limited. In other words, their scripts, which serve as the mechanisms for organizing and interpreting their everyday experiences (Berk 1996) are limited. Talking with these young children about exciting archaeology digs in distant or unfamiliar parts of this country or in the world will have little meaning to them.

Having these children engage in a pretend dig to discover recognizable "artifacts" in their sand table and helping them to make up a simple story about the people who might have used the objects will have a great deal more meaning for them and give them a better understanding about the field of archaeology. Children of this age love to be doing, making, trying, experimenting, taking things apart, or putting them together. Play, including pretend play, is both a window on the cognitive abilities of young children and the vehicle through which they often confront and master aspects of their world that are somewhat confusing. Vygotsky viewed play as a naturally occurring zone of proximal development in which children advance themselves to higher skill levels and more abstract levels of thinking (Vygotsky 1978; Berk 1994). Archaeology educators can take advantage of young children's curiosity, eagerness to know, and play modes to engage children in pretend play and other interactive activities that give them a hands-on feel for the world of archaeology and build in them an initial interest and excitement about this field of study.

The Concrete Operational Child (Middle Childhood: Grades 2–6, Ages Seven–Eleven)

With greater neurological maturity, more everyday life experiences and a few more years of formal schooling, children in the middle elementary and early middle-school grades have typically made significant cognitive gains. For Piaget, the hallmark of this stage was children's mastery of conservation tasks, an understanding that the amount does not change by mere transformations in shape or form. The logical reasoning necessary for successful completion of conservation tasks also is found in children's ability to engage in more complex classification and categorization tasks, such as matrix classification that entails an item being categorized along two dimensions simultaneously (Sroufe et al. 1996). Additionally, an understanding of conservation tasks is related to more sophisticated perspective taking skills.

By middle childhood, children have had repeated exposure and practice with some skills, and therefore are likely to have developed automaticity in some domains and not suffer the same working memory limitations as younger, less-experienced children. Automatic access to more knowledge and skills allows these children to devote more working memory space to increasingly sophisticated problems or ideas. Children in middle childhood have developed better memory and attentional strategies and have gained a greater refinement in metacognitive skills (Sroufe et al. 1996). For example, children gradually ignore irrelevant information and move from rehearsal as a sole memory strategy, to rehearsing selected information, to organizing and categorizing material to an elaboration or imagery scheme for remembering information (Berk 1996). Elaboration is a sophisticated memory strategy that often does not emerge until late childhood whereby we create a "relationship, or shared meaning, between two or more pieces of information" (Berk 1997:272). This can be accomplished through mental imagery. For example, if we were asked to remember a word list that contained the words "spoon," "dog," and "wagon," we could picture a dog feeding itself with a spoon riding in a wagon. Strategies like elaboration allow children to gather information into "chunks," enabling them to hold onto more information, and allowing working memory to be used more efficiently. Greater working-memory capacity and metacognitive advances allow children to engage in more systematic planning and implementation of problem-solving strategies.

However, although children at this age are more logical reasoners and show other significant cognitive gains, several limitations still exist. When confronted with a problem they are not usually exhaustive in their solutions, and, as with younger children, do not always use a skill they possess, especially if they must apply it across different knowledge domains or as part of a larger problem-solving system (Sroufe et al. 1996). This failure to generalize across situations and domains of knowledge is due to both limitations in their knowledge base and their difficulty in dealing with abstract concepts. Piaget's term for this period, Concrete Operations, is quite apt in that children's thinking in middle to late childhood tends to be held to things that are observable, manipulative things that they have experienced or, in other ways, things that are concrete.

Furthermore, even though these children may engage in the "scientific method" in school tasks, when faced with a new phenomenon they have a hard time letting go of prior beliefs even in the face of contrary evidence. They are also more likely to be influenced by coincidental events and not able to set up experiments to systematically determine the cause of an event (Santrock 1997). They tend to create their own theories about the happenings in their world by observing several specific instances or examples of an event and drawing some conclusion, often erroneously (empirico-inductive reasoning). But they are less able to start with a general theory, and systematically test particular hypotheses that emanate from that theory (hypothetical-deductive reasoning). Hands-on experiences continue to be important for learning, and, when confronting novel or complex ideas, they especially need a familiar basis from which to begin. Working with peers in cooperative endeavors is important for encouraging dialogue, challenging their thinking, and pushing them toward more advanced perspective-taking skills. Games with rules and cooperative play tend to supplant the pretend play ubiquitous to the preschool and early primary-school–age children. These types of play help challenge children's concept of rules and help them gain an appreciation for and practice with systematic problem-solving strategies.

The Formal Operational Child
(Preadolescence and Adolescence:
Grades 6–12, Ages Eleven–Eighteen)

For most individuals, adolescence brings with it the capacity for abstract reasoning. Young people are no longer held to the here and now, the observable, tangible, or manipulative. They are capable of considering multiple possibilities, of mentally manipulating abstract ideas and considering the relationships between them, and reasoning logically (Berk 1996; Sroufe et al. 1996). They show a greater capacity for metacognition and, on occasion, get lost in their own thoughts, thinking about their own thinking. Greater metacognitive capacity also allows for more self-regulation and better memory and problem-solving strategies, which include their ability to engage in hypothetical-deductive reasoning. They are now able to consider possible hypothetical situations and systematically go about testing possible solutions.

Factors such as greater neurological maturity, more knowledge in a greater number of subjects, more life experiences, and additional years of formal schooling where knowledge and skills have been repeatedly practiced allow greater automaticity across several tasks and knowledge domains (Case 1985). This automaticity, along with some of the aforementioned skills, allows adolescents to grapple with much more complex academic, social, and political problems and to gain an appreciation for increasingly sophisticated language and subtle meanings from poetry and literature (Berk 1996).

Although working memory may still become bottlenecked with too much information or too much novel or complex information, adolescents are less likely to suffer the working memory limitations found in schoolage children. Because so many more skills and concepts are retrieved automatically and effortlessly, more of working memory is available to tackle the novel and complex. Therefore, they can think about problems from multiple perspectives and begin to show greater flexibility in their thinking. Older adolescents, especially, begin to appreciate that there may also be many possible solutions to social and political problems, thinking which is clearly related to more advanced forms of moral reasoning. In addition, because of increases in knowledge across a variety of subjects, the adolescent has more anchoring points from which to consider new information. For example, the concept of preservation may be easier for adolescents to understand because many of them have also been introduced to similar concepts (such as ecology, which includes preservation of the world's resources) that serve as connecting points (see Frost, this volume).

However, while adolescents develop the capacity for such sophisticated thinking, research suggests that many adolescents and adults don't engage in formal operational thought on a regular basis. It appears as though abstract reasoning is most likely to occur in settings or situations in which individuals have had the greatest experience or training (Lehman and Nisbett 1990). Thus, although adolescents might be able to grapple with some of the complexities entailed in the study of archaeology, their initial introduction may still need to be done in concrete, hands-on form, again using their own or other reality-based experiences as the starting point for getting at the more abstract principles. Adolescents who have been lucky enough to have had continued exposure to archaeology will be better able to handle complex tasks and reason hypothetically about some of the moral or political issues.

Additionally, while I have lumped together children from approximately eleven to eighteen years of age in the formal operational stage, research suggests that formal operation skills develop gradually (Kuhn, Langer, Kohlberg, and Haan 1977). Younger adolescents may begin to show the capacity for some of these more sophisticated skills, but they are not fully developed nor do they use these consistently. Older adolescents are more likely to show fully developed formal operational thought and to use these skills more consistently (Sroufe et al. 1996). Whether older adolescents use formal operational skills seems to depend on their familiarity with the situation as well as on motivational, social and emotional factors. Although adolescents have at their disposal a much greater knowledge base, this, too, is not always used logically or organized into a coherent theory (Sroufe et al. 1996). Archaeology educators may need to point out explicitly the connections between areas of study or problem sets to help adolescents develop more coherent theories and to improve metacognitive skills.

At this level, social interaction and cooperative or collaborative work remain very important. Adolescents are more apt to understand situations if they can place themselves into these experiences through role-play or debates or other hands-on experiences. As they grow toward more independence and autonomy, they need increasing opportunities to make choices, to feel in charge, and to feel valued (Hamburg 1993; Takanishi 1993). Within this group, we are more likely to see individuals really "tuned in" or "tuned out." Therefore, enthusiasm and finding common ground continue to be important. These young people become capable of attaching emotionally to ideas and concepts, not just to other people. Archaeology educators can use this to help adolescents develop an appreciation of and respect for archaeology.

Conclusions

Archaeology educators are frequently engaged with school children with whom they have had no previous contact and are developing educational materials for the K–12 audience. The effectiveness of such materials and teaching experiences is much greater when they are designed with the developmental stage of the audience in focus. Not only is learning more likely to be enriched, but the upcoming educated generation will have had the opportunity to evolve the stewardship ethics that are necessary for preservation of the archaeological record.

RECOMMENDED READINGS

The following are recommended readings that provide an excellent account of human development. Although three of these are textbooks, the information is so thorough and well written that they are quite accessible for further information on cognitive, moral, and other aspects of development in children and adolescents.

Berk, L. E.
    1997   *Child Development*, 4th ed. Allyn & Bacon, Boston.
This text and the one below are fairly exhaustive in their coverage of children's development through adolescence. Each provides a wealth of information and up-to-date research on human development. This text is arranged topically, while the one below is arranged chronologically.

Berk, L. E.
    1996. *Infants, Children, and Adolescents*, 2d ed. Allyn & Bacon, Boston.

Coles, R.
    1997. *The Moral Intelligence of Children: How to Raise a Moral Child*. Plume, New York.
This popular book is more of a hands-on guide for raising moral children, but provides some background about moral development of children of different ages that can help educators better understand moral development on an everyday basis.

Sroufe, L. A., R. G. Cooper, and G. B. DeHart.
    1996. *Child Development: Its Nature and Course*, 3rd ed. McGraw-Hill, New York.
This text provides a chronological account of child and adolescent development. While not as exhaustive as the Berk texts, it is quite readable with interesting stories about children of varying age levels that introduce each chronological section.

VICTOR W. GERACI ■

Chapter Four
_____

Learning and Teaching Styles
Reaching All Students

Archaeology education, like all attempts to transmit information to an unknowledgeable audience, requires a clear understanding of two things: (1) a solid grasp of content and organization of the information that is being presented and (2) an understanding of how the audience receives and processes data. Children develop their ability to learn—to receive and process information—within specific age ranges, depending on a variety of factors that range from psychological to environmental. In addition, students of any age receive and assimilate data in different ways, called "learning styles."

While we can all learn in various ways, most people have a way that they most easily can take in new concepts and acquire new sets of skills. Some of us, for instance, learn best by writing notes or hearing the spoken word, while others relate best to pictures, physical movement, or problem-solving activities. Archaeology is both a science and a humanity. Further, it's a wonderful combination of sequential physical tasks done in the pursuit of intellectual and analytical goals. An archaeologist shovels dirt, all the while engaging in higher-order thinking using skills ranging from hypothesizing to information gathering through analysis. It is an excellent opportunity to allow students to manipulate knowledge and artifacts, be physical, utilize spatial skills, draw, quantify, write, verbalize, and visualize within the traditional curriculum.

In order to be effective in teaching archaeological concepts to students of any age, understanding how people learn is essential. This chapter provides a concise introduction to this aspect of educational psychology to help archaeology educators do the best possible job of helping people learn. Expressing concepts too complex for the learner or using language that is in advance of a child's developmental level will inevitably result in a bored, confused student and a frustrated teacher-archaeologist.

91

So, too, does presenting information in a way that only part of your class can readily assimilate. Using a variety of approaches, including activities, words, and even song or dance can help ensure that everyone learns about, and is excited by, archaeology and the archaeologist teaching it.

The Search for the Holy Grail

Throughout the twentieth century, educational reformers hoped to create an industrial model of a school whereby raw materials (children) entered the physical plant (school) and machines (curriculum) run by trained technicians (teachers) mass-produced graduates ready to assume their role in American democracy. At first, these researchers sought "lockstep" curricula and behavior modification techniques that would work with all students. For much of the century, this simplistic view of the process changed little, and many students did not succeed in this system.

The quest for better educational methodologies evolved with the proliferation of twentieth-century North American scientific scholarship. Early 1900 researchers, prompted by Social Darwinists and the new field of psychology, attempted to define the way students learned so that schools could produce uniform results. While the majority of researchers concentrated on the traditional singular mode, many educational leaders warned that humans were not machines. The idea that one-school-fits-all-learners came under scrutiny. As Emily Johnson has described in the previous chapter, educational specialists such as Jean Piaget, the noted French educational psychologist, promoted an active education whereby students constructed knowledge for themselves.

The belief that we learn in different ways gained little acceptance between the 1930s and 1950s as America's depression-era and war-burdened society concentrated on developing a curriculum that was society centered. Through the 1930s and 1940s, researchers spoke of the "cognitive style" of learning, whereby differences in the quality of environment and personality determined how students learned. Educational research emphasized individual intelligence and psychological differentiation. By the early 1950s, cold war setbacks caused Americans to doubt educational methodologies (Keefe 1987:4).

As a result of these setbacks, many professional educators began to realize that one style of teaching and singular curricular methodologies were failing to meet the needs of all students. New research that focused on the practices of successful teachers had demonstrated two important points: (1) Successful teachers have a natural gift for working with children, and (2) These gifted teachers successfully manage student learning through a pragmatic trial and error approach to curriculum. A "shotgun" approach, whereby a smattering of many techniques was used in the hopes that some would be effective, had taught these teachers that exchanging one singularly focused pedagogy for another left many students behind. So they adapted a philosophy of "There is more than one way to skin the cat." In other words, they agreed to use whatever method seemed to be the most efficient to maximize student learning (Orlich et al. 1994:63).

Using data from teacher success studies, educational professionals of the 1950s conceded that students learn in different ways and that no one style of teaching can meet all of these needs. By 1954, the term "learning style" was used to describe the dynamics of varied student learning. However, it would not be until the mid-1950s, when Benjamin Bloom proposed a school learning model, that progress was made. Bloom defined learning as the result of a mixture of cognitive behaviors (ways we think, perceive, and problem solve), affective characteristics (emotions, values), and instructional quality. Bloom's theory codified the fact that learning differences exist and that educators needed to develop varied strategies to meet the different needs of a range of children (Bloom, Krathwohl, and Masia 1956).

Reforms and liberalism of the 1960s and 1970s moved curriculum design toward an emphasis on the humane in schools. The era of social change and the Great Society widened the cognitive style to include factors like selection of strategies, open- and closed-mindedness, memory styles, risk taking, and sensory preferences. Student-centered trends embraced New Math, transitional grammar, learning centers, individualized instruction, and open-space classrooms. Yet, as the knowledge of multiple learning styles grew, educational pedagogy continued to concentrate on singular methods as the best means for handling large groups of students. These student-centered approaches failed to alleviate poor student performance, and a late 1970s backlash returned schools to a monocurricular "three Rs" revival of basic skills.

Tenacious apostles of differences in learning continued to develop pedagogical approaches that could address differences between student learning styles. In 1979, Anthony Gregorc observed that students' overt behaviors were biologically determined (for example, by nutrition, health, sex, environment). By the end of the 1970s, educational practitioners brought the Bloom and Gregorc ideas together and defined three factors that determine styles of learning—cognitive, affective, and psychological (Orlich et al. 1994:61–62).

The next two decades saw the development of numerous new educational theories. One of the oldest and most widely used approaches was Rita and Kenneth Dunn's work (1993). They identified four key differences in learning styles: (1) environment, (2) emotional support, (3) sociological factors, and (4) personal and physical elements (Dunn and Dunn 1992:passim). When developed around practical and pragmatic classroom experiences, their categorization system gained widespread acceptance. A psychological approach developed by Gregorc (1985) advocated using the hemispheric brain (right brain/left brain, concrete versus abstract perceptual preferences) approach with refinements for ordering abilities (ways of arranging, systematizing, and disposing of new information).

By the late 1980s, as educators and researchers began to classify and evaluate how students learned, they adapted a simpler pragmatic approach to the process of teaching. After evaluating diverse learning styles, they designed flexible modes of learning that accommodated the largest number of students.

Practical Learning Styles

Throughout the 1980s, educators sought practical methodologies capable of supporting the new learning theories. By the mid-1980s, Bernice McCarthy had developed the first of the new practical learning style approaches. McCarthy's system, like Gregorc's, was based on the premise that teaching activities should progress in a sequential four-step process that stresses both right and left brain activities and builds on Bloom's Taxonomy (McCarthy 1987; also see Table 4.1). The complicated system was difficult for busy classroom teachers to plan and execute.

A more practical approach came in the 1980s Multiple Intelligences work of Howard Gardner, which touted intelligence as being dynamic with many attributes that could be enhanced (Lazear 1992). By the 1990s, this theory became mainstream, and many practitioners designed practical means to teach to the seven basic intelligences of students. Gardner's research divided learners into seven groups, or "intelligences":

1. *Verbal Linguistic*: "The Word Player"—These are the students who learn best through verbal intelligence by utilizing vocabulary, verbal analysis, and complex verbal material and metaphors. They like to read, write, and tell stories and are good at memorizing and recalling facts. Most of them are good at teaching and learning and appreciate humor.
2. *Logical/Mathematical*: "The Questioner"—These students display mathematical genius and excel at inductive and deductive reasoning. They like to work with numbers, ask questions, and explore abstract patterns and are good at math, scientific reasoning, and logic.
3. *Visual/Spatial*: "The Visualizer"—Included in this category are learners who use and manipulate spatial objects. They like to draw, build, design, and create things and are good at mazes, puzzles maps, charts, and imaging. Many of them become architects and engineers.
4. *Body/Kinesthetic*: "The Mover"—Gardner determined that this group included students who thrive on physical activity and make successful athletes and dancers. They like to move around, touch things, use body language, and they are good at physical activities.
5. *Musical/Rhythmic:* "The Music Lover"—Musicians and songwriters shine as children in school in their ability to write, play, remember melodies, or sing music.

TABLE 4.1
*Instructional Objectives: Bloom's Taxonomy of Educational Objectives,
from Highest Level to Lowest Level (Bloom 1956)*

Cognitive Domain	Definition	Learning Outcomes (action verbs)	
Knowledge	Students recall knowledge such as facts, terminology, strategies, and rules.	define describe identify label list	match name select state match
Comprehension	Students show a level of understanding and restate readings, translate, see connections, draw conclusions, and see relationships.	convert estimate defend distinguish discriminate explain	generalize summarize infer paraphrase predict
Application	Students use previously acquired knowledge and apply it in a new setting.	change compute demonstrate develop modify operate	organize prepare relate solve transfer use
Analysis	Students identify logical errors or differentiate among facts, opinions, assumptions, hypotheses, and conclusions.	break down deduce diagram differentiate distinguish illustrate	infer outline point out relate subdivide
Synthesis	Students produce something unique or original with what they have learned.	categorize compile compose create design	devise formulate predict produce
Evaluation	Students form judgments and make decisions about the value or worth of methods, ideas, people, and products and state a basis for their argument.	appraise compare contrast criticize defend	justify support validate judge

Note: In the mid-1950s, Benjamin Bloom developed a taxonomy that categorized cognitive learning (intellectual ability and skills) into a six-step hierarchical schema referred to as Behavioral or Instructional Objectives. One of the assumptions was that educators could plan lessons that changed a learner's observable behavior. The six established domains provided classroom teachers with a means to plan effectively for the complex intellectual growth of their students. When teachers write their daily lesson plans, they are asked to think about the taxonomy and thus set intellectual/behavioral objectives for their planned activities. The practical classroom goal is to develop and execute teaching strategies that will enact behaviors that stimulate students to navigate through all six levels. Included in the chart are action verbs that teachers utilize to describe learning outcomes for their planned activities. Archaeologists planning teaching materials should utilize these domains and relate objectives to the included action verbs.

6. *Interpersonal:* "The Socializer"—Students in this group succeed by utilizing their gift of social intelligence or the ability to use subtle cues in their social environment with their families, friends, school clubs, and neighborhoods. They like to have lots of friends and enjoy talking to people, love to join groups, and are good at communicating and organizing people.

7. *Intrapersonal:* "The Individual"—Many students find their way in school through reflection and self-knowledge. They like to work alone, pursue their own interests, and follow their own instincts, and are original. Many of these students become religious people or philosophers.

Gardner's research also concluded that most teachers tended to develop the first two styles and discriminated against the other five (Gardner and Hatch 1989:4–10). The implication was that curricula needed to be more inclusive of all learning styles to enhance the total learning experience for the greatest number of students.

Teachers worried as to how they could meet the challenges of designing numerous activities that could bridge students' learning styles with the concepts required in the curriculum. How could they, on a daily basis, develop and execute a complex series of activities that met student learning styles, developed critical thinking, and promoted writing and cooperative learning, while intermingling their own teaching styles with environmental, social, cultural, political, and cultural factors?

Pressure was lifted from the backs of teachers as curriculum specialists developed practical methodologies and activities for all seven styles. Through trial and error, teachers discerned that as long as units of study addressed each modality, individual daily lessons only required limited modification. They also came to realize that students can sometimes learn in more than one mode or in a combination of styles. What teachers needed were curriculum specialists to develop a large array of activities for them to choose from and which could meet the numerous needs of their students.

Archaeologists as Curriculum Specialists

The task of developing multifaceted lessons to aid classroom teachers can be accomplished by archaeologists; they must approach the Herculean planning task by adapting strategies fostered by classroom teachers. Classroom practitioners brought order to this planning chaos by adopting a global perspective for their lessons. They view the social sciences as a pragmatic way to contextualize the world for each student. By using thematic approaches and "postholing" (going into depth on a topic), teachers integrated math, science, language, music, literature, art, and all the social sciences. This allowed students with every learning style to become active participants in the educational process (see Table 4.2).

Development of K–12 lessons for archaeology education entails designing multidisciplinary strategies. Archaeologists cannot plan for the individual needs of

TABLE 4.2

Seven Styles of Learning: Summary Chart

Learning Style	Teaching Activities	Teaching Materials	Instruction Strategies
Verbal Linguistic	lectures, discussions, word games, choral reading, journal writing, historical research—read about it, write about it, listen to it	books, tape recordings, primary source documents, artifacts	essays, written reports, newspaper and magazine articles, speeches, oral reports, journals, diaries, historic literature, poetry, debate
Logical Mathematical	brain teasers, problem solving, science experiments, mental calculation, number games, critical thinking, cause/effect—quantify it, think critically about it, conceptualize its uses	calculators, math manipulatives, science equipment, math games, primary source documents (census records)	time lines, computer databases of statistics, cost analysis, percentages, advantages/disadvantages, inquiry lessons, surveys
Visual Spatial	visual presentations, art activities, imagination games, mind-mapping, metaphor, visualization, video, film—see it, draw it, visualize it, color it, map it	graphs, maps, videos, block sets, art materials, slides, prints, posters, cameras, artifacts, atlas, almanac	cultural maps, physical maps, photo essay, video, organizational charts, political cartoons
Body Kinesthetic	hands-on learning, drama dance, tactile activities, sports that teach—build it, act it out, get a "gut" feeling, dance it, excavate it	building tools, clay, sports equipment, manipulatives, tactile learning resources, excavation tools, artifacts	build a model, role play, skits, demonstrations, field trips, board games, flip shutes, electroboards, body action wall and floor games, craft projects, archaeology excavations
Musical Rhythmic	super learning, rapping, songs that teach—sing it, listen to it	tape recordings, musical instruments, CDs, sheet music, lyrics	compose songs or lyrics to music based on history, create historic discographies, musical performances
Interpersonal	cooperative learning, peer tutoring, community involvement, social gatherings—teach it, collaborate on it, interact with it	board games, party supplies, role playing props, guest speakers	oral interviews, simulations, group projects, peer tutoring, mock trials, field trips, historical empathy, case studies, jigsaw activities, brainstorming, team learning
Intrapersonal	individualized instruction, independent study, self-esteem building—connect it to your personal life, making choices, values clarification	self-checking materials, journals, project materials, textbook, literature	geneology, create historical diaries, scrapbooks, journals, self-designed projects, learning centers, textbook activities, personal histories, tutorials, drill and practice, task cards, contract activity packages

SOURCES: Sitton, Mehaffy, and Davis 1983; Gardner 1993; Social Science Education Consortium, Inc. 1996.

every student; this must be left to the classroom teacher. But they can develop lessons with a thematic approach that incorporate all seven learning styles and address issues of age, ability, language proficiency, economic and cultural background, and geographic location (Wolynec, this volume). The bottom line is that archaeology educators must produce an array of multidisciplinary lessons that promote all seven intelligences and allow classroom teachers to adopt the appropriate strategies for their students.

Conclusion

Archaeology educators need to understand and apply methods and approaches used by teachers to ensure that they present their information in such a way that each and every member of the target audience can receive and process effectively. This means that they need to develop a precollegiate curriculum that fits well into the theoretical construct of Gardner's seven intelligences.

Gardner defined intelligence as the ability to find and solve problems and create products for one's culture. Since each student's cultural background differs, so, too, will his or her approach to learning. Be sensitive to cultural diversity and the different ways that people utilize spatial, linguistic, and logical skills.

Well-planned teaching strategies can be designed for the classroom, museum, or site visit. After developing strategies for an education program, ask yourself this question: Can these activities meet the needs of all learners? (Use the Learning Style column in Table 4.2 to help answer this critical question.)

Every activity does not have to have all seven styles, but together all the program activities should have some strategy for each style. Does your archaeology education program allow all students to touch, see, hear, and manipulate material culture, work individually and in groups, and then graphically, orally and in writing complete a task that helps them understand people from the past? Students construct knowledge for themselves in whatever learning style they primarily utilize. Provide teachers and their students with a large repertoire of activities and the ability to choose those that will meet the needs of their classes, and the program will be effective in conveying its educational and stewardship messages to the widest possible student audience.

Box 4.1 is a learning activity that incorporates all seven intelligences:

BOX 4.1
Activity Example

News Show about an Archaeological Site:

MATERIALS: Video camera, VHS tape, research materials, props, classroom materials

TIME: One to two weeks depending on the product desired.

GOAL: Have students complete individual and group historical research on an archaeological site. Students will delve into a particular era and become experts on the people and material culture of that era. Can be used in World or United States social science courses in upper elementary and secondary schools. Difficulty and grade level appropriateness can be modified by the selection of resources and adjustments for reading levels.

STRATEGY: The class will produce a News Magazine about a specific archaeological site.

PRE-ACTIVITY: The teacher divides the class into groups of four or five students based on their learning styles. Each group will contain a mixture of students (learning styles) and be responsible for a five- to ten-minute News Magazine presentation. Teachers can provide the class with a list of possible news stories.

GROUP RESPONSIBILITIES: Each member of the group should be assigned a task dependent on their learning style. Possible suggestions include . . .
1. Linguistic: These members of the group will conduct most of the written research, write the script for the presentation, and act as presenters.
2. Logical/Mathematical: These skilled quantifiers could investigate the site's artifact data, published reports, the Internet, and other sources to be used as part of the statistical data presented. Allow them to quantify, conceptualize, and hypothesize. They will provide data charts for the filming.
3. Spatial: These members of the group will design a set for their presentation and be in charge of lighting, film, and dub music. They need to interact with presenters and researchers and determine how to block stage activity and timing.

4. Kinesthetic: Have these students build the set and research and demonstrate a physical skill used by inhabitants of the site—sport, craft, dance, drama.
5. Musical: Allow these students to select appropriate background music for the presentation. If possible they should also research the music of the time and have a musical performance as part of the presentation.
6. Interpersonal: Serve as the group leader and peer tutor for those needing additional help. These students can be used to help out in areas requiring more input. Their style is being satisfied by the fact that they are collaborating in a group.
7. Intrapersonal: Students needing independent study can be assigned a self-designed project that ties something on the site to their personal life. They can present it, or the group can incorporate it as part of the presentation.

RESEARCH GUIDELINES: Have students use a minimum of five sources to do research on an archaeological site. Materials can be gathered from site archaeologists, school libraries, public libraries, historical societies, museums, and the Internet. Students need to view and study artifacts and the written record (primary sources). If possible, have them conduct oral interviews of actual participants or experts on the subject. Teachers should make available as many secondary sources as possible. A fieldtrip to the site could provide realistic footage for the actual presentation.

IF TIME PERMITS: Students could include commercials.

Chapter Five

Heritage Education for Special Students

Every child, whether gifted or not, shares our common human heritage. Yet a review of the current literature on archaeology education suggests that archaeologists have focused their attention on either gifted or talented children, on select groups such as Native American students, or on those perceived to have average abilities. In the process, much of the archaeological community appears to have systematically excluded students who may be perceived as more difficult to reach, who may require more effort, or who may consider that the subject matter is, in their opinion, inappropriate. Yet, today, it is likely that an archaeologist stepping before a group of students will face a very heterogeneous audience.

They can be faced with children for whom English is a second language and is therefore not understood, spoken, or read; children with learning, social, and physical disabilities; and children representing a great variety of socioeconomic and ethnic backgrounds. Because most archaeologists have no training in teaching methodologies, they are at a disadvantage when developing a program in today's complex teaching and learning environment. This chapter will explore the problems and challenges associated with teaching a highly diverse student body. The discussion will focus on aspects of multicultural education associated with exceptionalities, English as a second language, and contemporary immigrant perspectives.

Reaching the Learner

Know the Student Audience

At its most inclusive, multicultural education deals with self-esteem, family structure, ethnicity, religious groups, gender, children's issues, exceptionalities, values, age, socioeconomic status, and communication (Finazzo 1997: 99–105). Given the potential complexity of the audience, the archaeologist must be prepared to address the needs of as many children as possible. In this context, the archaeologist is a teacher and, as such, must treat every presentation very seriously. It is no longer enough to give a "canned" lecture and pat oneself on the back for how great it was. Even the shortest presentation requires preparation, which includes identifying who the students will be, their grade level, special needs, language abilities, and so forth. Interactive communication with the teacher (in the case of a one-time classroom visit) (Ellick, this volume) or with a curriculum development specialist (in the case of complex program development) is mandatory (MacDonald and Burtness, this volume). Ask specific questions. Many teachers don't volunteer information about the diversity of abilities or backgrounds represented by the students in their classrooms.

Lack of information about the composition of the class can lead to a poor learning experience. A slide lecture for a group including sight-impaired children may exclude them from fully appreciating and understanding a lesson. A prolonged lecture for students with learning disabilities such as Attention Deficit Disorder could become a painful experience for everyone concerned. A program that vilifies past members of an ethnic group may cause great personal shame, loss of self-esteem, or anger by students who are members of that ethnic group. An educator who uses only English lectures as the teaching medium, for a class with little or no English competence, will have wasted everyone's time. When developing any kind of program, the archaeologist must be aware of the needs and abilities of the student audience, how to meet these needs and make use of these abilities, and the message that will be conveyed and learned.

Know the Presented Message

In the process of preparation, archaeology educators must know their own values and be able to identify their feelings and perceptions about cultural diversity before they can teach children to do the same (Finazzo 1997:104) (see Box 5.1). Further, the archaeologist must be aware of the classroom teacher's perceptions of the field or subject matter. Each must be aware of any hidden agenda in the presentation. For example, some scholars have suggested that archaeology programs serve as a vehicle for forced assimilation and disparagement of Native American beliefs (Ahler 1994:454).

Stereotypes should be recognized and avoided. A teacher may think an archaeologist is a miracle worker if a class of children with Attention Deficit Disorder sits quietly for twenty minutes. The success of the lesson should not rest on their lack of activity but on what they actually learn from the lesson. "If the students are not learning, it doesn't matter how hard you're working up there in front of that class, there is no teaching going on" (McKenna 1988 in Smardz 1990:296).

Box 5.1
Teaching Cultural Diversity

In the process of preparation, archaeology educators must know their own values and be able to identify their own feelings and perceptions about cultural diversity before they can teach children to do the same (Finazzo 1997:104). This must include coming to grips with one's own cultural background (Tiedt and Tiedt 1995:21). "Although we almost all have an immigrant past, very few of us know or even acknowledge it" (Nieto 1992:xxv). Personal values, biases, and self-identity all have an impact on a teacher's effectiveness in a multicultural classroom (Tiedt and Tiedt 1995:xiv).

Sexism, racism, elitism, and any other form of prejudice have no place in the classroom. Replacing one "ism" with another, such as "Eurocentrism" with "Afrocentrism" continues the process of building-up one child's self-esteem at the expense of another's. Truly effective multicultural education should be human centered. Archaeologists may have just one chance to reach the students with their message. Will that message be about their personal prejudices or about more substantive material? As anthropologists, archaeologists would like to believe that they are relatively bias-free. But everyone has biases; social and economic class, race, gender, and ethnicity all may have an impact on what archaeologists will expect from the students and how they will relate to the students. Each archaeologist is a member of a society at large, often mirroring in teaching behavior the expectations of that society (Nieto 1992:29–31). "Recognizing our individual biases, their sources, and the way in which our cultural background affects our thinking is a crucial step toward multicultural understanding" (Tiedt and Tiedt 1995:xiv). To be effective teachers, archaeologists must recognize their own values, evaluate their impact on the students, and learn to set them aside if they will interfere with or bias the learning process.

First and foremost, the archaeology educator must define the message a lesson is intended to convey and then determine the best delivery system for the content of a presentation. A digging exercise will convey the message that archaeologists dig to gather their information. Depending on how it's done, such an exercise could also convey the message that archaeology is "kid-stuff," or that digging is the only thing archaeologists do. Certainly, children already have the message that archaeologists dig. Is this a message that needs reinforcement? (This is an issue of major debate among archaeology educators; various viewpoints on this topic are presented in Part III of this volume).

Lessons that include digging (excavation) as only a small part of the arsenal of techniques available to the archaeologist when studying the past might be more appropriate (Wolynec 1996). Overemphasis on any aspect of archaeological work, even preservation, can result in misunderstandings on the part of students. A role-playing exercise may convey a message of responsible site stewardship or foster attitudes condoning vigilantism. In developing any kind of short- or long-term program in archaeology, the overriding questions must be "What are the desirable learning outcomes?" and "Are the teaching tools being used appropriate to their attainment?"

Teaching and Learning

In a multicultural classroom, teaching must be student centered not teacher dominated. The successful teacher involves students in a variety of planned interactive activities which build on the student's past successes and develop self-esteem (Tiedt and Tiedt 1995:39). "Talking at" children is not effective. Neither is simply sharing lists or descriptions. Children must be encouraged to apply their critical thinking skills and to integrate the material presented with understanding (Tiedt and Tiedt 1995:52). Effective learning can be recognized when students want to continue to explore the material on their own to build upon their knowledge. "To be educative, a learning experience must not only generate fact, knowledge, or belief, it must also increase the likelihood that the learner will actually seek similar but expanded experiences in the future" (Dewey 1938 in Short and Burke 1991:17).

The archaeologist must be prepared to develop a diverse and flexible teaching toolkit in order to be an effective teacher in the heterogeneous multicultural classroom of today. This toolkit should include an assortment of teaching methods that engage the mind, body, and all of the senses. However, the application of these techniques may require special approaches because of the nature of student diversity (see Box 5.2).

Box 5.2
Student Diversity

Many immigrants to the United States and Canada have faced similar pressures in their countries of origin. Once here, these pressures continued, but in a more subtle way. By being labeled White or Asian, their specific histories and related identities were slowly erased from their perceptions of the past. Imagine a college student, in tears, declaring that white people like her should never be forgiven for what they have done to the Native Americans. She had learned of all of the very real horrors experienced during the long history of Native American ethnocide. Obviously, the educational system had not skimped on the horrors. That she felt guilty was an educational crime. She was the daughter of first-generation Slovak immigrants. Nowhere in her education did she learn about the early Slovak and Ukrainian immigrants who came to work in the mines of Pennsylvania in the 1800s and of their contributions to the growth of industry in the state. Her ethnic group had made an important contribution to the growth of this country, yet in sixteen years of going to school, no one had included this information in her education.

Although interaction and collaboration with trained teachers and curriculum development specialists are mandatory for the creation and delivery of effective archaeology education programs, they are insufficient for the purposes of developing successful teaching and learning experiences. Archaeologists must know something of education theory and methodology as well (not just what they experienced in the classroom while students themselves). The archaeology educator must be prepared to participate in some level of continuing education to achieve success in developing an effective teaching toolkit. Taking classes offered by a university department of education or special education, reading the specialized literature, and talking to other archaeologists about their experiences are important aspects of an archaeologist's teacher training. Several books cited in this chapter (Banks 1994; Miller-Lachmann and Taylor 1995; Tiedt and Tiedt 1995; Pierangelo and Jacoby 1996; Finazzo 1997) provide important basic information regarding the history, terminology, theory, methodology, problems, activities, and resources useful for teaching in a hetero-geneous classroom and are highly recommended as a starting point. Teaching students with exceptionalities, who speak English as a second language, or who identify with an ethnic group must always be a work in progress, one that requires a continuously developing sense of awareness of their special needs, abilities, and problems.

Challenges and Approaches

Exceptionalities

U.S. and Canadian laws mandate that students with exceptionalities must be educated in the least restrictive environment appropriate for the child. This often means including them with students who are not handicapped (20 USC Sect. 1412 (5)B) (Smith and Luckasson 1992 in Miller-Lachmann and Taylor 1995:156). Currently, the inclusion movement in special education tries to place all students with disabilities into a regular classroom situation. Whether the archaeologist is aware of it or not, the student audience may have a variety of disabilities. Therefore, archae-ology educators must familiarize themselves with the possibilities and be aware of teaching methodologies appropriate to each disability (see Box 5.3).

High-incidence disabilities are the most common. They include learning disab-ilities (the largest group), "speech/communication disorders, mild mental retardation, and emotional/behavior disorders" (Miller-Lachmann and Taylor 1995:163). Low-incidence disabilities include "hearing impaired and deaf, multihandicapped, ortho-pedic and other health impaired, visually impaired and blind, autism and traumatic brain injury" (Miller-Lachmann and Taylor 1995:174). Students with these disabilities can benefit from specific teaching methodologies that address their needs and learning styles (Miller-Lachmann and Taylor 1995:153–185).

BOX 5.3
Teaching Children with Disabilities

Preconceived judgments about the competence of children linked to their ethnicity, social class, disabilities, language abilities, etc. can create a self-fulfilling prophesy. Low expectations will produce expected results. Because a student is labeled "learning disabled" does not mean that the child can't learn. It does mean that other than standard approaches to teaching may be necessary for learning to take place.

No single teaching strategy applies to all or most cases because each child with a learning disability has individual characteristics. However, several strategies have been useful. Cooperative learning exercises, tapes of lectures, written outlines, memory enhancing devices, demonstrations, films, models, and lectures all belong in the teaching toolkit when working with children with learning disabilities (Miller-Lachmann and Taylor 1995:165). The teaching of archaeology and its resultant research are uniquely suited to developing and using this variable toolkit. For example, any of the activities found in *Intrigue of the Past* (S. J. Smith et al. 1996) are easily adapted to serve as excellent teaching and learning tools for children who are variously challenged. Archaeology can be a very useful vehicle for teaching students with disabilities necessary skills as well as concepts related to other disciplines. For example, it can be a "remarkably effective vehicle for teaching math, a form of therapy for hyperactive children, or even a valuable outdoor education experience for the physically challenged" (Smardz 1996:103).

High-Incidence Disabilities

The single most common learning disability is Attention Deficit/Hyperactivity Disorder or ADHD (Miller-Lachmann and Taylor 1995:164). ADHD children are easily distracted. They can fidget, fall out of their seats, impulsively blurt out answers or sounds, be angry, or withdraw from activity. Flexibility is an important key to success in working with a heterogeneous classroom that includes ADHD children (Rief 1993:5). Teaching archaeologists must be willing to alter their presentations as needed, in midsentence if necessary. Techniques that may have worked in one class may need to be altered in another classroom where the mix of students is different. However, a structured presentation is imperative.

ADHD children, as well as most others, find security in an ordered classroom where they know exactly what is expected of them academically and behaviorally (Reif 1993:19). Children are uncomfortable with disorder and respond to such with behavioral problems (Reif 1993:23). Expectations, rules, consequences, and follow-up must be clearly communicated to the students. Activities need to be broken down into manageable units (Reif 1993:6). Archaeology activities and presentations should be creative, interesting, and interactive to keep the attention of the children.

Children with dyslexia can benefit from similar teaching strategies. Beside difficulties in reading, dyslexic children may have problems in orientation and in determining days, time, distances, size, and right and left. They may also have poor motor coordination and delays in speech development (Pierangelo and Jacoby 1996:127). The key to enhancing learning for children with learning disabilities, including dyslexia, is variety in the teaching toolkit. Pierangelo and Jacoby list thirty-four different alternatives to obtaining and reporting information by students (1996:128–129).Together, they represent multisensory experiences that make students an interactive partner in the learning process and not just targets.

A diagnosed learning disability does not imply lack of intelligence. "Dumbing down" a presentation is rarely the answer. Dyslexic children, for example, have intelligence measured in the average to superior ranges (Pierangelo and Jacoby 1996:127). Teamwork between the archaeologist and teacher is imperative in the process of preparation and execution of the activity (Rief 1993:7). Multisensory instruction that gives students the "opportunity to work together and discuss with peers and who are actively, physically involved and participating in the lesson will have the most success" (Rief 1993:53). Activities that include auditory, spatial, verbal, and conceptual skills, among others, have the greatest chance of allowing the children to receive, understand, and retain the message that the archaeologist is trying to convey.

The second-largest group of students with exceptionalities includes those with speech and communication disorders. These include voice (pitch and loudness), articulation (speech sounds), fluency (rate and flow of speech), and language (form, content, and use) disorders (Miller-Lachmann and Taylor 1995:166–167). Students with speech and communication disorders can benefit from short two-step directions, succinct statements, avoidance of indirect commands and either/or statements, and instructions that show rather than tell what to do. In addition, students should be given extra time to answer questions. If they cannot express themselves verbally, some will benefit from acting out what they cannot say (Miller-Lachmann and Taylor 1995:168). By always calling on the student with the first hand up, the archaeologist may be excluding children who need time to develop a response mentally or who are hesitant to answer because of their speech or communication disabilities.

Students with mental retardation are the third-largest group. "Mental retardation is characterized by limitations in intellectual function accompanied by impairment in adaptive behavior" (Miller-Lachmann and Taylor 1995:183). Deficits may be in the areas of "communication, self-care, home living, social skills, community use, self-direction, health and safety, functional academics, leisure, and work" (Hallahan and Kauffman 1994 in Miller-Lachmann and Taylor 1995:170). Students may have problems with attention, long- and short-term memory, and making generalizations.

They can benefit from teaching styles that break down tasks into a series of steps ordered from easy to difficult, allowing for a high frequency of success. Learning goals should be specific and realistic. Tasks should always be explained by using concrete examples. Instructions must always be specific (Miller-Lachmann and Taylor 1995:170–171). The archaeologist should never assume that the student will be able to follow instructions to a logical conclusion, read between the lines, or understand with just one telling. Brevity, specificity, and repetition of instructions along with overlearning are often the keys to learning for children classified with mental retardation. Patience and tenacity on the part of the teaching archaeologist are prerequisites.

Students with emotional and behavior disorders comprise the last group included in high-incidence disabilities. These include students whose learning disabilities cannot be attributed to other causes, who cannot develop satisfactory interpersonal relationships with others, who exhibit inappropriate types of behavior or feelings, who consistently exhibit symptoms of depression or moodiness, or who exhibit physical symptoms or fears associated with aspects of everyday life such as school (Miller-Lachmann and Taylor 1995:172). Because these students have complex social and academic needs as well as differing abilities, the archaeologist should work with the teacher very closely to determine the teaching styles best suited to this audience.

Low-Incidence Disabilities

A small percentage of students comprise the low-incidence disabilities group. These include students who are hearing impaired (permanent or nonpermanent hearing loss, some hearing with or without a hearing aid), and deaf (no effective use of the sense of hearing); multihandicapped (two or more disabilities), orthopedic (physical disabilities), or otherwise health impaired (chronic or acute health problems); partially sighted (some functional sight) and blind (no functional sight); or who have autism or traumatic brain injury (Miller-Lachmann and Taylor 1995:174; Pierangelo and Jacoby 1996:74–75).

Students in the low-incidence disability group often require specialized techniques, equipment, or support staff (Miller-Lachmann and Taylor 1995:176–180). Hearing-impaired or deaf children should be seated close to and in front of the speaker to facilitate lip reading and use of their limited hearing abilities. Instructions or terms and definitions should be written out on blackboard and preprinted information sheets made available. A student partner can assist in taking notes. The archaeology educator should work with the American Sign Language (ASL) interpreter, in advance of the presentation, to ensure proper positioning of the teaching archaeologist, the ASL interpreter, and the student. Because archaeological terminology can be specialized, a list of such terms or the script of the presentation submitted in advance can give the interpreter an opportunity to prepare.

Partially sighted or blind children can benefit from an assistant who can take notes and describe events as they are taking place (especially important when viewing a video or participating in a demonstration or hands-on activity). Lectures can be audiotaped in advance of or during a lecture. Books can be read onto a tape. Handouts can be made available in Braille or in large-sized print. Instructions and definitions should be clearly stated and repeated.

Although archaeologists must always try to work closely or consult with the special education teacher or classroom teacher, they must be aware that children with low-incidence disabilities may require very special consideration, effort, and individualized instruction. Wheelchair accessibility is an obvious consideration. Less obvious is that students who are wheelchair bound because of severe cerebral palsy may not have the ability to control their bodies, but their minds may be as keen and sharp as that of a child active on the gymnastics team. Clearly, instructional tools that involve the mind and not the body are crucial to the child's learning success. Children with severe cerebral palsy may want to respond to questions either through verbalizing the answer or by means of a computer keyboard, sometimes one letter at a time. They must be given the time to do so. This can be a great challenge for the teaching archaeologist, because speech impairment may be so severe that the sounds are difficult to interpret. The abilities of autistic and brain-injured students should be evaluated individually and learning customized to fit the students' needs.

Above all, the safety of all students must be a primary consideration. Wheel chair accessibility, nonhazardous equipment, and safe activities must always be on the archaeologist's agenda. Even apparently safe activities such as cleaning whole glass bottles can become hazardous in the hands of a child with emotional problems who decides to the break the bottle and injure herself or himself with the broken glass. Adequate supervision is mandatory when working with a highly diverse student group. Although it is impossible to prevent all injuries, every possible effort should be made to do so. It is not acceptable for a child to be hurt during any educational activity.

Putting It into Practice: Preparing an Archaeology Experience for Special-Needs Children

Although this discussion may seem overwhelming, archaeologists should not be dissuaded from working with groups of children who exhibit exceptionalities. There are straightforward steps that can be taken to ensure a meaningful and comfortable experience for all concerned. When asked to give a presentation, the archaeologist should always ask the teacher if there are special-needs children, the nature of these needs, whether special equipment or individual assistants such as ASL interpreters will be available, the overall grade level of understanding of the class, and the special teaching tools that might be useful for the presentation. Because teachers often do not volunteer this information, the archaeologist must make the effort to ask such specific questions.

Unfortunately, classroom teachers are still trying to develop their own skills for dealing with inclusion and may not be very helpful in assisting the archaeologist with specific advice. In such circumstances, the key to enhancing learning in archaeology or about the results of archaeological research is to use a variety of teaching tools in each presentation. Therefore, a one and one-quarter hour middle-school presentation on the archaeological explorations of the Fort LeBoeuf Site at the Fort LeBoeuf Museum in Waterford, Pennsylvania, might include watching and listening to a slide show on George Washington's journey to the French fort in 1763 and the archaeological excavations that took place in the 1970s; learning how to pronounce the French name for the fort (Fort de la Riviere aux Boeufs); comparing Native American tools with equivalent European tools; brainstorming why the latter would have been attractive trade goods to be exchanged for beaver fur; touching a real beaver pelt; lecturing in a story-telling format that is divided into short sequential segments; giving students an opportunity to brainstorm answers to questions posed by the archaeologist; and looking for specific sources of archaeological evidence of the fort in the museum's display cases in cooperative groups. Throughout the presentation, students are also directed to specific research questions that they must explore after the visit to the museum. Tactile, visual, auditory, and critical thinking skills are used throughout the presentation, thereby ensuring that the children's attention is caught and held, and their desire to continue gathering information on the subject is engaged whether or not they exhibit exceptionalities. The key to learning success is diversity of teaching tools whether it be a one-time presentation or long-term curriculum.

English as a Second Language

As the variety of immigrant groups to the United States and Canada increases, the need for successfully dealing with language education becomes very important. There are two strategies currently in place that attempt to teach English as a second language: Native Language (MNL) and Teaching English as a Second Language (TESL) (Banks 1994:275–277). MNL is an approach that requires that the student study all subject areas in their native language. Proficiency in the native language is a prerequisite for starting in English-language studies. TESL focuses on developing immediate English-language skills. With TESL pullout, students leave the regular classroom for daily instruction in English language arts and then return for instruction in other subjects. With TESL intensive, students focus on English language arts for a prolonged period. First, the student learns to speak English and then to read English. Once successful, the student is returned to a monolingual English classroom. Total immersion involves no transition or maintenance of the native language. All subjects are taught in English immediately.

TESL continues to be controversial within the educational field. Many see it as an expedient and quick methodology that results in superficial knowledge of both the native language and English. The attitude about the first language is a negative one since the lack of English is considered a deficiency. The first language is perceived to be a "liability which interferes with the development of the second language, or English" (Banks 1994:277). Others believe MNL requires too long a commitment in time, but produces students with a thorough knowledge of each language including their deep structure. Irrespective of which method is used, the archaeology educator must develop programs that can address the needs of the MNL and TESL students. Indeed, the subject matter associated with archaeology can effectively be used by students to learn about the past while simultaneously developing their language skills.

Every student who has had an introductory level anthropology course knows that language and culture are closely interrelated. Yet the depth of this relationship is rarely understood. "Language is the heart of the students' identity" (Tiedt and Tiedt 1995:196). Many immigrants feel that to lose their language is to lose their culture. So, learning English can directly threaten one's cultural identity. It is perceived as a vehicle accelerating on a one-way road to assimilation. In the past, many European immigrants intentionally abandoned their native languages in favor of English because they intuited that this would hasten the assimilation of their children into the American melting pot. Because many contemporary immigrants choose integration, not assimilation, they insist on the right to maintain their own languages at home and in school. The "close tie between valuing one's language and self-esteem" (Tiedt and Tiedt 1995:3) is recognized in a series of state, provincial, and federal laws that mandate multicultural/bilingual education (Tiedt and Tiedt 1995:4–5).

Bilingual education provides an opportunity for all students, Native American or immigrant, to learn the mainstream language of English without abandoning the anchor of their identity, their own languages. Archaeologists who speak more than one language should consider giving presentations to students in those languages. A lecture on the life of archaic peoples in the lower Illinois River Valley in Ukrainian to Ukrainian immigrant children builds their knowledge of their adopted prehistory and history, in a language they can understand. A similar lecture in English might be poorly understood and underline their deficiencies in English, thereby diminishing their self-esteem and discouraging them from further learning.

Populations of bilingual and non-English-speaking cultures in North America are growing at a rapid rate. In 1992, more than 32 million Americans spoke languages other than English (Tiedt and Tiedt 1995:8). Shall children be excluded from heritage education because they can't speak English well or not at all? Are archaeology and the study of the past for the English-speaking classroom only? What about children for whom Black English is a first language, or children raised in extreme poverty whose only language is a regional or simplified form of English? Should they be disenfranchised from the rich cultural heritage of this continent or the world? Most archaeologists would respond to these rhetorical questions by affirming the right of all children to the best heritage education they can get. Archaeology educators who have the language skills should make the effort to use them in teaching and in developing curricula.

A public educated about archaeology and the past facilitates the research and preservation work of archaeologists. Archaeologists should be warned, the bilingual and non-English-speaking public is rapidly increasing in numbers and their positive or negative influence on archaeological resources will be felt. A major step in remedying the bias toward teaching mostly English-speaking students is to recognize just how multicultural both the United States and Canada really are. The second step is to develop archaeology programs now that recognize this increase in language and cultural diversity.

Immigrants and Ethnicity:
Today's Multicultural Classroom

If one believes the political rhetoric, then ethnic reality in the United States is basically Black and White, with a little Hispanic, Asian, or Native American thrown in if the political need arises. On occasion, terms such as Euro American, African American, or Native American intrude into the public consciousness. Such terms tend to falsely homogenize otherwise complex groupings of human beings. If one were to question contemporary college students of Euro American descent, few would identify themselves as Euro Americans of mainstream American culture. Many would identify themselves by the ethnic identities of their ancestors (Ahler 1994:456). Still others, especially immigrants or first-generation children of immigrants, would be most adamant about their ethnic affiliations. Although they may be of European heritage, they might consider themselves as different from each other as Norwegian Americans are from Polish Americans, as an Arikara is from an Ojibway (Ahler 1994:456).

Multicultural education is attempting to overcome this tendency toward cultural homogenization. Inclusion has much in common with multicultural education. They both strive to include all children in regular mainstream educational programs and emphasize "positive interdependence, respect, and valuing of all children's unique characteristics and needs in the regular classroom" (Dean, Salend, and Taylor 1993 in Miller-Lachmann and Taylor 1995:159). "A truly multicultural society should have traits of its constituent cultures that are shared for the benefits of all" (Blancke and Slow Turtle 1994:438). Unfortunately, dominant societies mold the image of a particular nation, often excluding histories of indigenous or minority peoples as the history of Native American societies in the United States has so graphically illustrated.

Archaeologists have been as remiss as historians in educating about the immigrant experience. It is not surprising that contemporary immigrants have a difficult time connecting with history on this continent. Archaeologists must recognize, through their research and educational programs, that this continent is a complex multicultural area throughout indigenous and immigrant history. By sharing what they have learned, archaeologists can make history more relevant to both the incoming and established immigrant communities. They can also further the causes associated with archaeology. For example, an archaeologist teaching about the values of archaeology (such as conservation and preservation of archaeological sites) can use examples of sites from the ethnic groups represented by students in the class to make the past personal and subsequently more relevant to them.

The Archaeological Resource Centre (ARC), founded by the Toronto Board of Education in 1985 and now disbanded, served as a model for inclusion of First Nations and immigrant ethnic groups in their public research programs (Smardz 1995). One of ARC's goals was to "give all residents of Toronto a sense of ownership in and value for the remnants of past cultures that we excavate" (Smardz 1995:3). For example, students explored the role of African Canadians in the building of Toronto. African Canadian children could develop a sense of pride in the accomplishments of the people being studied, while other immigrants could understand the drive to escape oppression experienced by these fugitive slaves. The project allowed immigrants to feel more at home and perhaps to identify new roots onto which they may be grafted in their new land. Concurrently, long-term residents of Toronto could appreciate the contributions of past immigrants to the growth of Canada. For immigrant children who may feel disconnected from mainstream life, this archaeological project fostered a sense of pride in both themselves and in the immigrants of the past.

The United States has been a country of immigrants since Columbian times. The past should belong to everyone, since it is the adopted (willfully or not) land of many. Yet, too few projects focus on the immigrant experience with an intent to share this information with the public at large. Few teachers think of the immigrant experience when they invite an archaeologist to do a presentation before a class. Their focus is predominantly on Native American or pioneer English-Irish-Scots societies in the past. But before any children (Native American, immigrant, or descended from immigrants) learn to appreciate others, they must first learn to appreciate their own cultural identities. "The multicultural curriculum begins with a study of self as students become aware of their own cultural backgrounds, their beliefs and attitudes, their eating habits, and other ways of behaving. Building from a sense of their own self-worth, students can then begin to compare and contrast their cultural identities with those of others in the classroom" (Tiedt and Tiedt 1995:33). The lesson plans in the first section of *Intrigue of the Past* (S. J. Smith et al. 1996) are ideally suited to meeting this compelling need for self-understanding with respect to other cultures. By personalizing the past, these lessons reinforce the fact that everyone has a past.

Multicultural education presents a very real opportunity for archaeologists to become involved in the educational process. Most states in the United States and the Canadian provinces have some kind of formal multicultural education programs. Of these, twenty-eight U.S. states have established a state-level position of responsibility for multicultural education. At least twenty insist that teachers meet certain requirements in multicultural education before certification (Mitchell and Salsbury 1996:339). Multicultural education is the law in many parts of the United States and a longstanding practice in Canada. It belongs in every part of the educational system including the sciences, mathematics, social studies, language arts, and fine arts.

Multicultural education should be an integral part of everything the educator does, and not an add-on (Banks 1992 in Reissman 1994:1). Unfortunately, archaeology is usually treated as an add-on. By becoming better educated in the multicultural education movement, archaeologists can make opportunities for developing and including the archaeological study of the past in local and state curricula. This level of involvement can be at every level of education from K–12 through college-level teacher education. Clearly, the educational community is committed to multicultural education. It is up to individual archaeologists to inform educators of the relevance of archaeological studies to multiculturalism and to take the time to work with them to develop programs effective across the curriculum. It is up to the academic archaeological community to recognize the value of these efforts when considering tenure and promotion. It is up to the contract archaeology community to include education programs into the time and costs of doing business. Teaching children to value the past and archaeological resources today will reap enormous benefits in protection of resources in the future.

Conclusions

To be an effective archaeology educator, an individual needs more than just a desire to address children on the issues of archaeology. Increasing student heterogeneity in the classroom requires that archaeologists become educated beyond their training in archaeology. They must be prepared to plan for each presentation with the special needs of their student audience and teachers in mind. They must be aware of their personal values and how they can enhance or detract from the message about archaeology which they are trying to present. They must be willing to teach in languages other than English and to address student audiences in nonmiddle- or nonupper-class neighborhoods. They need to be comfortable with multicultural audiences and issues. Ultimately, they must be willing to cooperate and interact with teachers and curriculum development specialists in developing programs for special-needs children, and learn to be flexible in their presentations.

Archaeology and its study of the past can be an exciting and useful teaching tool. It can help previously excluded children learn that they too have a heritage; it also helps all members of the community come to an appreciation of the heritage of the various cultural groups that make up our modern North American society. Archaeology has something to offer every child because every child has a past and a culture.

RECOMMENDED READINGS

Fullinwider, R. K., ed.
1996   *Public Education in a Multicultural Society: Policy, Theory, Critique.* Cambridge University Press, Cambridge.
A collection of essays that address the philosophical issues raised by multicultural education.

Jameson, Jr., J. H., ed.
1996   *Presenting the Past to the Public: Digging for Truths.* Walnut Creek, CA: AltaMira Press, Walnut Creek, California.
Nineteen essays that focus on conceptual and practical aspects of interpreting the past for the public in a variety of contexts.

Kottak, C. P., J. J. White, R. H. Furlow, and P. C. Rice, eds.
1996   *The Teaching of Anthropology: Problems, Issues, and Decisions.* Mayfield, Mountain View, California.
Forty-four essays that discuss the many complexities of teaching a variety of topics in anthropology in a variety of educational contexts.

Phelan, P., and A. L. Davidson, eds.
1997   *Renegotiating Cultural Diversity in American Schools.* Teachers College Press, New York.
Eight essays on the ongoing evolution of multicultural education in the United States.

Saravia-Shore, M., and S. F. Arvizu, eds.
1998   *Cross-Cultural Literacy: Ethnographies of Communication in Multiethnic Classrooms.* Garland, New York.
Eighteen case studies that focus on aspects of cultural diversity in a variety of educational contexts that represent an anthropological approach to dealing with diversity.

Stone, P. G., and R. MacKenzie, eds.
1999   *The Excluded Past: Archaeology in Education.* One World Archaeology Series, Routledge, London and New York.
Twenty-five case studies from around the world that focus on the sociopolitical consequences of good and bad archaeology education. This book was developed from papers

presented at the 1986 World Archaeological Congress held in England, and the authors focus on the exclusion or inclusion of certain aspects of the past as an exercise in control and power in education.

Stone, P. G., and B. L. Molyneaux, eds.
    2000   *The Presented Past: Heritage, Museums and Education.* One World Archaeology Series, Routledge, London and New York.
    Thirty-five case studies from around the world that focus on site and museum programs about the past. The authors developed the book from papers presented at 1990 World Archaeological Congress held in Venezuela; they are straightforward in their discussions of serious problems that archaeology educators face in specific cultural environments.

PATRICIA (PAM) WHEAT

Chapter Six

Developing Lessons about Archaeology
From a Teacher's Journal

The classroom teacher is the interface between archaeology education and students, the ultimate target audience. Teachers have discretionary time to influence students and shape their attitudes in the classroom. The individual classroom is where educational method and theory, standards, requirements, and politics converge; it is where the "rubber meets the road." It is true that the direction of that road is, in large part, guided by national, state, and local education agencies. It is responsive to many other forces, too, including the often conflicting demands of principals, curriculum specialists, social service agencies, parents, variously challenged students and, at least indirectly, politicians. All of these forces guide and limit what a teacher can present, but once that classroom door shuts, teachers are in charge. Despite the many strictures within which they work, teachers still have some freedom to design and present subject matter of their choice.

Archaeology has the opportunity to be part of a teacher's repertoire and many teachers are very interested in it, for reasons described throughout this volume. Still, teachers are generally hard pressed to add yet another subject area to their teaching load, especially one with which many are relatively unfamiliar. Therefore, it is important that archaeology educators understand the world of the classroom teacher and how a teacher weighs the introduction of a new subject into the curriculum. Teaching materials and lesson plans may then be designed so that teachers can and will use them within their burgeoning class structure.

This chapter will take you into the world of a teacher in the intermediate grades (4–6). Her journal entries for a normal teaching day are found throughout the chapter. They will give you, the archaeology educator entering the realm of the educator, a sense of the many responsibilities and concerns that teachers face each day. Learning

117

about the day-to-day operation of the classroom enables archaeology educators to work more effectively with teachers to promote archaeology as a curriculum topic. To create the best synergism, archaeology educators should meet teachers with a mutually beneficial agenda. When a teacher is interested in a topic, she or he will ask the following questions:

- How will this topic or lesson fit with my purpose in teaching?
- Why will my students be asked to learn about this topic?
- What specifically will my class gain from the study?
- How much time (in class, in preparation) can I devote to this study?
- Which instructional strategies will be most effective with these students?
- Which resources already exist and which do I have to locate or create?

The archaeology educator needs to understand how the modern educational system works, a point made throughout this book and explained by MacDonald and Burtness, and Davis, as well as in the introduction to this volume. With such a foundation, the archaeology educator can then focus on effective ways to design archaeology teaching strategies that can translate directly into classroom lessons. This is key to increasing the amount of archaeology that will be included in classrooms by teachers. To ensure that the archaeology program you present will actually reach the kids, not once but repeatedly over a teacher's career, teaching materials must be useful in meeting existing and acknowledged needs. Specifically, the lesson or activity must help the teacher meet curriculum requirements in specific subjects, or aid in developing desired skills at a particular age and ability level. Archaeology education needs to be seen as an asset to instructional planning rather than just another set of lesson plans that are going to mean more work for the teacher.

Planning to Teach Archaeology

Instructional planning is the key to successful teaching. Planning involves having a clear rationale for how one will proceed and what specifically one hopes to accomplish. It also incorporates what the students are to learn and why they are to learn it (Borich 1996).

> *5:45 a.m.*   *Up before the youngsters and husband. Wash a load of clothes, then have breakfast ready for an easy start to the day. Husband off to work, kids on their way to school; now I can get to school and assume the role of teacher. I've been intrigued by a program I learned about at the last state teacher's conference that used archaeology as an engaging way to teach a number of subjects and skills. But I wonder. . . .*
> *How will archaeology fit with my purpose in teaching?*

Archaeology can be used easily as part of a curriculum in intermediate classes (grades 4–6) and middle school (grades 6–8) where social studies and science are topical. Social studies topics are frequently chronologically arranged with prehistory in the fall of the year. Since information about prehistory is derived from archeological data, it is natural that archaeology be brought into the study (Banks 1984). An even stronger unit can be created if it is integrated with the science curriculum. The scientific process is a system of skills that can be taught using archaeological data, giving real-life application to the often dry and dull textbook theory.

7:45 a.m.   *Into the school building; scan the hall to shoo out any early arrivals; into the office to pick up notices from the mailbox; down the hall to the classroom. Twenty students due in the room at 8:13 a.m.*
Why should the students be asked to learn about archaeology? (See Box 6.1.)

BOX 6.1
Why Learn Archaeology?

Archaeology is an engaging topic that captures student attention and increases student learning. The skills taught in archaeology lessons are critical thinking processes that include analysis of evidence: therefore, student test scores often rise (Cooper 1994). Archaeology can be taught as an interdisciplinary unit with lessons focused on reading, writing, math, social studies, science, and art. It is most effective when taught across disciplines as an integrated unit (Lounsbury 1992; Schur, Lewis, LaMorte, and Shewey 1996). An important component of most archaeology units is the concept of stewardship. Therefore, stewardship becomes a topic upon which teachers and students can build community action (citizenship) activities and skills (Lewis 1991).

9:02 a.m.   *Time to collect milk money for the day to send to the office with attendance report. Begin group reading lesson.*
What specifically should the class gain from this study of archaeology?

Lessons and units that provide sound archeological concepts and clear teaching strategies are the most effective. Archeology educators should define for themselves the concept(s) important in a lesson. Often only one key idea per lesson should be developed. Topics that are successful in the classroom include: local cultural sequence, adaptation to the environment, observation of evidence, inference from data, classifying artifacts, interpreting patterns, ethics, and stewardship. While the complexity and interdisciplinary aspects of archaeology appeal to teachers, presentation to students should focus on one concept at a time.

> *10:44 a.m.* *Students respond to the assignment on the board with questions: "What do you mean? Do we get a grade on this?"*
> *How much class time can I devote to a unit on archaeology and how much time will I need to prepare?*

Since teachers have so many demands on their time, archaeology educators can assist by suggesting a "doable" class unit, such as six one-hour lessons to a six-week unit, or by helping to identify where the existing curriculum holds opportunities for archaeology to be injected. For example, where the curriculum requires students to discern between fact and opinion (often in language arts) or between observation and inference (science), one can offer a lesson that uses archaeology as the application. The topic then comes alive for the kids, which makes the teacher's job easier and more enjoyable, a key to ensuring the use of your materials. The easier and more "teacher friendly" the teaching resource is, the more classroom time it will receive.

Preparation time for the teacher can be minimized if the archaeology educator works closely with her or him to develop a joint plan. The plan should incorporate the priorities of both the teacher and the archaeologist so that the most important archaeological and stewardship concepts and educational goals can be realized. The archaeology educator thus must be a partner in developing new materials or in guiding the teacher to existing quality-tested materials. The archaeology educator can also supply background information and assist in teaching the lessons. These types of assistance to teachers are relevant at the one-on-one level and also when conducting teacher workshops.

> *11:21 a.m.* *Lunch period. Eat sack lunch from home for relief from cafeteria food. Review catalog of upcoming teacher workshops. Monitor playground for fifteen minutes*

Teachers must meet ongoing educational requirements to remain certified, to move into higher pay brackets, or to gain certification in another grade or subject area. One of the best ways to introduce teachers to archaeology and to establish a relationship with them is to offer a workshop, sometimes called in-service training or conference. In-service conferences are an excellent way to ensure that archaeological concepts such as cultural sequence, adaptation to the environment, observation, inference, classifying, interpretation, ethics, and stewardship will be understood by teachers. Workshops also provide teachers with opportunities to practice teaching new material and to gain confidence with a new subject. Some teachers attend workshops out of personal interest in the topic, but most are motivated to attend because they need the recertification credits, and only secondarily because the topic has appeal. While this may sound rather mercenary, *remember that it is the teachers who are not particularly interested in archaeology who make up the majority.* They can, however, become enthusiastic advocates and practitioners of archaeology education after a quality workshop experience. Accredited workshops reward teachers for going the extra mile to learn about archaeology and to structure it (with your help) for the classroom.

A first step in offering a teacher workshop is to find out how teachers learn about and receive credit for attending a workshop. Training may be validated or accredited by the state education agency, a university education or continuing education department, or the school district staff development office. Active teachers will often assist you in establishing the best vehicle for teacher training. Partnering with an established workshop venue, such as a local museum, is also a good strategy.

> *12:55 p.m.* *During when students go to physical education class, attend parent conference for student who does not turn in homework, and therefore is not successful in class. Which instructional strategies will be most effective with the students?*

Archaeology provides unlimited presentation opportunities. The discovery inquiry approach is demonstrated in the following sample lesson plan. Most lesson plans are structured with standard elements. When archeology educators under,stand and relate materials to the standard lesson plan, teachers will more readily respond to archaeology as a teaching topic because the information is being offered in a teachable familiar format. The lesson plan format shown in Box 6.4 is widely accepted.

Archaeology educators need to be aware that teachers face innumerable challenges in the course of their normal day. They are professionals, and education, like any vital profession, is always changing. There is the ever-present need to read trade journals and books and attend development activities, simply to stay professionally current. Schools are often expected to initiate programs that address societal ills, so drug and alcohol abuse, self-esteem, parenting responsibilities, work place preparation, and personal safety are now part of many school curricula, along with the traditional subjects. Teachers only infrequently receive adequate training or guidance in implementing these new subject areas. And, as the news media all too sadly reveal, many teachers face personal risk merely by doing their jobs, yet teachers are some of the most dedicated, enthusiastic and creative professionals with whom to collaborate (see Boxes 6.2, 6.3, 6.4).

> *1:20 p.m.* *Assistant principal arrives at door. Today is the day for the annual observation and evaluation of teaching techniques and classroom management. How will the new state form work? Will the students take advantage of an administrator being in the room and misbehave? Which archaeology education resources already exist and which will I have to locate or create?*

Lessons should not require materials that are hard to obtain or expertise that will cause teachers to feel overwhelmed or discouraged. Make it as easy and inexpensive as possible for teachers to find necessary information and supplies. These should be portable to the classroom because field trips are not easily arranged. It is helpful to the teacher to know of resources that can enhance the lesson, such as books, pamphlets, video tapes, games, teaching kits, Internet web sites, and local sites and museums to visit (KC Smith, Selig, this volume). One of the most requested resources is an archaeologist who is willing to be interviewed, either live, or by phone or e-mail.

BOX 6.2
Educational Terminology

ASSESSMENT: a way to evaluate knowledge and skills acquired in lessons; some assessment instruments include standardized tests, essay questions, and portfolios in which students place examples of their work such as reports, interpretive art work, and group projects (Martorella 1996; McNutt, this volume).

CURRICULUM: what to teach.

INSTRUCTIONAL STRATEGIES: how one teaches; the method of presentation, such as using didactic, inquiry, or discovery strategies, to mention a few.

INTEGRATED CURRICULUM: a free flow between subject areas that reflects the interrelatedness of knowledge.

SKILLS: process oriented; includes activities such as reading maps, constructing graphs, and drawing conclusions.

UNIT: a series of sequenced and related learning activities organized around one theme, issue, or problem. Typically, units may be designed for a duration of two to six weeks.

BOX 6.3
Components of a Lesson Plan:
The Focus of the Lesson

1. *A descriptive heading with:*
   a. Subjects areas identified (social studies, science, art, math, reading, language arts)
   b. Skills targeted
   c. Strategies used
   d. Time allotted
   e. Group size, and
   f. Grade levels targeted

2. *Objectives (state expectations clearly; relate the purpose of studying this)*

3. *Background information (teacher preparation)*

4. *Resources and materials (easily obtained, not complicated)*

5. *Procedure—teaching strategies and activities, including directions to students, questions to pose, and time sequence with teacher and student roles defined:*
   a. Set the stage (connect to previous knowledge, arouse curiosity, focus attention)
   b. State objectives of the lesson (expectations from above stated directly to students)
   c. Provide instructional input (how to, sequence of activities)
   d. Model the desired student behavior (demonstrate activity)
   e. Get feedback (check for student understanding)
   f. Provide for guided practice (short, in-class activity)
   g. Provide for independent practice (longer activity or homework)

6. *Closure (summary with transition to next lesson)*

7. *Extension (suggestions for further study and connections)*

Box 6.4
Example Lesson Plan: Artifacts Reveal Their Secrets

SUBJECTS: Social Studies, Science, Language Arts
Skills: Observe, Record, Infer
Strategies: Inquiry, Discovery, Cooperative Learning
Time: 45–60 minutes
Class size: 20–30; assigned to study teams of 3–4 students each
Grade level: 4th–8th

OBJECTIVES: Students will
1. Identify important events related to European exploration.
2. Use artifact drawings to acquire information.
3. Apply critical-thinking skills to organize and use information.
4. Make and record observations from artifact drawings.
5. Draw inferences and conclusions regarding the functions of the artifacts.

BACKGROUND: Archaeologists analyze artifacts (anything made or used by humans) to tell us about the lives of early people.
    In 1995 the wreck (1686) of the *Belle*, a ship sailed by French explorer La Salle, was located in Matagorda Bay, Texas. Four artifacts brought to the surface during test excavations were drawn and labeled with the site number 41 MG 86 and individual artifact numbers (Figure 1).
    The artifacts connect with four important interpretive themes:
1. navigation and maps: #00784 is a pair of dividers, a navigational instrument used to calculate distance on a map;
2. weapons and defense on sea and land: 00770 shows two views of the tip of a powder horn used to pour powder into a musket or cannon;
3. supplies for daily life in a settlement: #00760 is a hook used to suspend a pot over a fire; and
4. trade with Native Americans and the commercial nature of the voyage: #00759 shows two views of a hawk bell used for falconry in Europe and as a trade item with the American Indians (Karankawa and Caddo) in the New World.

RESOURCES AND MATERIALS: an artifact card and activity sheet for each team of students;

Articles: Fowler, G., La Salle's Lost Ship (*Texas Highways*, November 1997);
           La Roe, L. M., La Salle's Last Voyage (*National Geographic*, May 1997);
           Roberts, D., Sieur de La Salle's Fateful Landfall (*Smithsonian*, April 1997);

OR the 30-minute video, *Treasures of the Texas Coast: La Belle*, available from South Texas Public Broadcasting (512) 855–2213.

PROCEDURE:

1. Guide the lesson by saying, "Today we will look at artifacts—objects made or used by people—to tell us about the lives of past people. We will observe and record information using questions that archaeologists ask. Then we will extend the observation by inferring how each artifact was used."

2. Show a piece of chalk as an example of an artifact. Model the skills of observation and inference for the students. Observation: Give students a verbal description without naming the chalk. Use descriptors guided by the activity sheet: material, size, shape, color, and other. Inference: Tell students what inferences can be made about the chalk: how it was used, where it was used, how it was made, and where it was made. Ask for questions or comments from the students.

3. Ask students to make verbal observations about a pencil. What descriptors or measurements might help (material, size, length, width, shape, color, other)? The answers come from direct observation.

    Next lead students into inferences with the following questions: "What was the function (use)? How was it made? What technology was needed to make it? Where and when was it made?" The answers may be inferred; they are conclusions reasoned from evidence but are not directly observable.

CLOSURE:

Show color photographs of the *Belle* from popular magazines or a video. Ask, "What do you remember hearing about the *Belle*?"

Reinforce and add information from the background section so that students have an overview of the shipwreck and its recovery.

Assign three to four students to each team. Guide the students by saying, "Now we will observe and record information about an artifact recovered from the *Belle* during archaeological testing in 1995." Give each team one of the four artifact cards and an activity sheet on which to record observations and inferences (Figure 6.2).

Check work as they proceed. Ask students to share their observations and inferences with the class.

EXTENSION: Have students extend the themes represented by the artifacts.

Name _____
    student - lab technician
Date _____

ARTIFACTS REVEAL THEIR SECRETS

Site # _____   Artifact # _____
    state, county, number

OBSERVATION   ## SKETCH OR DRAWING

Description: _____

_____

_____

Material: _____

Size: length _____

       width _____

Shape: _____

Color: _____

Other: _____

INFERENCE

Look for clues that tell you more about the artifact than you can directly observe. What does it tell us about human behavior? Consider the following questions:

What was its function (use)? _____

Where was it used (location)? _____

How was it made (manufactured)? _____

What technology was needed to make it? _____

Where was it made? _____

What other inferences can you make about the people who used and discarded this artifact? _____

_____

_____

_____

Figure 6.1. Artifact cards of items recovered from the *La Belle* shipwreck excavation.

Artifacts Reveal Their Secrets

*Below are drawings of four artifacts recovered during the 1995 excavation of the La Salle Shipwreck. Select **one** to analyze using Activity Sheet 1.1. See back page for identification of artifacts.*

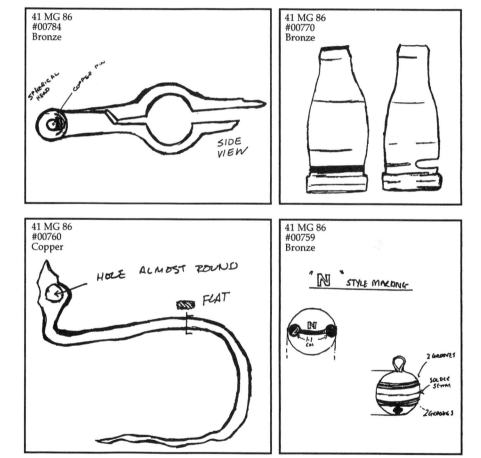

Figure 6.2. Activity sheet for recording observations and inferences about the *La Belle* shipwreck artifacts.

1:55 p.m.   Grade papers turned in during morning while students
are having art lesson with a special teacher in the room.
How do I assess student learning?

As a topic, archaeology promotes higher-level thinking and problem solving. Active teaching strategies include simulations, role-playing, and case studies, among others. Therefore, assessment will have to match both the presentation as well as student aptitudes.

Current trends in evaluation include a variety of options like portfolio development and project presentation, as well as traditional testing (McNutt, this volume).

3:10 p.m.   Reminder note arrives from co-teacher about the school
committee for establishing after-school clubs (maybe
one for archaeology?).

Archaeologists will enjoy collaborating with educators to prepare lessons that are useful and substantive. Teachers will enjoy using lessons that have the educational values to enhance their classroom teaching. And students will increase their knowledge and skills while becoming stewards of our archeological heritage.

3:20 p.m.   School dismissal. Monitor bus loading in the parking
lot.
Return to classroom to grade papers and collect
materials to work on at home, including a lesson on
archaeology. It matches my curriculum requirements so
well, and I can also see many areas where it will
enhance students' small group learning, affective and
cognitive skills. I can't wait to include it in my classes
for next term!

PART II

The Interface
Archaeologists Working with Educators

Part I of this book describes the cultural context of professional education within which archaeology education takes place, as well as providing information about how educational systems in North America are organized, funded, and administered. It also presents basic tenets of educational theory about how children of varying abilities and environments develop cognitively and morally. Archaeology educators need a basic understanding of the educational system's structure and the under-pinnings of pedagogical theory to approach teachers and administrators confidently and knowledgeably.

Influencing teachers to incorporate archaeology into their classroom strategies requires prior knowledge of what they need. Primarily, these needs must address educational system standards and the developmental requirements of their students, as outlined in Part I. Armed with exciting, targeted ideas for educational programs or well-designed teaching materials, the archaeology educator still has a challenge: How can I reach a wide audience of educators? Where will teachers get teaching materials and ideas?

Pam Wheat's concluding chapter to Part I begins to operationalize the theoretical into the actual, bridging Parts I and II. Part II discusses educational materials and programs and proposes effective strategies for getting accurate, quality materials into the hands of educators. In this section, we focus on archaeologists actively working in partnership with educators. The objective is to build a meeting place for the melding of archaeology and education. Part II also addresses evaluation, a critical and often-overlooked aspect of responsible educational programming. Assessing our work is essential for knowing whether it does what it is intended to do.

What do teachers know about the concepts, methods, and approaches used by archaeologists to discover and interpret our past? What sources do professional educators access most frequently to learn about archaeology? Dorothy Krass conducted a study to find out. In her chapter, she shares her findings about where teachers encounter archaeological information in the popular press and where they turn when deliberately seeking related teaching resources. She explores the messages that each source presents and challenges us to employ anthropological skills to examine our teacher audience and ourselves systematically.

One strategy for building the interface with educators is to intercept them during their formal college training. With initiative on the part of the archaeology educator, particularly one centered in academia, preservice teachers can become advocates of archaeology education during the formative period of their professional careers. By showing them the advantages of using archaeology as they develop their teaching philosophy and repertoire, they become better able to share myriad skills and concepts. Moreover, archaeology and its stewardship message have increased opportunities for transmission; lessons taught in the classroom will be heard by thousands of students over the course of a teacher's career. A corollary to this strategy is to offer in-service training and workshops to teachers already in the profession, who must take training courses to remain certified or to advance in their career tracks. Bob Brunswig's chapter describes his experiences in recruiting both pre- and in-service teachers to become involved with archaeology education. He shares the strategies of programs that are successful in building the relationship between educational theory and archaeology education.

Ruth Selig's chapter follows Krass's theme from another perspective: How does an archaeology educator ensure that program information is available in sources that teachers deliberately search for teaching resources? Selig's chapter is a resource guide for accessing the educational community through conferences, workshops, trade publications, newsletters, and journals. A companion appendix by Alana Kuperstein lists these resources with postal or web addresses for contacting them. Archaeology educators should use these vehicles to expand the audience of users; otherwise, we continue to "preach to the choir" of those teachers already committed to using archaeology.

Teachers and archaeology educators alike may use several existing avenues to acquire educational materials. Because many resources are good starting points and sound references for new programs, they can obviate the need for developing new materials. KC Smith provides a historical overview of the last decade's florescence of archaeology teaching materials and the nascent field of archaeology education. She offers suggestions about the future of archaeology education that challenge us to plot a course for this new hybrid discipline so that it will be a viable and relevant enterprise. An appendix presents an annotated selection of teaching manuals, books, and Internet resources.

As noted repeatedly in this volume, archaeology education programs and materials that actually will be applied in a teacher's crowded schedule must answer pedagogical needs dictated by government-imposed standards and modern educational theory and practice. In today's homes and classrooms, the speed with which computer-based technology is being adopted is nothing short of revolutionary. Computer labs, e-mail, the World Wide Web, and CD-ROMs will be part of most children's education and, for many, they already are. However, using the latest wizardry in electronic educational materials does not necessarily yield a quality, meaningful learning experience, nor is it always the most effective vehicle for transmitting the archaeological message. Joëlle Clark's chapter explores the roles and applications of educational technology and provides a model for using, designing, and evaluating computer-based materials. Through a series of questions, this model categorizes the types of learning outcomes from a particular product or program and helps to assess whether authentic learning has occurred. She also provides a glossary of "techno-terms."

Sometimes the first archaeology education resource that a teacher or students encounter is an individual archaeologist. This often happens in the context of a classroom talk or a meeting at a exposition booth or fair. In fact, your presence as an archaeologist or your forty-five–minute presentation may be the only exposure that a student ever has to archaeology. Carol Ellick's chapter gives advice on how to maximize the effect of these short-term encounters so that the archaeology educator has a positive and lasting impression on his or her audience. Focusing on a well-defined message, knowing the audience, and using active teaching strategies are some of the keys to success. She suggests several archaeological concepts and offers pragmatic and engaging ways to present them; her chapter demonstrates the application of many of the concepts presented thus far in the book.

The cultures of professional archaeologists and educators have many potential bridges between them, several of which have been explored in this section. Program evaluation provides the strengthening trestles for these bridges. A complete education program includes mechanisms for ascertaining whether goals were reached effectively and successfully. Nan McNutt gives an overview of several evaluation techniques available to archaeology educators. Evaluation is necessary and applicable at every stage of a program's development and implementation, from conception to several years after its presentation. Our cross-cultural efforts with the education community more likely will result in successful partnerships if reflection and evaluation are built into them. Evaluation is a part of the spiraling process of continually improving and honing our educational offerings.

Together, Parts I and II of this book give the archaeology educator an understanding of the culture of professional education and its interface with the culture of archaeology. In Part III, we will turn to the danger zones in this interface—the areas where misunderstandings and controversy are likely to occur, and we present ways to avoid the pitfalls or to turn them into "teachable moments."

DOROTHY SCHLOTTHAUER KRASS

Chapter Seven

National Geographic and Time Magazine as Textbooks
How Teachers Learn about Archaeology

Those of us who have seen archaeology-based school curricula blossom in the past decade know that there are many exciting and rewarding ways to use archaeology in schoolrooms and other traditional educational settings. We know that you don't have to dig to "do" archaeology. But we also know that for many people—including teachers—archaeology excavation is not merely a tool of archaeology, it *is* archaeology.

And this distorted view of archaeology intrudes into our attempts to introduce archaeology into the precollegiate curriculum. At one extreme, we meet the teacher who is raring to collect a bunch of shovels and launch a treasure hunt in the school's back yard; at the other extreme, we find many of the most thoughtful teachers excluding any idea of using archaeology because they assume it would demand that they lead their students in the field.

Aside from the issue of whether, or under what conditions, excavation is an appropriate tool for precollegiate education, the identification of archaeology as excavation contributes to its mystique as a subject too complicated or too expensive to teach in public school (Hawkins 1991; Chiarulli, Bedell, and Sturdevant; and Smardz, both this volume). It also works against our goals of teaching archaeological stewardship to the next generation of citizens.

If we archaeology educators are going to work effectively with teachers, we need to understand what teachers understand archaeology to be. We need to be aware of the distortions in their perceptions so that we are not stymied by them, but can work creatively with teachers to broaden their definition of archaeology to include analysis, interpretation, and the quest for an understanding of human behavior.

Sources of Information

Research among teachers has shown that few of them learned archaeology—or even anthropology—in their own formal schooling (Holm and Higgins 1985; Erickson 1990; Rice 1990). My own study of one high school found that none of its social studies faculty, not even the historian who teaches an archaeology unit in her upper-level elective in anthropology, had ever taken a course in archaeology (Krass 1995:100).

Teachers, like most members of the general public, are taught archaeology by the mass media. When asked how they learned about archaeology, the teachers I interviewed listed familiar sources of general information—*Newsweek, Time,* the *New York Times, National Geographic,* PBS, and the Discovery Channel—the reading and entertainment world of the educated American middle class (Krass 1995:61).

On the other hand, when asked where they look for information to use in their teaching, these teachers listed their professional journals, the meetings of their professional associations, their formal education, and the examples of their colleagues (Krass 1995). Research also indicates that even teachers who do use archaeology in their classrooms don't associate teaching it with the development and application of analytical skills, with source criticism, for example, or with teaching the scientific method. Few teachers use archaeology to illustrate how we know about nonliterate cultures or what we can learn about the majority of people who have lived outside the histories of literate societies: the women, the children, the poor, the unnoticed. Teachers don't make the connection between learning to analyze artifacts and their contexts, and learning to analyze historical documents and their contexts. By and large, teachers find archaeology useful for catching students' attention. They do not understand its relevance to what they often identify as the core goal of teaching: giving their students tools for analyzing and under-standing the world (Krass 1995:68–81).

Learning How Teachers Learn
about Archaeology

This chapter describes a preliminary study of how archaeology is presented in the periodicals teachers habitually read. The teachers themselves identified, in my interviews, the dichotomy between their sources of information about archaeology for their personal enrichment, and their sources of ideas for creating or modifying their lesson plans. I wanted to document a general impression of how the popular media portray archaeology, and to see if those images are repeated in teachers' magazines and journals. Are teachers being exposed to resources that demonstrate to them that, as Shurban said in 1989, "archaeology is more than a dig"?

My analysis was limited to the way archaeology is presented in the print media that teachers cite as sources of information they read on a regular basis —their daily papers or weekly news magazines, the magazines they relax with, and the professional journals they read to keep up to date. I did not include print resources (like handbooks, teachers guides, or in-service materials) to which teachers would turn to once they had decided to look more deeply into a specific topic. Nor did I try to analyze the images of archaeology teachers get from television, movies, or the Internet.

First, let's consider the general media and then let's look at the journals aimed specifically at teachers. Remember, teachers view these two different sets of sources as providing two different kinds of information. The first helps them develop their own personal knowledge, informs them about things in which they are interested individually, and serves as a pool of background materials into which they can dip for interesting illustrations, asides, or embellishments on lessons in their academic specialty. The second source provides ideas they can use in their classrooms. Produced by people they respect as their peers, it represents professionally authenticated ideas that can be legitimately used to contribute to classroom innovation.

The Popular Press

Among the teachers I interviewed, *Time Magazine, Newsweek,* and the *New York Times* were repeatedly mentioned among their major sources of news in general, and about archaeology specifically (Krass 1995:61). These teachers live in a rural community in the northeastern United States. Most read two daily newspapers, one large-circulation daily, the *New York Times* or the Boston *Globe,* plus the daily paper of one of two smaller cities closer to the school community. When I was preparing this paper, I did not have access to the *Globe* or to either of the smaller dailies. I used the nationally distributed index of the *New York Times* to assess its treatment of archaeology as news. For control, I also surveyed the index of another major city paper, the *Washington Post.* Its coverage of archaeology news during the same period was almost identical to that of the *Times.* I took this congruence of coverage to indicate that daily newspapers with large regional distributions would follow similar patterns of reporting on archaeology.

Beginning in 1988 and continuing through early 1996, *Time Magazine* published twenty articles about or including archaeology, and *Newsweek* published eighteen. This is only between two and three articles per year, although in several cases, these stories were featured on the covers of these national magazines. The *New York Times,* in contrast, ran ninety archaeology-related stories in each of 1992 and 1993; plus ninety-eight in 1994 and forty-nine in the first four months (January–April) of 1995.

Thus, the *Times* ran an archaeology story about every fourth day, while the news magazines averaged one story every four months.

The distribution of topics covered, however, was remarkably consistent among all three, and they will come as no surprise to most readers. The most frequently reported stories involved superlative discoveries: the largest Egyptian tomb, the oldest French cave paintings, the earliest hominid fossils, the oldest human sites in Europe or the Americas, the most spectacular tomb in the New World—the "-est" words fairly leapt from the headlines. Next came reports on Biblical topics: validating Biblical events, locating Biblical sites, or reporting on the political or religious conflicts surrounding archaeological excavations in the Holy Land.

The third most popular category of study is anything about mummies or frozen human travelers from the past: the Alpine Ice Man, the frozen Peruvian mummy, the Egyptian mummy undergoing a CAT scan. This last overlaps into the fourth notable category, which focuses on very high-tech means of discovering otherwise hidden history: satellites seeing the lost city of Ubar under the sands of Oman, or remote sensing identifying a funeral barge buried beneath the Great Pyramid at Giza.

The feature on the funeral barge is also the only story of the forty-five in these four categories that did *not* involve reporting on an excavation or a controversy stopping an excavation. Stories that combine excavation and controversy (setting up unreconcilable or polar positions) are highly popular as well: archaeologists prevented from excavating by orthodox or indigenous religious opponents, archaeological concerns hindering development projects at home or abroad, and repatriation issues around past or projected excavations.

Factoring out travel stories and obituaries (which contribute to the imbalance of frequency figures for the *Times* over news magazines), only a handful of the eighty-seven stories in the sample reported on archaeologists' analysis or synthesis of information from previously excavated materials, from standing monuments, or of ancient features of the landscape. One of these fell in the category of "unsolved mysteries" (a mysterious stone chamber in upstate New York); a second was a controversial interpretation of a frieze on the Parthenon; and a third featured Stonehenge at the solstice.

Of the eighty-seven stories that the teachers and the general public read about most, sixty-two centered on an excavation; twenty-eight were about an excavation that had set a new record; sixteen recounted a controversy; fourteen revealed a Biblical truth; four described applied technology in a surprising new way to discover a site. Or someone has accidentally found a mummy.

Is it any wonder the public thinks all we really do is excavate?

The Educators' Press

But teachers read professional and scholarly journals as well as the popular press. In fact, it is these regular communications from their peers that shape their notions of what topics are appropriate for their teaching (Krass 1995:108). Do the professional publications reflect the same bias toward excavation as the general media? The teachers I interviewed mentioned some twenty professional journals they read regularly for ideas about teaching (Krass 1995:61). Of these, only two were listed in the U.S. Department of Education's widely available database, the Educational Resource Information Center (ERIC), as having run articles about archaeology between 1986 and 1995. Altogether in those ten years, ERIC lists 175 entries including or about archaeology. Of these, 83 are journal articles. (Wanting to track the archaeological input in teachers' "normal" reading, I did not include books, monographs, and other print resources that don't arrive automatically by subscription.) Of the 83 articles in periodicals, 32 were either in general trade publications that were not on my teachers' lists, or were aimed at college or university faculty, or, unfortunately, were about dinosaurs. So, during this ten-year period, 55 entries in ERIC were (1) really about archaeology, (2) in periodicals, and (3) aimed at precollege teachers.

This is a biased sample, too. Publications are entered into ERIC primarily as a result of the author or publisher sending them in. Many journals aren't listed. *Archaeology and Public Education*, the newsletter of SAA's Public Education Committee, didn't appear in my keyword search; nor did the Smithsonian's free bulletin to teachers, *AnthroNotes*. None of the highly recommended curriculum guides like *Intrigue of the Past* (Smith et al. 1996), *Classroom Archaeology* (Hawkins 1991), or *Project Archaeology/Saving Traditions* (McNutt 1992) showed up in the search either.

What this limited sample did include about archaeology, however, was a surprise. Of the fifty-five articles, only nineteen included excavation as part of the education experience. Seven of those nineteen described lessons or units in which students dug in actual sites under the supervision of an archaeologist, seven involved simulated sites, and two featured field schools expressly for teachers. Thirteen lessons or units, on the other hand, involved classroom learning experiences, including four projects analyzing archived or previously reported materials. In nine of the fifty-five cases, the centerpiece was an exercise in inference from or analysis of contemporary material culture. Twenty-three of the articles described traditional text-based lessons or units, primarily around cultural history narratives. A list of these fifty-five references is attached as Appendix 1.

My impression from this very preliminary dip into the education literature is that, despite the fashion in education for hands-on, activity-centered, experiential learning, teachers are not being deluged with blueprints for digging.

What Can We Conclude?

It appears that there are published resources that can lead teachers to a wider understanding of archaeology and how it can be used in the classroom, resources that are placed in the journals that teachers respect as sources for classroom innovation. But the impact of fifty-five professional articles published over a period of ten years may be nearly invisible compared to the ninety-some published every year in the *New York Times* and the news magazines. When we archaeology educators work with teachers, we need to remember both kinds of sources: the professional sources that we can use to demonstrate the power of archaeology to teachers and the overwhelming popular emphasis on the archaeologist as digger.

We also need to ask ourselves what role we, as archaeologists, play in the pervasiveness of this emphasis on finding and collecting. What information do we provide to the journalists? It has been nine years since Milanich (1991) asked us to do our archaeology in the sunshine. What have we done since then to educate journalists about the real story of archaeology? Does the bias in favor of excavation stories start with us? As Keene (1993) asked, "What stories do we tell about what we do?"

As archaeology educators, we need to find out what teachers think we are telling them when we respond to their enthusiasm for field archaeology with resistance and with discussions of context and stewardship. Do they think we are "talking down" to them because we are jealous of our control over the "real archaeology," the dig? Or do they conclude that archaeology is so arcane, so difficult that there is no point in their trying to use it as a tool in their teaching kit?

In asking these kinds of question of ourselves and about our audience, we will have to dip back into our training as anthropologists. Despite that training, we archaeologists are only beginning to apply the tools of the anthropological craft to understanding what values and assumptions teachers bring to their teaching and to explore the culture within which teachers create their lessons. As more of us reach out to educators to encourage them to include archaeology in their classrooms, we need to remember our roots and to look at our audience and ourselves systematically and anthropologically. The alternative is to create lesson plans for ourselves and then wonder why no one takes us seriously.

APPENDIX 1
Archaeology in Educators' Periodicals:
A Sample Bibliography

Compiled by Dorothy Schlotthauer Krass
from the Educational Resource Information Center (ERIC) database
March 1997

Andel, M.
1991   Digging for the Secrets of Time: Artifacts, Old Foundations, and More.
. . . *Social Studies and the Young Learner* 3(1):9–11.

Audet, R.
1986   Marine Archaeology: Finders Keepers? *Journal of Marine Education*
7(4):33–36.

Backner, A. J.
1993   Making the Past Relevant for Today's Children: Connecting with Ancient
Civilizations. *Social Science Record* 30(1):27–36.

Borst, R. A.
1986   Bring Your Skeleton to Life. *Science Education* 53(4):42–46.

Brook, R., and M. Tisdale
1993   Mystery of the Mesa: A Science Detective Story. *Science and Children*
31(2):32–40.

Carroll, R. F.
1987   Schoolyard Archaeology. *Social Studies* 78(2):69–75.

Casey, J. E.
1989   Mummies and Magic. *Humanities* 10(1):1–21.

Creamer, W., and J. Haas
1991   Pueblo: Search for the Ancient Ones. *National Geographic* 180(4):68–83.

Danes, L.M.J.
1989   The Development of Cognitive Skills through Archaeology. *Social Studies
Journal* 18(Spring):43–45.

Danzer, G. A.
1991   The Earliest World Map, Babylonia, c. 500 BC. *European Social Education* 55(5):304–306.

Deal, W. F., III
1993   The Secrets of the Iceman: Technology Learning Activity. *Technology
Teacher* 52(4):34.

Devine, H.
1989   Archaeology in Social Studies: An Integrated Approach. *History and
Social Science Teacher* 24(3):140–147.
1991   The Role of Archaeology in Teaching the Native Past: Ideology or
Pedagogy? *Canadian Journal of Native Education* 18(1):11–22.

Dolph, G. E.
1989   Adventures in Ethnobiology. *Science Teacher* 56(1):57–59.
Duvall, J.G.I.
1988   Teacher-to-Teacher: Fieldwork for Teachers. *American Biology Teacher* 50(8):527–528.
Elbow, G. S.
1992   Migration or Interaction: Reinterpreting Pre-Columbian West Indian Culture Origins. *Journal of Geography* 91(5):200–204.
Elliot, I.
1994   Saying It with Flowers (and Wildlife, Too). *Teaching Pre-K–8* 25(2): 34–38.
Eve, R. A., and F. B. Harrold
1986   Creationism, Cult Archaeology, and Other Pseudoscientific Beliefs. *Youth and Society* 17(4):395–396.
Feder, K. L.
1986   Of Stone and Metal: Trade and Warfare in Southern New England. *New England Social Studies Bulletin* 44(1):26–41.
Gutierrez, E. D., and Y. Sanchez
1993   Hilltop Geography for Young Children: Creating an Outdoor Learning Laboratory. *Journal of Geography* 92(4):176–179.
Hall, K.
1989   Mystery in Progress. *Humanities* 10(1):8–9.
Hennessey, G. S., and R. Ballard
1988   Tut and the Titanic and Finding History Beneath the Sea. *Instructor* 97(6):84–87.
Hutchinson, B.
1991   Technological Clues to Ancient Mysteries. *TIES Magazine* Jan.–Feb.:12–17.
Kingsley, R. F.
1986   "Digging" for Understanding and Significance: A High School Enrichment Model. *Roeper Review* 9(1):37–38.
Laney, J. D., and P. A. Moseley
1990   Who Packed the Suitcase? Playing the Role of an Archaeologists/ Anthropologist. *Social Studies and the Young Learner* 2(3):17–19.
Lemmon, S. M.
1990   New Concepts for a Unit on the Maya. *Social Studies* 81(3):113–119.
Mathis, M. A.
1986   Mysteries and Relics of the Past Intrigue Kids. *PTA Today* 11(6):11–12.
Mull, K. V.
1990   Archaeology Informs Our Understanding of Ancient Texts. *Religion and Public Education* 17(1):51–61.

Nami, H. G.
    1992   Knapping Knowhow. *Science Journal* 59(2):14–18.
Ovoian, G., and D. Gregory
    1991   Can You Dig It? *Social Studies Review* 30(3):83–88.
Parmet, G. et al.
    1992   Across the Curriculum. *Learning* 21(3):15–22.
Pascua, M. P.
    1991   Ozette: A Makah Village in 1491. *National Geographic* 180(4): 38–53.
Passe, J., and M. Passe
    1985   Archeology: A Unit to Promote Thinking Skills. *Social Studies* 76(6): 238–239.
Paynter, S.
    1993   The Museum of Unnatural History. *Gifted Child Today* 16(4): 10–12.
Pollard, M.
    1991   Archaeology and the Environment. *School Science Review* 73(263): 33–38.
Russon, R.
    1992   Solstice Science: A Lesson in Archaeoastronomy. *Science Teacher* 59(9):14–17.
Sabato, G.
    1990   Touching a Moment in History. *Social Studies Review* 29(2):27–35.
Saindon, J. J., and C. M. Downs
    1992   Archaeology in the Classroom: An Intra-University Continuing Education Workshop for K-12 Teachers. *Innovative Higher Education* 17(2): 115–124.
Sanford, D. W.
    1994   Material Life in Revolutionary America: Artifacts and Issues in the Classroom. *OAH Magazine of History* 8(4):27–31.
Seager, R. D.
    1990   "Eve" in Africa: Human Evolution Meets Molecular Biology. *American Biology Teacher* 52(3):144–149.
Sentelle, S. P.
    1986   Digging to Learn: Teaching Science, History, and Social Studies through Archaeology. *Educational Leadership* 44(2):10–12.
Shade, R. A.
    1990   Grandma's Attic: Bringing Archaeology Closer to Home for the G/C/T Student. *Gifted Child Today* 13(3):10–12.
Shafer, M.
    1990   A Teachable Moment. *Religion and Public Education* 17(1):43–44.
Shamy, R.
    1991   A Museum Program: A Hands-On Approach to the Social Studies. *Southern Social Studies Journal* Special Issue(Summer):18–30.

Smardz, K. E.
1989   Educational Archaeology: Toronto Students Dig into Their Past. *History and Social Science Teacher* 24(3):148–155.

Steinman, M. C.
1993   The Earthmobile Project: Making Connections between the Past, Present, and Future. *Social Studies Review* 32(2):25–28.

Stuart, G.E.J.
1991   Etowah: A Southeast Village in 1491. *National Geographic* 180(4):54–67.

Swaim, G. E.
1985   Digging into Prehistoric Iowa. *The Goldfinch* (Magazine of the Iowa State Historical Department) 7(1):entire issue.

Tesser, C. C., and C. Hudson
1991   Before Oglethorpe: Hispanic and Indian Cultures in the Southeast United States. *OAH Magazine of History* 5(4):43–46.

Trygestad, J., and J. Nelson
1993   Project Marco Polo: Experiences Applying Geography. *Journal of Geography* 92(4):170–175.

Watts, L. E.
1985   They Dig Archaeology. *Science and Children* 23(1):509.

Welsh, C.
1994   Digging through History. *Gifted Child Today* 17(1):18–20, 42.

White, H. R.
1992   An Exercise in Field Archaeology for the Gifted: Fake Mound, Genuine Scholarship. *Gifted Child Today* 15(5):2–6.

White, J. R.
1995   Empty Lots as Modern Classrooms: Using Archaeology to Enrich the Gifted Curriculum. *Gifted Child Today* 18(5):12–16, 42.

Wygoda, L. J., and A. V. Cain
1994   Motivational Mysteries. *Science Teacher* 61(8):30–33.

ROBERT H. BRUNSWIG, JR. ■

<hr>

Chapter Eight

Including Archaeology in K–12 Teacher Education

An important way to encourage the inclusion of accurate, engaging, and effective archaeology programming in today's classroom is to introduce archaeology to preservice educators at teachers' colleges. Archaeologists involved in teacher education play particularly critical roles in influencing perceptions and directions of the public on cultural heritage and cultural preservation issues. This chapter addresses teacher education and archaeological education from my perspective as a research archaeologist and university teacher involved in teacher training, twin roles too seldom found in academia.

Since I began recruiting in-service teachers for summer archaeology field schools more than a decade ago, my philosophy on integrating teachers (in-service and preservice) into professional archaeology research has evolved considerably. Part of that evolving perspective has paralleled a growing national trend of involving avocational archaeologists and, often, inexperienced John Q. Public in academic and government-sponsored archaeological research. A number of government agencies, under shrinking budgets and legislative pressure for increased reliance on volunteer workers, have developed low (or no) budget volunteer programs under the aegis of heritage tourism. Those programs represent both best and worst case scenarios of how the public may be incorporated into archaeological research and heritage stewardship roles. At best, such programs encourage members of the public to become enthusiastically involved in cultural preservation, developing a growing appreciation of the human historical-cultural record and the rich diversity of human heritages. At worst, some programs, usually from lack of funding, adequate volunteer training, and sufficient professional supervision, may lead to damage and loss of the irreplaceable cultural resources the programs seek to document and preserve.

Part of the insurance against the dangers of such programs, and threats to our national and international cultural resources in general, lies in integrating archaeological concepts and the meanings and values of cultural heritage in our nation's precollegiate school curricula. Simply put, our children are the future. Without effectively providing our young people with the knowledge and tools for understanding the roots and foundations of human cultural history, we cannot expect them to appreciate and wish to preserve them. Schoolteachers have the ability to reach out effectively to millions of young people throughout North America. But first our teachers must be given the knowledge and tools to educate the youth of today and tomorrow. And therein lies our challenge with respect to archaeology education.

Getting Teachers to Teach Archaeology

With the current turmoil over "re-structuring" social studies education in the United States, often overwhelmed K–12 educators are likely to ask archaeologists why they should consider incorporating archaeology content into their classrooms. That question is particularly important in light of two considerations: (1) Archaeology (and its parent discipline, anthropology) is seldom addressed in either preservice or in-service teaching training programs, and (2) Time and resources for teaching "required" subjects in precollegiate classrooms are limited enough without adding a seemingly esoteric knowledge area like archaeology.

There are many sound reasons for including archaeology in the K–12 curriculum. For instance, archaeology's approaches and methods promote problem-solving and creative-thinking skills; its interdisciplinary focus can effectively integrate a variety of social science, math, and science skills and knowledge areas; and it teaches about diverse cultural histories and backgrounds, the latter promoting respect and awareness of our nation's and our world's diverse ethnicities (i.e., multiculturalism). Finally, the most valuable aspect of incorporating archaeological topics into the precollegiate classroom is that it is almost universally considered exciting and mysterious by students of all ages. That appeal can serve as a magnet to encourage young people to learn about exciting archaeological subjects while being taught a multitude of practical skills and content knowledge in core areas such as geography, history, math, earth sciences, and biology. Once teachers decide that using archaeology in the classroom is a valid exercise, they (and archaeology educators involved in teacher training) must consider how its integration can be accomplished without adding unduly to teachers' already heavy workloads and satisfy state and school district graduation requirements and standards (see Davis, this volume).

Historically, attempts to integrate archaeology and, more generally anthropology, into precollegiate school curricula have met with mixed success. In fact, the ambitious Anthropology Curriculum Project of the mid- and late 1970s attempted to design a stand-alone anthropology curriculum for social studies programs in K–12 school systems (Collier 1975; Haas 1976; Fenton 1991). For various reasons, including public and interest group resistance to the teaching of many anthropology subjects such as cultural diversity and human evolution, the project largely collapsed without implementation by the early 1980s. Less volatile disciplines such as history and geography continue to dominate social studies and social science programs with little reference to anthropological (and archaeological) topics. This "head-in-the-sand" attitude, based in part on dominant culture biases in the United States, is a phenomenon we are only just beginning to address at national and state levels of K–12 education in terms of learning standards. Even so, reluctance to deal with social and cultural diversity in the nation's school systems remains problematic and: "As a discipline, anthropology is disquieting to school curriculum makers for three reasons: (1) evolution, (2) culture, and (3) values. Unless these three factors are recognized, they cannot be addressed as problems to be solved" (Rice 1995:222).

With the rise of standards-based education philosophy in the late 1980s and 1990s, precollegiate teacher preparation and K–12 education entered a new era of "back-to-basics" school curricula, reformulating nineteenth- and early twentieth-century fundamentals teaching approaches in late twentieth-century technology-rich classrooms (Bragaw 1993; U.S. Department of Education 1997a). Present standards-based initiatives in K–12 education are only now reaching their maximum expression in U.S. school systems and must be taken into consideration in attempting to incorporate archaeology and cultural heritage content into precollegiate classrooms of the next decade and beyond.

Archaeology and School Curricula:
Teaching Standards and Guidelines

The development of teaching standards and knowledge goals, integrated with rigorous assessment rubrics, is now driving precollegiate education at national, state, and local school district levels. I believe that the integration of archaeology (and other anthropology knowledge areas) in K–12 curricula can particularly benefit from two approaches at the preservice teacher education level: development of teaching curricula and resources specifically supporting (and being integrated with) geography and history standards goals and content matter, and development of curricula and resources designed to highlight archaeology as a valuable focus for multidisciplinary teaching in the nation's classrooms. Teacher education programs at universities should be encouraged to include archaeologists and archaeological educators in developing and offering courses addressing geography, history, math, and science standards.

The powerful movement toward the integration of multicultural content into K–12 curricula can also benefit from the use of archaeological topics as "core themes" in the multicultural courses favored among university students in teacher education programs. One of the most popular and useful classes for preservice teaching students at the University of Northern Colorado (UNC) is an anthropology course on multiculturalism, taught from an anthropological perspective. The course, which provides a fundamental background on the history and composition of ethnic communities in the United States, also addresses the historical and archaeological origins of those communities. The teaching of archaeologically derived histories of ethnic groups, particularly of less-advantaged minority communities, is increasingly becoming an avenue for raising levels of self-respect within those communities and more enlightened awareness of the rich achievements of their ancestors (see Scott and Connor 1986; Harrington 1992).

Archaeology Education for Preservice Teachers

A large and growing number of teacher education institutions require content-based degrees, in contrast to more pedagogically oriented (methods) education degree programs of the past. The shift in focus toward more content-enriched teacher education represents a new opportunity to develop courses designed to provide preservice teachers with a foundation based on skills and quality-focused archaeology content.

My experience in teacher training at the undergraduate level includes developing courses on the Archaeology of Colorado and Teaching Anthropology in K–12 Classrooms, both designed for teaching K–12 students. The first course, Archaeology of Colorado, provides both basic information and teaching resources for prospective teachers. Through the years, I have always found it odd that although nearly every school district required elementary grade level teaching blocks on culture and archaeology of Native Americans or other ethnic and historical groups (usually specific to a region or state), teachers were seldom given adequate training or resources to deliver quality instruction on those subjects.

At UNC, we now provide basic instruction for preservice teachers, preparing them for teaching those "archaeology-based" topics. An important element of the Archaeology of Colorado course is its focus on our state's long multicultural history, from the prehistoric and early historic encounters of often quite different Native American cultures and belief systems to a rich, and seldom addressed history of ethnic group interactions (i.e., Spanish and French explorers, African-American mountain men and farmers, Chinese railroad workers, and Japanese farm laborers).

The course Teaching Anthropology in K–12 Classrooms is a very recent innovation and is designed to address important K–12 subjects such as global and national cultural diversity and the historical development of humanity from the origins of the earliest human species to the present. The course focuses on placing the human condition and the diversity of cultures in the past and present within a perspective of cultural relativity, a central tenet of modern anthropology that teaches that different cultures and their societies should be viewed within their unique cultural contexts derived from a series of adaptations through time. Along with content, the course provides a variety of teaching resources for all grade levels, including exposure to a growing number of anthropology education Internet sites and valuable teacher resources such as the Smithsonian's *AnthroNotes* and teaching modules (see Smithsonian Institution 1990–1997; Selig and London 1998; also see Selig, this volume). Archaeology teaching resources, lesson plans, and course materials are provided for class participants in part by use of the Bureau of Land Management's teacher's guide, *Intrigue of the Past* (Smith et al. 1996).

Both anthropology and archaeology content courses for teachers at UNC remain electives for content-focused social science and history teaching majors. Social science (or social studies) and history teacher training at the university are coordinated through our Institute of History and Social Science Education. The institute administers undergraduate, content-based teaching degree programs in elementary, middle-school, and secondary-school education. Students in those programs take a variety of required and elective content courses along with a smaller number of methods and student teaching and internship courses (Professional Teacher Education Program/PTEP) in the College of Education. The above courses provide at least some training foundations for prospective teachers for the eventual inclusion of archaeological and anthropological subjects in K–12 school curricula.

A second avenue for the integration of archaeology into precollegiate curricula is through in-service teacher education, frequently in the form of continuing education programs driven by periodic postgraduate certification (or licensing) requirements at the state level. In-service teacher education programs offer an even more immediate means of integrating archaeology into school curricula by addressing archaeology and anthropology-associated elements of the history and geography standards, because in-service teachers are directly involved in standards-based curricula planning and implementation at the school district level. Commonly, such in-service programs involve workshops and summer institutes that provide continuing education credits for teacher recertification and relicensing, and access to the latest classroom concepts, teaching materials, and aids (see Wheat, this volume).

In-Service Archaeology for Professional Educators: Workshops and Summer Courses

At UNC, we are addressing in-service teaching training through special workshops and summer courses. One approach has been to recruit in-service teachers in field research activities during the summer. Since 1987, I have been directing field projects in northeastern Colorado. In most summers, I have had in-service teachers involved in those projects, either for graduate credit in formal field schools or simply as volunteers.

As participants in field projects, those teachers have not only been valuable contributors and resources for our research, but their experience and background have contributed to the education of younger college students working with them. The teachers themselves have direct contact with "dirt archaeology" and, when they return to their classroom, enrich their classrooms with descriptions, videos, and slides of the practical (and some say romantic) side of archaeology. Our most recent version of a course for in-service teachers is a graduate class called Teaching Colorado Archaeology: Addressing the Geography and History Standards. The course is taught over four, eight-hour days, on both the campus and, mainly, at a field site in the Rocky Mountains. It incorporates a general review of Colorado's archaeological record; a short introduction to archaeological methods (using the above-discussed *Project Archaeology* curriculum); a review of state history, geography, and science standards addressed by archaeology topics; and an outline of student assessment strategies related to the standards. Two valuable aspects of the course for in-service teachers are that it provides access to a wide range of archaeology education curriculum resources and materials, and it involves a hands-on, though brief, participation in ongoing research projects within a few minutes drive of the classroom (see Photos 8.1 and 8.2). When the teachers complete the course, they are encouraged to join the state's avocational society and are instructed how to volunteer for field projects conducted every summer by Colorado academic institutions and government agencies.

Recently, archaeology education at the university was integrated into a long-term program of K–4 teacher workshops. The team-taught workshops involve the participation of anthropology, geography, history, and education faculty and master teachers from regional school districts and the Colorado Department of Education. The workshops are designed to address content and assessment requirements of Colorado's newly adopted Geography and History Standards (Colorado Department of Education 1997). My role in the workshops, as an archaeologist, was to describe and address elements of the standards that are largely or in part derived from anthropology and archaeology. At least twenty-nine of those standards requirements are directly related to anthropology and archaeology content knowledge. Some of the standards that are directly related include statements that students should know and understand "how culture and experience influence people's perceptions of places and regions," "the nature and spatial distribution of cultural patterns," "the general chronological order of people, groups, and events in the history of Colorado," and "how various societies were affected by contacts and exchanges among diverse peoples."

Conclusion

My experience in the workshops has convinced me that they are an effective way for university anthropologists and archaeologists to contribute to postgraduation teacher training and to inculcate anthropology and archaeology subjects into precollegiate curricula. One of the most important strengths of archaeology (and anthropology as a whole) is its holistic, interdisciplinary approach. That strength is emphasized when

Photo 8.1. Teachers excavating a 3,000-year-old rock shelter site in the Rocky Mountains, Colorado.

Photo 8.2. A high-school teacher mapping artifacts at a 1,500-year-old campsite in the Colorado mountains.

university archaeologists participate in interdisciplinary team teaching efforts, such as the UNC workshops. Our most recent effort in that regard was a *National Geographic*–sponsored workshop, focused on Colorado geography standards, and centered on a theme of grassland ecosystems in three world regions (the U.S. high plains, the East African savannah, and the Ukrainian steppes). Using thematic content on multiple regions with their diverse ecologies, histories (some of it archaeologically derived), and geography, the workshop effectively integrated concepts and knowledge bases from physical and economic geography, archaeology, and history to provide a cross-disciplinary resource base for teachers.

I suggest that in the future academic archaeologists and archaeological educators involved with teacher education programs at all levels become thoroughly aware of state and national standards and tailor courses, workshops, institutes, and lesson plans and materials to address those standards. In doing so, archaeology (and associated knowledge areas in anthropology) can increasingly make an impact on U.S. precollegiate education. Archaeology educators, working from archaeology's greatest strength as a multidisciplinary, multifaceted discipline of study, can most effectively contribute to current standards-based efforts for education reform at the precollegiate level.

RECOMMENDED READINGS

McCarthy, Gloria, and Molly Marso
  1984 *Discovering Archaeology.* United Educational Services, Buffalo, New York.
  An educational curriculum on archaeology as a tool for integrating different areas of study and knowledge in the precollegiate classroom. Student and teacher versions are available from either United Educational Services, Inc., D.O.K. Publishers, P.O. Box 1099, Buffalo, NY 14224, or The Teachers' Room, 259 Mamaroneck Ave., White Plains, NY 10605. (ISBN# 0–88047–194-8) (teacher) (ISBN# 0–88047–195–6) (student).

McNutt, Nan
  1992 *Project Archaeology: Saving Traditions: Archaeology for the Classroom,* 2d ed. Sopris West, Inc., Longmont, Colorado.
  Project Archaeology is a curriculum that uses skills learned in science, social studies, math, and language arts for archaeology study. The curriculum is composed of three units. The book's focus is to provide an introduction to archaeology, ancient lifeways, and materials (for example, pottery, stone tools, bones) in North America during the prehistoric and historic periods. It is for grade levels 6–8. To order, contact: Sopris West, Inc., 1120 Delaware Avenue, P.O. Box 1809, Longmont, CO 80502–1809; tel.: (303) 651–2829; fax: (303) 776–5934.

O'Brien, W., and T. Cullen
  1995 *Archaeology in the Classroom: A Resource Guide for Teachers and Parents.* Archaeological Institute of America, Boston.

An excellent guide to teaching resources of all types for introducing archaeological/ anthropological topics to K–12 classrooms. For more information and ordering, contact the Archaeological Institute of America, 656 Beacon Street, Boston, MA 02215–2010.

Selig, Ruth O., and Marilyn R. London, eds.
   1998   *Anthropology Explored: The Best of AnthroNotes.* Smithsonian Institution Press, Washington, D.C.
   A compilation of selected articles on anthropological topics from the Smithsonian's well-known *AnthroNotes* teacher's bulletin. Designed for teacher content use and student classroom use, the articles simply and informatively present ideas and discoveries in anthropology (including archaeology) to readers from the age of 8 up. The edited volume provides an excellent teacher resource and abundant materials and topics for classroom use. Order from the Smithsonian Institution Press at Washington, DC 20560.

Smith, Shelley J., J. M. Moe, K. A. Letts, and D. M. Paterson
   1996   *Intrigue of the Past: A Teacher's Activity Guide for Fourth through Seventh Grades.* Reprint. Bureau of Land Management, Anasazi Heritage Center, Dolores, Colorado.
   This guide is part of a nationwide education program known as Project Archaeology. The text provides an introduction to basic archaeological concepts (for example, chronology, context, and culture) and the processes of archaeology (for example, field mapping and recording, artifact classification, pollen analysis, dating techniques, and experimental archaeology). A section covering the issues surrounding archaeological conservation completes the guide. The guide is designed for grades 4–7 but can be used for both lower and higher grades. Many states have prepared a companion state-specific supplement. For more information on *Project Archaeology* contact: Project Archaeology, Anasazi Heritage Center, P.O. Box 758, Dolores, CO 81323; tel.: (970) 882-4811; e-mail: projarch@co.blm.gov; Web: http://www.co.blm.gov/ahc/projarc.htm.

Time Education, Inc./Time-Life Series
   Time-Life, Inc. has published a book series of archaeological interest that would be beneficial as K–12 school curricula resources. Among the more useful volumes are:
   1. *Lost Civilizations*, which explores the daily life, social structures, economic systems, and religions of ancient civilizations from North and South America, Africa, Asia, and Europe.
   2. *The American Indians*, which explores the history, everyday life, customs, and social institutions of Native Americans.
   3. *Time Frame*, which provides a view of the simultaneous development of diverse civilizations around the world.
   For ordering information, contact: Time-Education, Inc., P.O. Box 85026, Richmond, VA 23285-5026; tel.: (800) 449–2010; fax: (800) 449–2011.

Williams, Martha
   1989   *Strategies for the Classroom.* Society for Historical Archaeology, Falls Church, Virginia.
   Curriculum development guidelines for teachers focusing on historical and historical archaeology topics. Available from Society for Historical Archaeology Education Committee, 7129 Oakland Avenue, Falls Church, VA 22042.

Chapter Nine

Brokering Cultures
Archaeologists Reach Out to Teachers

Archaeologists Reach Out to Teachers. Copyright © 1999, by Robert L. Humphrey.

Archaeologists and teachers operate within two quite separate professional worlds. An anthropologist studying these two worlds might even designate them two separate cultures because their languages, values, goals, modes of operation, and professional identifications are so dissimilar. Despite the gulf between these two worlds, increasingly one can find "cultural brokers" like the editors and authors of this book who are comfortable crossing from one of these professional worlds into the other. Archaeology educators can move smoothly from the world of archaeology into the world of education and back again; however, such cultural brokers rarely designate the "education" portion of their identity as primary. They generally will identify their primary affiliation with archaeology or anthropology rather than with the profession of education. The exceptions are professionals who consider their identification as archaeologist (or anthropologist) and educator as equal.

As an anthropology educator, I spent a decade teaching social studies, history, and anthropology to junior high and high-school students, another decade teaching teachers, and as much time again working at the Smithsonian Institution with colleagues in the Department of Anthropology, developing museum-university teacher training programs which have been described in detail elsewhere (Selig and Lanouette 1983; Selig and Higgins 1986; Selig 1991, 1995). By working in both areas, I have experienced firsthand the many benefits of offering anthropology to precollegiate audiences. As I have said before:

> When teachers are taught anthropology, they are offered a perspective and a framework within which they can better understand the many seemingly diverse fragments of their curricula, enabling them to approach their subjects— geography, social studies, world cultures, history, biology, earth science, language, literature, and the arts—in a more coherent and less ethnocentric fashion. [Selig 1997:300]

This chapter explores how archaeologists can better understand and gain access to the professional world of teachers. By learning more about the professional organizations teachers join; the conferences and workshops they attend; the journals, newsletters, bulletins, and other publications they read; and the Web sites they access, archaeologists will be better positioned to enter the world teachers inhabit in order to persuade them to introduce more archaeology and anthropology into their classrooms. Hence, the goal of this chapter is to provide practical strategies and specific avenues through which the archaeological community can more effectively introduce their subject matter, curriculum units, resource materials, and teacher training workshops to the community of K–12 teachers. In addition, it describes major anthropology and archaeology organizations and publications. Appendix 1 offers a full listing of major educational as well as anthropology and archaeology organizations and their publications and resources, including Internet Web sites.

Education in North America

Public education in North America is decidedly a local matter, with curriculum determined by district, county, or urban school systems within parameters established at the state and provincial levels (MacDonald and Burtness, this volume), although a movement toward the establishment and application of National Curriculum Standards is well underway (see Davis, this volume). Limited national testing is in the early stages of debate and development in the United States, while Canadian schools are seeing an increase in interest in general achievement and skills-based tests at the provincial level.

If one wants to know what curriculum is actually taught at the local elementary school, junior high or middle school, or high school, there is only one way to find out: Call that local school, or the subject matter curriculum specialist, or consultant (social studies or science, for example) for that school district. Similarly, to learn what specific local in-service training or workshops are being offered, one must canvass the local school system. Often individual school systems have newsletters announcing in-service training, local opportunities for teachers, new teaching resources, conferences or workshops that teachers might find of interest. As Pam Wheat explains earlier in this volume, any archaeologist interested in working with local teachers should do some on-the-ground investigation into the local school system before venturing further.

That said, however, there are national education organizations, publications, and resources to which teachers regularly turn, and that anyone can access quite easily, thereby becoming more familiar with what is happening in schools across North America. National organizations are a good place to begin, since each has its own membership, publications, conferences, teacher services, and newsletters through which they reach vast numbers of teachers, offering them information about curriculum resources and opportunities for teacher training. Today, it is particularly easy to identify these organizations, since virtually all of them have Web sites, and the research can be done almost entirely on the World Wide Web, a one-stop shop for anyone seeking to learn more about the professional world of the K–12 educator.

The archaeologist in search of this information can do his or her own "participant observation" via the Web and, from this initial entry into the world of teachers, expand beyond by seeking out and interviewing professional educators, whether they be local teachers, social studies curriculum supervisors, state or provincial curriculum specialists, museum educators, or professional staff at national organizations. This combination of Internet exploration and interviews with key individuals was the approach used to gather information for this chapter, thereby providing a research model for other archaeologists to pursue.

Major Education Organizations, Publications, and Resources

For archaeology educators, the most effective way to reach the largest number of teachers is through the professional organizations, conferences, and journals that serve educators. National, regional, and local education conferences and seminars are excellent venues to introduce archaeology education materials and activities to teachers in their own milieus. Workshops, poster sessions, displays, and papers all provide direct and relevant access to the teachers archaeology educators most want to reach.

Publications such as newsletters and journals aimed at the various teaching disciplines in elementary and secondary schools, as well as at educational administrators, can be vehicles for letting teachers know of opportunities and resources for archaeology education. Archaeology educators writing for this audience would do well to utilize the vehicles that serve the needs of the education profession.

The National Council for the Social Studies (NCSS) offers the most important entryway into the world of the social studies teacher, and its Web site (www.nscc.org) is one of the most comprehensive. There one will learn that the NSCC is the largest association in North America devoted solely to social studies education, with members in all parts of the continent as well as in sixty-nine foreign countries. The National Council is further divided into more than 110 affiliated state and local councils, each of which organizes activities and offers resources for teachers. The NCSS Web site offers teaching resources categorized in the ten themes of the Curriculum Standards for the Social Studies (both "Culture, and People," "Places, and Environments" relate to anthropology and archaeology); a separate section lists an enormous number of professional development opportunities, including summer institutes and workshops, annual meeting sessions, grant and awards providers, and so forth. In addition, the NCSS hosts an annual five-day conference during which teachers from all over the country gather to participate in sessions both as presenters and audience; at this conference, a huge exhibit hall displays published curriculum resources and textbooks.

The NCSS produces three major publications: *Social Education*, published seven times a year with a circulation of 25,000, primarily geared for high-school teachers; *Social Studies and the Young Learner*, published four times a year especially for elementary-school teachers (with a circulation of 8,000); and *The Social Studies Professional*, the NCSS newsletter published six times a year.

The National Education Association (NEA) of the United States, with head-quarters in Washington, DC, is a major organization of teachers from throughout the country, organized by state and then nationally. The NEA lobbies on behalf of teachers at state and national levels, and produces the publication, *NEA Today*, published monthly except in the summer. The Canadian Teachers' Federation and the Canadian Education Association are Canadian equivalents to the NEA. Finally, The

Society for Curriculum Study is a major organization for curriculum specialists and supervisors and produces the publication *Educational Leadership*.

The National Science Teachers Association (NSTA) is the largest science teachers' organization in the world; its membership in 1998 included 53,000 science teachers, science supervisors, administrators, scientists, business and industry representatives, and others involved in science education. Among other things, the association publishes five journals, a newspaper, many books, and a new children's magazine, *Dragonfly*.

NSTA holds national and regional conventions that attract more than 30,000 attendees annually, in addition to professional development workshops and educational tours. NSTA has a World Wide Web site with links to other science education organizations and an on-line catalog of publications. Since archaeology can link as easily to science as social studies classes, archaeologists need to become aware of both the science and social studies organizations that work with educators in North America.

Although Canada has no single organization comparable to the National Science Teachers Association, two provinces have similar organizations: British Columbia and Ontario (see Appendix 1). Many Canadian teachers belong to equivalent U.S. organizations as well. Some local educational organizations such as teachers' federations and disciplinary subject groups have their own publications. For example, The Science Teachers' Association of Ontario publishes both *Crucible* and *Elements*, aimed at secondary and elementary science teachers, respectively.

In addition to these organizations and publications, there is another that particularly serves the teaching profession in private schools: the National Association of Independent Schools, a U.S. organization. The NAIS holds conferences, and like NCSS, offers workshops, teacher presentations, and large publishers' exhibitions at its annual conference. The Federation of Independent Schools in Canada serves a similar purpose.

Several publications produced outside any single organization target social studies teachers. *The Social Studies* is a widely read journal by history and social studies teachers in the United States and Canada alike; it includes essays on teaching as well as book and curriculum resource reviews. *The Teaching Professor* is a monthly newsletter containing articles on teaching skills and activities and on current issues and technologies. Finally, *Instructor Magazine* and *The History Teacher* target professional educators in the social studies and history.

On a more general level, there are many publications aimed at teachers and students that can serve to publicize archaeology education information to different age and grade levels. Two publications for teachers and young students that often have anthropology- and archaeology-related articles are *Cobblestone: The History Magazine for Young People* and *Faces: The Magazine About People*—both are published by Cobblestone Publishing, Inc. Canadian equivalents are the magazine for very young children, *Chickadee,* and the associated magazine for the middle-school set, *Owl,* published by Bayard Presse, of Toronto, Canada.

Major Anthropology/Archaeology Organizations, Publications, and Resources for Teachers

The larger anthropology and archaeology organizations in North America have put ambitious public outreach initiatives in place, establishing offices and publications that target teachers; unfortunately, these are not yet used heavily by teachers who probably are unaware of their existence. It is important that archaeologists become aware of these various outreach efforts since some teachers are utilizing these resources to learn about opportunities for their classrooms. However, the plethora of curriculum requirements facing today's teachers, coupled with the downsizing and budget cutting that many district boards of education are experiencing, means that educators are more likely to use materials that are provided through their normal access channels than those produced by professional organizations in other disciplines.

The Society for American Archaeology (SAA) is the single most active and effective organization for archaeologists, heritage resource specialists, and interpreters teaching the public about the value of archaeological research and resources. Although the SAA scholarly publication would be of little interest for most K–12 teachers, the Public Education Committee of the SAA has for the past few years published a marvelous newsletter entitled *Archaeology and Public Education.* It includes teaching activities as well as news of multiple opportunities and resources for teachers; it is evolving into two new formats, one of which is available through the SAA Web site (www.saa.org). There are also plans for a theme-based publication series of booklets aimed at educators. The Mississippi Valley Archaeology Center (MVAC), in La Cross, Wisconsin, publishes a highly useful newsletter, *The Mississippi Valley Archaeology Center Archaeology Education Newsletter,* with information about learning materials, workshops, and resources for teachers (see Christensen, this volume).

The Archeological Institute of America publishes a bimonthly publication of general interest, *Archaeology,* that contains both scholarly and public interest articles as well as book reviews and other materials of interest to educators. They have available an annotated bibliography of archaeological teaching resources entitled *Archaeology in the Classroom: A Resource Guide for Teachers and Parents* (O'Brien and Cullen 1995). An updated version is currently being prepared for publication in 1999. The Society for Historical Archaeology produces a newsletter announcing conferences, workshops, and publications, while its yearly conference has many sessions of potential interest to teachers. This important organization is also engaged in developing videos for classroom use and encourages a public archaeology approach in historical archaeology projects.

Within the field of anthropology, there are several publications that target either teachers or a general audience. The American Anthropological Association includes a General Anthropology Division that publishes a bulletin, *General Anthropology*, focusing on articles and book reviews of material of general interest to teachers at all levels. *The Canadian Journal of Archaeology*, produced by the Canadian Archaeological Association, is also available through university libraries and by subscription to interested teachers. The Society for Anthropology in Community Colleges (SACC) produces a newsletter that promotes teaching anthropology, creating a forum through which teachers and educators can exchange ideas and learn of new resources and curriculum units. *Practicing Anthropology* is the vehicle of the Society for Applied Anthropology; it includes short articles that elucidate anthropology in action, particularly in applied settings.

One of the longest-standing publications aimed at teachers and produced by anthropologists is *Teaching Anthropology Newsletter (TAN)*, published by the Anthropology Department at St. Mary's University in Halifax, Nova Scotia. The newsletter promotes precollegiate anthropology and archaeology by providing curriculum information for teachers, reviews of new materials, advertisement of upcoming events teachers would find of interest, and articles describing innovative programs in North America.

Teachers and Museums: A Learning Experience

National, state or provincial, and local public institutions are important sources of information for elementary and secondary schoolteachers who wish to introduce archaeological information and concepts into the classroom. Often, field trips to museums are the first introduction to archaeology for students and teachers alike. Many museums have educational staff to produce instructional media, teaching kits complete with replica artifacts and age-appropriate lesson plans, and more general curricula for use in schools (see Lea, Kwas, this volume).

In Canada, provincial museums from coast to coast offer invaluable advice and resources on archaeology and related disciplines for use by the classroom teacher. The National Museum of Civilization has a useful Web site, while Internet resources such as those offered by the Nova Scotia Museum and Head-Smashed-In-Buffalo-Jump, a World Heritage Site in the prairies, are available to educators everywhere. The Royal Ontario Museum has a large education staff, including personnel dedicated to the design and maintenance of traveling teaching kits on many subjects of interest to the classroom teacher.

American museums and historic and living history sites are very important sources where teachers gain information about archaeology. For more than twenty years, the Smithsonian Institution's Department of Anthropology has targeted teachers as a major audience to be served. A separate office of Anthropology Outreach offers a variety of materials for teachers, including classroom ideas, bibliographies, teachers' packets, and resource and fieldwork opportunity listings. The department publishes *AnthroNotes* twice a year and distributes it free of charge. A compilation of essays published over the years is available in *Anthropology Explored: The Best of Smithsonian AnthroNotes* (Selig and London 1998). The volume is especially strong in its archaeology section.

Conclusion

Archaeologists and educators have worked together successfully over the last several decades, as evidenced by several exemplary model programs throughout the continent and beyond; many of these are highlighted in this volume. However, in general, these programs have tended to grow from the enthusiasm and hard work of individual teams of archaeologists and educators. They have evolved far outside the mainstream of the professional literature and venues for teachers, which focus very little on either anthropology or archaeology. The relative absence of archaeology in mainstream journals and forums contrasts with the parallel success and visibility of individual model archaeology programs.

Archaeologists must work more within and with the mainstream organizations for teachers if they want to build more than single model programs in various locations across North America. For archaeology programs to be more than occasional "success" stories in unusual circumstances, archaeologists have to convince large numbers of teachers, curriculum supervisors, and editors of mainstream publications that archaeology is a necessary and wonderfully appropriate subject through which educators can introduce students to the rich heritage of their past and the exciting potential of their future.

APPENDIX 1
A Listing of Education and Archaeology/Anthropology
*Organizations and Publications**

Alana S. Kuperstein

I. Education Organizations, Publications, and Resources

The National Council for the Social Studies (NCSS)
3501 Newark St., NW, Washington, DC 20009
tel.: (202) 966–7840 or (202) 328–5800; fax: (202) 966–2061; Web: www.nscc.org
Publications: *Social Education*
    Social Studies and the Young Learner
    The Social Studies Professional

The National Education Association of the United States (NEA)
1201 16th St. NW, Washington, DC 20006
tel.: (202) 833–4000; Web: www:afj.org/mem/nea
Publications: *NEA Today*
tel.: (202) 822–7282

Canadian Teacher's Federation
110 Argyle St. West, Ottawa, ON, Canada K2L 1B4
tel.: (613) 232–1505; fax (613) 232–1886; e-mail: info@ctf-fce.ca

Canadian Education Association
#8–200, 252 Bloor St. West, Toronto, ON, Canada M5S 1V5
tel.: (416) 924–7721; fax: (416) 924–3188; e-mail: acea@hookup.net
Publications: *Education Canada*
    (published quarterly)
    CEA Newsletter
    (published nine times per year)

The Society for Curriculum Study
1250 N. Pitt St., Alexandria, VA 22314–1453
Publications: *Educational Leadership*

The Centre for the Study of Curriculum and Instruction at the University of British Columbia
2125 Main Mall, Vancouver, B.C., Canada V6T 1Z4
tel.: (604) 822–6502; fax: (604) 822–8234; Web: www.scci.educ.ubc.ca

The National Science Teachers' Association (NSTA)
1840 Wilson Blvd., Arlington, VA 22201–3000
tel.: (703) 243–7100; Web: www.nsta.org

Publications: *National Science Teachers Association Reports*
                (newspaper of science education)
                Science and Children
                (for elementary teachers)
                Dragonfly
                (new science magazine for children)
                Science Scope
                (for middle-level science teachers)
                The Science Teacher
                (for high-school science teachers)

British Columbia Teachers' Association
Member of the British Columbia Teachers' Federation
#100, 550 6th Ave. West, Burnaby, BC, Canada V52 4PZ
tel.: (604) 871–1848; fax: (604) 871–2291; Web: www.bctf.bc.ca

The Science Teachers' Association of Ontario
P.O. Box 771, Dresden, ON, Canada N0P 1MO
tel.: (800) 461–2264; fax: (519) 683–2473
Publications: *Crucible*
                Elements

The National Association of Independent Schools (NAIS)
1620 L St., NW, Suite 1100, Washington, DC 20036
tel.: (202) 973–9700; fax: (202) 973–9790
Publications: *Independent School Magazine*
                The National Association of Independent Schools Newsletter

Federation of Independent Schools in Canada
9125 50th St., Edmonton, Alberta, Canada T6B 2H3
tel.: (403) 469–9868; fax: (403) 469–9880

Other Publications:
                The Social Studies
Heldref Publishing, 1319 18th St., NW, Washington, DC 20036–1802
tel.: (800) 365–9753; Web: www.heldref.org

                The Teaching Professor
                (yearly subscription, $49)
Magna Publications, Inc., 2718 Dryden Dr., Madison, WI 53704–3086
tel.: (608) 246–3580, (800) 433–0499; fax: (608) 246–3597; Web: www.magnapubs.com

                Instructor Magazine
P.O. Box 53896, Boulder, CO 80322

The History Teacher
California State University, Department of History, 1250 Bellflower Blvd., Long Beach, CA 90840

Cobblestone: The History Magazine for Young People
Cobblestone Publishing, Inc., 7 School St., Peterborough, NH 03458
tel.: (800) 821–0115; Web: www.cobblestonepub.com

Faces: The Magazine About People
Cobblestone Publishing, Inc., 7 School St., Peterborough, NH 03458
tel.: (800) 821–0115; Web: www.cobblestonepub.com

Chickadee and *Owl* Magazines
The Owl Group, Bayard Presse Canada, 179 John Street, Suite 500, Toronto, Canada M5T 3G5
tel.: (416) 340–2700; fax: (416) 340–9769; e-mail: owlcom@owl.on.ca

II. Archaeology/Anthropology Organizations, Publications, and Resources

Society for American Archaeology (SAA)
900 2nd St., NE #12, Washington, DC 20002–3557
tel.: (202) 789–8200, fax: 789–0284; e-mail: headquarters@saa.org; Web: www.saa.org
Publications: *American Antiquity*
                  (published quarterly)

                  Archeology and Public Education
                  (a Web-based newsletter of archaeology education)
See Web site cited above.

Mississippi Valley Archaeology Center (MVAC)
1725 State St., La Cross, WI 54601
Web: www.ulax.edu/colleges/mvac
Publications: *The Mississippi Valley Archaeology Center Archaeology Education Newsletter*

Archaeological Institute of America
135 William St., New York, NY 10038
tel.: (212) 732–5154; fax: (212) 732–5707; Web: www.archaeology.org
Publications: *Archaeology*
                  Archaeology in the Classroom: A Resource Guide for Teachers and Parents (1999)
Subscription Service, P.O. Box 50260, Boulder, CO 80321
tel.: (800) 289–0419

Society for Historical Archaeology
Web: www.sha.org

Publications: *The Society for Historical Archaeology Newsletter*
Department of Anthropology, College of William and Mary, P.O. Box 8795, Williamsburg, VA 23187–8795

American Anthropological Association (AAA)
General Anthropology Division, 4350 North Fairfax Dr., Suite 640, Arlington, VA 22203
tel.: (703) 528–1902; Web: www.ameranthassn.org;
Publications: *General Anthropology*
David McCurdy, ed., Department. of Anthropology, Macalester College, St. Paul, MN 55105
tel.: (612) 696–6587; fax: (612) 696–6324
Patricia Rice, ed., Department of Sociology and Anthropology, West Virginia University, Morgantown, WV 26506
tel.: (304) 293–5810; fax: (304) 293–5994

Canadian Archaeological Association
Space 162-Box 127, 3170 Tillicum Rd., Victoria, BC, Canada V9A 7H7
tel.: (250) 478–1147; fax: (250) 388–7373
Publications: *Canadian Journal of Archaeology*
(published annually)

Society for Anthropology in Community Colleges (SACC)
2005 Arkeny Blvd., Arkeny, IA 50021
tel.: (216) 987–4513; fax: (216) 987–4404
Publications: *The Society for Anthropology in Community Colleges Newsletter*
tel.: (515) 964–6435; fax: (515) 965–7301; e-mail: ljmil@aol.com

Society for Applied Anthropology (SfAA)
P.O. Box 24083, Oklahoma City, OK 73124
Publications: *Practicing Anthropology*
Alexander M. Ervin, ed., Department of Anthropology and Archaeology, University of Saskatchewan, Saskatoon, Saskatchewan, Canada S7N 5A5
tel.: (405) 843–5113; fax: (404) 843–8553; e-mail: ervin@skyway.usask.ca

Human Organization
Robert V. Kemper, ed., Department of Anthropology, Southern Methodist University, Dallas, TX 75275
tel.: (214) 768–2928; fax : (214) 768–2906

SfAA Newsletter
Michael B. Whiteford, ed., Department of Anthropology, 319 Curtiss Hall, Iowa State University, Ames, IA 50011–1050
tel.: (515) 294–8212; fax: (515) 294–1708

Teaching Anthropology Newsletter (TAN)
Department of Anthropology, St. Mary's University, Halifax, Nova Scotia, Canada B3H 3C3
tel.: (902) 420–5628; fax: (902) 496–8190; e-mail: mlewis@shark.stmarys.ca

III. Museums

The Smithsonian Institution, Department of Anthropology, Washington, D.C. 20560
Publications: *AnthroNotes*, The National Museum of Natural History Publication for
Educators
e-mail: kaupp.ann@nmnh.si.edu

Teachers' Packet in Anthropology
The Department of Anthropology makes available, free of charge, materials including:
bibliographies, leaflets, activities, and teachers' packets.
tel.: 202–357–1986; Web: www.nmnh.si.edu/anthro

Anthropology Explored: The Best of Smithsonian AnthroNotes
Ruth Osterweis Selig and Marilyn R. London, eds., Smithsonian Institution Press, 1998
tel.: 800–782–4612
National Museum of Civilization, 100 Laurier Street, P.O. Box 3100, Station B, Hull, Québec,
Canada J8X 4H2
Web: www.civilization.ca/cmcchome

Head-Smashed-In-Buffalo-Jump, Box 1977, Fort Macleod, Alberta, Canada T0L 0Z0
tel.: (403) 553–2731; Web: www.head-smashed-in.com/home

Nova Scotia Museum, Museum Services Division, 1747 Summer Street, Halifax, Nova Scotia,
Canada B3H 3A6
Web: www.ednet.ns.ca/educ/museum
Web: www.museumlink.com/canada

Provincial Museum of Alberta, 12845 102d Avenue, Edmonton, Alberta, Canada T5N 0M6
Web: www.pma.edmonton.ab.ca

Royal British Columbia Museum, 675 Belleville Street, Victoria, British Columbia, Canada
V8W 9W2
Web: rbcm1.rbcm.gov.bc.ca

The Manitoba Museum of Man and Nature, 190 Rupert Avenue, Winnipeg, Manitoba, Canada
R3B 0N2
Web: www.manitobamuseum.mb.ca

The Newfoundland Museum, P.O. Box 8700, St. John's, Newfoundland, Canada A1B 4J6
Web: www.nfmuseum.com

Royal Ontario Museum, 100 Queen's Park, Toronto, Ontario, Canada M5S 2C6
Web:www.rom.on.ca

The Québec Museum, Parc des Champs-de-Bataille, Québec (Québec), Canada, G1R 5H3
Web: www.mdq.org/fr/Anglais

*Listings follow the order discussed in the chapter.

Note: Information on Canadian organizations and resources was provided by Paul A. Erickson, Department of Anthropology, St. Mary's University, Halifax, Nova Scotia, Canada B3H 3C3.

Chapter Ten

From Context to Content
Instructional Media for Precollegiate Audiences

Historical Overview

Efforts in the last decade to bring archaeology into precollegiate classrooms have been supported by a florescence of educational materials to assist teacher instruction and student exploration of the discipline. Not only have conventional resources —such as books, magazines, teaching manuals, games, videos, and teacher in-service—increased in number, precision, and creativity, but they also have been augmented by new media—such as traveling trunks, computer simulations, World Wide Web sites, and living history interpretations at archaeological sites. In addition, papers from conference symposia, journal articles, and theses and dissertations that address and analyze archaeology education strategies increasingly are available to discerning educators.

Because the use of the discipline in precollegiate contexts has emerged so dynamically in recent years, archaeology educators have struggled mightily to keep track of new materials and programs as they have been developed. The National Park Service Archeological Assistance Division published two volumes of *Listing of Education in Archeology Programs: The LEAP Clearinghouse* (Knoll 1990, 1992). This endeavor required a full-time staff person to maintain the database and prepare the reports, which summarized more than 1,200 products and activities generated for the public between 1987 and 1991 in twenty-one categories of media—from brochures and tours to community outreach and school curricula.

Building on a list developed for a Society for Historical Archaeology education symposium (Smith 1990), the Society for American Archaeology (SAA) Public Education Committee (PEC) began in 1990 to maintain a bibliography that includes precollegiate books, teaching manuals, resource guides, periodicals, games and simulations, and audiovisual resources, pertaining primarily to the Americas. Its compendium now consists of more than 200 entries (Smith 1991a, rev. ed. 1997). In 1995, a resource guide published by the Archaeological Institute of America expanded the field by including educational programs, organizations, and publications world-wide (O'Brien and Cullen 1996). Local lists also have been produced by agencies or individuals in many states and provinces in North America (Williams 1989; Peñalva 1994).

Beyond the resources that are readily available through commercial, organizational, or governmental outlets is a vast array of items that fall into the category called "gray literature." While these lesson plans, activity ideas, and program outlines may be academically relevant and pedagogically sound, they do not have widespread distribution because they have been designed for specific and often limited educational programming—for example, by an individual teacher, museum, or archaeological site. Information about these products often is shared in local newsletters or papers presented at regional conferences, although as electronic and interpersonal networks have developed, the trail of these "hidden" efforts has become easier to track.

Among the educational resources that are readily accessible, some are site specific, and others focus on regional cultures and traditions. Some emphasize broad conceptual or methodological aspects of archaeology, while others highlight specific topics such as physical anthropology or underwater research. Although most items are geared for social studies instruction in grades 4–8, the full spectrum of resources enables teachers to use archaeology to share knowledge and skills in all subject areas and at all precollegiate levels.

While the bulk of instructional materials has been developed in the last ten years, teachers have been experimenting with classroom archaeology and sharing their ideas at least since the early 1970s. A seminal publication by Holm and Higgins (1985) not only examined the emerging archaeology education trend, but also summarized much of the early literature, which consisted primarily of method and theory articles published in educational journals. But it was not until the mid-1980s that archaeologists really began to grasp the extent to which teachers were using the discipline to enhance classroom instruction.

Their attention was prompted in part by professional concern over the rapid destruction of archaeological sites, and the recognition that the general public—including well-tutored youths—could help protect and preserve cultural properties. More important, it had become clear that the earnest and enthusiastic efforts of some teachers were yielding strategies and resources that were inappropriate or inaccurate. To address this, concerned archaeologists began to work more closely with educators to improve the direction and precision of materials. As this interaction coalesced and moved into the 1990s, resources began to focus on interpretive, analytical, and con-servational aspects of research as highlights of the archaeological process, rather than on fieldwork. The results are seen in the current array of products, which are more accurate, ethical, and pedagogically effective. The ubiquitous crossword puzzles, word searches, and simple drawing exercises have given way to activities that develop critical thinking skills, provide real-world but nonintrusive experiences, and foster a sense of stewardship about cultural properties. Hands-on opportunities still are encouraged, but not necessarily through schoolyard digs; rather, they are presented as explorations that require consideration of all of the elements of an archaeological project.

In 1991, members of the recently formed SAA Public Education Committee met to examine the course of archaeology education efforts and to discuss ways in which the PEC could contribute to these ventures. Among other projects, the team began to construct an "ideal" set of information that precollegiate resources and programs might include. After much revision and review, its summation was presented in *Guidelines for the Evaluation of Archaeology Education Materials* (SAA PEC 1995a), which suggested basic theoretical, editorial, methodological, and curricular concepts that would present archaeology responsibly to youths, facilitate the use of materials, and dispel myths and misconceptions. Although the guidelines were designed primarily with print media in mind, they nonetheless represented a starting point for defining professional and pedagogical standards.

Based on a small number of evaluations returned by teachers, the guidelines have been used to develop and assess instructional items for individual curricular needs. Their only widespread application has been to evaluate commercially available archaeology games, a project completed by the PEC with a grant from the U.S. Department of the Interior, Bureau of Land Management (Wheat and Colón 1997). In 1999, the PEC started a long-term project to use the guidelines to evaluate print materials in its bibliography, "Classroom Sources for Archaeology Education." As the evaluations are finished, they will be posted on the SAA Web page (www.SAA.org).

Further recognizing the importance of evaluation in the public awareness process, the PEC sponsored a symposium at SAA's 59th annual meeting that presented a cross-section of efforts to assess materials and strategies (Krass 1994). Speakers not only reviewed area-specific endeavors, but also described feedback from classroom teachers, who reconfirmed the unique value of the discipline as an instructional motif.

Archaeology Education Resources in the Future

This overview of the history and status of precollegiate archaeology education media necessarily leads to a single question: Where do we go from here?

Given the current volume and accessibility of resources, it may be time to focus further on evaluation, rather than production. Myriad excellent models exist that have been generated by teachers and archaeologists and that are classroom tested. Perhaps the next step is a widespread assessment of materials and an outline of needs for the future, with an eye on certain questions. Archaeology educators must ask themselves: Are current devices really promoting preservation? Are they enabling teachers who have varying backgrounds in archaeology to present the discipline responsibly? To what extent do materials mesh with existing or emerging national and local curriculum standards? Are efforts targeted primarily at gifted students rather than all students? Is there a need for multilingual products? Are aspects of the discipline, such as underwater research, underrepresented?

In addition, as the Internet becomes more omnipresent, untold reams of information about terrestrial and underwater archaeology are at one's fingertips; however, most of it remains geared for adults. The extent to which teachers access this data has not been measured, but that question may be academic. The real issue may lie in how frequently precollegiate students use the Internet to learn about archaeology, and whether on-line resources are sufficient to guide their exploration and discovery. It may be that the next wave of archaeology education products ought to be geared toward kids, who probably have more time and opportunity to "surf the net" in class and at home than their teachers have.

This is not to say that print and hands-on media should be jettisoned. A recent Internet-based teaching manual reports that 40% of public secondary schools and 35% of public elementary schools have access to the Internet, based on a U.S. Department of Education study (Roerden 1997). This is not a sufficient level of Internet dependence to abandon conventional resources. Moreover, the highly unscientific "word on the streets"—that is, informal conversational feedback from teachers to professional archaeology educators—suggests that teachers cannot and do not yet rely on electronic outlets for their students' primary educational experiences.

Archaeology's elegance as an instructional vehicle is multifaceted: It is interdisciplinary, interactive, culturally awakening, and pedagogically effective. Materials and programs that support its application are critical to its purpose and efficiency. Enough time, productivity, and experimentation have passed since the onset of this movement for archaeology educators and teachers to determine whether their efforts are meeting intended objectives.

Educators strive to prepare students intellectually and affectively for their future. Archaeologists strive to save past cultural resources for future discovery and study—by these same youths and their descendants. The instructional resources and programs that teachers have at their disposal for sharing archaeology with youths are the keys to the attainment of these objectives.

Sample Resources

It is not possible in this chapter to review all of the educational media available to precollegiate teachers. Examples listed below suggest the range of content and creativity that have been incorporated into resources, but their inclusion does not imply a commercial, professional, or organizational endorsement of any kind.

Teaching Manuals

Gregonis, Linda, and Lee Fratt
    1992   *Archaeology: Window on the Past.* Tucson Unified School District,
    Tucson, Arizona.
    A revision of the seminal 1985 publication, "Archaeology Is More Than a Dig," this
manual and its predecessor were designed to complement an archaeology component at Camp
Cooper, the Tucson Unified School District's field experience for elementary students.
Understandably, the section on culture history focuses on past populations in Arizona and the
Southwest, but the excellent presentation of archaeological theory and method could be used
as a guide for teachers or students in any location. Written with fifth-grade youths in mind,
information is thorough, concise, and well illustrated. A section on preservation discusses
federal and local legislation as well as ethics. Text is augmented by a long bibliography,
glossary, and nearly twenty classroom activity ideas.

Hawkins, Nancy
    1991   *Classroom Archaeology. An Archaeological Activity Guide for Teachers,*
        rev. ed. Louisiana Department of Culture, Recreation and Tourism,
        Division of Archaeology, Baton Rouge.
    One of the earliest comprehensive manuals for teachers, this collection of resources,
games, and activities has evolved in its previous printings in 1984 and 1987 to reflect changing
philosophies about classroom strategies. Instructions for a simulated dig in the first edition have
been supplanted with a nonintrusive activity in which students record and interpret an actual
site. A fundamental concept behind the manual's design is the recognition that teachers often
have limited knowledge about archaeology and few academic and financial resources to assist
them. Thus, activities are flexible: They can be used singly or sequenced as a unit; and, while
they are targeted for middle school, most can be adapted for younger or older audiences. The
culture history and many supporting resources focus on Louisiana archaeology.

McNutt, Nan
    1992   *Project Archaeology: Saving Traditions,* 2d ed. Sopris West, Inc.,
        Longmont, Colorado.
    A curriculum for middle-school and gifted elementary-school students, this resource
offers a multidisciplinary approach to classroom archaeology, with activities that draw on social
studies, science, mathematics, and language arts. Overall, there is a strong emphasis on
stewardship. In addition to an introductory section for teachers, the manual presents the
discipline in three educational units: The Artifact, The Site, and The Culture. Activities in each
unit are complemented by student workbooks; auxiliary components, such as games and
audiovisual media, can be purchased separately. While the culture history focuses on the Pacific
Northwest, the lesson ideas can be adapted to any region. (Note: These materials are distributed
by the Association for Archaeology and Historic Preservation, Seattle, Washington, rather than
the publisher.)

Moyar, Joanna T.
    1993   *Archaeologists at Work: A Teacher's Guide to Classroom Archaeology.*
        Alexandria Archaeology Publication Number 48, Alexandria, Virginia.

Archaeologists at Work offers an example of how an archaeological agency can develop educational materials and programs that make use of local resources and that have the local school system in mind. Prepared with the prospect that teachers will arrange an Alexandria Archaeology museum tour or classroom outreach, the publication contains scheduling details and pre- and postvisit activity plans. Additional classroom ideas and information about historic Alexandria are tied to local educational objectives. Three sections in the notebook provide general information about archaeology, commonly asked questions about the discipline, selected articles, and other educational and local resources.

Prentice-Hall, Inc.
1997   *The Wreck of the* Henrietta Marie. Interdisciplinary Explorations series, Upper Saddle River, New Jersey.
This three-part packet, based on the study of a slave-trading vessel that wrecked in Florida in 1700, is one of the few teaching manuals that deals with an underwater site. A student workbook leads kids through discovery activities; a supplemental reader is intended for teachers and students; and a teacher-planning guide explains curriculum philosophy and classroom procedures. Although it addresses a particular aspect of culture history—the transatlantic slave trade in the early eighteenth century—this packet provides an excellent interdisciplinary model for educators who want to use maritime archaeology and history as a linchpin for instruction.

Smith, Shelley, Jeanne Moe, Kelly Letts, and Danielle Paterson
1996   *Intrigue of the Past. A Teacher's Activity Guide for Fourth through Seventh Grades.* Reprint. Bureau of Land Management, Anasazi Heritage Center, Dolores, Colorado.
Intrigue is the cornerstone of Project Archaeology, a component of the Bureau of Land Management's Cultural Heritage Education Program. Building on an earlier, similar publication that was oriented toward Utah archaeology, the updated version is less specific geographically. Twenty-eight classroom-tested lesson plans are presented in three categories: Fundamental Concepts, The Process of Archaeology, and Issues in Archaeology. Collectively, the activities emphasize ethics, preservation, and nonintrusive aspects of archaeology, rather than fieldwork. Lesson plans also correlate well with national standards in history, geography, and scientific inquiry. Information is available at the Web site: http://www.co.blm.gov/ahc/projarc.htm

Wheat, Pam, and Brenda Whorton
1991   *Clues from the Past. A Resource Book on Archeology.* Texas Archeological Society, Austin; Hendrick-Long Publishing, Dallas.
Although currently out of print, this teaching manual provides an excellent model for presenting methodological aspects of archaeology to students. While the culture history is Texas based, most lesson ideas are founded on such basic principles that they can be adapted to different regions and contexts. Moreover, each phase of archaeological research is addressed— including survey, excavation, analysis, interpretation, replication, reporting, and preservation —with activities that are geared for grades 3–12.

Books

Cork, Barbara, and Struan Reid
1984   *The Young Scientist Book of Archaeology. Discovering the Past with Science and Technology.* Usborne Publishing, Ltd., London; EDC Publishing, Tulsa, Oklahoma.
There isn't much about archaeology that is overlooked in this easily readable and brightly illustrated book. Sixteen general themes and myriad subthemes address archaeological history, methods, tools, field and lab techniques, artifacts, burials, dating, conservation, replication, and much more. Although geared for middle-school readers, the book is suitable for older audiences who want a quick but thorough overview of the discipline. This resource will enhance any classroom library or school media center.

Macaulay, David
1993   *Motel of the Mysteries.* Houghton Mifflin, New York.
Buried during a catastrophic event in 1985, the culture of the ancient country of Usa is brought to light through the efforts of amateur archaeologist Howard Carson, who begins excavating Tomb 26 at the Motel of the Mysteries in the year 4022. Macauley's classic description and drawings of this endeavor, and of Carson's wholly erroneous interpretations of finds, are as much a spoof of archaeology as they are of contemporary society. Suitable for secondary and older readers, this book is an excellent companion to classroom archaeology units.

McIntosh, Jane
1994   *Archaeology.* Dorling Kindersley, London.
One of the useful Dorling Kindersley "Eyewitness Guides," this book offers a well-illustrated overview of the discipline for secondary-level and older readers. As she did in her earlier popular text, *The Practical Archaeologist*, the author discusses major themes in archaeology—for example, preservation, landscapes, documents, why and how excavations are undertaken, conservation, dating, and interpreting daily life—in two-page summaries. Brief statements about each theme are embellished by photos that exemplify the concepts. Most examples are drawn from Old World contexts.

Samford, Paricia, and David L. Ribblett
1995   *Archaeology for Young Explorers. Uncovering History at Colonial Williamsburg.* The Colonial Williamsburg Foundation, Williamsburg, Virginia.
Using Colonial Williamsburg and nearby sites as a focus, this book for upper elementary readers presents an outstanding introduction to historical archaeology, beginning with an explanation of the discipline and ending with a discussion of the knowledge that is derived from research. Activities for readers are interspersed throughout the pages to reinforce text information. The book also is enhanced by excellent drawings and photographs, many of which show young people involved in archaeological research.

Internet Resources

Anthropology on the Internet for K–12
http://www.sil.si.edu/SILPublications/Anthropology-K12/anth-k12.htm
    Maintained by the Smithsonian Institution Libraries, this site features anthropology-related links in more than ten different categories, including a separate listing for archaeology. The network of resources ultimately leads to considerable information about anthropology.

Archaeology Resources for Education
http://www.interlog.com/~jabram/elise/archres.htm
    This privately maintained site lists links to other resources or Web sites. Click on "Resource Menu" at the bottom of the page to get twelve categories of links, such as historical research, virtual sites, resource lists, on-line journals, teacher resources, career information, and short articles about the discipline.

ArchNet
http://archnet.uconn.edu
    ArchNet is the World Wide Web virtual library for archaeology, providing access to resources available on the Internet. Information is organized by geographic region or subject, and home pages are available in six languages other than English. The site also includes lists of academic departments, museums, and publications, and common ways to search for different types of archaeology information.

History/Social Studies Web Site for K–12 Teachers
http://www.execpc.com/~dboals/boals
    More than thirty searchable topics are included in the History/Social Studies Web Site for K–12 Teachers. The Archaeology/Anthropology page provides a comprehensive list of related locations, divided into eight categories: news groups, university pages, journals, organizations/museums, digs and site/regional reports, concept sites, teaching sites, research fields, and general information. The site is suitable for teachers and older students searching for archaeological resources.

Southeast Archeological Center (SEAC)
http://www.cr.nps.gov/seac/links3.htm
    The Web site of this National Park Service regional center includes information about parks, publications, educational programs, training, and a host of other topics. However, one of its finest features is its list of more than 200 links to other archaeology web sites worldwide, grouped under such headings as education and outreach, search sources, professional information, institutions and academic departments, Native Americans and other indigenous peoples, and links for kids.

Chapter Eleven

Teaching Archaeology with Educational Technology

> As long as there have been people, there has been technology. Indeed, the techniques of shaping tools are taken as chief evidence of the beginning of human culture. On the whole, technology has been a powerful force in the development of civilization. [American Association for the Advancement of Science 1989:39]

Teaching archaeology to today's technologically sophisticated elementary and secondary school students requires much more than an Indiana Jones hat and a slide carousel. The cutting-edge educational archeologist needs to be able to keep up with the incredible pace of technological development, particularly in the area of communications technology, and understand how this is revolutionizing the way modern teachers teach and modern students learn.

Technology is nothing new to archaeologists who are trained to scrutinize the form, function, and changes of human-made materials over time. However, to many nonarchaeologists, the term "technology" refers to the medium and the technical process of using multiple forms of electronic information (for example, new *technology* for accessing information via the World Wide Web) and this is the operational definition of technology that will be used in this chapter. To educators, technology means having the ability to turn on and use a computer for word processing and spreadsheets, to have voice mail and e-mail, to surf the Internet, to use a video or laser disk, or to use an educational CD-ROM. There is no doubt that these electronic changes are revolutionizing every aspect of the education system.

Students in today's classrooms are downloading data from the Internet as fast as it is being uploaded elsewhere. They are designing and conducting their own research and communicating their results with other students worldwide. They are using CD-ROMs to explore tropical rainforests and ancient civilizations and to suggest solutions for environmental problems.

Similarly, more and more archaeologists are using the Internet to communicate their research in forms that range from daily excavation reports to full-scale interpretive models recorded for public interest and peer review. The question then is, "How can archaeologists involved in K–12 education best use, design, develop, and evaluate educational technology?" This chapter will offer a model for archaeology and educational technology within the current national efforts of education reform.

The Context of Educational Reform

Archaeologists consider one of the most important concepts in the discipline to be that of context; this means that artifacts, features, and other findings are analyzed and interpreted in light of their association with one another. If archaeologists are to become archaeology educators and immerse themselves in educational technology, we must understand the role and uses of educational technology in the reform of today's schools. This is the context for doing archaeology education in modern schools.

Today, educational reform is based in systems theory in which the entire educational system (infrastructure, policies, practices, parents, teachers, students, support staff, and administrators) works together to improve student learning and achievement (Sabelli and Barrett 1993; Bybee 1997). This vision of educational reform was first communicated in *A Nation at Risk*, a U.S. government report that outlined the problems within the K–12 school system; it demanded changes in curriculum content and methods of teaching and called for the development of national education standards (National Commission on Excellence in Education 1983; Davis, this volume). For student learning, this means changes in the traditional teaching methods and in the roles of students and teachers (see Table 11.1).

These reform efforts and national mandates have caused educators to examine and reflect on the content, methods, and evaluation for what students should know and be able to do as part of their learning experience. For educational technology, this means that the focus is on learning with, not about, technology (The President's Committee of Advisors on Science and Technology 1997). Educational technology provides the tools to help improve instruction, to connect to the world outside classroom walls, and to gather, process, and communicate information (Lane n.d.; Means 1994; Grégoire, Bracewell, and Laferrière 1996). Used in this way, educational technology also has the ability to meet individual student needs regardless of learning style, economic level, or special needs (Gonzales and Roblyer 1996; Birman et al. 1997).

Integrating technology into the curriculum isn't easy. Traditionally, technology has been applied by using overhead projectors, television, video recording and viewing, basic word processing, spreadsheets, and databases. New techniques and developments have expanded these uses to include computer-assisted instruction (CAI), Integrated Learning Systems (ILS), graphing calculators, distance learning, desktop publishing, simulation games, laserdiscs, audio-visual presentations, data entry and analysis, CD-ROM disks, and Internet and electronic communications (Martin 1997).

TABLE 11.1
Educational Reform Changes in Student Learning

Traditional System Moving from . . .	. . . to a Reformed Educational System
Instruction is teacher directed	Instruction is interactive with students
Learning is by subject matter with little interdisciplinary connections	Learning is authentic: based on real-world problems with multiple opportunities for inter-disciplinary applications
Learning is viewed as a change in observable behavior, which occurs through stimuli and response. The world is objectively fixed and meanings are common; therefore, teachers deliver truths and "facts" to students.	Learning is viewed as a process of gaining or changing insights, outlooks, expectations, or thought patterns. The world is knowable to individuals, but meaning is not necessarily understood; thus, understanding is constructed.
Learning is a mental process that occurs within the individual.	Learning is a social process wherein the input of others is an important part of changing ideas.
Learning in Traditional Student Groups:	Learning in Cooperative Student Groups:
• One leader • No interdependence • Homogeneous membership • Assumption of effective social skills • Responsibility for individual achievement • Emphasis only on task • Direction by teacher • Individual products • Individual evaluations	• Shared leadership • Positive interdependence • Heterogeneous membership • Instruction in cooperative skills • Responsibility for all group members' achievement • Emphasis on task and cooperative relationship • Support and guidance by teacher • One group product • Group evaluation

All this technology can become quite overwhelming and difficult to manage. To help organize how educational technology is used, Means (1994) and Means et al. (1994) have devised four classifications: tutorial, exploratory, application, and communication. This classification along with the basic structure for educational reform provides a model framework for how technology in archaeology education should be used, designed, developed, and evaluated:

- *Tutorial* technology teaches students directly by advancing them as correct responses to questions or problems are achieved. It is used for repetitive skill development and is not considered as effective as other technological uses.
- *Exploratory* use of technology allows students to gather and manipulate resource information in a one-way learning environment. Within this type of technology, students utilize multiple sources to gather information about a particular topic.
- *Application* involves the use of technology as a tool to assist in word processing, data analysis, graphing, or other such operations. With this type of technology, students can manipulate information or data in ways that help them better understand a problem.

- *Communication* allows students to send and receive messages and information through networks, satellite, and cable. This form of technology allows the students to disseminate what they have learned or to ask questions to further clarify what they are learning.

A Model for Teaching Archaeology with Educational Technology

Incorporating technology into a model for teaching archaeology at the K–12 level should be a process of directing "authentic learning." Authentic learning implies that students do something that is closely related to real world problems and is of relevance and interest. Students need to be working with archaeological concepts, processes, and data using techniques appropriate for their research. Depending on their cognitive level, students should be able to pose questions, gather information, create explanations, manipulate data, make interpretations, and develop models or simulations based on their interpretations.

The following model proposes a process through which educational technology could be used, designed, developed, and evaluated for archaeology education in K–12 settings. The model is based on the classification of educational technology and authentic student learning. As with any educational materials, there should be clearly defined learning outcomes (see McNutt, this volume).

Ideally any authentic learning experience would include:

1. a way to incorporate or elicit students' prior knowledge and experiences;
2. opportunities for students to develop a plan for how they will gather information;
3. allowing students to observe phenomena;
4. collecting and organizing the data and then using it to conduct experiments;
5. enabling students to propose interpretations, or solutions for their work; and
6. encouraging students to apply, or "do something" with their research.

Table 11.2 ranks criteria in a presence/absence format. The information that this table provides will help with making decisions about selecting, designing, or evaluating a particular form of technology in archaeology education. Not every question needs to be affirmed; rather it is meant to present an overarching philosophy of presentation, strategy, and content that makes for effective education. The following questions guide the ranking selections:

- Does the form of technology use multiple technology applications or approaches (tutorial, exploratory, application, and communication)?
- Is the technology user friendly? Is it easy to follow, navigate, and visually attractive?

- Are the materials educationally appropriate (pedagogy, grade level)? To answer this question, one must refer to the context of educational reform and to the content, grade levels, and teaching strategies supported by the reform efforts (see Johnson and Geraci, both this volume).
- Does the technology engage students in active learning? Do the thinking skills progress in a manner consistent with developing critical thinking skills (what do you know and how do you know)?
- Does the form of technology have real-world applications or simulations that involve archaeological research and protection?
- Does the technology allow students to explore or manipulate the information?
- Does the content information provide exposure, information, or manipulation with multiple disciplines, perspectives and ways of knowing?
- Is the information accurate and does it provide sufficient archaeological information?

TABLE 11.2
Model for Teaching Archaeology with Technology

Questions about Learning	Tutorial		Exploratory		Application		Communication		Rank
User Friendly	Yes	No	Yes	No	Yes	No	Yes	No	
Educationally Appropriate	Yes	No	Yes	No	Yes	No	Yes	No	
Engage Students in Active Learning	Yes	No	Yes	No	Yes	No	Yes	No	
Authentic Learning Experiences	Yes	No	Yes	No	Yes	No	Yes	No	
Student Exploration and/or Manipulation of Data	Yes	No	Yes	No	Yes	No	Yes	No	
Multidisciplinary	Yes	No	Yes	No	Yes	No	Yes	No	
Provide Accurate and Sufficient Information	Yes	No	Yes	No	Yes	No	Yes	No	
Rank									

Yes = 1; No = 0
The final ranking across the rows will provide information about student learning. The final ranking down the columns will provide information on the multiple uses of the technology.

Conclusions

Educational technology is becoming an integral, if not pivotal, part of every student's educational experience. Archaeologists, too, are becoming more interested in and intrigued by techniques for collecting, manipulating, and disseminating research using electronic media. As these methods are developed and explored, archaeologists should participate in developing their potential use in K–12 educational settings. For instance, data used in generating a model of prehistoric regional land use can be given to students via the Internet to enhance their classroom research in geography and history. And as more and more archaeological sites are being threatened by development, tourism, looting, and vandalism, students and teachers can use archaeological data in virtual situations without ever stepping foot or scraping trowel on the actual site.

To facilitate interaction between archaeologists and educators, there needs to be continued professional development for teachers in the uses of educational technology for the transmission of archaeologically derived information, as well as in the concepts and processes of research inherent in the discipline. Likewise, archaeologists need to educate themselves about what is involved in designing quality educational experiences and in what is involved in producing educational technology. Having a model such as the one proposed here provides critical guidelines for reviewing, using, and designing educational technology in archaeology. From this starting point, archaeologists can contribute to educational reform efforts and provide relevant media through which K–12 students can learn about archaeology.

TECHNO-TERMS

CD-ROM (Compact Disk Read Only Memory): A computer disk that can store large amounts of information in digital form for computer access (Kearsley et al. 1992).

CD-I (Compact Disk Interactive): A multimedia technology that does not use a computer; rather it has its own microprocessor and uses a television or video monitor. Users of this technology control and interact with material on CD-I disks with a remote control or joystick (Skolnik and Kanning 1994).

CD-R (Compact Disk Recorders): A special type of CD-ROM disk with the capability of allowing large amounts of data and multimedia information to be recorded, written, stored, and retrieved (Sengstack 1997).

DVI (Digital Video Interactive): Transforms a full-screen video into one that has been digitized and compressed onto a CD-ROM disc or computer hard disk. These types of disks have the capability of storing other digital information as well (Skolnik and Kanning 1994).

E-Mail (Electronic Mail): Allows user to send and receive written messages via the Internet (Dockterman 1997).

FTP (File Transfer Protocol): The standard format of sending a file from one computer to another via the Internet (Dockterman 1997).

Gopher: A menu-based system for browsing the Internet that can be used to search by subject headings; mainly used for articles (Dockterman 1997).

HTML (Hypertext markup language): A programming language of the World Wide Web (WWW) used to create documents (Dockterman 1997).

Hypertext: A text link to other documents on the Internet that contain more or related information on a topic (Dockterman 1997).

Internet: A global network of networks that connects more than 2 million "host" computers. Internet allows e-mail access, Telnet, gopher, WWW exploration, and FTP (Dockterman 1997).

Internet Service Provider (ISP): Any organization that provides access to the Internet. ISPs often offer technical assistance to schools that want to become Internet sites and place their information on-line (Dockterman 1997).

LAN (Local Area Network): A group of computers that are connected together directly by cables and without the use of telecommunications (Kearsley et al. 1992).

Laserdisc or Videodisc: A multimedia product that is an optical storage medium that allows multimedia information to be accessed by computers (Skolnik and Kanning 1994).

List Serv: An automated mailing list that use e-mail as a way to distribute messages via the Internet. You must subscribe to a list to get messages (Dockterman 1997).

Modem: An electronic device that attaches to a computer and links it to the Internet via a phone line (Dockterman 1997).

Multimedia: The integration of more than one medium into a form of communication, usually with the use of a computer controlling some combination of audio, video, animation, graphics, still photography, sound, and text (Skolnik and Kanning 1994).

Netiquette: Actually a pun on the word "etiquette" referring to proper behavior on the Internet (Dockterman 1997).

Operating System: The software that manages all input/output files and operations for a computer (Kearsley et al. 1992).

Telnet: Service that allows you to access remote computers and their information (Dockterman 1997).

URL (Uniform Resource Locator): The standard addressing format for any resource site on the Internet that is part of the World Wide Web, for example: http://www.saa.org (Dockterman 1997).

Usenet Newsgroups: A system of thousands of special interest groups to which readers can send or "post" messages; these messages are then distributed to other computers on the network. Usenet registers newsgroups, which are available through Internet Service Providers (U.S. Department of Education 1997b).

Virtual Reality: An interactive technology that simulates the actual (real) world controlled through computerized sensors in three dimensions (Skolnik and Kanning 1994).

WWW (World Wide Web): A browsing system that allows you to click words or graphics with your mouse to retrieve information on the Internet (Dockterman 1997).

World Wide Web browser: A software that allows users to access and investigate the World Wide Web (Dockterman 1997).

RECOMMENDED READINGS

Bradsher, M., and L. Hagan
   1995   The Kids Network: Student-Scientists Pool Resources. *Educational Leadership* 53 (2):38–43.
   The National Geographic Kids Network involves elementary and middle-school students in learning about scientific and geographic concepts using technology. The curriculum that accompanies the program is based on units that study real-world phenomena, such as "What's In Our Water?" Students across the country study the units simultaneously allowing them to ask questions, investigate problems, and communicate their thoughts and findings with each other.

Bybee, R., W., C. E. Buchwald, S. Crissman, D. R. Heil, P. J. Kuerbis, C. Matsumoto, and J. D. McInerney
   1989   *Science and Technology Education for the Elementary Years: Frameworks for Curriculum and Instruction*. The National Center for Improving Science Education, Washington, D.C.
   This report outlines frameworks for curriculum and instruction in science and technology for elementary education. Technology is viewed as a process in problem solving. The report emphasizes using relevant and authentic hands-on activities that provide a variety of experiences leading to developmentally appropriate conceptual development.

Collis, B., and G. Carleer
   1992   Summarizing the Case Studies of Technology-Enriched Schools. In *Technology Enriched Schools: Nine Case Studies with Reflections*, B. Collis and G. Carleer, eds., pp. 135–144. International Society for Technology Education, Eugene, Oregon.
   This chapter summarizes nine case studies in schools that improved education through using technology. The nine case studies were compared with each other in terms of how they began using technology, how technology is integrated with instruction, the level of support offered at the school, and assessing the effectiveness of using technology.

Converse, R. E.
   1996   Technology and the Science Program: Placing Them in the Proper Perspective. In *Issues in Science Education*, J. Rhoton and P. Bowers, eds., pp. 49–56. National Science Teachers Association and National Science Education Leadership Association, Arlington, Virginia.

Technology's role in the reform of science education should be determined by the effectiveness of using technology in facilitating curriculum, instruction, and assessment efforts. Technology research indicates that one should approach the utilization of technology to promote this vision, not to entrench undesirable practices or to use technology for technology's sake.

Copen, P.
1995   Connecting Classrooms Through Telecommunications. *Educational Leadership* 53 (2):44–47.
The article describes and provides examples for the global telecommunications network, I*EARN. The network is used by K–12 students working on joint social and environmental projects. One such project involves students in Washington helping a village in Nicaragua through fund raising after learning about problems with water acquisition.

Cradler, J.
n.d.   *Summary of Current Research and Evaluation Findings on Technology in Education.* On-line. http://www.fwl.org/techpolicy/refind.html. 29 November 1997.
This on-line report outlines the major student and educator outcomes from using technology to support classroom learning, particular features of technology-based resources critical for effective classroom use, local, state, and national factors to support effective technology applications, and considerations for expanded research for educational technology.

Dockterman, D. A.
1994   *Cooperative Learning and Technology.* Tom Snyder Productions, Watertown, Massachusetts.
Cooperative learning and technology can be effective in the classroom with planning in how interdependence among students is fostered, the type of technology and information being used, and strategies for resolving conflicts and developing shared responsibility.

Lonergan, D.
1997   Network Science: Bats, Birds, and Trees. *Educational Leadership*, 55 (3):34–37.
Network science is a project developed by teachers in New Hampshire for students in grades 2–8 to use technology to collect and share scientific data on bats, birds, and trees. The results and findings from this project indicate the importance of making science relevant, timely, valid, and interdisciplinary.

McCarthy, R.
1990   Integrating Technologies to Enhance Learning in Science and Math. In *Technology in Today's Schools*, C. Warger, ed., pp. 93–102. Association for Supervision and Curriculum Development, Alexandria, Virginia.
The Voyage of the *MIMI*, a multimedia program used in many classrooms to teach science and mathematics, is described as a method for successfully integrating technology, educational concepts and materials, and instruction.

Means, B., and K. Olson
1994 The Link between Technology and Authentic Learning. *Educational Leadership*, 51 (7):15–19.
Authentic learning in technology involves students beyond the computer-assisted instruction model into tasks that are relevant and interesting to them. It also involves teaching in a different manner, coaching students and promoting collaborative student work.

National Academy of Sciences
1995 *Reinventing Schools: The Technology Is Now!*
On-line. http://www.nap.edu/readingroom/books/techgap/index.html. 26 November 1997.
The National Academy of Sciences and National Academy of Engineering sponsored the conference, "Reinventing Schools: The Technology Is Now," in 1993 to discuss issues of technology in K–12 education. The article describes the results of this conference and is a reflection of the sometimes opposing views and effects of the infusion of technology in today's schools.

O'Neil, J.
1995 On Technology and Schools: A Conversation with Chris Dede. *Educational Leadership* 53 (2):6–12.
Chris Dede is an expert in technology and education. In this interview, he shares his ideas on the status, future, and role of technology in K–12 schools, particularly in the case of students and teachers using the Internet.

Peck, K. L., and D. Dorricott
1994 Why Use Technology? *Educational Leadership* 51 (7):11–14.
The article provides the need for encouraging teachers to integrate technology into learning. The importance of technology in accessing, evaluating, and communicating information and the ability of students to solve complex problems are some of the reasons cited.

Shinohara, M., R. Wenn, and A. Sussman, eds.
1996 *Tales from the Electronic Frontier: First-Hand Experiences of Teachers and Students Using the Internet in K–12 Math and Science.* WestEd, San Francisco.
This is a compilation of ten stories of teachers in K–12 classrooms using the Internet in science and mathematics education. The stories focus on different aspects and benefits of using the Internet.

Willis, E. M.
1996 Where in the World? Technology in Social Studies Learning. *Learning and Leading with Technology* 23 (5):7–9.
The article describes three study projects in which technology was used to teach social studies. One of the projects was the Archaeotype Study conducted by the Teachers College of Columbia University (New York) and Dalton School (New York). Archaeotype is a computer-simulated archaeological site to dig up artifacts, research on their finds, and apply their simulation. These students created explanations for observations and data representation, but needed to learn more strategies for manipulating data.

Chapter Twelve

Against the Clock
Introducing Archaeology in
Time-Limited Situations

At some point in their careers, just about every professional archaeologist is invited by a precollegiate teacher to be a classroom speaker, provide a tour of an excavation, or help with a career day or science fair. This is an opportunity to expose an entire new audience to the excitement of learning about the past while transmitting a stewardship message. How do you convey your enthusiasm for archaeology, and a career's worth of knowledge and experience within the normal 45-minute class period? This chapter offers some concepts and techniques that help maximize the impact of such time-limited presentations. The brief encounter is likely not the format most archaeologists would choose to convey such important concepts as the value, meaning, relevance, and stewardship of the archaeological record, but it is the most frequent opportunity we have to reach the public.

The methods used to introduce archaeology and historic preservation to the public are as diverse as the audiences being addressed. Expertise in archaeology and cultural history is not sufficient to capture the imagination and hold the attention of an adult, let alone a room full of six year olds. It is the manner in which the narrator communicates the message that is key. He or she alone stimulates the imagination, captures the attention, and holds an audience.

Although audience, time limits, and location determine the best method of presentation, the overall concepts and principles remain the same. Regardless of the situation, there are some broad concepts that can be presented. There is no single right way, or single message. In a short-term contact, you can not cover everything of importance; at best you can correct some of your audience's misconceptions, invite their interest, and offer them the next step.

Initial contact is an important moment for you and your audience. It may be the first time they have come face-to-face with a professional archaeologist. In this capacity, you have an opportunity to say the first words and plant the first well-grounded ideas. Up until now, their understanding of archaeology may have been pieced together from commercial presentations of the thrilling suspense of *Raiders of the Lost Ark* or the detailed investigations on the Discovery Channel.

You are fighting a battle against preconceived notions and the clock, but don't be discouraged—initial contact is exciting! By sharing your experience, students will begin to see how math, science, and social studies relate to real world jobs. You will open eyes, change minds, and leave them questioning.

Sizing Up the Situation

Situations where archaeologists can encounter a K–12 audience, or their teachers, may include classroom visits to every grade level from preschool through graduate school; booths, displays, and lectures during state archaeology weeks; teachers' workshops; site tours; or even appearances on the local news. Each situation represents an opportunity, and although the situations and the methods of interaction differ, the information to be presented is basically the same.

Collecting background information about the intended audience is imperative to appropriately tailoring the presentation. First, find out who the group is, how many people will be present, and the age range or grade level. And find out the room size, location, and seating arrangements. Do you need a table on which to place your props? Do you prefer to sit or stand? Will you need a blackboard, dry eraser board, or easel and paper? Will the organizer need to provide these or will you? How much time will you have for your presentation? What kind of audience preparation has been made in anticipation of your presentation? Find out if the group has been studying archaeology, cultural history, or some related topic. Will you be addressing a homogeneous audience with regard to age and abilities? Will there be students with special needs, and if so, how can you adapt the information to fit the situation (see Wolynec, this volume)? Discuss with the person making the arrangements any special requirements that will help maximize the benefits of the experience.

Many presenters find it useful to have the teacher cover some basic concepts with the students before you arrive; provide her with the resources to do so. A previsit packet is a useful resource to have already prepared and available for teachers. Include in it background information relevant to your presentation, lesson plans or suggestions for teaching the information, and stage-setting materials such as posters and bookmarks (see Lea, this volume). A previsit packet helps maximize your time with the class. You then know what most of the students already understand about your topic and that the teacher has covered such basics as vocabulary words and definitions.

You can also have the teacher establish any guidelines, rules or expectations you have (such as taking care in handling the artifacts) before you arrive and reinforce them once you arrive.

Setting up a simple form listing the above considerations is an easy way to make sure that all of your questions are answered (Figure 12.1). In this way, each time you receive a request all you need to do is fill in the blanks. How and what you present and the props you use will be based on this initial information.

Date of Contact:	Presentation Date:	Time: _____ to _____
Contact Person:		
Name of Group:		
Address:		
Directions to location:		
Phone:	Fax:	E-mail:
Group Size:	Age Range:	Room Set Up:
Focus of presentation:		
Current area of study:		
Special instructions, needs, guidelines:		

MATERIALS CHECKLIST:	BRING:	PROVIDED:
flip chart and markers		
dry erase board and markers		
artifacts and tool kit		
information packet		
table for props		

ADDITIONAL INFORMATION:

Figure 12.1. Previsit form.

Hear It, Touch It, Do It, Learn It

Preparing for the presentation involves more than knowing a topic. To be truly successful, you will need to use a few basic teaching strategies. First, by checking with the organizer beforehand and knowing what has been studied, you will be able to connect their knowledge with the new information you wish to present.

Activity Example: You've been invited to talk to a group of second graders. They have been studying paleontology. (Oh no, here we go again—archaeologists study people, not dinosaurs! This is one of those myths that archaeologists constantly encounter). How do you turn around this misconception, use it to your advantage, and give a presentation on archaeology? Answer: While paleontology and archaeology study two entirely different subject areas, the tools and the techniques for data recovery are very similar. Start your program here. A few sentences will get the kids (and the teacher) on the right track.

To deliver a message effectively, you need to do more than lecture. A few notes, with a couple of artifacts held up in front of the group, along with bits of information scribbled on the board, may be easy but it's hardly effective. The problem with lecturing is that auditory learning imparts the lowest level of memory retention. To reach the greatest number of kids and accomplish the highest level of retention, learners must hear, see, touch, and do. An educator, no matter what his or her personal learning style, must utilize all teaching styles, as Geraci tells us earlier in this book. This is difficult, because educators tend to teach using the style with which they themselves learn most effectively.

Activity Example: Dress like an archaeologist. Catch their attention by walking into the room with a sun hat on your head, hiking boots on your feet, a screen and a dig kit in one hand, and a box of artifacts in the other. Right there you have your props, a basis for discussion, and their attention. Using these tools, you'll be providing auditory, visual, tactile, and kinetic learning opportunities.

Keep the age of your audience in mind. For instance, younger children have a shorter attention span and think concretely. Although it is difficult for them to think of information in abstract terms, it is not impossible. It just means that you have to be prepared to build the images for them, or produce the "scaffolding" as Johnson describes in her chapter in this volume. With any audience, an interactive format works better than straight lecturing. Bring things such as artifacts, models, and tools that people can touch.

Activity Example: Pass out artifacts, such as pottery sherds to the group, or lay them on your display table. Let students use their senses and observation skills to describe the objects. Based on their observations, let them name the objects. Move them into a discussion of the importance of observation and inference in the scientific process.

Ask questions of your audience and let them answer. Some are very quick to raise their hands, others take a bit more time to process information. After asking a question, wait . . . count off at least five seconds before you call on someone. Alternate between boys and girls. Pick someone in the front, then the back, then the middle, and let them come up with the answers for you. Encourage them. Keep your questions open ended, ask things that require more than a "yes" or "no" answer, and accept more than one answer. This engages everyone in an exciting learning experience.

Misconceptions and Concepts

Sometimes, you need to undo the ideas that people already have. This is probably one of the most difficult parts of any presentation. These misconceptions usually don't need to be gone over point by point, but rather your counter to them can be embedded in your presentation. A good reference for basic information on archaeological concepts and dispelling common myths the public has about archaeology can be found in the SAA Public Education *Guidelines for the Evaluation of Archaeology Education Materials* (1995a). Also see Hawkins for a discussion about archaeological concepts commonly presented to schoolchildren, and Krass (both in this volume) to gain an idea about where teachers go to acquire information about archaeology.

What are the basic concepts that could be included in a brief presentation? The choices are infinite, but the following suggestions are based on my personal voyages into countless classrooms. The concepts constitute a progression relating archaeology and material culture to human behavior. The culminating message is one of preservation. At each step, the audience actively participates in the learning process. Don't overload your audience; present only three–five well-chosen concepts per session.

Concept: What is archaeology?
- This leads to a discussion of archaeology, archaeological sites, features, artifacts, and behavioral inferences.

These topics can be easily related to people's lives by comparing an archaeologist's work to looking in someone's house whom you've not met. By looking in each room, you can guess the number of people who live there, their approximate ages, hobbies, interests, and even what they like to eat.

Concept: What is culture?
- Identifying basic human needs isn't the goal of archaeology or anthropology. Archaeology studies past cultures by systematically recording and analyzing their material remains. Through these, we

determine how people meet basic biological, social, and psychological needs.

Ask students what people need to survive: food, water, shelter, communication, companionship, artistic expression, love, family, and a social structure. A discussion of basic needs introduces the idea of culture. Relating basic needs to material objects leads to the question of what archaeologists find that helps them describe a culture.

Concept: Where did people live?
- This is a problematic question because for some reason, children and even some adults think that archaeological sites are found only in far-off places.

Tie into the discussion on basic needs for food, water, and shelter. Let them tell you that people lived close to rivers, or other water sources. This discussion builds the base by looking at the importance of showing information in context, then moves the group into a discussion of site formation and the archaeological process.

Concept: What are the steps of the archaeological process?
- There's more to archaeology than digging.

Relating the archaeological process to the scientific process works extremely well with students. By the third grade, many children are doing classroom experiments and writing reports on science fair projects. By relating this experience to archaeologists' work, you can quickly bridge the gap between what they know about the scientific process and how it applies to a field new to them—archaeology.

Concept: Preservation
- This is the crux of archaeological education. From an archaeologist's perspective, the incentive behind most archaeological education programs is the possibility that vandalism and destruction to archaeological sites can be reduced.

We want to teach about archaeology and cultural history, but we don't want to leave the audience thinking that they are qualified to dig a site or that people can own artifacts. By putting excavation into the context of the archaeological process, excavation is deemphasized. We want to empower the public to help protect sites. By educating people about the alternatives to collecting and by providing access to archaeologists, we help preserve the archaeological resource. Encourage people to use a camera or a piece of paper and a pencil to record where an item was found. Tell them to mark the site so they can take the archaeologist back to the artifact, instead of bringing the artifact to the archaeologist.

Activity Example: Create a scenario. You are out wandering out-of-doors when you come across an artifact. You note its location and tie your bandana to the branch of a tree to mark it so that you can find it again. When you get home, you know you need to call an archaeologist, but how do you find one? Answer: The phone book.

Ask the group how they would find an archaeologist. Let them brainstorm answers till someone comes up with the Yellow Pages. With a teacher's permission, assign homework to look in the Yellow Pages. They need to look under "archaeologist" or "environmental specialist." (Sometimes, in smaller communities, archaeology is not listed separately.) Students then report back on how many listings they find. In the 1997/1998 Tucson phone book, there were ten listings under the category "archaeologist." In addition to the listings under archaeology, most federal and state or provincial land managing agencies have staff archaeologists who could be contacted.

Present a Negative as a Positive
(Avoid "Don't" and "Can't")

Correcting misconceptions and introducing the preservation ethic can be the most difficult aspects of a presentation, especially if you avoid using no, don't, and can't. Statements like "archaeologists don't study dinosaurs," and "no, you can't do your own dig" stop the audience from listening. These messages are much better received if they are embedded positively in the context of the discussion. The following example deters a negative activity but is presented through a positive process that allows the audience to draw their own conclusions and come up with solutions.

Activity Example: This technique introduces artifacts, archaeological sites, decay, reuse over time, and preservation. It takes very little time, connects all of the basic concepts outlined above, presents information in a visual format, and is interactive.

Using artifacts and "artifakes," lay out a mock site on the floor or on the table in front of the group. Set up patterns within the site by grouping the artifacts, for example, place a hammerstone with a piece of leather, an antler tine, flakes, a core, a couple of stone tools, and an arrowhead. Next to the lithics, place a basket and grinding stone, then some decorated and undecorated sherds (if ceramics were produced in your area) and some cotton or examples of other prehistoric perishables. Create a story about who lived at this site and what types of activities occurred during occupation. Discuss abandonment and decay ("It rains, the wind blows, organic materials don't survive." "What decays and rots?") Let them tell you what rots. Remove the perishables.

Continue your story, now set in the year 1986. Some kids are out on a picnic. They wander off to a clearing and set up an army base with their set of toy soldiers and other toys. Add some historical-period artifacts to the "site" on the table—a metal spoon, a small bottle, and some plastic soldiers.

Now it is 1996, I (always put yourself in the position of the bad guy) am out on a hike and "Wow, I always wanted to find an arrowhead." Pick up the bifaces, the painted pottery, and anything else that is neat, and put them into your pocket.

It is now today. Archaeologists have just finished studying this site before a highway is built over it. They conclude that the inhabitants were a simple, vegetarian people who had no time for art.

Let the group tell you what is wrong with your conclusion. The audience provides the rationale against casual collecting and for preservation. You can also get into a discussion of soil, pollen, and macrobotanical samples by directing attention at the places where the organic materials decayed.

Humanize the Data

Archaeologists study people, something that can get forgotten in the piles of sherds, reams of computer printouts, and office cubicles. Archaeology is the study of people based on their material remains. In the office and in technical reports, archaeologists tend toward conservatism. Qualifiers frequent every paragraph of text in a technical report, but when presenting archaeology and cultural history to your audience, use the data to build pictures, create scenes, and imagine the possibilities. You have to tell a story, a human story, one to which your audience can relate.

Alternate Venues

Presentations aren't always verbal. Circumstances may limit the presentation style. At archaeology fairs and expos associated with State Archaeology Week or provincial Heritage Month celebrations, you will have space to present your message. Think of the possibilities. Picture children clustered around a table trying to see what's going on. It's active, that's what draws them. There are artifacts to draw, measure, and weigh under an archaeologist's supervision. The visitors receive their own form. At the bottom of the paper is a preservation message and the phone number of the State Historic Preservation Office or for Canadian provinces the Ministry of Culture's Archaeology Branch or the Department of Canadian Heritage. They take the paper home, not the artifact. A freestanding display shows the cultural history chronology and information on your agency or organization. Copies of popular books and archaeological reports line the other end of the table along with information on public programs and a sign-up sheet for those who want to become more involved. People walking by, spending no more than five minutes, can take away three very specific concepts.

What are the messages? (1) By participating in the laboratory process, people learn that there's more to archaeology than digging. It puts archaeology into a scientific perspective. *Concept:* What is archaeology? (2) Between the hands-on activity and the static display, the archaeological process is related to the human history of the area. *Concept:* What is culture? (3) By taking the paper not the artifact, people leave with a preservation message. Along with the preservation-oriented activity, they have information to apply to possible future situations. *Concept:* Preservation.

It Doesn't End When You Walk Out the Door: Leave Them Wondering

Before walking out of the room, leave the teacher with a resource packet. Include a list of archaeological parks open to the public, classroom lessons, books, and volunteer opportunities. Let the teacher know where to get more.

In just a few minutes, you can grab students' attention, spark an interest, inspire ideas, and get kids energized, but you can't teach then everything that's important about archaeology. You can present three to five basic concepts. If the audience walks away knowing a little more, you've made an admirable stride. If you leave them excited, they will keep continue asking questions, reaching, and wondering. Through this process, today's students become an active and informed public and ultimately, support the preservation of our heritage.

Chapter Thirteen

Assessing Archaeology Education
Five Guiding Questions

Third- and fourth-grade students huddling around a large floor map of the world are engaged in a game of cultural development. In this imaginary world they live as early people occupying specified regions of the world. One group, the Yotals, whose territory is located within a tropical forest, secretly strategize to obtain a rich source of copper from nearby mountains. Their neighbors, the Wasics, oblivious to the plot, celebrate their recent success in the domestication of dogs. Six groups of children all working as different cultural groups are deeply involved in the game.

In this narrative, the teacher enthusiastically describes the month-long simulation as an experiential way of teaching a wealth of information about cultural development to young students. His excitement, as well as that of the students, is contagious. What is so apparently missing in this description is information regarding student learning or plans for assessment.

Evaluation is crucial to the success of any educational program. Professional educators have established criteria and evolved methods for assessment of curricula, instructional media, and program delivery that can significantly improve the impact of any teaching program. It is an essential step in teaching. Archaeology educators are not exempt from the need to evaluate and assess the effectiveness of curriculum materials, with a view to ensuring that students receive the best learning experience possible. This chapter discusses some concepts that underlie assessment techniques, and demonstrates their application to the teaching of archaeology to young people.

Archaeology is a subject that engages and enthralls people of all ages. The neophyte archaeology educator often mistakes the excitement of a student group's first exposure to archaeology as evidence that the program he or she has devised is successful. Active engagement of students is a critical aspect of education, but active engagement alone does not guarantee that students have been able to make the connections that are necessary for conceptual development, nor does it guarantee that the concepts the archaeology educator is trying to so hard to transmit are actually being appropriately received by the students.

Learning involves making meaningful connections between action and consequences; Dewey described this connection as *thought* (1963). In their eagerness to get students excited about the subject matter, educators, archaeological or otherwise, sometimes ignore the significance of making connections, and they fail to define the knowledge and concepts they hope to nurture. Without clearly defined goals and objectives, and without a comprehensive plan for assessing whether those same goals and objectives have actually been achieved over the course of the program, educators are unable to evaluate whether the students are acquiring desired skills and assimilating the desired concepts. As they say, "If you don't know where you are going, any road will take you there." This chapter, therefore, seeks to explain why educators must help students build connections through the curricula they design and why assessment is vital to the development and survival of archaeology education programs.

The Reasons for Evaluation

Assessment or evaluation can be a scary proposition because it forces educators to look hard at their curricula and face up to the possibility that they are falling short of their goals. Further, assessments often call for changes in instruction and change is not only time consuming, it is uncomfortable. Like educators in other disciplines, many archaeology educators enjoy curriculum development and want to believe that the activities they find stimulating and satisfying are received with equal enthusiasm and interest by their students. They want to believe that the lessons they design and teach are effective. Assessment in education is always two pronged; the evaluation of student learning is both a critique of instruction (and the instructor) and an assessment of the students' performance. Some instructors just don't want to know that their lessons and instruction are anything less than perfect.

With few exceptions, archaeology education programs have been assessment free, so why spoil a good thing? To begin with, there is the question of legitimacy. Learning can and should be fun, but "fun activities" don't automatically result in learning. Sound educational programs include assessment, not because it is an expectation of educational bureaucracies—although this is usually true, but because the educational process is incomplete without it. Those outside the educational profession can have trouble seeing this. An inadequate understanding of the complex nature of learning and a lack of training in the field of education can lead to the mistaken notion held by much of the public—that teaching is easy. In order to have archaeology education programs be viewed by the larger educational community as more than an entertaining type of enrichment, they must include analysis and assessment. If archaeology is more than a dig, then education is more than an activity or a lecture.

Another reason for assessing archaeology education is related to contemporary learning theory. Simply put, what gets taught is not directly congruent with what gets learned. A naive understanding of education involves the notion that the teacher provides instruction around a certain topic and students will learn that particular content within a certain range of accuracy (0–100%). If only it were this simple. Constructivist theory tells us that each individual possesses prior knowledge that will affect the way the new information will be processed. The question is not how much of the new information will be retained, but how the new information will be integrated with prior knowledge and how it will affect the way the student conceptualizes the given topic. The only way to grasp what learners are doing with the information taught in archaeology education programs is through assessment or, more appropriately, through educational research. Truly excellent educators will embrace the role of researcher because they understand that learning takes place in the minds of students and, unless student understandings are examined, the act of teaching is no more than a performance.

Educational Assessment: The Basics

Educational evaluation falls into two primary categories based on the purpose of the evaluation. These are: *formative* and *summative.*

> Summative evaluations serve the purpose of rendering an overall judgement about the effectiveness of a program, policy, or product for the purpose of saying that the idea itself is or is not effective, and, therefore, has the potential of being generalizable to other situations. . . . Formative evaluation on the other hand, is limited entirely to a focus on a specific context. Formative evaluation serves the purpose of improving a specific program, policy, group, staff, or product. [Patton 1990:151–152]

Summative evaluations are not particularly useful for providing insight into why a particular program or project fails or succeeds, but they are often a requirement of foundations and other agencies that provide funding. Because such organizations are generally interested in improving education for all children, they need information that can be considered to apply generally across various groups and in different settings. Formative evaluations are important to educators who want to understand and improve their programs. In addition to summative and formative evaluations, educational research also includes basic research, applied research, and action research. Although such a discussion strays beyond the scope of this chapter, it is important to mention that research in archaeology education should not be limited to summative and formative evaluation. Basic research contributes to the development of fundamental knowledge and theory for a given field. Although evaluation is important to specific programs and sometimes for informing other programs, a deeper knowledge of how students form concepts about the past and process information about time and culture are essential to the maturity of the discipline.

Designing a Plan for Assessment:
Five Guiding Questions

1. What are the goals and objectives for this curriculum/lesson?

At the heart of any educational program is a statement of goals. Goals guide the educational objectives, concepts, projects, and assessment criteria. Goals are far-reaching with broad achievements that often cannot be measured. When clearly stated, a goal is all encompassing, yet it is also the seed; for example:

> *Project Archeology: Saving Traditions (PAST)* engages intermediate students in archeology, effectively combining the disciplines of social studies, science, mathematics and language arts with special emphasis given to the students' development of higher-level thinking skills (McNutt 1992:1).

Program goals, as well as the objectives, concepts, tasks, and assessment criteria, should be sensitive to the nature and needs of the population for whom the program is being developed, and should directly relate to the reason the program is being conducted. They should also be mindful of the constraints that those implementing the program will need to address, such as state/provincial or national education standards (see Davis, and MacDonald and Burtness, this volume). The goals of the program may be considered to be the two or three main skills and concepts that you wish to instill in your student body and that therefore provide focus for the development of curriculum and for individual lessons.

Questions that one might consider in the development of program goals include:

- What concepts do you wish the students to assimilate?
- What are the background knowledge and skills students are expected to acquire?
- How do state or provincial or national learning standards correlate with the program goals?
- What kind of tasks can lead to the realization of these goals? Is it important to include the process for constructing archaeological knowledge, or should the program be more focused on the findings of archaeological research (the process versus the story)?
- How will I know if the goals of the program have been achieved?

The essential task is to capture program goals, objectives, concepts, tasks, and assessment criteria in writing. The importance of this can not be over emphasized. Too often, goals and objectives are identified but not actually recorded. And, when in the thick of program implementation and assessment, the once-clear intent becomes muddled. Written goals and objectives are the backbone for program development and assessment.

2. *How will I know what students are learning?*

Assessment brings to mind the pop quiz or the term exam where good testers score well and those wrought with fear have trouble finishing. There will probably always be single-right-answer tests that have the power to invoke nightmares in individuals who are long past their school years but, in truth, this sort of assessment is valuable for revealing certain kinds of information. However, a wide range of approaches to assessment exists, and the correct choice will vary depending on the purpose of the assessment.

When constructing a plan for assessment, it is also important to consider the validity and reliability of assessment instruments and methods. In very general terms, validity refers to the *extent* to which an instrument or method actually measures or reveals what it was intended to. The question of an instrument's validity must always be considered in the context of the particular situation and purpose for which it was designed; this is true for both quantitative and qualitative approaches to assessment

Reliability refers to the degree of *consistency* with which an instrument or method measures or reveals what it was intended to. A highly reliable instrument would yield very similar results each time it is used with the same individual or group of individuals. In quantitative approaches to assessment, reliability is determined through a statistical analysis of variation. Qualitative approaches use methods of triangulation to establish validity. For example, three different researchers might be asked to analyze the same set of data independently.

The development and use of assessment instruments in large educational programs is essential. A professional evaluator can be engaged at the time that a program is proposed to establish the standards and guide the formal evaluation process. Evaluators who consult for educational projects in schools, museums, outdoor facilitates, and other informal education settings, can be located by calling the education department at a university, the state department of education, or a large school district. Fees will vary according to the tasks they are asked to accomplish.

In 1975, when *PAST* staff developed and validated two tests (McNutt 1992), a professional evaluator was involved to design the research component, identify and guide the validation process for the tests, and analyze the data. These tests measured statistically significant gains in knowledge and skills exhibited by middle-school students who had been involved in the project. These statistically measured outcomes illustrated how well this project was teaching the identified concepts, content, and skills; they reflected the project's level of success.

Quantitative evaluations measure certain outcomes, but they do not answer the multitude of questions that teachers mull over, such as, "What patterns do I see in students' learning?" "What are the successes and where are there holes?" "What were the children's thoughts as they worked on their projects?" " What sort of techniques did this child use to accomplish her or his results?" "How did that child go about assessing his or her work?" "What would assist me in documenting and measuring students accomplishments over time?"

When asking such questions, it is important to recognize that they are process related, thus requiring a qualitative approach to assessment. Within the realm of qualitative methodology, it is also important to understand the distinction between knowledge and the way that knowledge is expressed. This is directly related to variation in student learning styles, discussed at greater length by Geraci (this volume). Those students who possess strengths in writing may compose an essay; others who are more visually expressive may create drawings; the verbally expressive child may convey thoughts well through an in-depth interview. Triangulation, a method for establishing validity in a qualitative project, may use multiple methods for examining the same question. These multiple methods should allow for variation in expressive style.

Portfolios can be used for both program and student assessment. These consist of work that students have chosen to show their understanding of specified concepts or skills. Students themselves are involved in selecting the work they feel best expresses their mastery of the subject. Evaluation that includes use of student portfolios is less threatening than more standard types of testing and is an excellent way to gather qualitative data in an educational setting. Portfolios can reflect the quality of instruction as well as the quality of student work. Yet, "portfolios are more than collections of students' work to be used as tools of standards and assessment. Not only do they contain the evidence of individual student's accomplishments for others to see, they also give the students real data upon which to reflect as they come to understand themselves as thinkers, knowers, producers, and learners" (Kamii 1996:60).

Portfolios bring students into the assessment process, asking them to think about what defines their "best work" and where they need help. Because standards, tasks, and criteria are explicit, students can discuss them, refer to them, and address them in their own work. When students are brought into the discussion of standards and criteria, they see themselves as owners of assessment. In a classroom climate where students are honored as thinkers, knowers, producers, and learners, they demonstrate what they know and eveal their conceptual understandings. They recognize what constitutes good, better, and best work, and they will strive to do their best (Barton and Collins 1997). Following are guidelines for developing a focused assessment of portfolios (Herman et al. 1996).

- Define the purpose of your assessment. Is it solely to assess the student's progress? Consider that you may also want to use it to communicate with parents or even use the information to conduct an evaluation of your program.
- Identify the tasks that should be reflected in the portfolio collection. Include statements which define the outcomes and products for each task. Suggest appropriate tasks that are linked to the goals of your program.
- Standards or criteria must be established. These should be sensitive to your instruction, developmentally appropriate for the student, and meaningful and credible to the student, parent, and you.
- Consistency in scoring is crucial in all assessments. Whether you are focusing on holistic overall achievement, or developing specific criteria that help you analyze particular aspects of a task, scoring can be accomplished by using a quality continuum.

3. *What do students already know about archaeology and what do they wonder about?*

When South Carolina archaeologist Christopher Judge asked his archaeology camp participants, aged seven to fifteen, to draw a picture of an archaeologist doing what they thought an archaeologist did, he tapped into a wonderfully effective way of getting into kids' minds. In doing this activity and repeating it weekly, he prepared himself for how and where he would guide the students in their study of archaeology. This activity was a good example of front-end analysis, a way of examining prior knowledge, concepts, and questions (Judge 1988).

"Front-end analysis" is an evaluation of existing knowledge on the part of a student audience prior to delivery of an educational program. This step helps educators understand how to guide a program that is meaningful and relevant to students and that reflects their knowledge and organization of the subject matter. Front-end analysis uncovers students' misconceptions, detects information gaps, and explores all levels of interest. It enables educators to assess prior knowledge, and to learn what students bring to the program. It does not dictate the goals, objectives, and concepts of the program, but helps the educator prioritize and structure information.

Students can be asked what they know about archaeology and what questions they would like to have answered about the subject at the beginning of a program. If they are asked to record their knowledge and questions on large sheets of paper, this may be considered a survey, a very effective means for collecting data that can inform instruction. Then, if students enter this information into their journals, the journal entries can themselves become the platform for portfolio assessment. By reflecting on such entries and surveys, educators can identify strengths and recognize gaps in understanding. This process contributes to the development of programs of instruction that have direct relevance to students and that can build their development of concepts. As an example, photo sorting can be used as a means for gauging the interest of a variety of audiences, including museum visitors.

By giving visitors a stack of photos of artifacts and asking them to make a pile of the pictures they find most interesting, you can get a quick "take" on the objects most likely to stimulate visitors' attention. . . . It won't tell you why they find them interesting, but it will tell you when they agree and disagree with your opinion of what they should be interested in. [Taylor 1991:21]

A poster entitled *PASSAGES: A Timeline of Southeast Alaska* (McNutt 1993a) was intended to represent the cultural development of Southeastern Alaska in both visual and textual form. The content, however, was significantly restructured because of the insights gained from a front-end survey mailed to teachers and staff members of cultural institutions. The survey asked each participant to order statements pertinent to archaeology according to importance. The analysis from the returned questionnaires indicated that the audience was more interested in understanding prehistoric daily life than in learning about the science of archaeology, which had been the project's original intent. Even with this shift in perspective, the educational objectives of the sponsoring organization, the U.S. Forest Service, were still met, but the visual and written material on the poster was presented in a way that piqued the interest of the intended audience.

The front-end analysis instrument is also highly useful for institutions such as museums. The California Academy of Science conducted a visitor survey early in the development of an archaeology exhibit. Fifty randomly selected individuals, aged six and older, were interviewed. Responses were tape recorded to capture the exact words of the visitors. Analysis of these data provided valuable information to the staff as they moved through the planning process. Following are the survey questions (MacKinney 1994):

1. Is this your first visit to the California Academy of Science?
2. Do you have any particular interest, knowledge or training about archaeology?
3. What comes to mind when you hear the word "archaeology"?
4. What would you expect to do, see, feel, and find out about in an exhibit about archaeology?
5. What do you think archaeologists do?
6. Have you ever done anything like that?
7. What issues are you aware of concerning archaeology?
8a. What comes to mind when you hear the term artifact?
8b. What comes to mind when you hear the term stewardship?
8c. What comes to mind when you hear the term archaeological record?
8d. What comes to mind when you hear the term antiquities trafficking?
9. Do you think archaeological sites are endangered?
10. Is there anything else you'd like to add?

Surveys, photo sorting, and drawing are just a few ways in which front-end data can be collected to ascertain prior knowledge. Mail and telephone surveys are less reliable because of the low success rate with obtaining responses. Of primary importance is the willingness of the evaluator to put aside assumptions and ask, "I wonder what my audience has to say about this."

4. *Do the selected instructional materials clearly address the intended goals and objectives?*

The daily assignments and activities that are developed for a particular unit of study should provide experiences that build conceptual development and help students achieve identified goals and objectives. An adequate assessment of instructional materials and activities cannot be carried out without field testing. Field testing, the term used for materials under development, puts the educational prototype out for the audience to assess, be it in the form of a presentation, exhibit, written material, or other form of instructional media.

When field testing new materials, it is essential that student perspectives be included in the assessment. In conducting field tests, the instructor must consider the students' active behavior, the nature and content of their questions, and their approaches to problem solving. Students can act as editors, circling words and passages that are unclear in written materials and recommending different ways of illustrating information. The idea here is not to assess student work but, rather, the effectiveness of the instructional materials and their delivery. Student interviews that focus on the clarity of materials and on their appeal can also provide valuable insights.

Student work also provides data for assessing activities and materials. Questions to consider include, "Is there a pattern in the students' responses?" "Were they able to apply knowledge, skills, and concepts?" "To which concepts, tasks and criteria were they not able to respond?" " Were the materials and instruction designed to elicit the kind of information needed?"

Field testing is necessary to assess the design and implementation of all curriculum materials and instruction. The most difficult aspect of it is inviting outside review. Although this may result in minor embarrassment for the program design team or instructor, the process is far less painful and costly than producing a finished product that is not understandable or that is quickly passed over and seldom used.

During the 1992–1993 school year, field testing was conducted with previously published materials, a selection from which would be included in *Action Archaeology: Tracing Our Past* (McNutt 1993b), a small activity packet focusing on stewardship. It contained three lessons and a number of extended activities for teachers of grades two through four. Eight teachers who were involved in the project responded to questions related to three areas of focus. To field test the materials, these teachers were asked to teach the lessons and critique the materials, using the following criteria:

1. In looking at the concepts, tasks and criteria of the activities, please comment on the appropriateness of individual activities for second through fourth

graders. Also, please comment on the appropriateness of the whole packet for this level.

2. How usable were these materials? (Please indicate your previous instruction in archaeology.) Be specific, red mark the materials and indicate how you changed the process of instruction.

3. Please include samples of work from individual students, and from group work, and your comments on student response to the materials.

Following are some of the teachers' comments regarding ways they personalized the lessons for their classrooms. These variations were included in the final publication.

As a follow up and reinforcing the concept of ownership to a past, I had student make a book about their family artifact(s). They needed to interview a family member who could tell a family story about the artifact. After they recorded the story, they draw pictures for the story and combine the two. I laminated the pages and bound their stories with a comb binder. Then I further reinforced the concept by having the students read their stories to the entire class over a period of time. [Sally Reimer, personal communication 1993]

Field testing showed some students needed more investment of their own creativity in one lesson. Their teachers responded with an adaptation to the lesson:

We started an archaeology stewardship poster contest for our school. To our surprise, when we shared with other schools, it became a contest for our city. (Penny Marksheffel and Tom Hunt, personal communication 1993)

Archaeology education, especially that which takes place out-of-doors, in living history settings, or on actual archaeological sites, can benefit from methods of field testing drawn from the field of museum studies. Field testing, when applied to museum education initiatives, can be a very versatile assessment technique. The three most common methods are: (1) timing the visitors' interaction, (2) observing the nature of visitors' interaction, and (3) interviewing the visitor. While timing and observation can be handled discreetly, interviewing visitors is perhaps the most intrusive in that the visitors' experience is being interrupted. Some visitors may need to be reassured that a wide range of visitors' opinions, skills, and knowledge are useful in helping museum staff understand how an exhibit will actually be used. The intent of field testing is to focus on the specifics of an exhibit that is already in the stages of development. The interview process can take two forms: *cued testing* and *uncued testing*. In cued testing, the interviewer and the visitor work together as a team. In uncued testing, the interview takes place after the visitor's interactions have been observed and recorded.

In *Evaluation Techniques*, Samuel Taylor provides some helpful suggestions for interviewing museum visitor, such as this introductory phrase:

Excuse me . . . the museum is in the process of renovating its exhibits. We have a mock-up of one part of the new exhibit set up today and we want to get some feedback from visitors before we go any further with the design. Would you be willing to help? [Taylor 1991:53]

Whether the interview takes place while the visitor is interacting with the exhibit or afterwards, the questions used are the same:

- What is this exhibit about?
- Do you think that visitors will understand it?
- What can we do to make this more interesting and understandable to visitors?
- What parts were confusing?
- Do you think visitors will understand what to do here? [Taylor 1991]

5. How can the long-term effects of the program be evaluated?

It is a miserably rainy day, even for Southeast Alaska, when Beth, Bryson, Codie, and I approach the site where Beth had two years earlier found fragments of a jadite adze blade and basalt maul. We were returning with Beth to draw a sketch of the site and to locate where she had found the artifacts. Five years earlier, both she and Bryson were part of an archaeological study that emphasized the importance of the past, the development of archaeological strata over time, and site stewardship. Just a year following their study Bryson reported a find, a complete jadite adze blade and, with the assistance of an archaeologist, located the site on a map. Bryson did not relinquish the artifact or make a report, but my hope, and that of the archaeologist, was that he would do this. But it wasn't until the summer of 1998, when yet a third child, Codie, found a bone harpoon on the tidal flats in front of his house and the weekly newspaper announced that he was keeping the artifact, that I set myself in motion.

As I guided the three students through their recollections of how and where they had found the artifacts, I began to reflect on how two of these students who had gone through a stewardship study could have collected artifacts and not turned the artifacts over to an archaeologist. I wanted to believe that the guidance provided by their teachers and the archeological materials used were excellent. Yet, somehow, we missed the mark.

As I watched Beth, Bryson and Codie so eagerly measuring and drawing the artifacts and writing down their discovery stories, my disappointment ebbed away. I began to assess what these students knew about archaeology, evaluate their level of involvement, and think about the process that brought them to this stage of knowledge. What I concluded was that we did not fail, we had simply faltered. We gave the students a good start through the introductory studies. They showed a growing interest in archeology and the importance of the past. And now, they were enthusiastically writing reports to send to the SHPO, to the local tribal association, and to the museum. Their eagerness spilled into a plan to create an exhibit showing others how to record newly discovered sites. All of the previous educational pieces were successful, it was the process that was incomplete. We were negligent in not providing the ongoing structure to support their efforts in helping to save the past.

This brief summer visitation was not an assessment of the students, but of the educational process used to increase students' knowledge and ethical orientation toward archaeological sites and artifacts. The initial activities were effective; those in charge of the project simply fell short by thinking that the job was done—that these students learned the importance of saving the past and could continue to carry on, independent of adult support.

This narrative highlights the value of pairing assessment and instruction in such a way that they occur simultaneously. We, as archaeology educators, can use this strategy to our advantage by examining student work in the context of the instructional situations. By keeping an on-the-spot running record of assessment, instructors and students can create a valuable set of data for later reflection. Again, student portfolios provide one opportunity; they serve as tools for assessing student thinking on a daily basis, as well as over time. The portfolios can be used as a form of longitudinal assessment; they can become time-captured, concrete representations of the success and commitment each student has toward archaeology.

Long-term assessment is both the prime indicator of lasting attitudinal and behavioral changes archaeology education programs have encouraged, and notoriously difficult to conduct. The effectiveness of our efforts can be assessed by measuring our students' retention of stewardship concepts years after they have been exposed to an archaeology education program. Archaeology educators should continually seek opportunities for such longitudinal evaluation.

Conclusion

The summer experience with Beth, Bryson, and Codie provided the opportunity for longitudinal assessment of previously developed materials, and raised an important question that we, archaeologists and educators, must ask ourselves, "What do I know about my students' archaeological knowledge, and how do I know it?" When federal funds were first provided for archaeology education in the mid 1980s, too many in the profession began scrambling to produce materials and programs, but few of these programs were designed to assess learning and the effectiveness of curricula, instructional materials, or teaching methods. As archaeology education has matured and has entered into the larger arena of professional education, the glaring lack of information about what is learned through these initiatives has become painfully obvious. What can be learned from this is that a plan for assessment must be developed at the start of every program or project.

A plan for assessment can be developed through a consideration of the five guiding questions presented in this chapter:

1. What are the goals and objectives for this curriculum/lesson?
2. How will I know what students are learning?
3. What do students know about archaeology and what do they wonder about?
4. Do the selected instructional materials clearly address the intended goals and objectives?
5. How can the long-term effects of the program be evaluated?

The act of creating educational materials and programs is not a one-time happening but a continual process of assessing clarity and effectiveness. Continual evaluation brings a level of confidence to archaeology education efforts because it demonstrates the adjustments made to focus the materials or programs and to accommodate the audience's needs.

We, as archaeology educators, must be able to clarify what we are doing for our students and for archaeology. We must be willing to take a close look at our work and become committed to building a true educational foundation for the teaching of archaeology.

PART III

The Danger Zones
Issues in Teaching Archaeology

A foray into another culture can be enlivening and broadening; it also can invite misunderstanding and controversy. The interface between archaeology and education has zones of sensitivity that can inflame passions, cause anguish, and derail the best archaeology education program. Teaching people about their heritage and trying to impart ethics such as site stewardship and respect for other cultures treads very near many peoples' most basic personal and religious values. Certain archaeology concepts and professional convictions may be in direct conflict with children's—and their parents'—dearly held beliefs. Archaeology educators should be very aware of this when designing and delivering educational programs. Whether or not acknowledged and deliberate, all archaeology education has the potential to challenge religious, ethical, cosmological, and doctrinal beliefs. As we caution in the introduction to this book, archaeology educators have a grave responsibility to reflect on the possible effects of their programs and prepare to address the consequences.

Part III identifies common areas of controversy that veteran archaeology educators have experienced. It offers approaches for preparing for them and solutions for turning calamities into positive educational experiences for the student as well as the archaeology educator. We shouldn't shy away from these encounters because, through them, we learn what our audiences need. Dialogues on controversial topics are vehicles for making data gleaned from archaeological sources relevant to modern life. Many people care greatly about what our work reveals about our collective past. And, a stated objective of archaeology education is to instill an ethic in audiences for protecting and valuing the record of past cultures. We must be prepared to challenge values that run counter to achieving this central professional goal.

Sometimes the belief systems that archaeology education programs challenge are held by other professional archaeologists; the worth of archaeology education still is doubted by some within the profession. Even among archaeology education supporters, there is debate about the appropriateness of including school-age children and interested members of the public in the actual excavation process. Proponents of hands-on excavation programs cite enhanced respect for heritage resource conservation, a sense of community involvement in research, a clearer sense of the multidisciplinary process that archaeology entails, and the greater impact of activity-based learning on a student. Opponents range from those who believe that excavation programs for the K–12 audience increase the perception that archaeologists do nothing more than dig, to those who generally are supportive of the pedagogical aims of hands-on dig programs. However, the latter group has reservations about student digs because of possible threats to delicate resources and the additional staffing, program structure, field time, and funds that they require. Between the two camps lie adherents of the "simulated dig," who want students to have the experience of participating in the excavation process without the complications of using a real site. Instead, a constructed site, either indoors or out, becomes the archaeological "classroom."

In the first three chapters of Part III, experienced archaeology educators present their views of the pros and cons of digging with kids, and offer important information about how best to design programs to fit the educational goals at hand. Nancy Hawkins discusses the constraints of focusing on excavations, real or virtual, as vehicles for transmitting messages about archaeology and stewardship. Her chapter outlines issues to consider when planning an excavation experience and proposes alternative means of getting archaeology information to students. She reports on Louisiana's experience of offering teaching materials that are not dependent on a physical site.

Other archaeology educators believe that simulated excavations can offer a meaningful learning experience, given the appropriate procedures and format for assuring this positive outcome. Beverly Chiarullli, Ellen Dailey Bedell, and Ceil Leeper Sturdevant, proponents of the simulated excavation, outline the educational benefits that it can offer. They also report the assessment results of what students learn about archaeology through three types of exposure: classroom programs delivered by visiting archaeologists, a visit to a real excavation, and participating in a simulated excavation.

Karolyn Smardz, a long-time advocate of conducting excavations on real sites with students, discusses the issues attendant on this educational approach. While she cautions that this is not suitable for every site and that a carefully structured, integrated educational and research plan is mandatory, she offers practical advice for conducting excavations with children that allow for scientifically sound research and enriching educational experiences.

This suite of chapters on digging with children represents the spectrum of opinions among archaeology educators. There is, of course, no correct universal answer. Each type of program can be exceptionally effective. Which is appropriate in a given situation depends on the archaeological, financial, and supervisory resources available; the character, age, and ability level of the students to be taught; and—this is the critical piece—the educational objectives of both teacher and archaeology educator. Collectively, the chapters offer a way to review archaeology education goals and resources objectively and select the type of program best suited to the situation.

Another major issue is the need to recognize the inherently political nature of archaeology education. At its core, it is a propaganda program. We are trying to change the public's attitude toward archaeological preservation. We want people to value what the past can tell us and to care for the sources of this data—archaeological sites and collections. The archaeological profession urgently needs to encourage and ensure the continuity of public support for archaeological endeavors. Unless the public chooses to pay for research, curation, and site management and protection through contributions or tax revenues, and unless individuals choose not to loot sites, collect artifacts, or purchase antiquities, the profession cannot survive. Government funding and site protection legislation are directly contingent on politicians' perceptions that there is public support for such enterprises. In its broadest sense, archaeology education is the way that the profession shows the public the value of what we do and urges them to share our concern for site stewardship.

An archaeology education program in schools asks children to form values and ethics of stewardship. Working with values education in schools is the subject of Jeanne Moe's chapter. She outlines the historical development of what is now termed "character education" or "citizenship" within the education system. By providing archaeological examples for several widely used values education methods, she prepares readers to take on this critically important aspect of archaeology education. This approach gives archaeology educators "airtime" in the classroom, since it helps a teacher to meet the need for real-life ethical issues within values education programs. Moe's chapter shows how stewardship, a topic of vital concern to archaeologists, has a niche within our schools that can be used for the benefit of educators, students, and archaeologists. However, she cautions that the success in affecting an individual's attitudinal change is a difficult outcome to measure. Her chapter links with Johnson's (this volume) discussion of moral development in children.

Perhaps the most volatile issue in archaeology education concerns archaeological interpretations that conflict with traditional, religious, or ethnic precepts. Commonly held theories such as the origins of North America's native peoples or general cultural history sequences, and basic concepts like the nature of time, can conflict with fundamental and traditional views. Innocently presented teaching strategies, like guided imagery, are regarded by some as akin to brainwashing, and their use has prompted a backlash from parents. Marjorie Connolly's chapter identifies some of these flash points and offers constructive advice about how to include alternative interpretations of the past. She suggests addressing these issues through an experiential education approach.

The issues presented in Part III are ripe for discourse. Since archaeology education is a budding subdiscipline, issues only recently are surfacing and being defined. An editorial chapter by Anne Pyburn concludes Part III and links archaeology education issues with larger ones within the professions of archaeology and anthropology. Pyburn's provocative discussion offers readers much to reflect on and examine as they prepare for and deal with the "danger zones" inherent in interpreting cultural heritage to the general public.

Part IV concludes the book, and that is where we explore the various arenas in which archaeology education takes place. In Part I, we gained an understanding of the educator's world, and we explored the interface of archaeology and education in Part II. Part III alerts us to potential pitfalls in this interface. Part IV brings strands in the previous sections together and demonstrates their points and principles as they play out in real-world places.

Chapter Fourteen

Teaching Archaeology without the Dig
What's Left?

Archaeologists and educators who are contemplating ways of introducing students to archaeology may consider excavation to be a fundamental part of any archaeology unit. To many, archaeology is synonymous with excavation. However, important concepts of archaeology can be taught without ever having students participate in actual or simulated excavations. Issues to consider when planning a precollegiate excavation activity and ideas for alternative activities are described below.

Actual Excavations with Precollegiate Students

Archaeologists and educators can easily cite reasons to excavate real sites with students. Excavations can provide engaging, hands-on, interdisciplinary learning experiences (Smardz 1991). When conditions are good, the projects are rewarding for both archaeologists and students (Dawdy 1996a, 1996b).

Several factors are conducive to a positive experience for the participants. The first is ensuring a low ratio of students to archaeologists. This allows for excellent supervision, teaching, and quality control. The second is an excavation that is planned to answer research questions, rather than just to give students a chance to dig. This teaches that the purpose of excavation is to learn about people in the past, not to provide entertainment, or even to teach excavation skills. The third is choosing a site with at least some areas that have uncomplicated stratigraphy and few features, so students with limited skills will be less likely to miss critical information. The fourth is a site location appropriate for the group participating. For example, if students are traveling from school to the site on a bus, the site must be relatively near the school, with adequate bus parking.

Logic and experience show that these conditions are difficult to meet, especially in rural areas where many well-preserved prehistoric sites are located. They are more likely to be achieved in urban areas, where schools are close to sites, so that transportation, parking, and rainy days are not big problems. Further, at historical urban sites, students will almost certainly uncover something recognizable, a major asset in helping students understand the meaning of material culture in the site context within a time-limited program period.

Although field experiences for precollegiate youth are rewarding when circumstances are suitable, relying on them as the primary way of reaching a lot of students is unrealistic. For example, imagine the difficulties of trying to give all eighth-grade students who live within a one-hour drive of a town a chance to excavate at a site. The students would come from many socioeconomic backgrounds, have differing levels of interest in archaeology, and some may have various physical and behavioral abilities that would require alternative program design within a single site context.

Consider the challenge of finding one or more sites in the area that are already slated for excavation because of land development, research, or other priorities, and that are large enough, simple enough, and convenient enough for the student project. Envision, further, identifying a lead archaeologist motivated to integrate educational, logistical, safety, and supervisory objectives with research and management objectives. Finally, imagine the difficulties inherent in obtaining funding sufficient to support the planning, analysis, interpretation, and reporting for the complex project.

There are other problems: Could the project be repeated in the coming years? Should hands-on excavation programming on real sites be repeated annually and all over the continent? Is this the appropriate way to teach care of scarce archaeological resources? Does it teach protection of sites? Does it teach that archaeology is normally conducted by highly trained scientists and that students are not encouraged to go out and try this themselves, either on their own or with their teacher?

Unfortunately, it is very uncommon for an excellent archaeological research project also to be an excellent educational project for a large number of students. One major reason is the difficulty of balancing educational objectives with research goals. Another is the cost in time and money to process and interpret artifacts, samples, and field records from students, and then to prepare a comprehensive professional report. Exemplary projects are usually well funded and serve a small number of students.

While these noteworthy experiences are great for the few who participate, they are not the way to reach most students. Because of this fact, many educators and archaeologists have turned to simulated excavations.

Simulated Excavations with Precollegiate Students

There are three reasons why simulated excavations are appealing:

1. They can be created almost anywhere.
2. They hold the potential for teaching concepts of archaeology (context, techniques) without disturbing actual sites.
3. They can be excavated without the assistance of professional archaeologists.

Two basic kinds of simulated excavations are used. One is small, simple, and primarily illustrates the law of superposition. Into this first category fall activities like the trash can excavation (Adams and Gronemann 1989), the earth cake (Nobles 1992), and the dig box (Des Jean 1990).

The second type is a more realistic excavation designed to simulate a more complex, but usually single component, nonstratified archaeological site (Ellick 1991; KC Smith 1991c; Williamson 1991; McNutt 1992; Mitchum and Giblin 1995). Excellent ones are labor intensive to set up, use a lot of space, and are supervised by archaeologists. The complex simulated excavation activities teach techniques of excavation, mapping, screening, analysis, and interpretation. They also introduce concepts of artifacts, features, and context.

However, even the most complicated ones rarely include many aspects of archaeology. For example, sites are usually unrealistically simple, without complex or ambiguous features and stratigraphy. During a simulated excavation, there is no need for collection of samples for specialized analyses. Even when analysis, interpretation, and some form of reporting are included, they are necessarily simplified and superficial. Simulated excavations may give students the idea that archaeology is intuitive, simple, and straightforward: something they can do as well as professional archaeologists.

Just as with actual excavations, simulated excavations led by archaeologists are not practical, primary ways of reaching a lot of students. Not every student can visit a museum or university with a professionally led simulated excavation.

Simulated excavations led by teachers and nonarchaeologists are also problematic. They tend to mutate into treasure hunts for exotic artifacts, recovered for exhibition, instead of for less glamorous clues about how ordinary people lived, which is exactly the opposite message to the one archaeologists and educators are trying to transmit (Hawkins 1996).

In sum, excavations (real or simulated) are not practical for introducing a large number of students to archaeology. Further, they provide a simplified version of the techniques of field archaeology. The experience may overlook or even negate messages about importance of site preservation. Students involved in a field phase may not learn about the pre- or postfield phases of a project (like background research, analysis, and report writing). Through a real or simulated excavation experience, students may not learn what the site tells about people, and, most troubling, students may get the idea that they are ready to excavate a site alone after they have worked on a simulated or actual site.

Alternatives to Excavation

What can be done, instead, to reach a lot of students, even with limited money, teacher training, and staff? The only way the majority of students can be reached is through their teachers. There just aren't enough archaeologists available for students to have direct contact with them. But personal interaction with archaeologists and excavations are not critical to learning about people of the past, any more than direct contact with astronomers, astronauts, or space travel is critical to learning about our galaxy.

Archaeologists can take three simple steps to help get information about archaeology to students through their teachers.

1. They can compile materials and resources that teachers can use (Christensen 1995). They can collect, develop, and distribute activity guides, kits with lessons, posters with lessons, audiovisual materials, and booklets or other background information that teachers can convert into lessons.
2. They can be a source of information for teachers who want to know about materials that other organizations distribute. Archaeologists can prepare locally appropriate lists of information about archaeological sites and museums to visit, books for various ages (KC Smith, this volume), audiovisual materials, articles from major magazines (*Science News*, *National Geographic*, *Smithsonian*), and Internet sites (Clark, this volume). They also can consult with teachers who are developing classroom materials and activities about archaeology.
3. They can go where teachers are to link with them (Selig, this volume). They can attend, display, and present at teachers' conferences. Archaeologists can lead workshops, offer to give presentations at meetings held by related organizations (like the Geographic Alliance), and offer to lead in-service and preservice training for teachers (Brunswig, this volume).

Many alternatives to actual excavation are available to help teach students about the fundamental concepts of archaeology. Quite a few of them are suggested in chapters throughout this volume.

Selecting the Messages for Archaeology
Education Projects

As educators and archaeologists launch new archaeology education projects, it is helpful to identify the special issues in the area (public vs. private land; visible vs.

hidden sites; types of threats to sites), to set priorities among archaeological goals, and to define the geographical scope (city, region, nation, world).

Archaeology is a very big, very complex subject. The purpose of archaeology education projects need not be to translate a college-level course into precollegiate activities, or to train teachers or students to become archaeologists. The objective of archaeology education is to find ways to teach fundamental concepts and information that relate to the defined special issues, priorities, and geographical scope of interest to the project designers.

What are the "fundamental concepts of archaeology"? Have basic themes and content been identified that always should be included? I suggest that four broad concepts emerge in most education projects that archaeologists have helped develop (Wheat and Whorton 1990; Blanchard 1991; McNutt 1992; Smith et al. 1996) (see Box 14.1).

BOX 14.1
Fundamental Concepts of Archaeology

1. Archaeology is the study of material remains such as artifacts and features and their contexts.
2. The purpose of archaeology is to learn about past peoples, their cultures, technologies, and adaptive behaviors.
3. Archaeologists have lengthy, specialized training and use scientific methods. Their work is different from that of untrained excavators and treasure hunters.
4. Archaeological sites are fragile and irreplaceable. They should be protected from vandalism, unscientific digging, and destruction by natural forces.

In developing ways to introduce these concepts, it is helpful, but not critical, for archaeologists and educators to collaborate. Many successful projects, however, have been developed by archaeologists who knew little about formal educational theory and by educators who never had an archaeology course or field school. Just as not all students are alike, neither are all teachers alike nor are teaching situations alike, so there is not a single right way of getting information ready for use.

What Has Worked Well in One State

Louisiana's statewide archaeology education program was initiated in 1981 through the state archaeologist's office, which is part of the State Historic Preservation Office.

Existing printing and office supply monies were made available, and a staff archaeologist was assigned approximately one-third time to it. The educational effort has continued throughout the years with steady, but limited, funding and staff time. A lot has been learned about what can work well in a statewide, low cost, nonlabor-intensive approach.

Experience has shown that teachers use materials like posters, activities, booklets, and artifact kits that are ready to give to the students. For example, Louisiana developed, printed, and continues to distribute a series of five posters about Louisiana prehistory. Each poster has a timeline, drawings, and text describing artifacts, settlements, and foods. Several classroom activities are distributed that are linked to the posters. These are well received because they can be used in multiple ways.

Teachers also welcome information about other resources available to them, such as sites and museums to visit, and accurate books and videos to use with students. Information of this type was first compiled for the Louisiana project in the early 1980s and was included in the 1984 activity guide, entitled *Classroom Archaeology* (Hawkins 1991, revised ed.). Teachers who use the guide report that this is the section they refer to most frequently. Information about resources is regularly updated.

Classroom Archaeology also included short, self-contained activities about archaeological processes and concepts, games about Louisiana prehistory, and activities about recording a site, interpreting a site, and conducting a simulated excavation. The simulated excavation activity was removed after teachers reported using the instructions to excavate real sites. Educators say that the games, and the activities about recording and interpreting a site, are less frequently used than are the short activities that focus on concepts like chronology, artifacts, context, and on the processes like inference, scientific analysis, and relative dating.

Classroom Archaeology is still requested and still distributed, but teachers more frequently ask for activities that include specific information about archaeological sites in Louisiana. The interest in local information is attributed to two factors: (1) The teachers often are including the material in Louisiana history classes, and (2) Louisiana has some spectacular prehistoric and historic sites that are not widely publicized. Teachers are excited to learn about them and want more information to pass along to their students.

So, locally specific activities are now displayed and distributed at teachers' conferences and workshops. The best-received activities can stand alone (are nonsequential), inexpensive to implement, and usable even without previous background in archaeology or workshop training. Teachers appreciate lessons that are appropriate for cooperative learning groups, that are hands-on, and that are interdisciplinary.

The primary messages focus on:

1. Our state's rich cultural past and examples of important archaeological sites that tell about the people who once lived here.

2. How archaeologists have found out about these sites through careful scientific study.
3. What artifacts, features, and context are.
4. How students and other residents can help report and protect sites.

Newly developed lessons are linked with background resources such as books, articles, posters, or artifact kits. Whether intended for use in science, social studies, or interdisciplinary settings, they focus on what archaeologists have found out about people in our state, rather than on general processes of archaeological principles such as inference, drawing conclusions, or classification. This works well with our state-specific audience and our goal of enhancing appreciation for, and protection of, the state's important archaeological sites.

Conclusion

There is no single right way to introduce students to archaeology. Especially when archaeology education materials and activities are prepared for teachers to use independently, few activities are guaranteed to be successes or failures. Therefore, the best advice for the archaeology educator is, don't wait to become an expert in both archaeology and education, to develop an innovative curriculum guide, or to identify the perfect situation for a student excavation.

Instead, take a step toward sharing archaeology with students. Identify a small number of key preservation messages or archaeological concepts. Then borrow an activity from someone else, give information about already existing resources, or develop one or two activities, talks, or handouts. Like everything else, teaching about archaeology gets easier with experience. Taking the first step is what it's all about.

RECOMMENDED READINGS

Boy Scouts of America
   1997   *Archaeology.* Boy Scouts of America Merit Badge Series. Boy Scouts of America, Irving, Texas.
   This handbook gives a good introduction to the field of archaeology, career options, and study topics. Available from local Boy Scout council or BSA Direct Mail Center, 1–800–323–0732. Good for middle-school and high-school students.

Buco, Deborah
   1999   *Poverty Point Expeditions.* Division of Archaeology, State of Louisiana, Baton Rouge.
   This guide has activities related to the 3,500-year-old Poverty Point earthworks site in northeast Louisiana. The unite introduces the Poverty Point culture through hands-on activities

that integrate basic curriculum areas and higher-level thinking skills. Each activity is both interdisciplinary and linked to the Louisiana Curriculum Standards. Appropriate for upper elementary- and middle-school students. Available from the Dvision of Archaeology, P.O. Box 44247, Baton Rouge, LA 70804, 225–342–8170.

Duke, Kate
    1997 *Archaeologists Dig for Clues*. Let's-Read-and-Find-Out Science Series. HarperCollins, New York.
    This thirty-two–page cartoon-style book tells a story about children helping archaeologists excavate a complex archaic site. The book has a lighthearted tone, yet contains an incredible amount of accurate information. It tells about both archaeological techniques and what research has revealed about life at the site 6,000 years ago. The back cover says the book is for ages five–nine, but the vocabulary and concepts are appropriate for older elementary- or even middle-school students.

O'Brien, Wendy, and Tracey Cullen
    1995 *Archaeology in the Classroom: A Resource Guide for Teachers and Parents*. Archaeological Institute of America, Boston.
    This guide is a compilation of teaching resources relating to archaeology worldwide. Available from Kendall/Hunt Publishing Company, 1–800–228–0810.

Samford, Patricia, and David L. Ribblett
    1995 *Archaeology for Young Explorers: Uncovering History at Colonial Williamsburg*. The Colonial Williamsburg Foundation, Williamsburg, Virginia.
    This beautifully illustrated book tells about the methods of historical archaeology and their use in the study of eighteenth-century Virginia. Although most photographs and examples are from Williamsburg, the book gives a great introduction to archaeology in general. Photographs in the book show elementary-age children participating in excavation. The reading level is upper elementary and middle school.

BEVERLY A. CHIARULLI ■
ELLEN DAILEY BEDELL
CEIL LEEPER STURDEVANT

Chapter Fifteen

Simulated Excavations and Critical Thinking Skills

As public interest in archaeology has increased, many teachers have created simulated excavations. Some use archaeology as entertainment; others use archaeological data in multidisciplinary programs to develop students' critical thinking skills. What makes an effective archaeological education program? What message do we as archaeologists and educators want students to gain from an educational program? What do we want students to learn? These are questions that we all face as we develop archaeological education programs and that we need to answer during the process. We want students to learn that archaeology is about people. It is more than entertainment or things, and, of course, it is not about dinosaurs. In our ideal program, students will learn about context and method and that uncontrolled excavations are destructive. Our goal as archaeologists and educators should be to develop programs that teach these lessons.

In this chapter, we discuss factors to consider in creating a simulated excavation experience and describe how we implemented and evaluated such a program.

Simulated Excavations and Educational Goals

What kind of program is most effective in transmitting important messages about archaeology education? The most common programs that students experience, beyond archaeology lessons taught by a classroom teacher, are classroom visits by archaeologists, class visits to archaeological excavations and archaeological exhibits in museums, and simulated digs. Each type of program has advantages and disadvantages. We believe that a simulated excavation provides the most opportunity for a meaningful learning experience for the following reasons:

1. A simulated archaeological excavation is the perfect forum for interdisciplinary education. It utilizes the scientific method and integrates many disciplines—almost any you can think of—such as geology, botany, economics, mathematics, art, computer technology, history, and, naturally, archaeology.
2. It teaches students the effective use of primary source material. They excavate artifacts, ecofacts, and features, and use this primary source material to reconstruct culture. Educators have emphasized the use of written primary sources in schools, but have largely ignored the importance of material remains in analyzing ancient civilizations.
3. Students learn to appreciate another culture—for example, The Ellis School simulation is based on a Native American culture, the Anasazi. By replicating the artifacts from this culture, students are able to understand better that these people had to manufacture everything they used in their daily life and that they often made these things in a distinctive way. The students therefore begin to understand the significance of the material culture of a different people.
4. A simulation not only introduces students to the techniques of excavation, but also encourages them to apply deductive reasoning and other high-level thinking skills. They are trained to use the scientific method and to appreciate the importance of context and association in archaeological investigation. Students soon realize that unless they find artifacts in association with each other, they cannot say anything meaningful about the behavior patterns, social structure, or ideology of the people who lived on the site.
5. Students learn to cooperate and work as a team. They work in groups during the making, investigation, and analysis of artifacts; and they cooperate in putting together a site report. Each student is able to contribute something to the site report, depending on the student's interest and experience.
6. This type of project provides an alternative assessment method for student evaluation. Such an alternative is beneficial to students who do not perform well on tests.
7. Students gain an understanding of the need to preserve our cultural heritage. They realize that pot hunting is not only illegal but also destroys the historical and scientific value of artifacts.

The other advantage of a simulated excavation is that it can be taught independently by a classroom teacher. With adequate training and facilities, a simulated excavation can be a yearly component of a teacher's curriculum.

We have experience in developing simulated excavations for elementary and high-school students. At The Ellis School, an independent all-girls school in Pittsburgh, Pennsylvania, a simulated archaeological excavation is part of the ninth-grade history curriculum. The simulation is an elaborate, multistrata dig in which students learn to use the scientific method and to appreciate the importance of context and association in archaeological investigation. Ellen Bedell and Ceil Sturdevant created a "site" in a large sandbox. This box, which measures 6 feet x 8 feet x 2 feet and contains four tons of sand, is made of treated wood and cost approximately

$450.00 to build. It was made by a professional carpenter and has a reinforced bottom and a heavy lid that protects the site when it is not being used. At Bushy Run Battlefield, near Pittsburgh, Beverly Chiarulli used single-level sandboxes containing artifacts from different historical periods as part of an introduction to archaeology for elementary students. We think that both of these projects have been very effective in educating precollege students about archaeology.

In this chapter, we will describe how you might create a comprehensive simulated excavation. It draws on both of our programs, but uses the details from the simulated excavation at The Ellis School, developed by Bedell and Sturdevant. We will then present the results of several follow-up surveys that compare the view of archaeology gained by students in simulated programs to the view gained from other program types.

Archaeology at The Ellis School

Soon after Ellen Bedell started teaching an archaeology unit at The Ellis School, she realized that her students were victims of the mass media and popular culture. They tended to see all archaeologists as clones of Indiana Jones, running through the jungle clutching valuable artifacts to their breasts, and dodging the arrows of hostile tribes. These archaeologists teach a few classes between adventures. This romantic image is not new; our parents thought that archaeologists wore pith helmets and ran screaming from mummies who were suddenly revived from the dead by a concoction of tana leaves. And then there is the ongoing saga of Tutankhamen and the mummy's curse. Updated versions of this theme are still frequently seen on cable television. How could high-school students be convinced that archaeology is a serious scientific pursuit, and not a quest for the Holy Grail?

Bedell had worked at several sites in the Middle East and the United States, and she began teaching archaeology by showing students slides of various activities on these excavations. She tried to explain to them the importance of provenience and data clusters, and got a lot of blank stares. She decided that the only way students could get a feel for what an archaeologist does is for them to actually go through the excavation process themselves.

As a history teacher, Bedell was also disturbed by the fact that students completely trust secondary sources. In an experiential archaeology project, they would have to use primary source material exclusively to reconstruct a culture. But what culture? Even though her academic field is Egyptology, she couldn't imagine putting some kind of replica of the temple of Karnak in a sandbox. She decided that Anasazi culture would lend itself to this kind of project. There are distinctive types of artifacts in each period of Anasazi history, and it was feasible to build part of a kiva wall in a sandbox. It was also obvious, though, that she needed help with this project, because she had to somehow manufacture the artifacts.

Bedell went to the art department for help and found that the ceramics teacher at Ellis, Ceil Sturdevant, was very interested in ancient pottery styles. Sturdevant had been interested for some time in Zuni and Hopi pottery. In fact, she had recently gone to the School of American Research in Santa Fe, New Mexico, and had seen their extensive collection of American Indian pottery, which included Anasazi pottery. She had also visited Santa Clara pueblo and saw demonstrations of how ancient people fired pottery in pits in the ground. Her students were already familiar with ancient firing techniques and Native American pottery designs. The two teachers decided to collaborate and create a sophisticated simulated excavation at The Ellis School.

Creating a Simulated Excavation

A simulated or experiential excavation is an archaeological program in which students excavate in an environment created or controlled by the instructor. Many activities are classified as simulated excavations including sandbox digs, tabletop excavations, garbage can digs, and even computer simulations like "Fugawiland" or "Excavating Ockaneechee Town" (Price and Gebauer 1996; Davis et al. 1998). Our definition of a simulated excavation is that it is an experiential project organized by a classroom teacher that has an educational goal of reconstructing human behavior using archaeological techniques. A program should include the following elements:

1. *Background preparation:* Preparation should begin approximately six months before your scheduled classroom program. First, decide where it will fit into your curriculum. Is it history or science or both? What culture will you investigate? Do you need help from a professional archaeologist in planning the activity? Consider the logistics and the space available at your school. What will the weather be like at the time of excavation? Can you create an excavation area in the ground or will you need to construct some kind of box?

As preparation for the Ellis School excavation, Bedell and Sturdevant attended the teachers' workshop at Crow Canyon Archaeological Center, an archaeological research and educational facility near Cortez, Colorado. Crow Canyon is dedicated to teaching adults and children to respect our cultural heritage. Many students who go through one of their programs actually help excavate an Anasazi site. The teachers learned how successful the experiential method of teaching archaeology was, but they had one problem: They didn't have an archaeological site in their backyard. The Crow Canyon program uses a single-stratum sandbox to teach young children about the process of archaeological data recovery and recording. The Ellis solution was to create a simulated excavation on the school grounds at Ellis.

There are other solutions. Some schools have land that can be used to create a replica of an actual site. The teachers are able to place artifact replicas in the ground in a protected area. The Western Beaver School District in Beaver County

Pennsylvania took this approach (in 1995) and created an area measuring 3 x 12 meters replicating a Late Woodland village. Another approach is to build a tabletop site that creates a smaller version of an excavation. As described by Baker, Cardennis, and Miller (1996), the tabletop excavation can be very elaborate. One recent version contained four stratigraphic layers and reflected the environmental changes in an area resulting from deforestation and nineteenth-century industrialization.

2. *Set the stage for your students:* What do students need to know to understand the culture they are investigating? Students should conduct research on the culture or cultures that they will be investigating. Sometimes this can be done effectively by having one set of students create the culture which another group will investigate. In addition to learning about the relevant culture, the students must be introduced to archaeological concepts and techniques. The first eight lessons of the Bureau of Land Management curriculum *Intrigue of the Past* (Smith et al. 1996) provides an effective approach to learning archaeological concepts. Other lessons in this valuable guide are designed to teach students archaeological techniques such as how to grid a site or measure for provenience. This can also be the time that students develop a research design or plan to define the questions their excavation will answer.

In May (1993) of the school year preceding the first scheduled excavation at The Ellis School, art students made artifacts from five periods of Anasazi history (i.e., Basketmaker II–Pueblo III). Most artifacts were of clay and included: side-notched projectile points, animal figurines, plain gray pottery, corrugated pottery, black-and-white pottery, pipes, feather boxes, manos and *metates*, kiva jars, and water jars. In addition to clay replicas, the students made coiled baskets and brought shells, bones, gourds, corn, turkey feathers, and other items from home. The students then buried the artifacts in the proper stratigraphic order and in distinct behavior clusters.

While the students were making artifacts for the simulated dig, art teacher Sturdevant discussed the cultural significance of the objects, the importance of good craftsmanship to survival, and the function of various artifacts. She also discussed cultural innovation and mythological inspiration. Bedell, in the ninth-grade history class, which was the setting for the excavation, then used the *Intrigue* lessons to introduce the students to such archaeological concepts as the personal importance of objects, cultural universals, archaeological context, observation and inference, stratigraphy, and attribute analysis.

3. *Create the excavation (or use an excavation created by a group of students):* Once you have finished your preparation, it is time to construct the excavation area. Locate the area where the excavation will be placed. If you plan to do this on a yearly basis, try to find an area where the excavation can remain undisturbed from year to year (i.e., not in the lacrosse field). Remember that a box filled with sand is very heavy and can't easily be relocated. Where will the artifacts come from? Is there an art teacher in the school who would be

interested in working on the project to create artifacts in his or her class? Is there a woodshop at the school? Would that teacher join the team and either produce the box or other equipment such as screens? Successful programs, like successful excavations, bring many other disciplines into the project.

At The Ellis School, the art students who made the Anasazi artifacts buried them in the permanently installed sandbox. They created three strata in the box, as follows:

Bottom of Box:
    Squares 1 and 2 = Basketmaker II
    Squares 3 and 4 = Basketmaker III
Next level:
    Squares 1 and 2 = Pueblo I
    Squares 3 and 4 = Pueblo II
Top level:
    Squares 1 and 2 = Pueblo III
    Squares 3 and 4 = Pueblo III

These periods were not distinctly divided in the middle of the box. The artifacts were placed in more of a random fashion as if people actually lived in the area. The whole top level (Stratum I) contained artifacts from the Pueblo III period, as if in this period the population greatly increased and people occupied the entire site. During the excavation, each stratum was color coded so that the students could keep better control of the material. Stratum I (top of the box) was red, Stratum 2 (middle level) was green, and Stratum 3 (bottom of the box) was purple. Red pens were used to label artifact bags from Stratum 1, green pens for Stratum 2, and purple pens for Stratum 3. The students also constructed various features on the different levels, such as sections of kiva walls, made from Belgium blocks (dressed limestone blocks), and a *sipapu* (a small hole in a kiva floor thought to have symbolic meaning), made with a bulb digger and Sakret mortar mix. They created different textures in the sand by plastering the floors of grain storage areas with mortar.

In the art studio, the students designed activity areas for placement in the sandbox. In the Stratum 1 kiva, they placed several burned roof beams, a feather box, bone awls, a kiva jar, pipes, red-ware pottery (trade ware), and a *sipapu*. On the patio outside the kiva and room block structure, they created a food preparation area. They included a clay *mano* and *metate*, stone scrapers, ears of Indian corn, corrugated pottery containing kernels of corn, a water jar, and children's toys. In Stratum 2, they placed a pottery-making area and a corn storage facility with a paved floor. In the Basketmaker level, they included a kill site with deer bone, obsidian scrapers (made from pottery with a shiny black glaze), a fire pit containing charcoal, and an atlatl.

4. *Purchase equipment for the excavation:* After the artifacts are buried, you should purchase the equipment that your students will need to excavate the site.

It cost about $150.00 to purchase equipment for The Ellis School dig. Purchases included excavation tools such as mason's pointing trowels (eight Marshalltown trowels), small brushes of assorted sizes, dental picks, whisk brooms and dust pans, and a plumb bob, line level, and tape measure for determining provenience. String and screws and a screw driver to set up a grid system (four squares), as well as four buckets (one for each square) and several screens to sift the sand from the dig for small artifacts were also required. Laboratory needs included two plastic dishpans, nail brushes and toothbrushes for washing artifacts, and a bottle of white glue to repair the broken artifacts. Graph paper for the site map, a field notebook, and red, green, and purple marking pens completed the equipment list.

> 5. *Organize the students:* Which class will be excavating the site? How many students will be working at a time? Will they all need tools? How will they record their information? Will they work as teams? Everyone may only want to excavate at first, but a successful excavation has a lot of jobs. Archaeology is teamwork.

At The Ellis School, students (a different group than those who made and buried the artifacts in May) excavated the site for the first time in September 1993, three months after the artifacts were buried. The ninth-grade students who excavated the site had never seen any of the artifacts before and were completely unaware of what they might encounter in the excavation. They first studied archaeological terminology and techniques in the classroom. They saw slides of various archaeological sites and did exercises involving clusters of archaeological data. They learned how to determine behavior patterns, social structure, and ideology from primary source material. They also learned the importance of context and association. They studied Anasazi culture and knew what types of artifacts they might encounter. Thus, the students were well prepared for the excavation before they ever picked up a trowel.

The students were assigned different positions on the excavation team, such as chief archaeologist, excavator, screener, photographer, mapper, pottery washer, recorder, and the like. The positions were rotated so that each student had a chance to excavate and to perform at least two jobs in the laboratory. Each student knew what her job description was and what was expected of her. On the day of the excavation, assignments and the times when the rotations would take place were posted. The job descriptions are as listed in Figure 15.1.

> 6. *Excavate the site:* How do archaeologists excavate a site? Why do they dig square holes? What are they measuring?

In an actual excavation, archaeologists excavate slowly in a way that allows them to record carefully information about what they are finding. Excavations are square to fit into a grid system so that all the artifacts can be tracked. Horizontal and vertical measurments are recorded for each item found. This may be the stage at

EXCAVATION: 8 students (2 in each square)
    a. Dig with trowels, brushes, dental pick, etc.
    b. Fill out site forms
SCREENING: 4 to 8 students (1 or 2 assigned to each square)
    a. Empty buckets into screen held over large tarp
    b. Put artifacts in bags
    c. Label each bag (color code) (level and square)
    d. Take bags to laboratory for washing
    e. Help excavators measure artifacts and features in the box (line level, plumb bob)
FIELD NOTEBOOK: 1 student for each stratum *(chief archaeologist)*
    a. Draw artifacts and features in notebook
    b. List artifacts
    c. Preliminary thoughts on behavior indicated by artifacts, ecofacts, and features in association
SITE MAP (GRID): 4 students for each stratum (1 student for each square)
    a. All important artifacts and features are drawn to scale using graph paper
    b. Each student is responsible for one square
    c. The four sheets of graph paper will be put together on a poster board to make a site map for each stratum.
PHOTOGRAPHY: 1 student for each stratum
    a. All important artifacts and features must be photographed in situ using a digital camera
    b. The student photographer for each stratum will download the pictures into the computer for use in the site report
LABORATORY: 4 long (cafeteria) tables
POTTERY WASHING: 2 students
    a. Washing pottery and other artifacts
    b. Use soft nail brushes and toothbrushes
RECORDING AND DESCRIPTION: 3 students
    a. Each artifact and ecofact must be described in detail
    b. Keep together all data from the same square and stratum using colored markers and color-coded boxes
SORTING AND IDENTIFICATION: 2 students
    a. Sort *(classify)* and identify each artifact by style and period
    b. Pictures of pottery styles from each period will be provided (Match the pottery style to the period) *(cross-dating)*
DRAWING POTTERY: 3 students
    a. Draw pottery outline (rim sherd etc.)
    b. Draw decorative or incised patterns
REPAIRING POTTERY: 2 students
    a. Glue together pottery fragments to try to reconstruct vessels
    b. White glue
COMPUTER DATA ENTRY: 4 students
    a. Use lap-top computers
    b. 4 computers set up at end of lab tables
    c. Enter data from lab forms into database fields
BOXING: 12 boxes
    Put all artifacts from a particular square and level in one box so they can be reburied

Figure 15.1. Archaeological excavation assignments

which you need to consult with someone who has archaeological experience. If students dig in a fast, uncontrolled way, they will miss the point of the excavation, which is to discover clues about the past. But if the students are prepared in advance, and assigned jobs which include mapping and measuring, and recording information, most teams naturally slow down to record the information.

Before the dig at Ellis, Bedell and Sturdevant used a hose to wet the sand so that it was the right consistency for digging. The students then divided the sandbox into four squares with the datum on the north side of the box and carefully excavated with trowels and brushes (Photo 15.1).

They used their math skills to measure the provenience of the artifacts using a line level, a plumb bob, and a tape measure, and they recorded the location of each artifact and feature on a site map. They recorded both the horizontal and vertical measurements from a fixed point (datum) so that they could later determine exactly where the artifact was found (Photo 15.2). After a level was brushed clean, and everything was recorded and photographed, the artifacts were removed and put in paper bags that were labeled with a color coded site designation. Bedell adapted the Smithsonian code for site designations and used as the site designation 36ALEL1SQ1.

36 = Pennsylvania
AL = Allegheny County
E = Ellis
L = Level 1, 2, or 3
SQ = Square 1, 2, 3, or 4

This designation was on every bag containing an artifact coming out of the site. It was also on every form filled out by the excavators. The designation was written in red on all bags and forms from Stratum 1, in green on all bags and forms from Stratum 2, and in purple on all bags and forms from Stratum 3. The students also used a digital camera, and the images were downloaded into a computer, to record each level and square. One of the student archaeologists working in each square filled out a site form when they finished excavating. They used the form shown in Figure 15.2.

7. *Beyond digging:* In an archaeological project, the excavation is the smallest part of the experience. Students working on a simulated excavation should spend more time on the site analysis and report than on the excavation. This is the stage in which the students reconstruct past behavior.

While The Ellis School site was being excavated, some students were assigned to the adjacent field lab. Bags containing artifacts were taken from the site to this laboratory area which consisted of four long tables. The artifacts were washed and sent through the laboratory process with a sheet of paper on which

SITE DESIGNATION: _____

DATE: _____

EXCAVATED BY: _____ ASSISTED BY: _____

SQUARE WORKED: (#) _____

FEATURES FOUND OR WORKED: _____

DESCRIPTION: _____

COMMENTS AND OBSERVATIONS ON FEATURES: _____

ARTIFACTS FOUND (BE SPECIFIC IN DESCRIPTION AND SKETCH BELOW)* ____

COMMENTS AND OBSERVATIONS ON ARTIFACTS: _____

INTERPRETATION OF FINDS: _____

*SKETCH:

Figure 15.2. Site form.

Photo 15.1. Students at the Ellis School excavating a simulated site.

Photo 15.2. Students recording the provenience of artifacts in an excavation unit of a simulated site.

the students recorded the stratum and square the artifact came from, and a description, period identification, and drawing of the object (Photo 15.3). Large posters of pottery from various periods of Anasazi history were taped to a wall near the tables so that the students could compare their potsherds to pottery from other sites. They were able to use this information to provide an approximate date for their pottery. The form used is shown in Figure 15.3.

The students put the information from these forms into a database using lap-top computers. There were four computers set up on a table at the end of the laboratory. The students were trained to enter the data into the various fields in the database before the dig. They would eventually be able to paste the digital pictures that they took of artifacts and features into the correct section of the database. The picture would match the artifact description and would be used in the site report.

At the end of one full day of excavation, the students were divided into groups and they put everything back into the box for future excavations. The excavated sand was sifted over a large tarpaulin so that the students could put it back in the box at the conclusion of the dig. They used the site maps and the chief archaeologist's field notebook to place the artifacts in the correct position in the sandbox. This exercise also helped the students understand the context in which the artifacts were found. They did not remove any features from the box. The students worked around each feature and left enough sand to support the feature. The chief archaeologist from each stratum supervised this operation.

After the students returned to the classroom, they wrote a site report using all the evidence collected from the dig. They had site maps, field notebooks, photographs, and all of the site forms, laboratory forms, and the computer database forms on which to base their conclusions. The site report included a site description, an analysis of excavation methods, and a detailed section on excavation finds, including drawings of features and artifacts, photographs, and a clear description of artifacts.

The students wrote their conclusions strictly based on the evidence found during the excavation and attempted to answer their research questions using this data. They then compared their data to similar material found on other sites and to relevant ethnographic material. The procedures the students used for preparing their site report were as described in Figure 15.4.

This unit on archaeology at Ellis is five weeks long, and the actual excavation takes a full day. On the day of the dig (usually the third week in September) the students are excused from other classes so they can spend the day excavating, working in the laboratory, and putting the dig back together for the next year.

Photo 15.3. "Laboratory" processing of artifacts recovered from the simulated site excavation at The Ellis School.

STRATUM_____ SQUARE_____

ARTIFACT DESCRIPTION

ARTIFACT IDENTIFICATION

DRAWING

Figure 15.3. Identification form.

A site report must include procedures used during the excavation, a list of artifacts and features discovered, and conclusions based on the excavated data. The sections of the report should be as follows:

I. INTRODUCTION
The introduction should include information on the reasons for selecting the site, who worked on the site, and the culture of the people who are thought to have occupied the site.

II. SITE DESCRIPTION
Details of the site should be included in this section of the report. Any history that is relevant to the excavation should also be given in this section.

III. METHODOLOGY
In this section there should be complete descriptions of the excavation methods used, the way records were kept, and the forms used to record information.

IV. EXCAVATION FINDS
This section should present evidence and facts about any artifacts and features uncovered during the excavation, and any data that was gathered during the analysis stage of the excavation. Conclusions about the site should not be put in this section.

An unbiased presentation of the discoveries made at the site is required in a final report. This section should be as follows:
    A. Description of the stratigraphy of the site
       1. Report any disturbances
       2. Include the grid map
    B. Report of features (hearths, pits, walls, etc.)
       1. Draw typical features
       2. Illustrate unusual features
       3. Include photographs
    C. Report of artifacts (All of this information has already been put into the computer database. Hard copies of these sheets should be printed for inclusion in this section of the site report)
       1. Clearly describe all objects
       2. State the provenience of the objects (precise vertical and horizontal location in the excavation)
       3. Divide the artifacts into categories
          a. lithics
          b. pottery
          c. bone
          d. wood
       4. Include photographs

V. CONCLUSION
Conclusions should be based strictly on the evidence found during the excavation. Inferences can be drawn from similar material found on other sites and from relevant ethnographic material.

Figure 15.4. Preparation of an archaeological site report.

Assessment

In assessing the value of the simulated excavation at The Ellis School, the students' personal responses to their experience are significant. Comments from the ninth-grade students who excavated our Anasazi site are listed in Tables 15.1 and 15.2. As the students said in their own words, they will remember this experience and will not become the future pothunters of America.

We also used two other methods to assess what students learn about archaeology from different types of programs. Each year, the Pennsylvania Archaeogical Council sponsors an archaeological essay contest. Students are asked to write on the topic "What is an archaeological site and what can we do to protect sites?" Several classes that participated in the contest also participated in archaeological programs in preparation for the contest. Table 15.3 provides a comparison of elementary students' understanding of archaeology derived from having participated in one of the following types of programs:

1. classroom programs given by professional archaeologists;
2. visits to archaeological excavations, primarily to the Archaeology Week excavation on City Island, in Harrisburg, Pennsylvania; or
3. participation in the "Archaeology in Action" simulated excavation program at Bushy Run Battlefield.

The comparison used information provided by the students regarding their understanding of the subject of archaeology and of the activities of archaeologists. The data used for the analysis were collected from two sources: the classes that had an archaeologist visit the classroom and the group that visited the excavation. Instead of being questioned directly about archaeology, both of these fifth-grade classes participated in Pennsylvania's archaeology week essay contest. Essays submitted for the 1995 contest in which students were asked to explain what archaeological sites are and why it is important to protect them were used for the analysis. In addition, a third-grade class that had attended the simulation program at Bushy Run was asked to answer two questions: (1) What is archaeology? and (2) What do archaeologists do?

While these groups differ in age and length of time spent in understanding archaeological concepts and follow-up, each of these programs were conducted by the same archaeologist. All of the responses were then reviewed and are summarized in Table 15.3.

In general, the groups of students had similar ideas about archaeology after participating in the various programs. Archaeology is firmly associated with excavation for all of the students. This is certainly not a surprising result since in all of these activities, archaeologists either show slides of excavations, show an actual excavation, or direct a simulated excavation. The differences are in the level of detail about archaeological investigations gained by the students' view of

TABLE 15.1

The Ellis School Student Responses to the Question
"What did you learn about archaeology?"

"I learned the importance of all records, especially site maps, because once you move the stuff, it is out of context/association forever. I also learned about the different jobs—washing, bagging, digging."

"It is very destructive. If you goof and take an artifact out before it gets recorded you can never put it back in the exact way it was."

"I learned that archaeologists are more thorough than you think. They aren't all Indiana Jones like I dreamed they would be."

"You can't just learn archaeology from a book, there is so much to learn, like excavating and washing the artifacts."

"I learned that archaeology is not just digging in the dirt, archaeology is difficult, particularly the identification process."

"I learned that there is a lot more to it than just a few weeks of digging up artifacts. I didn't realize there was so much recording—it was so carefully done."

TABLE 15.2

The Ellis School Student Responses to the Question:
"Do you like this form of hands-on learning?"

"Yes definitely, it was so much fun. I usually can't remember everything I read in the sheets, but I will and do remember everything from the dig."

"Yes, I learned so much at the dig, stuff that I didn't quite understand from the notes."

"Yes, very much—you had to apply everything you learned."

"Definitely! This hands-on experience taught me more in a day than I learned the whole time in the classroom."

"Yes, it is more realistic than learning from books."

"I love it! Can we do this every Monday?"

Note: Photographs and a description of The Ellis School Simulated Excavation can be found on The Ellis School Social Sciences Department Web site: http://www.ellis.k12.pa.us/WorldClass/sites09/html

archaeology. For example, 20% of the students who visited the excavation on City Island still associated archaeology with finding dinosaurs—the same percentage as indicated archaeology is about people in the past.

More revealing is the question about what archaeologists do. While all of the students report that archaeologists dig, 54% of the students who participated in the simulation connect this with the archaeologist studying, recreating, or learning about the past. It is also interesting to note that the students who heard the speaker and the group who visited the site had other ideas about archaeologists. The group who heard the speaker strongly connected archaeologists with scientists. Sixteen percent of the site visit group had a view of archaeologists as detectives collecting clues.

TABLE 15.3
Comparison of Student Ideas about Archaeology
After Three Types of Classrom Programs

Archaeology is about . . .	Speaker	Site visit	Simulation
People in the past	12 (27%)	11 (20%)	7 (20%)
Research	0 (0%)	0 (0%)	1 (3%)
Finding things	11 (24%)	7 (16%)	3 (7%)
Digging up things	21 (47%)	22 (39%)	19 (54%)
Dinosaurs	1 (2%)	11 (20%)	1 (3%)
Fossils	0 (0%)	5 (9%)	4 (11%)
Total	45	56	35
What do archaeologists do?			
Study the past	21 (47%)	22 (45%)	14 (54%)
Dig	10 (22%)	12 (24%)	9 (35%)
Find things	5 (11%)	4 (8%)	2 (8%)
Investigate clues	2 (4%)	9 (18%)	1 (4%)
Make great discoveries	0 (0%)	2 (4%)	0 (0%)
Archaeologists are scientists	7 (16%)	(0%)	(0%)
Total	45	49	26

Conclusions

As archaeologists and teachers develop programs about archaeology, we need to be aware of the messages that we will leave with our audiences. Even when we are most clear about our subject, a sizable minority of our listeners will retain the misconceptions they already hold. Each time we ask students to participate in an elaborate archaeological exercise, such as a simulated excavation, however, we come closer to making students aware of the complexity of an archaeological investigation.

Chapter Sixteen

Digging with Kids
Teaching Students to Touch the Past

Perhaps no issue in public archaeology has engendered more debate—indeed, more outright hostility between members of the profession—as whether or not educational programs involving kids should be conducted on real archaeological sites.

It's not a topic on which many archaeologists remain neutral. Opponents of the concept contend that hands-on excavation programs endanger the resource, waste valuable time and money that could be spent on much-needed research, teach kids the wrong thing—that all archaeologists do is dig—and promote the idea that public archaeology projects will "create a generation of pothunters." Proponents cite the proven educational impact of hands-on and experiential education in a variety of fields, the potential for attitudinal change offered by involving children in heritage conservation at a young age, and the importance of public interaction with professional archaeologists within the actual research context, so that archaeologists are the one interpreting their own discipline directly, rather than through the various media.

So doing real archaeology with kids is not without its down side. It's nerve wracking, potentially dangerous, and likely to get you lynched by your colleagues the first time a member of the media doesn't read your press release and publishes a headliner that reads "Schoolkids dig for buried treasure!"

So why do it at all? In the preceding two chapters of this volume, Hawkins and Chiarulli et al. have made excellent cases for nonintrusive archaeology education programming. Both offer compelling cases for using alternative means for transmitting archaeological information, without encouraging children to think that excavating real sites is something in which they or their classmates ought to engage during the summer holidays. This chapter offers another perspective; it shows that a carefully crafted system of data recovery and recording, coupled with a comprehensive curriculum based on sound pedagogical principles can produce a superb experiential learning experience for kids, and excellent archaeological research at the same time.

Thus, although I concur with my colleagues as to the validity and value of their respective approaches, we have an important point of divergence: I think that in certain, very special cases, and only in those cases, archaeological techniques and ethics are actually best taught by real archaeologists in the context of a real archaeological site. There is simply no other method that has this kind of educational impact. It can be done, and done well, while archaeologists operate a full-scale research excavation at the same time. This is predicated on a number of conditions being met and on the premise that the people running the program are well versed in both archaeological education principles and in pedagogy in its own right. In other words, they are archaeology educators who have a clear sense of what they are trying to teach in the on-site program, how they are going to teach it, how they are going to ensure the safety and well-being of both the site and their neophyte excavation crew, and what they intend each and every student participant to go away with at the end of the day (and it shouldn't be an artifact!).

As an acknowledged hard-liner of the proexcavation school, I could not pass up the opportunity offered here to present some basic information about hands-on archaeology programs in the field and how they can be effectively and productively conducted. Yes, it is possible to do good, scientific research in a fully public context. Yes, there are ways of informing children and adult visitors alike that "archaeology is more than a dig." Yes, I believe that doing archaeology with kids can be a rewarding experience for both the children and your site stratigraphy. But it is expensive, it is very labor intensive, and it requires enormous dedication to the tenets of both professional archaeology and professional education to make it a viable means of transmitting the stewardship message to a large proportion of the population. It is not something that can be done on every site; it is not something that should be carried out by every archaeologist. But, in the right place and at the right time, doing archaeology with kids is the single most effective means both for marketing our professional goals and ethics to the general public, and for ensuring that children are exposed in appropriate and effective ways to the method and theory of archaeological research. The clearest rationale for doing public, educational archaeology with real live student participants is that hands-on programs engenders a sense of ownership of, and value for, fragile heritage resources that no amount of preaching or teaching can match.

In the early 1980s, when I first started doing archaeology education in the field, what I was doing in downtown Toronto was not new. The programs at Crow Canyon Archaeological Center and The Center for American Archaeology at Kampsville, Illinois, were under way. Dedicated teachers and archaeologists all over North America and beyond had been working together for years, offering individual programs on individual sites scattered across the continent. However, since I was completely unaware of the existence of such programs, in good crusading spirit, the

Toronto Archaeological Resource Centre was established. Meeting with great interest from the education profession, and with a certain degree of success with raising money to do public archaeqqology through the school system itself in downtown Toronto, I was unprepared for the storm of criticism that descended on me from my professional colleagues. They really hated the idea.

While we veterans of public archaeology's pioneering days are grateful for the criticism and for the questions now, I didn't appreciate my colleagues' skepticism at the time. Operating a large-scale public archaeology program in the center of Canada's largest city, in the nation's biggest school board, within what the UN has designated the "most multicultural city in the world," was challenge enough without having to deal with potshots from archaeologists who considered doing archaeology with kids as something akin to having school children carry out brain surgery.

But opponents to public archaeology were, to a great degree, expressing the same kinds of concern that dedicated professionals do whenever there is significant change in method or approach in any discipline. They wanted to make sure that the archaeological resource was protected, and that the public perception of their discipline was one that reflected truth rather than the highly romanticized fiction portrayed by such media as the Indiana Jones films that were just coming out at the time. I knew that good, effective educational archaeology would achieve the stated goals of both archaeology and education. But I had to prove it to my colleagues. And this, more than anything else, made the ARC's staff, to borrow an expression from the New Agers, "live—and work—consciously."

The program to which I am referring is, of course, the late and lamented Archaeological Resource Centre (ARC) of the Toronto Board of Education. The ARC was the 1993 victim of a reorganization of the Metro Toronto school system, coupled with its own success. (It got more publicity than all other school programs combined, so it was a good demonstration piece when budget cuts came around. Logic at the board's executive level held that the public would notice that the board was downsizing if it cut its highest-profile public program.)

For many years, the Centre was the only school board-based hands-on archaeology education facility in the world. Under the supervision of a core staff of seven professional archaeologists, a great many archaeology students and professionals, teachers and administrative staff from the educational system, and members of the general public from fourth grade through senior citizens participated in, honed, and changed the programs of the ARC over its nine-year existence. It was a wonderful laboratory for the development of hands-on archaeology programs, and because it operated both in the public eye and under the gaze of highly critical professional colleagues, it was better than it might have been. I am grateful to those critics—they forced us to test, prove, and articulate every goal and objective; hone every program; and polish our method and theory to a high shine so that we could prove that archaeology education was a Good Thing (Smardz 1990, 1991, 1997; Fagan 1995).

Of course, not everyone was agin' us. We had lots of help from professional educators at all levels of the school board, so that every aspect of the curriculum reflected the best and latest of pedagogical method and theory. Strong support from the provincial archaeology authorities at the Ontario Ministry of Culture deflected some of the criticism and provided us with advice and input throughout the ARC's evolution. The generosity of archaeologist and educators alike from not only Canadian and U.S. programs and projects, but from colleagues around the world, ensured a steady influx of information, ideas, and methodological approaches, many of which came to be incorporated into the ARC's curriculum and field strategies. People visited, too, to learn what we were doing and took away with them ideas and approaches and technique of educational archaeology in multicultural settings that influenced program development in many other places, from Zimbabwe and South Africa to Japan.

What did we learn? Doing archaeology in the field, lab, and classroom with schoolchildren and members of the public—more than 10,000 participants per year —taught us a great deal about how to teach archaeology as well as about how people learn about archaeology. We learned that having highly educated professionals in a specific discipline teach their subject to thousands of the uninitiated has many pitfalls, and that we got better at it the more we talked to teachers, curriculum experts, and educational theorists. We discovered, too, that what people hear is not necessarily what you think you are telling them. Since the objective is to have students understand and internalize the archaeological principals you're trying to transmit, it is best if you understand how people absorb and process data, at different ages and ability levels, and in different contexts.

Most of all, we learned that to do educational archaeology effectively, we had to learn to be good educators as well as being good archaeologists. And that pedagogy is a profession thousands of years older than archaeology, with its own rules, beliefs, values, language, and methods.

That said, how does one operate an effective program for kids in the field? Let's look at some of the methods and approaches to public archaeology that are tried and true. This is not meant to be a complete instruction manual, simply a sharing of methods, techniques, and concepts that might help a budding archaeology educator get started. Not all of these come from my own experience—many are learned from other archaeology educators and then tried and proven in my own context. Working together, we all become both better educators and better archaeologists.

Public Archaeology in Context: The Marketing Branch of the Profession

Archaeology education is about the past, the real past. It is about the most primary source material there is—the objects and structures and living spaces and patterns that humans left behind hundreds or thousands of years ago. It is the quest for evidence of that past, and the means for making the silent clues speak to us. Usually, arch- aeologists acquire access to that evidence through excavation. So, most people who think of archaeology think of digging into the ground to discover the remnants of past civilizations. That's what they usually see on TV, read in popular magazines, and view on the Internet about archaeology.

Public archaeologists—people who consciously educate the public about archae- ology and its objectives—often use the romance of discovery inherent in archaeology as what the advertising industry calls a "hook." The idea of recovering mysterious evidence of past cultures and peoples is what makes archaeology exciting, so that is what most of us start with in trying get our unknowledgeable audience in the door. Once we have them, we can teach them that archaeology is a painstaking, careful, and immensely complex process beginning with a hypothesis and ending with some hopefully testable conclusions—the "it's not what we find, but what we find out" underlying archaeological principle, to paraphrase David Hurst Thomas. But the idea of discovering the past on an archaeological site has an undeniable appeal for people of all ages, and it is the first, most familiar, and most attractive idea the majority of people have about archaeology. So that is what public archaeology often uses as the entry point for beginning lessons or media campaigns aimed at ordinary citizens.

Hard as it may be for archaeological purists to swallow, most people think archaeology is about digging anyway. However much archaeologists would like to make everyone believe that "archaeology is more than a dig," the truth is that we our- selves are the ones who have created this impression. We are also the ones who continue to use the romanticism and mystique that goes with the profession as a means for getting public interest, money, and political support for meeting archaeological goals. It's pretty hard to get a newspaper reporter excited about a lab slide of a thin section of pottery at the same time you're sending in that all-important grant application. You show her a dig and some of the neat stuff coming out of the ground, a little interpretation, tastefully presented with just the right degree of scientific gravity, and abracadabra! There's your article (if you're lucky, "above the fold" in a prominent section of the paper) and, hopefully, the grant money.

Given that the most fascinating part of archaeology to the uninitiated is the excavation side of the process, and following the age-old pedagogical adage of "work from what they know to what they don't know," the dig is a pretty logical place for archaeology education to start. Get 'em in the door, get 'em young, and then teach them what archaeology is REALLY about. This is a basic premise behind doing real archaeology with kids, that having schoolchildren take part in a real dig is the best way to engender a sense of awe and wonder about how complex and important archaeological conservation is; how each and every site belongs to all people in any community; and why site damage and destruction, whatever the cause, takes away something real and valuable from every one of us. Digs give archaeology educators a chance to teach both science and stewardship, while getting great publicity to boot.

How does one go about ensuring that the message one is trying to transmit is the one that the students and the public are receiving? A daunting fact of education is that teaching people anything can be a bit like the kids' game of "telephone"; one person speaks into a paper cup with a string on the end and the next person listens to what they have said through a cup on the other end of the string. As you go around the circle, the story changes and then, when told aloud by the final participant, everyone sees how much the original story has changed. As Bilbo said in J.R.R. Tolkein's wonderful book, *The Hobbit,* "the tale grows in the telling." Archaeology education can be like that also. Too many kids have gone home and told their parents that they "dug up a dinosaur bone today" at your archaeological site to believe this isn't an occupational hazard of educational archaeology, if one that we are trying mightily to avoid.

Learning about how people learn is probably the single most important thing an archaeology educator can do. If we understand what messages we are getting across when we craft a public archaeology program to be conducted on a real site, we can develop programs that will actually achieve the effect we want—firmly establishing the stewardship ethic in our multiaged audiences and developing a value and appreciation for the remnants of past cultures that will enhance our students' respect for both living peoples and archaeological remains.

Public field programming is teaching. First and foremost, good education entails the development of effective and relevant curriculum materials, coordinated and cohesive lesson plans (which are followed!), and a clear understanding of our own educational objectives in offering the programs in the first place. These are concepts far from what archaeologists usually think about when they set out to dig a site. When one does experiential archaeology programs that involve excavation, one needs to develop a project that integrates both good archaeological method and theory and pedagogical method and theory. This has to be prepared well in advance, with the aid of expert help from the teaching profession.

Frankly, archaeologists who decide to "have a few schoolkids in for the day —we'll just let them screen" often do more harm than good in enhancing public perceptions of archaeology and archaeologists. Or do we want them to go away thinking that "archaeologists do all the fun parts themselves, but we found neat treasures in the screen"?

When archaeologists enter the field of pedagogy, we are borrowing methods, theory, and skills that took thousands of years to evolve. Education is a much older discipline than is archaeology, and it should not be entered lightly by would-be archaeology educators. Fortunately, educators are generous with their time and their information about how to teach, and they're really interested in the multidisciplinary educational potential of archaeology as well. Working together, we can do an excellent job of teaching archaeological principles to schoolchildren and do good field archaeology at the same time.

Doing Field Archaeology with Kids

There are several basic principles of archaeology education in the field context that are tried and true. They won't all work in every context or on every site. But they are tested methods that generally have the desired effect—they help you conduct real and scientifically sound archaeological digs, with dozens if not hundreds of schoolaged children not only looking on, but digging in.

Program Design

1. Begin your program with the design of a full-scale educational curriculum that meets the needs of professional educators who will be bringing their students to your site. Work with teachers, curriculum consultants, and others to discover the educational priorities in your nation, state or province, local school district, and school so that what you are teaching fits what the kids are learning elsewhere and how they are being taught (Macdonald and Burtness, and Davis, this volume).
2. Have clearly defined educational goals for each phase of the program you are going to offer. Most archaeologists doing their first hands-on program try to teach far too much in too short a space of time. The kids don't need to remember every attribute of Mimbres pottery. They need to know that archaeologists differentiate period and culture through examination of the art and technologies represented in pottery. Make sure the examples you use result in the children comprehending the concept rather than the particulars.
3. Try and define three concepts with which you want each child to leave your site and stick to teaching students skills and approaches regarding those three concepts. Examples might be: Archaeology uses scientific methods to collect clues that help us learn more about people who lived in the past; archaeological sites are destroyed by digging them; everyone has a responsibility to keep archaeological remains safe.
4. The tried-and-true method for lesson planning is the "who, what, when, where, how" approach. It greatly resembles the "scientific method" you used in lab experiments in high school:

   WHO   Who is your audience, what is appropriate to their age and ability levels, what do they already know, and what can they learn in this space of time?

   WHAT   What do you want them to know when they depart from your program?

WHEN   What is the timeframe you have available, and how are you going to structure the lessons so the kids meet your learning objectives within that time?

WHERE   What are the advantages and disadvantages of the learning context?

        You're in the field—how many kids can you get into that excavation unit without having the stratigraphy compromised? How can you use topography, nearby resources and settlement pattern data to demonstrate how people lived here in the past?

WHY   In what way will what you are trying to teach benefit the children who are your audience? (If you can't answer this question—and the old "enhancing their quality of life" isn't enough anymore—then you need to clarify your teaching objectives much more thoroughly.)

HOW   What are the methods of teaching you are going to use, and how are you going to ensure the information you transmit is what the students receive? What methods of reinforcement are you going to use to ensure that they learned it, and how will you assess the program after it is completed?

5. Provide clear, concise directions for each activity in which you want students to engage. Make sure every supervisor is using similar methods of transmitting these ideas.

6. Set a strict timetable so that each child has an opportunity to participate in all phases of the program and make sure that staff are familiar with your learning and teaching objectives for every activity before you bring your first group of kids on-site.

7. Hire your staff with public archaeology in mind. Individuals, however expert they may be in excavation or other site skills, who do not enjoy working with the public will do considerably more harm than good in a public education context. A happy, enthusiastic set of site supervisors is the critical component of a successful public archaeology project.

Preproject Liaison with Teachers and Students

1. An important aspect of your educational program is the development of introductory materials for the teacher to use before the site visit. Children should have a clear idea of your expectations for them when they participate in the archaeology program, as well as a sense of the purposes of the project as a whole. Background information on the cultural group represented at the site, an explanation of the process in which they are going to participate, and a short synopsis of what you, the archaeologist, intend to learn from the excavation can be included in the previsit packet. So can a list of site rules.

2. Don't focus introductory materials on purely verbal or lecture-type presentation. Reading levels vary widely, as does language comprehension. Quizzes and games and lessons that involve doing (such as laying out objects on a tile floor and then transferring the information to graph paper), and role-play exercises are far more effective with children (and adults) than simply providing a sheet for the teacher to read to the class.

3. Make sure that students know what to wear and bring—hard-soled shoes, sunblock, hats, water bottles, bug spray if needed, and so on.

4. Be sure you know of any important allergies or illnesses among the children. Creating a health form for parents to fill in is one way of dealing with this issue. You need to know if children are allergic to bee stings, for instance. In some areas, forms to parents may need to be in a variety of languages—consult the teacher on this matter. Schools may have all this information on file, or have field trip forms made up for the purpose, already translated into the appropriate languages represented by the student population.

5. Having a cell phone on site is mandatory for any public program, even in an urban location. Emergencies can happen anywhere.

6. If you expect the media during a program, have a publicity photo form for parents to fill in for every child before they come to the site. You need to know if there is a reason why certain children or their names should not appear in newspaper or television coverage. Sometimes children's lives may be endangered if you forget this step—it's really important.

Setting Up the Excavation for Public Archaeology

1. Choose a site that is suitable for public archaeology programming. This means that it's suitable for both the purposes of archaeology and of education. It needs to be physically accessible, not actively dangerous (i.e., not a salvage site with bulldozers on the periphery, or a very deep site with unstable underlying layers), and sufficiently interesting to engage and hold the attention of nonarchaeologists. In practical terms, this means that the kids are going to find something, and are likely to be able to understand what their findings might mean. The significance of negative evidence is very hard to explain to a nine year old who has worked all day in the hot sun. Choose sites where you expect a reasonable amount of artifactual evidence, preferably in the context of comprehensible features and stratigraphy. It's hard to hold the attention of kids when they have no idea what you're talking about and when there isn't enough evidence in the ground for them to even imagine what life used to be like for the people who occupied the site in the past.

2. Choose a site that has a comprehensible "story" attached to it, either one that you know because of historical documentation or oral tradition, or one where you can build up a set of images about what people did there in the past based on the evidence you uncover. Humanize the findings as you go. Most people think archaeology is about people—it is. Let's not be so scientific that we forget to explain our findings in clear English, so that we help our audience

understand what our findings may mean in a given context. Archaeologists are the only ones who believe that pottery "migrates" all by itself—don't forget the people behind the objects.

3. Don't mix your messages or your objectives. If you intend to teach good, careful archaeological process to your students, don't try and run an educational archaeology project on a salvage site unless you have a very long timeframe. Encouraging children to work slowly and carefully is not compatible with their watching a bulldozer cut trenches across another part of the site. Likewise, having kids piece plot (which is an excellent way to teach technique and math at the same time) doesn't make sense if you have archaeologists shoveling into screens within full view of the class.

4. Lay out your site with the educational program in mind. Do you need a wider walkway in one area to allow for site tours, moving wheelbarrows to a screen, or simply walking kids from one place to another? Are 1 x 1 meter squares appropriate for the physical size of the children you will be teaching? Sometimes trenches divided into one meter intervals with string are easier to supervise and for the kids to see what they are doing, for instance. They can kneel on either side of the trench, and your supervisors can watch every pair of hands at once. You won't be drummed out of the archaeology club for digging in differently sized units than the ones you used in field school, lo those many years ago!

5. Deep units are not suitable generally. They're dangerous, hard to see in, and tend to fill with water when it rains. Sites with a lot of shallow demolition rubble (for historic work) plus some deeper units where more experienced volunteers and archaeology staff are exposing structural features might provide a good context for a public archaeology dig. The resource is being impacted by public programming in shallower layers while comprehensible structural findings are being recovered in deeper units, benefiting both the scientific and educational goals of the project. Yet, everyone is doing "real" archaeology, which is key to maintaining the educational impact of the program.

6. Make sure that the needs of the children and volunteers are met appropriately. People do not learn well if they are uncomfortable or frightened. Providing large enough digging units, using smaller buckets for smaller people to carry; not having the backdirt pile too high for little people to climb carrying buckets; using relatively shallow excavation units and keeping poison ivy, insects, and pesticides away from the edges of excavation areas all contribute to the students' concentrating on the dig program rather than on the degree of physical discomfort they are experiencing.

7. Match methods to your site context and to the fact that you have a public program in operation. Be creative. You don't have to do everything the way you first learned how to in university. For instance, on one very large site, I experimented with using spaghetti strainers beside each unit to screen each trowelful of dirt into the buckets. The sifted dirt was then dumped into strategically placed wheelbarrows later removed by staff, rather than having dozens of people walking over baulks all the time. This was important for site preservation, but also provided an opportunity to text excavation programs for

physically challenged children. They didn't have to leave their unit, but still experienced each aspect of the archaeological process.
8. Safety is always first. Small people dehydrate quickly, so make sure they drink lots of water. Have regular bathroom breaks, provide shade, and make sure kids come equipped with hats and sunblock. Have a good first aid kit and trained staff who know how to deal with emergencies. Clean, accessible bathroom facilities are a must; some school districts require the availability of separate boys' and girls' facilities, so check the regulations before you set up your site. And don't forget liability insurance. Make sure the school or organization that is bringing the groups to the site has insurance and inform your company (in writing) that the excavation will include children.
9. Make your site as safe as possible. Stakes with nails sticking up can put out an eye. Lay strings flat, pound in nails, and set datum points flush with the ground. Look around your site with the eyes of a parent—what could possibly hurt a child? Then fix whatever it is. No site, artifact, or project is worth a serious injury to one of your participants.

Tips and Techniques for Public Archaeologists

1. Understand that young people have short attention spans. Vary the activities and the skills being taught and the method of teaching. Keep the lesson parts short, have kids rotate through a series of different activities, and help them feel a sense of accomplishment at each level.
2. There are many aspects of the actual excavation process in which kids can participate. In general, working with trowels and having children map every artifact in place works very well for conveying the care taken by archaeologists in recording their data, and for teaching two-coordinate graphing skills at the same time. I use meter sticks rather than tape measures because they are easier for little hands to manage. Screening is well within their grasp, but remember that children do not know what a flake looks like and have no experience with tiny bits of pottery, so maintain a sharp eye on their screens. Moving children between excavation and screening activities helps keep them interested, while an artifact table showing items already recovered will help them understand what they are looking for.
3. Remember: You are not trying to create young archaeologists, but to expose kids to how the process of archaeology helps us learn about the past. Have clear pedagogical objectives for every lesson and include appropriate means for assessing whether students have assimilated the information, skills, and concepts before moving on to the next stage. Sum up and reinforce the lessons at the end of the educational session, so the kids go away feeling they have not only learned something new, but have accomplished something while they were learning it.
4. Age and ability levels affect how people learn concepts and both acquire and practice skills. Work with professional educators to ensure that your lessons and program are age- and skill-level appropriate. Everyone can benefit from

archaeological education programming (it's not just for gifted students), but your expectations of what a specific class can accomplish cannot outstrip what their abilities will permit (Wolynec, this volume). That's discouraging for everyone. Make sure that everyone understands what you expect them to do, then encourage them to enjoy the process of discovery. The best educational experience is one that the students enjoy and one where they feel they are achieving a significant goal through their participation.

5. Don't tell kids that the methods and procedures are too complex for them to engage in—that's insulting and makes people defiant ("I can go do this myself, if they won't let me do it here!"). Using clear, simple recording forms rather than notebooks, having kids learn how to piece plot before they put artifacts in bags, and having them write their own names beside the word "excavator" on both notes and bags helps children understand that heritage conservation is a responsibility that everyone has in a society, and that everyone can contribute to preserving our past. Archaeology staff can augment the notes later, but I am a firm believer in having people do things that are REAL, not simplified or created especially for them.

6. You catch more flies with honey than vinegar. Tell kids "what a good job" they are doing, and that "it might be even better if they try it this way," for instance. Admonishing kids for not being expert excavators during their first experience is discouraging for them and creates a very unpleasant atmosphere for the operation of the program. Kids should feel like they are achieving something positive. Don't let a class go away feeling that the whole process is beyond them.

7. On the other hand, don't make it a game. Archaeology is a scientific discipline that, while fun to do, has an important series of skills and methods that have to be applied by every participant. It is critical that kids do not see this as an educational exercise set up for their benefit, and that they see you, the archaeologist, as a professional with specialized knowledge. Hammering this home helps contribute to both the learning process and to making sure that kids go away with the idea that they can't go out and start a dig in their own backyard. Archaeology can be education per se, but it should never be "edutainment," unless you *do* want to create a generation of pothunters.

The End of the Lesson

1. Explain what you're going to do with all this information after the dig is finished (I usually use an artifact-handling and discussion session to show students how archaeologists date, analyze, and interpret site findings). Make sure that all your participants understand that archaeologists spend much more time in the lab than they do in the field, and that every artifact, map, photo, and other piece of data is going to be used to help interpret what people used to do at this site, a long time ago.

2. Always thank students and volunteers for helping "to save the past for the future" by participating in your dig. Make them feel privileged for having the opportunity to do this special thing with real archaeologists—not in an

arrogant way, but so as to engender respect—so that kids go away feeling special and also that this is NOT something they can just go out and do in their own backyard.
3. Give them something to take home—a button or badge or label. This enhances the students' experience while giving them a centerpiece for discussing with parents, siblings, and friends the exciting experience they had on an archaeological dig. Not only do you increase the educational impact of your program on the student, but the things he or she learned will be transmitted to the child's entire family circle. Marketing the message of stewardship is the point, and this really helps.

It's helpful to provide follow-up materials for the teacher or even to invite students to view a display in a public location that demonstrates what the excavation produced in the way of new information about their community's past. If at all possible, students should be involved in the artifact-processing and identification phase of your project. This reinforces their involvement and demonstrates that archaeology is, indeed, more than a dig. Don't worry, washing bits of ceramics in a bucket of cold water with a toothbrush is well within the abilities of a fourth-grade child. Data entry, sorting, identification of objects using reference collections and typology books, and certain conservation activities are skills-based learning exercises that teachers will be pleased to have you conduct with their students.

It is important to convey a sense that the children have actually contributed to heritage conservation during their time at the site, and that they can be active in stewardship efforts in the future. Again, if at all possible, students should have a chance to learn what you have discovered from analyzing the site data. The likelihood of their reading your site report is, ah, limited, so providing easily accessible follow-up information for all your program participants is both good archaeology education and good marketing for archaeology in general.

Conclusions

There are literally dozens of other components to the operation of public archaeology projects that have not been discussed here. I have concentrated on those elements that will help ensure a successful educational experience for your young participants. Excellent research results can be obtained from projects where such programs are offered, provided the staff maintains vigilant watch over students who take part. The excavation will be remarkably slow (it's rather like digging with a teaspoon), but if you convey to the children that you are trusting them to do a careful job, and that they are going to be the very first person to touch an artifact that has been in the ground for a hundred or a thousand or ten thousand years, you will find that the archaeology education program is an asset, not a liability, in the real site milieu. Besides, there is nothing that earns the interest and support of a politician more effectively than inviting him or her down to the site to excavate alongside the grandchildren. Guaranteed grant-getting material, I assure you.

One very important aspect that I have not discussed is how to deal with the media while you are operating a program for forty hormonally challenged eighth graders on your site. The key is keeping the kids focused and being well prepared yourself—press kits already made up, a special box of artifacts found at the site around which you can center an interview, and some general statements to which you and your staff all agree in advance, will go a long way to making a media visit a positive event for your and your little diggers (Comer, this volume).

I hope that I have conveyed that archaeology education can include on-site programming that is successful, effective, and practical. It is, as you can see from the points I have given, time consuming, expensive, and very demanding on your staff. The operation of a public archaeology project that includes school participation is a value judgment that has to be made in light of your objectives as an archaeology educator. If you have a suitable site, sufficient means, and a supportive community atmosphere, by all means do archaeology in public, with the public. It's incredibly rewarding, and ensures that everyone who takes part goes away feeling that archaeology is important to them, personally, and that anyone who destroys or loots an archaeological site is removing something of immense value from our collective community heritage. That's why I do public archaeology, anyway.

Basically, when it comes to the "to dig or not to dig" debate, we have a choice as archaeological educators: We can meet the expectations that our own profession has established in the minds of the public, or we can attempt the (difficult at best) task of altering what the public has been told that it should expect from archaeology. You see, the archaeological profession is at least partially guilty of creating the image of archaeologist-as-seeker-of-ancient-treasure. We can't entirely blame Hollywood or the popular press for this impression.

What do we read in the newspapers, hear on the radio, or see on TV whenever archaeologists are interviewed? "See what I dug up at this really neat site? It's the oldest/biggest/most mummified/most Biblically correct set of artifacts/things/goodies in the oldest/biggest/most culturally advanced/most-likely-to-make-my-career ancient site that you can possibly imagine! And here's a picture of me digging it up!" I hope the more conscientious of my colleagues will forgive me, but you must admit that there is enough of this kind of media coverage to ensure that millions of ordinary people are going to want to come out and dig up neat things, too.

We can try and alter this perception and steer our audiences into the ways of righteousness by teaching them that archaeology is a destructive process, so we are always seeking new and better ways to explore our heritage without excavation, that excavation is only one aspect of a long research process that follows the scientific method, and that data recovery ought to be done only by trained and experienced archaeologists. Or we can take our audience into the field with us, demonstrate through structured and well-supervised experiential learning the scientific approach that archaeologists take to data recovery and conservation, and try to transmit the same messages in the most realistic learning environment possible—the actual archaeological site.

As archaeology educators, we have a range of teaching opportunities— computer and Web-generated lessons; media articles, be they books, films or interviews; classroom, museum, archaeological park, or field trip teaching; archaeology kits and laboratory experiences; simulated excavations; and actual participatory public dig programs. As we have seen throughout this book, all of these have great value and each is suitable to a different teaching environment and to meeting a specific set of educational goals.

In my view, good archaeological education encompasses all these methods of reaching and teaching our public. I do not and never have recommended hands-on digging programs where even the tiniest part of a real site is sacrificed for educational purposes, nor do I believe that participatory programs should be offered in any but the most highly structured, well-supervised, and thoroughly thought-out combined research and public education program. That said, there is a place for the public archaeology excavation, complete with hands-on program opportunities for people aged eight to eighty. This kind of project, properly executed and appropriately publicized, achieves a level of popular understanding and support that is almost unattainable by any other means. You just have to be very, very careful how you do it.

In the final analysis, perhaps the most important part of the teaching you do at the site may be to make sure that every group of kids has a happy memory of their day at the archaeological dig. After all, this may be the only experience each of those children may have, ever, of an archaeological site. In fact, *you* may be the only archaeologist those children will ever meet—so their impression of archaeology for the rest of their lives may rest on your performance. A daunting thought, isn't it?

Chapter Seventeen

Archaeology and Values
Respect and Responsibility
for Our Heritage

Archaeology education has many goals: to demonstrate scientific processes; to show how archaeology contributes to scientific and historic knowledge; and to connect people to their own heritage, to name a few. However, the most important endeavor for much of the emerging field of archaeology education is to teach citizens to value the tangible evidence of the past, sites and artifacts, and to protect them (Smith 1991b; Smith et al. 1996; Moe 1999). Archaeology educators teach people that there are laws protecting antiquities and more important, why these laws exist. In other words, we are teaching people to respect our shared cultural heritage and to behave responsibly in regard to archaeological sites and artifacts.

While archaeologists have been busy developing and implementing programs to promote appreciation of archaeological resources, some educators have been seriously reexamining the role of moral education in schools and how values are transmitted to children (see Nucci 1989; Lickona 1991; Kilpatrick 1992; Wynne and Ryan 1997). They cite growing crime rates, drug use, and pregnancy among young people as evidence of moral decline in the United States and throughout much of the Western world. They contend that values should be taught in schools and that instilling ethics in young people is both achievable and necessary.

The implications of the renewed interest in values education for archaeology education are significant. There are new opportunities for including archaeology in the curriculum, especially archaeological protection. At the same time, we need to evaluate the effectiveness of existing archaeology curricula and find out if it meets the needs of classroom educators.

History of Values Education

Values have always been a part of education, whether by design or default. Hence, the history of values education is as long as the history of education itself. Since Plato and Aristotle, Western societies "have made moral education a deliberate aim of schooling" (Lickona 1991:6). Thomas Jefferson, Benjamin Franklin, and other founders of the United States recognized that morality was essential to democracy and must be instilled at an early age. John Dewey, the great early twentieth-century philosopher of education, probably said it best:

> The devotion of democracy to education is a familiar act. The superficial explanation is that a government resting upon popular suffrage cannot be successful unless those who elect and who obey their governors are educated. Since a democracy repudiates the principle of external authority, it must find a substitute in voluntary disposition and interest; these can be created only by education. But there is a deeper explanation. A democracy is more than a form of government; it is primarily a mode of associated living, of conjoint communicated experience. [1963:87]

Similarly, early twentieth-century French sociologist Emile Durkheim (1962) recognized the importance of moral education for society. And in *Look to the Mountain*, Gregory Cajete (1994), an Indian educator, demonstrates that most of Indian education is moral education.

In recent decades, two approaches to values education have dominated the field: values clarification (Raths et al. 1966; Simon et al. 1972) and moral reasoning or moral dilemmas (Blatt and Kohlberg 1975; Kohlberg 1976, 1978). Archaeology educators, along with most other educators, have adopted these approaches to make students aware of problems in archaeological conservation and to help them determine appropriate behavior regarding protection of sites (Smith et al. 1996). Both approaches have come under severe criticism in the last decade. Concomitantly, accepted practices in values education have evolved and archaeology educators need to move forward along with everyone else.

Values Clarification

Values clarification appeared on the education scene during the late 1960s and was used extensively during the 1970s. Its proponents realized that didactic methods such as lecturing or moralizing or simple slogans do little or nothing to transmit ethics and morals, so they focused on thinking processes instead. In values clarification, students go through a seven-step process and determine and clarify their own set of values (Raths et al. 1966; Simon et al. 1972). There is no distinction between right and wrong. The teacher is merely the facilitator of the process and must accept whatever values the students choose.

So what does the teacher do if the students arrive at the wrong value? What if a student determines that cheating or stealing is all right? Or that vandalizing an archaeological site is acceptable behavior? Over the years, many teachers have faced this problem (Lickona 1991:10–11) and the approach offers no way to address the discrepancy between the student's chosen value and widely held ethics or the laws of the land. For this reason, values clarification has been largely discredited as an effective form of moral education. It was well researched and widely used but didn't work very well because it was based on the idea that values are completely relative. This implies that everyone can do whatever they want, even if it violates the law or hurts someone.

Moral Reasoning

The moral reasoning approach is based on the notion that children go through the same stages of moral development just as they go through the same stages of cognitive development (Kohlberg 1976; see also Johnson, this volume). Kohlberg found that progression through the stages was not solely dependent on age and concluded that the child's "moral atmosphere" influenced moral development. Thus, by stimulating moral development, children would advance to a higher moral stage. Moral dilemma discussions were successfully used to stimulate thinking and advance participants to higher stages (Blatt and Kohlberg 1975).

Like values clarification, the moral reasoning approach focuses on thinking processes, thus making it an attractive educational tool. However, it assumes that students already value honesty, property rights, and human life (Kilpatrick 1992:86), and that they have enough information about laws and related issues to make good decisions. In addition, some dilemmas used by Kohlberg and his colleagues have little relation to children's lives and are so problematic that they "would stump Middle East [peace] negotiators" (Kilpatrick 1992:85).

Amy Gutmann recognizes both the positive and negative aspects of moral reasoning in democratic education:

> People adept at logical reasoning who lack moral character are sophists of the worst sort: they use moral arguments to serve whatever ends they happen to chose for themselves. . . . But people who possess sturdy moral character without a developed capacity for reasoning are ruled only by habit and authority. . . . Education in character and moral reasoning are therefore, both necessary, neither sufficient for creating democratic citizens. [1987:51]

Although there can be problems with moral dilemmas, when designed and used properly they are an effective tool for teaching archaeological stewardship, a topic I will discuss in a later section.

Character Education

Beginning around 1990, values education received renewed interest and a new name—character education. Leaders of the character education movement cite rising juvenile crime rates, cheating, peer cruelty, teenage pregnancy, and self-destructive behavior, to name a few, as reasons to teach values again in our schools (Lickona 1991; Kilpatrick 1992; Wynne and Ryan 1997). Judging from the plethora of literature on the subject and a nationwide pilot project (Fink 1997; U.S. Department of Education 1998), character education is one of the hottest topics in education in this decade.

Character education is defined as "the long-term process of helping young people develop good character, i.e., knowing, caring about, and acting upon core ethical values such as fairness, honesty, compassion, responsibility, and respect for self and others" (Character Education Partnership [CEP] n.d.). In a more general sense, it is viewed as a return to traditional values such as respect, responsibility, integrity, honesty, justice, and tolerance; values that are believed to have been lost or diminished in the latter half of the twentieth century (see Box 17.1).

When the subject of teaching values arises, especially in the context of public schools, the first question is usually, "Whose values do we teach?" Character education assumes that universal core values exist. Do they? Many scholars including philosophers, anthropologists, theologians, psychologists, and educators have examined this question (Kluckhohn 1955; Edel and Edel 1968; Redfield 1973; Schirmer 1988; Nucci 1989; Kidder 1994; Bok 1995; Matthews and Riley 1995; Lewis 1996; Wynne and Ryan 1997; Fluehr-Lobban 1998).

In the 1940s, C. S. Lewis (1996:30–31) identified basic concepts and values that connected past civilizations in a common morality, which he called the *Tao*. Rushworth Kidder (1994), founder of the Institute for Global Ethics, interviewed hundreds of individuals from many different countries and cultural and ethnic groups. He asked them what they valued most. From the interviews, he identified eight universal values: love, truthfulness, fairness, freedom, unity, tolerance, responsibility, and respect for life (Kidder 1994:309–320). In a chapter entitled "Cultural Diversity and Common Values," Sissela Bok (1995:12–23), a Harvard University ethicist, identified three widely recognized values that are necessary to human survival: mutual support, loyalty, and reciprocity; restraint from harmful action; and fairness and justice in cases of conflict. Larry P. Nucci (1989), a developmental psychologist, found that children form similar and strongly held values regarding justice andcompassion regardless of specific religious affiliation or even a complete lack of religious affiliation.

BOX 17.1
The 24 Values Identified by Baltimore's Task Force on Values Education and Ethical Behavior (CEP n.d.)

compassion
courtesy
critical inquiry
due process
equality of opportunity
freedom of thought and action
honesty
human worth and dignity
integrity
justice
knowledge
loyalty
objectivity
order
patriotism
rational consent
reasoned argument
respect for others
responsibility
responsible citizenship
rule of law
self-respect
tolerance
truth

Note: Within the character education movement, values taught vary from school to school and even teacher to teacher, but the two that top most lists are respect for others and responsibility.

Anthropologists have long recognized the vast cultural differences in accepted conduct and assume that those diverse practices are ultimately based on culturally held values. However, many anthropologists share the view that a common moral base can be found (e.g., Edel and Edel 1968:27–28; Schirmer] 1988). Clyde Kluckhohn (1955:669) asks: "Are there universals or near universals of any sort that cut across cultural boundaries?" and answers it as follows: "There is good agreement that there are—in some form or other." Kluckhohn points out the universality of moral standards in general and shows that cultural patterns (such as the ubiquity of the family unit) are very similar. Robert Redfield explores the universally human and culturally variable and concludes that "[T]here is a central tendency, a disposition, for the content of all moralities to vary around basic similarities" (1973:143). In examining the interface between cultural relativism, the idea that practices must be studied within their cultural context, and universal human rights, Carolyn Fluehr-Lobban uses the idea of "avoidance of harm" as a key standard: "When reasonable persons from different cultural backgrounds agree that certain institutions or cultural practices cause harm, then the moral neutrality of cultural relativism must be suspended" (1998:16).

It is possible to affirm the common values of a nation, such the belief of most Western nations that it is the citizen's responsibility to participate in a democratic government, and respect diversity at the same time.

> People in different cultures will never come to share any one of the complex religious and political traditions that have evolved over many centuries; and we shouldn't want this to happen. The uniqueness of so many different traditions enriches all of our cultural heritage, and cultural diversity may be as important as biological diversity for the purposes of surviving and thriving. [Bok 1995:23]

Archaeology has long been used to teach cultural diversity and tolerance. "Public archaeology is an educational vehicle and device through which we learn tolerance, banish fear of diversity, and acquire knowledge that helps us deal with the multicultural populations that make up our present world" (Smardz 1995:15; see also Wolynec, this volume). Perhaps, even more important, archaeology can help students understand and embrace the commonalities of being human, including our widely shared values (Messenger and Enloe 1991; Smith et al. 1996).

Values are formed within a community. Think back to your own childhood and remember how your values were formed. You may recall ethical lessons learned within your family or perhaps in the classroom or school, or within a group such as 4-H, Boy Scouts, or a church group. Not surprisingly, research shows that all effective values education must be grounded in a community of some kind (Kohlberg 1978; Leming 1993:69; Matthews and Riley 1995:17). The hallmark of character education, and the prerequisite to all other instruction, is the moral school, a place were core universal values are practiced by everyone (CEP n.d.; Lickona 1991, Wynne and Ryan 1997). Much of the literature in character education focuses on establishing and maintaining moral schools and classroom communities where ethics can be absorbed.

Along with establishing moral schools and developing values-related skills, proponents of character education insist that the entire curriculum be grounded in the core values. Thus, traditional academic subjects can be used to create a planned context for moral discussion (CEP n.d.; Lickona 1991:183). For example, English literature is often used to provide models of self-discipline, honesty, or courage, while history and social studies are good venues for teaching a nation's guiding principles and the laws derived from them. Many teachers have made ethics the underlying and unifying theme of instructional units or the entire academic curriculum (Lickona 1991:161–181)..

Numerous surveys indicate that young people in the United States seem to have few if any heroes. "When they can think of someone they would like to identify with, it will quite often be a high-salaried entertainer—a Madonna, a Michael Jackson, or an Eddie Murphy. Many if not most of these figures are admired not for their virtues but for their success" (Kilpatrick 1992:106). Character education advocates think that children need more positive role models to emulate. Science, history, and many other subjects are replete with heroes and stories of their lives and accomplishments can easily be included in the curriculum.

In sum, character education is a broad approach to values education emphasizing core universal values that can be described as those values that define us at our best as humans. Because education already has a moral dimension, academics and values must be deliberately woven together. In the United States, public schools were founded to teach academic literacy as well as moral literacy because the founders recognized that democracy requires morally literate citizens. Character education encourages tolerance of cultural differences as the basis of a pluralistic society and world, while reinforcing the commonalities of a nation's citizens. We may not agree on everything, but tolerance allows us to debate our deepest differences with respect and civility.

In practical terms, character education encompasses developmental theory, the moral reasoning approach, and recognizes that values cannot be transmitted by didactic methods; the student must be actively involved in the process. It can be delivered to students using a variety of methods including conflict resolution, cooperative learning, and teaching values through the curriculum (CEP n.d.).

Character education currently enjoys widespread support in the United States, and recent Supreme Court decisions have determined that it is an appropriate part of education (Boyd 1996). Twelve states (California, Connecticut, Iowa, Kentucky, Maryland, Missouri, New Jersey, New Mexico, North Carolina, South Carolina, Utah, and Washington) have been chosen by the U.S. Department of Education to develop effective character education programs that could replicated in other states (Fink 1997:1; U.S. Department of Education 1998). Under current plans, ten more states will soon follow with new programs.

Character Education Under Scrutiny

Character education is not without its critics. Robert Nash (1997), a philosopher of education, maintains that while character education has much to recommend it, it is deeply flawed. He asserts that it is inherently authoritarian in its convictions, a trait that may preclude the very virtues that make a democratic society possible.

> [C]haracter educators blissfully ignore the fact that modern, constitutional democracies must continually find new ways to resolve the inevitable clash of values that is the heart and soul of democratic living. . . . Pluralism frequently gives rise to unruly public disagreements and intractable divisions. And people more than ever need the skills and dispositions to deliberate effectively together. . . . [Nash 1997:11]

For Nash, character education, as it is currently conceived and practiced, cannot produce citizens capable of democratic deliberations in a pluralistic society. He proposes an alternative to character education that is based on "democratic dispositions," those capacities essential for constructing and maintaining a democratic society. Similarly, Patricia White (1996) also uses the idea of democratic dispositions, as a basis for moral education. While character educators routinely cite democracy as the basis for values education, both Nash and White focus more directly on the virtues required for the actual *practice* of democracy.

James Leming (1993) evaluated several character education programs and discovered that many are very effective at fostering good character. However, "studies that have used multiple classrooms have detected considerable variations in program effects between classrooms" (Leming 1993:69). Some educators have reported that character education programs have not been effective in some schools and districts (Black 1996). Schools or classrooms where character education is less than effective may be traced to how the program is actually implemented. For example, if the program is based on slogans and codes, methods that do not work, it probably won't cause notable changes in behavior or attitudes. Or programs may have been tried in schools that do not possess a community where core universal values can be fostered.

Character education has not yet developed a "grand theory" (Leming 1993:70). The lack of a theory and research based on it hampers efforts to develop uniformly effective programs, thus creating variable evaluation results. "Character education needs to develop a more coherent view that can integrate research, provide a focus for the movement, and guide curriculum planning . . ." (Lemming 1993:70). More recently, Nash (1997) confirms that many teachers are still confused about character education and don't know how to implement it in their classrooms. Despite all this, it seems that character education can improve the behavior of students when well implemented. In the meantime, best practices are certainly improving all the time and good materials are more widely available (The Master Teacher, Inc., 1998; Rusnak 1998; Wiley 1998; Ryan and Bohlin 1999).

A few educators still question whether public schools should tackle the issue at all because values education places such a heavy burden on the system, especially teachers (Black 1996). Teaching ethics in school may occasionally place teachers in awkward positions because parents sometimes object when values they disagree with are presented in classrooms. Some states have not implemented statewide character education programs. For example, character education was not included in the Texas core curriculum, which was adopted less than two years ago (Ann Rogers, Texas Education Agency Social Studies Coordinator, personal communication). In that state, individual districts may adopt character education programs, but thus far it is not widely used in the schools. In Texas, and probably many other states, some teachers may not know exactly what "character education" is, hence values may fall under a "citizenship" strand instead.

Regardless of any shortcomings of character education specifically, and the difficulties of teaching values generally, almost all educators argue that academics simply cannot proceed in an environment that lacks mutual respect and respect for authority, responsibility, and honesty, and therefore consider values as part of their mission (Lickona 1991; Kristin Fink, Utah Character Education specialist, personal communication). Most teachers include values in their curricula even though they may not refer to it as "character education."

Interface between Archaeology and Values Education

Archaeologists want people to help protect archaeological sites and artifacts. We want them to report illegal excavation and vandalism, and we want them to refrain from vandalizing, digging, or buying artifacts themselves. How can we use the educational system and the character education movement to change behavior in prescribed ways? We need to change attitudes about archaeology and preservation along the way, but that is not enough—we want people to act appropriately. Issues of archaeological conservation can be taught through traditional classroom curricula including science, social sciences, language arts, mathematics, and art using methods employed by values educators: moral reasoning (dilemmas), cooperative learning, examples of archaeological "heroes and heroines," problem-solving exercises, and community service directed toward archaeological protection (see Boxes 17.2 and 17.3).

Archaeology through the Curriculum

Teaching values, while also teaching academic skills and content, is an emerging trend in education (Lickona 1991). *Project Archaeology*, a nationwide archaeology education program, allows educators to teach archaeology within the existing curriculum (Moe 1996, In press; Smith et al. 1996; Moe and Letts 1998). In training

Box 17.2
Changing Behavior—Strategies that Don't Work
(Adapted from Leming 1993 and Matthews and Riley 1995)

1. Didactic information such as brochures.
2. Focusing on awareness of the problem only.
3. Persuasive communication of any kind.

Box 17.3
Changing Behavior—Strategies that Work
(Adapted from Leming 1993 and Matthews and Riley 1995)

1. Long-term exposure to conservation at school or another venue and involvement with specific issue.
2. Responsible action to protect archaeological sites: peer teaching, education campaigns, solving a problem and implementing a solution, being a site steward.
3. Student involvement in archaeology clubs or volunteer programs.
4. Encourage ownership of the problem and empower students to solve it.

workshops, teachers are encouraged to infuse ethics such as responsibility for our shared legacy and respect for the diverse cultures who lived on this continent in the past, into lessons in science, social studies, language arts, and art. For example, in a series of lessons on prehistoric rock art, students discover the significance of the art, make their own "rock art," experience vandalism of their own work, and discuss how damage of the archaeological record might harm sites and objects that have value for Native Americans, as well as damage archaeologists' work. Not only do students learn about art and cultural history, they also discover the emotional impact of senseless vandalism. Many character educators are looking for good ways to teach values in the context of real world problems and issues, in addition to using exercises designed solely for addressing values.

Teachers also need ways to address ethical issues in science. Archaeology itself is replete with ethical issues such as responsibilities to other interest groups, stewardship, the obligation to share information with the public, and the use of "looted" data for research or in museum collections, for instance (Lynott and Wylie 1995b). Some of these issues might form the basis for a discussion of scientific research and ethics. Human remains issues, especially the case of Kennewick man (see Kaupp [1997] for a review), have been highly publicized recently and could be used to show the relationships between the science of archaeology, the responsibilities of archaeology to Native Americans, and applicable federal laws (see Box 17.4).

BOX 17.4
Archaeological Heroes

A famous archaeologist.
A local archaeologist.
An archaeological preservation hero.
A student or group of students who have protected a site.

Moral Reasoning

When used in context, moral reasoning or moral dilemmas can be a good tool for stimulating discussion of values especially as they relate to personal conduct. Dilemmas present a morally ambivalent situation and the reader/student must decide on a course of action (Blatt and Kohlberg 1975). Here is an example of a moral dilemma involving archaeological resources (adapted from Smith et al. 1996:110):

> You are on a trip to a national forest to visit an old historic ghost town. Your youth group leader takes you into an old building where there are a lot of relics lying around including bits and pieces of pottery. Your teacher has informed you that historic places are protected by law and that you should take nothing but pictures and leave nothing but footprints. As you are leaving, you notice that your leader is picking up several pieces of pottery and some other artifacts. Several children are doing the same thing. When you tell the leader what your teacher said about not taking artifacts, the leader answers by saying, "Taking little things like broken pottery doesn't count." What do you do?

A list of options may be added to help younger students with the reasoning process:

1. Act as though you saw nothing, let them take the pottery pieces home.
2. Pick up just one piece of pottery as a souvenir.
3. Do nothing, knowing that you were obeying the law by not taking anything.
4. Find another youth group.
5. Ask your parents to report the leader to the U.S. Forest Service or appropriate Canadian ministry.
6. Ask a professional archaeologist to come and talk to your youth group.
7. Other.

In this dilemma, the student knows that it is against the law to take artifacts. However, knowing that removing artifacts from sites will damage the archaeological record and our ability to learn from it, may help the reader decide on the best course of action. In other words, students need some knowledge about archaeology and the laws that protect antiquities to use the moral dilemma method effectively. If they are going to engage in moral reasoning, they need something of substance to reason about and the knowledge to reason with. Other personal dilemmas that may be posed include reporting vandalism, refusing to buy artifacts, or reporting an important discovery.

Research has shown that moral reasoning is effective in advancing children from one moral developmental stage to another, but it has not been demonstrated to change behavior (Leming 1981, 1993:64–65; Emler 1996:125). It does, however, offer an opportunity to open ethical discussion in a planned context. When linked to other information such as laws and the scientific value of the archaeological record, it gives teachers a useful tool for addressing conservation issues.

Cooperative Learning

Cooperative learning teams students for group projects and teaches values and content at the same time (Lickona 1991:186). Students working together in teams of two or more or even as whole classes to accomplish a goal, builds community in the classroom and teaches the value of cooperation.

Many cooperative learning teachers divide students into teams of four to six students and each student plays a specific role (for example, recorder, reporter, illustrator, or reference librarian). Archaeology educators can capitalize on this popular classroom strategy by modeling how teams of archaeologists work together on projects or to solve a problem. One student could be a ceramicist, one a lithics specialist, one an expert on textiles, and so on. Interdisciplinary cooperation, which is usually a part of archaeological inquiry, could also be modeled for cooperative learning groups. For example, each student could take the role of a specialist (geologist, ethnobotanist, or zoologist). Many existing lessons such as those used in *Project Archaeology* (Smith et al. 1996), can be adapted to cooperative learning. We cannot directly teach archaeological conservation using cooperative learning, but by making lessons and activities compatible with the cooperative strategy, it is one way to get "air time" in the classroom.

Community Service

Community service forms the basis of many character education programs because it provides a way for students to learn to care while giving care.

Archaeological conservation lends itself well to a variety of community service projects. In the classroom, students can design and implement educational campaigns for their community or school (see Smith et al. 1996). In rural communities, classes might organize site-monitoring programs to protect nearby cultural resources.

When immersed in the research process, participants learn the importance of protecting the archaeological record (Heath 1997). Students and teachers can assist archaeologists with field and laboratory projects through organizations such as Earthwatch Institute or the Passport-In-Time program sponsored by the U.S. Forest Service. Students and teachers may also attend learning centers such as Crow Canyon Archaeological Center (Colorado), the Center for American Archaeology at Kampsville (Illinois), or Dig Afognak! (Alaska) and work with archaeologists on long-term research projects.

Involving the Community

The community can significantly reinforce values that students learn in school (Lickona 1991). Speaking to a class of fourth graders about archaeological conservation will show them that someone beside their teacher thinks it is important to protect sites and artifacts. However, the experience must be placed in context to be effective. The teacher needs to prepare the class by covering basic concepts, then when a guest speaker arrives they will be ready to learn about conservation issues.

Similarly, if students see that local businesses, government agencies, and other organizations support archaeological resource protection, it will reinforce the conservation ethics they have learned in the classroom. Land-managing agencies, for example, might sponsor public projects to fence sites that are being damaged. In California, Utah, Nevada, Pennsylvania, and Wyoming, the state professional archaeological associations are assisting with establishing and maintaining state *Project Archaeology* programs. Sponsorship sends an important message to teachers and students: professional archaeologists are willing to spend their own time and money to support archaeology education.

Considerations for Archaeology Educators

Be realistic. Archaeology is certainly part of traditional academic subjects, but it will never be more than a small part of the K–12-grade curriculum. Most teachers will not teach entire units on archaeology or devote more than a few lessons to ethics even though they may be required to cover prehistory or may have a personal interest in the subject. They simply do not have the time to cover archaeology extensively.

Although we can't expect much teaching time to be devoted to archaeology and conservation ethics, we can transmit the stewardship message to educational settings effectively. Archaeological conservation exemplifies several core universal values: respect, responsibility, and good citizenship. By pairing these with scientific inquiry, culture history, and problem solving—requirements that teachers already need to cover—archaeological protection can be infused into the curriculum (Davis, this volume).

Teachers are our most important and effective link to the young citizens we are trying to reach. They create the classroom community in which values can be taught and ultimately decide what will be taught and how. If teachers are advocates for archaeological protection, they can instill the conservation ethic in their students through the curriculum presented, but more important, through the long-term relationships established in the classroom. A teacher can reach hundreds or maybe thousands of students during his or her career. Therefore, it is essential to prepare teachers to teach archaeology and particularly ethics (see Brunswig, this volume).

With in-service and preservice training for teachers, we can model the relationship between content—basic archaeological principles and culture history—and the ethics of preservation—respect for archaeological sites and the people who are connected to them and responsibility for our shared cultural legacy. We must emphasize values during workshops or teachers will not emphasize them to their students. After all, no one automatically links archaeology to ethics; rather, most people think of ancient objects, excavations in tombs or ancient cities, or museum collections. Teachers might think about scientific inquiry or culture history, subjects that they are required to teach, but probably won't jump into conservation issues unless they are inspired to do so.

Teachers are understandably hesitant to tread on the thin ice of controversy, especially when they aren't conversant with the issues. Showing them how to address ethics in the classroom will increase their confidence and ultimate success. Imagine that you are a teacher who has just presented a lesson that demonstrates the importance of leaving artifacts in context to a fourth-grade class. A student asks if it is all right to pick up a single arrowhead she has found on public land. It is difficult enough to answer the question when you are an archaeologist—believe me. Think how difficult it would be for a teacher with no training, who is covering archaeology for the first time. Working through some of these issues and dilemmas in a workshop can help a teacher in some difficult situations.

About 90% of teachers who complete Project Archaeology workshops list ethics or values as a primary objective for teaching archaeology in their classrooms. After nearly ten years of instructing workshops, I have come to believe that the mere presence of an archaeologist helps lead teachers to advocacy. Most archaeologists are not afraid to show how much they love their work and the pieces of the past that they study. Teachers quickly pick up on their enthusiasm and passion and most of them become advocates for protection before leaving the workshop.

Archaeologists can work directly with students in a number of ways. Boy Scouts can earn a merit badge in archaeology (Skinner 1997; Skinner et al. 1998) and each scout needs a mentor throughout the process. Some archaeologists work directly with schools to schedule field trips or volunteer projects for students. Emphasizing ethics during classroom visits will reinforce the values already taught in the classroom.

Conservation issues should always be presented in an open atmosphere. Federal and state laws protect antiquities, and everyone needs to know that, however it is crucial that people understand the reasons behind the laws. Open ethical discussion should be encouraged in teacher workshops and the classroom so that everyone has a chance to understand the sometimes complex issues involved in archaeological conservation. Voluntary compliance is the goal.

Sometimes values in home and school don't match, and the discrepancies can place children in difficult situations with their parents or other relatives. The illegal collection of artifacts is not unlike the conflicts that arise when a parent smokes or doesn't use seat belts while their son or daughter is learning the dangers of such behaviors in school. Students often want to talk about collections owned by relatives or bring them to class for show and tell. Experienced teachers already know how to turn a conflict in values like this into a productive discussion. Teachers often call these situations "teachable moments" and use them to illustrate points or change thinking (see Box 17.5).

Sometimes young people become strong advocates for archaeological protection and want to act on their convictions. Occasionally, differing ethical viewpoints can place children at odds with their relatives and friends (see Box 17.6). Both archaeologists and educators should help children find the most positive outlets for their enthusiasm. Students can design educational campaigns to protect sites, implement a site-monitoring program, conduct a community problem-solving exercise involving archaeological resources, or many other productive projects (Smith et al. 1996).

If you've been around education for more than ten years, you will know that programs and trends can change radically every few years. Character education may evolve into something else and some alternatives have already been proposed, but values have always been part and parcel of education. As research progresses and best practices change, "character education" may look different and even have a different name, but values education will always be with us. For these reasons, you should base your program or project on the most current information and be prepared to make changes as educational practices change and improve. If you use your own most deeply held professional values as your guide, you probably won't ever be too far wrong. Indeed, archaeology can offer many effective ways to implement values education in the classroom and help character educators improve their practices.

BOX 17.5
Linda Stott, 4th-Grade Teacher, Cottonwood Elementary,
Salt Lake City, Utah

Mike: Miss Stott! Miss Stott!

Linda: Yes, Mike.

Mike: My Grandpa and I were out hiking last summer and I found an arrowhead.

Linda: Hmmm. That's really interesting, Mike. Was it fun to find that artifact?

Mike: Yeah, it was. We were just walking along the canyon bottom and all of a sudden, there it was, all black and shiny.

Linda: Yes, I'll bet it was fun to see it there on the ground. What did you do with it?

Mike: I took it home. Grandpa said it would be the first arrowhead in my collection.

Linda: Oh, I see. Hmmmm. What else can you tell me about where you found it?

Mike: It was on our vacation so we were in southern Utah. I think there was a creek because we saw some grass and trees, too.

Linda: Why do think the arrowhead was there?

Mike: Maybe someone lived there and dropped it.

Linda: Wow! You found a site—a place where an artifact tells us that someone may have lived or hunted or worked in that very spot. So you really discovered information as well as an artifact. How about your best friend, John? Do you think he would have liked to see that arrowhead all black and shiny there in the sand?

Mike: Yeah, I guess so. It was really fun to discover it.

Linda: But, John won't be able to see it where it was left in that beautiful place in the desert.

Mike: No, but he can come over to my house and see it.

Linda: Will that be as much fun? I wonder if John will appreciate the artifact and the site like you can. What do you think?

Mike: No, I guess not.

Linda: What will you do if you find another arrowhead?

Mike: Uh . . . uh . . ., I don't know. I guess maybe I'll just leave it there so other people can see it.

Linda: What a great idea! I know that was a hard decision because I've had to make that choice before. But it sounds to me like you'll be prepared for the future now.

> BOX 17.6
> *Letter to Ronald J. Rood, Assistant State Archaeologist,*
> *Salt Lake City, Utah**
>
> Text of letter reads as follows:
>
> *Dear Mr. Rood:*
>
>   *Thank you for talking to our class about archaeology. I liked the picture of the pottery pieces. My uncle has pottery that he digs up. I know it is wrong but be says it is not. He lives in Cortez.*
>   *I liked looking at the skulls and learng (*sic*) about plant eaters and meat eaters.*
>   *You could call my uncle and tell him not to dig. His number is* _____.
>
> *Thank you.*
>
> Ron asked a class of fourth graders to imagine that they were 95 years old and had a great-granddaughter who wants to be an archaeologist. He told them that if all the archaeological sites had been vandalized, there wouldn't be anything for the great-granddaughter to study. In fact, there wouldn't be any sites for anyone to see and enjoy. Ron's argument convinced the author of this letter that archaeological sites were worth saving, even if her uncle got "a talking to."
>
> *Letter reproduced with the permission of Ronald J. Rood

The strategies that work best for instilling respect for the past and responsibility for protecting it require the involvement of archaeologists and well-prepared educators. Neither teachers nor their students will become advocates for historic preservation by reading brochures or books or by exploring the Internet. Values are transmitted from person to person within communities, communities that are formed in teacher workshops—however fleetingly—in the classroom, or through programs and projects that bring educators, archaeologists, and students together working for common goals.

RECOMMENDED READINGS

Lickona, Thomas
  1991   *Educating for Character: How Our Schools Can Teach Respect and Responsibility*. Bantam Books, New York.
  This book kicked off the character education movement. Lickona explains the theoretical underpinnings of character education and describes practical classroom applications.

Matthews, Bruce E., and Cheryl K. Riley
  1995   *Teaching and Evaluating Outdoor Ethics Education Programs*. National Wildlife Federation, Vienna, Virginia.
  This useful guide provides a brief description of character education and applies it to teaching and evaluating outdoor ethics education programs.

Nash, Robert J.
  1997   *Answering the "Virtuecrats": A Moral Conversation on Moral Education*. Teachers College Press, Columbia University, New York.
  Robert Nash criticizes the character education movement and offers an alternative to values education.

Chapter Eighteen

Who Paints the Past?
Teaching Archaeology in a Multicultural World

Archaeologists are often invited into classrooms to explore the past with students and teachers. In this role, we frequently talk about cultures that differ from those that we have experienced. How do we teach about a culture that is not our own? How can we teach archaeology and include alternate perspectives on the past? This chapter explores several key elements for teaching an archaeological curriculum to diverse audiences. These include first, a better understanding our own cultural heritage and that of our students, and second, the development of an experiential curriculum that incorporates community involvement and traditional and historical perspectives. These elements allow for exploration of contemporary issues in a constructive manner, making archaeology relevant to students.

Background

Archaeological curricula are based on the scientific investigation of past cultures and life ways. The past comes alive for students when they can understand how the artifacts and features unearthed by archaeologists were created and used by people long ago. A meaningful curriculum is an artful compilation of content, instructional methods, chaos, and laughter. The lessons change as our discipline, students, and teaching methods evolve.

Over the years, some archaeological curricula have grown to be inclusive of different interpretations of cultural history. In these approaches, archaeology is defined as one of many ways to know and interpret the past. In addition to archaeology, written records, oral histories, and religious traditions are widely recognized as valid means of providing information about the past. The need to emphasize inclusivity has arisen from an uncomfortable realization that the scientific interpretation of the past that we were teaching was quite often different from what some students were learning at home. If, for example, students are raised with the knowledge that their ancestors have always been in the place where they now live, why should they be interested in learning about the migration of Native Americans from Asia across the Bering Land Bridge? If students believe the world was created in seven days, why should they be expected to accept an evolutionary perspective?

Reflecting on Our Own Cultural Identity

Context is essential to the work of archaeologists. For archaeology educators, understanding both our own personal cultural contexts, and those in which our students live and learn is crucial to being able to interpret and transmit information about our human heritage to a modern audience. Our backgrounds and cultures affect the learning environments we create; thus, to become effective educators we must reflect on our own past. We all bring our own cultural biases to the table when we begin to study and analyze the cultures of the past. So does each student in the archaeology classes that we teach, whether they are ten years old and are being exposed to archaeological concepts for the first time or graduate students planning on a career in the discipline. We should think about the origin of ancestors, family traditions, and other insightful personal experiences we can share with students to help them understand their own cultural context. Often, teacher education programs omit cultural training, so it is up to us as educators to develop methods for connecting our own culture with that of our students.

Examination of students' differing backgrounds is especially important in the highly multicultural classrooms of modern North American schools where the majority of teachers are white women: Only about 10% are of African American, Asian, Native American, or Hispanic descent. However, estimates say that by the year 2000, approximately 40% of the U.S. student population will be nonwhite (Viadero 1996:39). Teachers need to understand the communities in which they teach and make students aware of the differences and similarities that characterize those communities. The understanding of context and culture with respect to the classroom community allows student accessibility to those concepts in their study of the past. Students need to be able to differentiate between aspects of their ethnic and family backgrounds, and those of the larger society that we all share. By being open with students about our own experiences, educators and archaeologists can encourage students to share their cultural identities with others. In turn, this sharing and learning experience will go a long way toward helping students understand both the cultural contexts in which past peoples operated and the way that our own cultural biases and background filter and change our interpretation of archaeological remains, however objective we attempt to be.

The examination applies not only to the everyday life of the students, but also to the lifeways developed and experienced by the peoples who lived before us. Activities can be developed in the classroom that explore family histories, stories, arts, and traditions. Such cultural investigation not only provides an opportunity for students to develop an appreciation for their own culture, but also exposes them to the cultural characteristics of those from different backgrounds. These experiences encourage students to be open to and interested in studying about past cultures.

An Experiential Approach

An experiential education philosophy is an excellent method to encourage students to explore the past in a variety of ways. Kraft and Sakof (n.d.) define experiential education as "all those environments where the learner is actively involved in his or her own learning and is not just a passive recipient in the knowledge of the teacher." Archaeology educators have discovered that hands-on activities stimulate students' interests, encourage critical thinking, and stimulate meaningful dialogue.

In an experiential curriculum, each student is encouraged to express what he or she is learning and thinking. This process, known as reflection, encourages a safe participatory learning environment, contributes to academic skills, aids in students' personal development, and strengthens student-teacher relationships. Educators have observed that once students learn some aspects of a past culture, it serves as a point of intersection for discussing cross-cultural issues affecting the present.

Students at all levels can be introduced to evidence uncovered in archaeological research. Such evidence provides knowledge of specific components of prehistoric and historic lifeways. Trade, subsistence activities, social and political organization, and archaeological indications of status can be addressed in the classroom. An activity demonstrating the ways in which students' families obtain the food they regularly consume can be followed by a discussion of hunting and gathering and its implications. An exploration of modern medical practices could be followed by an ecology hike to examine plants used for medicinal purposes, based on plants remains in the archaeological record. Such experiences show students the commonality of all cultures, in that each has a culturally prescribed unique way of meeting universal human needs.

Issues in Teaching Archaeology

Certain elements of an archaeological education program may present points of sensitivity for some people. There is no one curriculum to address the diversity of issues that arise when teaching archaeology. Educators need to be aware of the social, intellectual, and religious traditions in their areas.

Until the past decade, archaeology in North America had rarely included the voices of the people who were being studied. Studied groups have long been denied a voice in archaeological excavations, museum exhibits, and educational programs (Lea, this volume). Aspects of this problem changed in 1990 for Native Peoples in the United States when the Native American Graves Protection and Repatriation Act (NAGPRA) was passed. The Canadian archaeological community, with leadership from the Canadian Archaeological Association, is following similar guidelines, even though these are not currently written into law. The act and practice have significantly changed the approach of archaeologists and anthropologists in their study of human remains, grave goods, and items related to cultural patrimony As more archaeologists become sensitized to Native American concerns, these issues should lessen.

All cultures have deeply held beliefs about the appropriate treatment of the dead; this topic is very emotional for many groups, especially when discussed in a secular setting. The excavation, treatment, analysis, and curation of human remains are particularly sensitive issues. These issues have long been part and parcel of archeological investigations, but should be approached with great care and sensitivity in the classroom. Even photographs of human remains and sacred objects can be disturbing to living cultural descendants and should be avoided in an archaeological education unit.

Some students from conservative Christian backgrounds may object to any archaeological explanation that differs from the belief that the world was created in its present form. For those students, evolution is an untenable hypothesis. These beliefs can provide a teaching opportunity to explain the principles of culture. Teachers and archaeology educators should be careful not to challenge any student's belief system, but to work to help students learn to be tolerant of the beliefs of others.

Different interpretations of time present another area of concern. Archaeologists create a picture of the past through excavation and observation, often producing linear chronologies for prehistoric cultures. Some groups may view historical settlement and migration events as sacred and therefore could be offended by archaeologists' assignation of calendrical dates to these events.

One approach to studying time in the classroom is to ask students to express their own concept of time. What does "old" mean to them? Demonstrate to students how to develop a time line based on their own life events. When applicable, have the students develop their time lines to include the cultural chronology of the area.

Honoring Oral Tradition

Archaeology educators can find valuable teaching resources in their own areas. These are community elders, local historians, and others who gather and transmit the oral heritage of an area, cultural group, or community. Archaeology and oral tradition can be overlapping or conflicting ways to look at the past. They both have validity when taught in their own cultural context. Archaeology is a science that investigates how people lived in the past and it is based on scientific rules of evidence. Oral histories contain historical, religious, and traditional information that is passed from one generation to the next. Some oral histories may be thousands of years old. Historical archaeologists often seek advice and information about artifacts and cultural practices from elderly residents of an area or practitioners of a craft or trade, such as carpenters, potters, and butchers.

Using oral history in an archaeological curriculum is an excellent way to connect the present with the past. People who can make history come alive for all of us live in our communities. The best way to share oral traditions with students is to invite elders into the classroom. An elder person, who remembers "what it was like when I was a child," can give an interesting overview of the not-so-ancient past. Students can then compare their lives with that of those who lived in their area in earlier times.

Storytelling is an excellent medium for sharing traditional histories and engaging students in a past culture (Praetzellis and Praetzellis 1998). Students love to know where the stories originated and quickly imagine themselves outside the classroom walls. When researching a story, the archaeology educator should recognize that some libraries contain outdated books that may not contain authentic renditions of traditional stories. When attributing a story to a particular Native American group, be aware that in the United States alone there are more than 500 recognized tribes, Alaskan villages, Hawaiian organizations, and several groups not recognized by the government, each with a distinct culture. Accuracy is important and stories should be referenced correctly. For some cultures, there is a seasonality to storytelling and there may be restrictions on telling religious stories at certain times of the year; violating these parameters can cause some students to experience emotions ranging from uneasiness to anguish.

Involving Community Members in Curriculum Development

Whether teaching a unit about the neighborhood surrounding a historic site, Native American or Native Canadian cultures, or a local immigrant group, such as Chinese railroad workers, it is beneficial to seek out, early in the planning stages, community members who would like to help. Involving community members at the beginning of a project will help educators and archaeologists identify sensitive topics and will strengthen community support.

Another important resource to consult when developing materials for pre-collegiate audiences is the professional archaeological community; many members will have had experience in working with various traditional, religious, or ethnic groups. The professional community includes the State Historic Preservation officers' staff, Department of Canadian Heritage and provincial archaeological staff, academic archaeologists at nearby colleges and universities, research archaeologists who work for private contract firms, archaeologists employed by tribal governments, and archaeologists who work in agencies of the federal governments. Such agencies might include the U.S. Forest Service; National Park Services in both Canada and the United States; the U.S. Bureau of Land Management; the Bureau of Reclamation; the Army Corps of Engineers; the Tennessee Valley Authority; the archaeological and heritage services of various regional municipal governments, such as the Ontario Heritage Foundation; and museum-based archaeological groups such as those at the Nova Scotia Museum and the Prince of Wales Northern Heritage Centre in Yellowknife, Northwest Territories, Canada. Museums, historical societies, and other interest groups might also be willing to assist in developing material suitable for classroom use.

Archaeology educators should make every effort to provide teachers with the opportunity to expose students to archaeology, and they should offer to visit classrooms and talk about the work that they do. Exchanging ideas with a wide range of individuals will greatly enhance the archaeology educator's ability to carry out curriculum development and have it accepted in the classroom setting. It will also help archaeological educators build important relationships with many elements of the community (a point Christensen, this volume, also emphasizes). These sources can assist the archaeology educator in understanding, interpreting, and teaching about past and present cultures. This exchange of ideas and cultural experiences better prepares everyone to understand, interpret, and teach about the contemporary group's life and culture, and forms a basis of trust and understanding that allows us to teach effectively about archaeological topics to a wider range of students.

In Sum

Who paints the past? We all do. Our perspectives on the past define who we are as a people. Archaeologists are often invited into classrooms to paint a picture of past cultures for students and teachers. Both teachers and archaeologists need to be aware of the range of cultural backgrounds which characterize themselves and the students they address. Before we create an archaeological curriculum, we need to learn as much as we can about the students and the community where we will be teaching. By creating an environment where students are free to express their own cultural backgrounds, it will be easier for everybody to understand and appreciate the culture being studied.

Use hands-on methods as much as possible. Bring archaeology alive by including all perspectives, and be prepared to discuss controversial topics in a positive way.

RECOMMENDED READINGS

Darder, Antonia
    1991   *Culture and Power in the Classroom: A Critical Foundation for Bicultural Education.* Bergin and Garvey, Westport, Connecticut.
    This book explores the concepts of critical pedagogy and transformative education. It is a must-read for anyone trying to understand today's students and the challenges within the education system.

McIntosh, Peggy
    1989   White Privilege: Unpacking the Invisible Knapsack. *Peace and Freedom,* July/August.
    This short article explains the concepts of white privilege. Readers explore their own education and the advantages the dominant culture has within the education system.

Swidler, Nina, Kurt Dongoske, Roger Anyon, and Alan S. Downer, eds.
    1997   *Native Americans and Archaeologists.* AltaMira Press, Walnut Creek, California.
    A compilation of papers given at the 1997 SAA meeting in New Orleans. The most up-to-date resource on the relationship between Native Americans and archaeologists.

Warren, Karen, Michael Sakof, and Jasper S. Hunt, eds.
    1995   *The Theory of Experiential Education.* Kendall-Hunt Publishing Co., Dubuque, Iowa
    An excellent resource for anyone interested in articles written by the leaders in the experiential education field.

Chapter Nineteen

Gatekeeping, Housekeeping, Peacekeeping
Goals for Teaching Archaeology in
the Public Schools

Most people think that teaching archaeology is simply retelling important aspects of culture history, with some interesting caveats about using material cultural data. But history records many voices, and the political present asks many different questions about the past. What are we really teaching when we teach archaeology?

Archaeology is a wonderful teaching tool; I call it "brain candy." People from many cultural backgrounds are fascinated by the archaeological record and the mystery-solving techniques archaeologists use to get a peek at an ancient reality. Golden tombs and fabulous jewels titillate the imagination; but the real appeal is the sense of humanity across time and the feeling of an almost cosmic "connectedness" that people get when they hold a tool that killed a rabbit in 320 AD, or look into a pot that cooked the dinner of a family now dead for 3,000 years. When I tell the story of discovering an ancient Maya hearth that preserved the recipe for a stew no one has tasted for 1,200 years, I hold my audience spellbound. But why? What is the point? Is it really worthwhile for me to teach American Rotarians or Belizean schoolchildren or Danish marketing professors that the ancient Maya ate boiled snails?

The truth is that culture history is only a part of what we teach. And the details of human experience that are common across centuries and miles of territory are important not in and of themselves, but for what they teach us about humanity and human values. We use the past to teach lessons, sometimes implicitly, sometimes unconsciously, but the lessons are always there. Deciding what route to take into the distant past determines at least to some extent what students who follow will take back with them into their daily lives. How do we make that choice? How do we know what to teach?

Gatekeeping

At the most general level, which I call gatekeeping, epistemology (How does science work? What is history?) and ethics (Who owns the past? What is the value of science?) provide the philosophical underpinnings of the discipline of archaeology. Several of the papers in this chapter treat the manner in which archaeological work is related to gatekeeping. Many teachers use archaeology to teach values and to discuss the power and the limitations of science. These are certainly the most important uses of archaeology: understanding the implications of what we claim about the past; learning the deeper meaning of our perspectives in the modern world; and developing critical thinking among students of all ages are surely projects to which I would contribute my own bones!

But it is also important that as educators we understand the origins of the values that we promote and the messages we teach. This is particularly discussed in the essay by Moe, who recognizes the importance of "values education." In addition to the points she makes, I would add that there is a profound but subtle difference between cultural relativism and ethical relativism. Understanding this difference entails the realization that the study of other cultures without objectivity is voyeurism; we are simply entertaining ourselves with exoticism and the extension of our own cultural perspective into unknown territory. In the absence of understanding, both racial prejudice and romantic admiration have potentially evil political repercussions. Admiration of tradition should not be justification for marginalization and poverty of First Peoples in the modern world. The desire for modern amenities and economic opportunity are not bad for "them" but good for "us," nor does material improvement equate with a "loss of traditions." A cultural relativist perspective gives an essential basis for communication, respect, and education; it doesn't entail the disapproval of cultural change, which is normal among all cultures (Said 1978), or the automatic approval of violence or torture in any cultural context (Salmon 1997), no matter how "traditional."

It has been my experience that North Americans generally fail to understand this distinction or to know that its underpinnings are philosophical and not necessarily religious. Well-meaning, but naive, educators sometimes believe that a relativistic perspective means all belief systems should be given equal weight; they may introduce the beliefs of Christianity or Buddhism into their culture history classes out of a spirit of evenhandedness. Usually this comes with the desire to teach something besides "just" the scientific view, as though religious knowledge were an equivalent or an alternative to a scientific understanding.

But this is misguided; all religions can never be included, and many teach intolerance of other beliefs that cannot be both honestly and neutrally portrayed. Some children will always be left out of the discussion and made to feel different. The goal of science is to disprove its own tenets; successful scientists change their beliefs about the world regularly. No religions take such a contingent approach to reality. It is important that teachers understand that science is not just another belief system, that it has some characteristics, both freedoms and limitations, that distinguish it from Creation Science, Christian Science, or other sources of absolute truth. Scientific truth is always provisional; scientific theory can never be proven to be true. Religious truth is another thing altogether, deserving of respect, but also requiring distance from the intellectual tolerance that must exist in a classroom.

Archaeology provides an excellent context for teaching about these issues, because local students may have strong motivations to discuss issues that have no easy answers or ready solutions. One very important reason for teachers to distinguish between science and religion is that science has historically been tremendously enriched by having practitioners from many religious and cultural backgrounds. If science is styled as antithetical to religious beliefs and explanations, young people may feel that an interest in science is a betrayal of their cultural heritage. Science certainly suffers from the narrowed perspective of a monocultural constituency, and emphasis on questions of particular interest to minority groups languish without the drive and enthusiasm of members of those groups trained in scientific disciplines. Young people need to be encouraged to consider a career in science a possibility no matter what their religious or cultural background.

Housekeeping

The second set of goals for teaching archaeology in public schools includes what I call housekeeping. This type of teaching serves the professional discipline of archaeology through a direct emphasis on protecting the archaeological record—in effect, keeping our "house" in order. These goals have recently been elaborated and carefully presented by the ethics committees of both the Society for American Archaeology and the Archaeological Institute of America. Differences of wording and thrust are very minor; both organizations resolve that the first commitment of a professional archaeologist is to stewardship (Lynott and Wylie 1995a).

The issue of stewardship is taken up by the papers in this chapter through discussions about the appropriateness of excavation or simulated excavation as teaching strategies. The problem with excavation-oriented teaching, as Hawkins (this volume) so clearly points out, is that it can easily send the wrong message, since if inappropriately presented, it can have the undesirable effect of taking the focus off analysis, research design, and report writing, and may dramatically oversimplify what archaeologists do. The truth is, many aspects of serious archaeological research, which includes ethnographic research and educational outreach within the local community; statistical sampling; specialist analysis of bone, pottery, stone, and other material types; and computer storage of analytical data, as well as excavation, cannot be done by children. In fact, children would not enjoy some of these activities very much. Chiarulli et al. (this volume) demonstrate clearly the advantages of using a simulated excavation experience to present the process of archaeological research to the student, without the potential difficulties inherent in using the actual site context to accomplish the teaching objectives. The impact of hands-on programming is preserved, without either the danger to the resource that can ensue from running a public site, or the financial and staff outlay required to do actual dig programming effectively.

Although there are aspects of excavation that children can do, that anybody can do, we must be careful not to give undue emphasis to these aspects when teaching about archaeology, lest we encourage people to try excavations for themselves. As Smardz (this volume) has shown, while excavation with kids is sometimes appropriate, and if carefully handled can be a very important educational vehicle for transmitting the stewardship message, it creates much more work for professionals, rather than less! However, if we exclude the public from excavation, we risk alienating our audience and being charged with elitism and snobbishness. After all, everybody knows how to dig a hole. So, we either have to invest the time and energy required to operate participatory excavation programming on real sites, with the carefully structured system of safeguards in place that Smardz advocates, or we have to offer something exciting in place of excavation that also makes clear our emphasis is on stewardship.

Housekeeping is tacitly recognized in these papers when they discuss reasons to dig or not to dig with students; it is important to note that these issues are very much central to the modern discipline of archaeology.

Peacekeeping

The third set of goals for teaching about archaeology I call "peacekeeping," and include the need to teach the history of local areas. As Connolly (this volume) discusses, archaeological knowledge is especially important in this effort because it is much more inclusive than traditional history, which emphasizes the deeds of white men to the exclusion of all else. Children get the idea that women have not contributed much to the modern world and that people who are not White have no history (Wolf 1982). Encouraging respect for women and minorities is ineffective unless children are taught history that recounts the accomplishments of many kinds of people. Often, the people most interesting to a local community left little or no written history, so archaeological reconstructions are the only sources of information. For example, in Indianapolis, Indiana, African-American and Anglo-American children are learning about the life of African Americans in the city at the turn of the century by excavating in a historic neighborhood with houses dating back to the Civil-War period. Although many documents exist for this period, none were produced outside the control of Anglo-American editors, so the reality of some kinds of human experience is poorly known through history books. In this case, the research design of the project is a simple one, because limited data are available, and the program is being directed by the state archaeologist in collaboration with a local high school. A community center with both display and storage space was created before excavations were begun, and the areas of digging were slated for construction. Without the participation of the youth of the community, much of the information would certainly be lost, so this is a situation where the inclusion of children is appropriate.

In this context, archaeology students can be stimulated to think about the construction of history and what biases a traditional historical perspective may contain. Although suitable only for older students, this level of critical thinking is possible for students in their early teens and can result in greatly enhanced enthusiasm for understanding the past. After all, documents are artifacts, too, and their cultural context defines them as surely as it defines any other artifact.

Archaeology can be used to teach critical thinking, values, science, and culture history. Professional archaeologists must balance all these issues, but they are also relevant to the general public. Teaching students to work through the complex information and ethical dilemmas posed by the archaeological record prepares them for the time when they will take the future of the past into their own hands.

The Provenience
Archaeology Education in the Real World

Archaeology education is occurring in numerous locations outside the classroom. Some venues, such as museums and archaeological parks, are nearly synonymous with archaeology in the public's eye. In Part IV, we look at arenas in which archaeology education is taking place outside the traditional classroom setting that has been been examined extensively in this book. Our focus is still on heritage education aimed at a K–12 audience. The locations discussed in this section all incorporate programming for schoolage children. Each has unique features that the archaeology educator must consider, whether working in urban sites, museums, research and public outreach centers, or university anthropology departments.

Peter Stone discusses several themes that emerge from the Part IV chapters. Indeed, many of these themes—the political nature of archaeology education and the responsibilities that archaeologists have to diverse publics, to name two—thread throughout the book. The manifestations of the marriage of education and archaeology presented in Part IV are the basis for Stone's analysis of issues about the nature of that union and its relationship to the parent archaeological profession.

Concepts and practical approaches relating to archaeology education presented in the first three sections should equip an archaeology educator to offer programs in any venue, and to do so creatively and effectively. The exciting and engaging archaeology education programs described here, that are bringing the benefits of archaeology to the public, should provide readers with both guideposts and inspiration.

Chapter Twenty

Applying the Message to the Medium

The chapters in this section raise issues that are fundamental to the effective achievement of successful, viable, long-term links between archaeology and education. They require us to look beyond the notion that it is "a good thing to do some public archaeology" and force us to formulate a clear rationale and methodology for the creation, development and long-term success and viability of public archaeology programs. In doing so, they touch on issues that many archaeologists would perhaps feel happier not discussed: Implicitly at least (and explicitly in some cases), they raise issues that are absolutely fundamental to the organization, nature, and role of archaeology as a discipline and profession. As such, they do not make easy reading.

Joanna Lea asks us to consider the belief that "educators changed the balance of power in the museum world, and with the change came different definitions of archaeology." Elizabeth Comer presents a clear example of archaeology being instigated not for archaeological but rather for, in this instance apparently benign, explicitly political reasons. Bonnie Christensen and Mary Kwas give clear arguments that show the public (and especially school teachers) are interested in archaeology *for their own reasons* rather than for the greater glory of archaeology (or archaeologists)—an essential point for those archaeologists wishing to work in public archaeology to grasp quickly and early in their careers (and see, for example, Zimmerman et al. 1994). Nancy White implicitly, yet almost devastatingly, demonstrates the lamentable failure of most M.A. courses in archaeology to help students prepare for what is accepted, certainly by all contributors to and, I suspect, most readers of—this book, as an increasingly critical role for many professional archaeologists. Finally, Stuart Struever demands that we step back from the comfortable world of public service and address the possibility that the future of archaeological research and educational projects lies in privately, rather than publicly, funded programs. None of this is for the faint hearted and none of it is unique to the North American situation (see, for example, various chapters in Stone and MacKenzie 1990; Stone and Molyneaux 1994).

Struever's four-point argument why archaeology occupies, and will continue to occupy, a marginal status in the minds of most Americans is depressing yet compelling reading for all archaeologists, especially for those who rely on public funding. It is perhaps even more depressing for archaeologists based outside the United States, as the philanthropic culture clearly present in this region is sadly lacking in most other parts of the world. Struever's commentary on the need for enhancing archaeology's image to attract private resources is all too cogent in light of the recent trend toward economic streamlining and personnel downsizing, which impacts heritage funding as it does all other areas of public life.

Whether Struever is correct in his analysis or not, his argument raises a number of crucial points reflected in the other contributions in the section. These are, in no particular order of importance, the need for:

- public support for archaeology
- effective management of public archaeology programs
- clear goals for public archaeology education.

I will discuss these aspects in a little more detail in the rest of this chapter.

Public Support for Archaeology

This is obviously one of the central issues addressed by this book and this group of chapters make some general, yet crucial, points with respect to public support. First, several authors, including Christensen, Kwas, and Lea, make the vitally important point that there is not one public sitting "out there" waiting expectantly for archaeologists to present the findings of their latest excavation or research project. Rather, there are many publics with varying needs and interests and we need to tailor our work to each if our expectation of public interest is to be met (also see, for example, Molyneaux 1994; 5ff). This is not news to anyone who has been involved in public archaeology for more than a few weeks. However, it is certainly my experience that it *is* news to many, if not the majority, of archaeologists. We tend to lead lives cocooned in an environment of like-minded people. I frequently attend international meetings of archaeologists who gather to discuss one or more particular issue. I usually leave with a warm feeling of mutual support, sure in my knowledge that I'm doing good work that is appreciated by my peers. It is usually only on the plane home that it dawns on me that it was supposedly an *international* meeting and yet perhaps only thirty countries were represented; those, usually self-selecting, colleagues who were present may have applauded my work—but what of the thousands of archaeologists who did not attend? Was our consensus a real consensus of the archaeology profession or just of those particular individuals present at that specific meeting? This is an overly simplistic example that ignores all manner of issues including practicalities such as costs, ability to travel, and so on, but one that, I hope, makes a point. If we talk among ourselves about the importance of public archaeology, we may convince each other that everything is fine and that we are doing a good job. However, we have left out the single most important group: the public and their reaction to our attempts to provide for them. Many of the following chapters emphasize the need for the proper evaluation of our public archaeology programs and stress the point that we need to interact with the many faces of the public, not only to gauge how well we have done, but also to find out what other issues we should be addressing.

This leads directly to my second point. Once we accept that we have to address a multiplicity of publics we also have to accept that we are passing on some level of control over our subject matter to these groups. No longer can museums put on exhibitions written by (and frequently for?) archaeologists using jargon and levels of English totally unsuitable to most nonacademic people. This is where Lea's argument becomes crucial. *If* educators become the central, pivotal staff in museums (and I am, sadly, rather skeptical that this has happened yet in any but a very few isolated instances anywhere in the world), then it really will mean a *complete revision* of what archaeology is. I do agree with Lea that the *process* of education being taken more seriously has begun in many—but by no means all—museums and that, as a result, education should, inevitably, take on a more central role within museums. As this process becomes more widespread, archaeologists will no longer be able to "tell it like it was" but will have to be open to various interpretations and beliefs that may, on occasion, go directly against what we, as archaeologists, believe the "truth" to be.

This questioning of archaeological truth is already taking place within some academic circles (see, for example, Shanks and Tilley 1987; Shanks 1992; Hodder et al. 1995) and in a number of educational and museum-based projects (see, for U.K.-based examples, Stone 1994; Anderson et al. 1996). I suggest that NAGPRA and other, similar, recent developments around the world (for example, the development of Keeping Places for human skeletal remains in Australia and the ongoing revision of criteria for Cultural Sites and Landscapes within the World Heritage Convention) are direct results of the acceptance by some archaeologists of their responsibilities toward the wider community and of the feeling of various groups making up that wider community of "being robbed of their material culture." Such initiatives may or may not be welcomed by the archaeological profession, but one crucial factor in their development has been the failure of archaeologists to address particular segments of the public and to convince them of the importance of archaeological research. As increasing numbers of archaeologists accept their responsibilities toward the public, as encouraged by Lea, and accept that archaeology is essentially a subjective discipline, others will have to follow suit: The myth of archaeologists working in an objective way and *knowing the answer* has been exposed, and the profession as a whole has to accept this development, however unpalatable it may be.

Some archaeologists will (have) argue(d) that the examples I have chosen above are not illustrations of public archaeology but rather the politically motivated use or possible abuse of archaeology as a lever for wider political or social goals by active minority communities. This may or may not be true, and this is not the place to discuss this particular controversy, but these examples serve to introduce my third point. What is relevant here is that, whatever the motivation, archaeology is, has been, and will continue to be, used for political ends (see Ucko 1987; Gathercole and Lowenthal 1994).

Archaeology itself may not be political (although Struever clearly commits himself to such a purpose—and perceives the mission of the Crow Canyon Center to be so), but the long-term goal of achieving a "multicultural, pluralistic society" is an explicitly political objective. However, as archaeologists, we work—perhaps more than most other academic colleagues—within a *political context.* Comer describes one such project in detail. In this example, the political motivation appears to have coincided benignly with archaeological interests and the two (politics and archaeology) mutually supported each other. But walk into a hypothetical world with me if you will and ask what could the archaeologists have done if the postexcavation political interpretation or use of the site had clashed with the archaeological?

We may court political support and hope that the high media profile that is a central part of the political world can be manipulated and used for the greater good of our public archaeology program. We must realize, however, that unless we are particularly fortunate in finding a politician who is personally interested in our subject and who has the time—and is allowed—to get involved, politicians will only support archaeology for their own reasons and own political agendas: Archaeology may be *our* own final goal, but it will almost certainly be only a means to an end (usually nothing to do with the archaeology per se) for politicians. I'm not saying that we should avoid working with politicians—as Comer and countless others have shown, such collaboration can have extremely positive results—but we must, as a profession, be aware of the potential dangers that such collaboration can bring.

An extreme example of the political abuse of archaeology appears to have happened recently in India. Excavations carried out over a number of years at the Babri Masjid mosque in Ayodhya have been documented in an interim report, which clearly states that there was no archaeology of significance below the extant mosque (Lal 1976–77). This report was ignored by the BJP, a right-wing Hindi political party, which argued that the mosque had been built on top of a Hindu temple marking the birthplace of the god Ram. The BJP appears to have been instrumental in the management of riots that eventually resulted in the destruction of the mosque, as well as the deaths of hundreds, if not thousands, of people in street riots, in 1992. The destruction of the mosque helped develop a substantial grassroots Hindu following for the BJP, which recently gave it the majority in a coalition government. Since the destruction, a number of senior Hindu archaeologists apparently closely aligned with the BJP (including the original excavator) have claimed that there was archaeological evidence for the temple and have supported the extreme line that this justifies the destruction of the mosque. Whatever the reality of the particulars of the Ayodhya situation, it is a clear example of archaeology being used by politicians for political ends (also see, for example, Rao 1994; Golson 1996; Shrimali 1998).

By opening the discipline to public involvement, we open it to being far more easily abused and misused. Public archaeology is, potentially, an extremely dangerous avenue to follow as we lose sole, undisputed, control over "our" data. In the U.K., Barbara Bender (1998) has identified what she believes to be a friction within English Heritage (the official advisory body to government on all matters to do with the heritage) that epitomizes the potential problems within public archaeology world wide:

> One of the really interesting things is that the English Heritage Education Program is radical. . . . But the trouble is that there seems to be a total split between the education department and the rest of management. My guess is that the education section has a degree of autonomy which has allowed it to be much more innovative. Maybe history for the kids is also seen as harmless—although that's patently a mistake. Maybe, too, it's about particular individuals that have stood up for a different way of doing things and thinking about things. . . . The problem is that it stays at the level of the Teacher's Handbook. It doesn't seem to filter down—or rather up. The minute management are involved, or more formal presentations, all the incertitudes and questions drop away and all the platitudes and desire to control reassert themselves. [Bender 1998:177–179]

Public Archaeology is about "enfranchisement" (Comer, this volume) and "control" and "empowerment" (Lea, this volume). These are laudable and, in my view, essential aims. Yet we must not think they do not have the ability to question the very fundamentals of our discipline and of our profession.

Effective Management of Public Archaeology Programs

The second aspect of public archaeology raised by these chapters is that of effective management. No longer can overworked archaeologists agree to do the odd "one-off" class with a local school or an occasional public lecture and claim to be doing anything but the most basic of public archaeology. As more and more archaeologists begin to recognize their responsibilities to the public, the various elements of the public are beginning to expect more and more from archaeologists. Christensen, Struever, and Kwas give some excellent advice about the realities of developing public education programs that should be heeded by anyone beginning to work in this field.

Basically, it's not easy; don't try to develop programs without significant preparation; don't try to do too much too quickly—start small, get good, and then increase and develop your commitment and programs; know your audience and what they want from you; and make sure you have put in place the necessary management systems to make your program work. Such management systems relate not only to the organization of the archaeological input to the program, but also to the management of, for example, the various groups of the public with which you are dealing; any political aspects of your program; any press or other media interest; the actual resource (be it excavation, archaeological park, or box of artifacts); and so on.

All these are critical areas of public archaeology. If we do not manage them correctly and efficiently we will end up alienating various groups of the public by failing to give them what they want—or raising expectations we cannot meet; potentially exposing our work to the subjective excesses of politicians; having our messages distorted and misappropriated by the media; and potentially putting at risk the actual archaeological record. Opening archaeology to the public opens our work to all of these, and many more, potential risks. We must learn to manage our work to minimize the risks and maximize the huge potential for good.

Struever emphasizes that anyone trying to set up a privately funded program anywhere near the scale of Crow Canyon needs to be ready to sacrifice their archaeological or educational career. In effect, anyone contemplating such a step needs to be *ready, able, and willing* to give up their present career (my words). To me, *ready* means that there are no old excavation reports to complete or books to finish; *willing* means that the individual is committed to a new life and to giving up the old and—most importantly—*able* means that the individual will be taken seriously *as an expert* in their field by at least one side of the archaeology/education debate. If you are not in such a position, then why should anyone listen to you, let alone part with their money to support you?

Clear Goals for Public Archaeology Education

If, as argued above, public archaeology has the ability to affect fundamentally the discipline of archaeology, and if those at the forefront of the work need to be recognized as experts, then, as archaeologists, we need to address how we teach those who are to take our place as the professional archaeologists of the future. This issue is addressed specifically by Nancy White and Stuart Struever. Both authors clearly perceive the need for effective proactive management and expertise as crucial elements of an archaeological education. If we are claiming that public archaeology is such an important aspect of modern archaeology, why do most of us fail to teach it to those students wishing to join the profession? There is no point in individuals rising to the top within archaeology or education to change career and immediately begin to reinvent the wheel and make all of the same, basic mistakes that those practicing public archaeology have already made over the past twenty or more years. We need to specifically train the next generation of public archaeologists *as public archaeologists*.

The suggestion that we should be teaching the skills and methodology of public archaeology to archaeology students raises the issue of who should be doing this work—a point addressed specifically by Kwas. We do not, for example, expect all archaeologists to be equally knowledgeable in all periods and geographical areas or equally proficient at excavation, survey, and synthesis writing. Nor should we expect everyone to be equally as good—or even interested in—public archaeology. I agree that *all archaeologists* should be taught and should understand the value of public archaeology and that they should perhaps understand the basic requirements of good public archaeology programs so that they will understand and be able and willing to support their colleagues who are involved in this aspect of the discipline.

However, not all archaeologists should be heavily involved in public archae-ology. Some are just not suited to this type of work and shouldn't be forced into it. As long as they realize the importance of public archaeology programs and help where they can (for example, in providing data; slides of their work, perhaps unprovenanced finds; and checking texts to be used in public archaeology programs), they should not be coerced into doing more. This is a critical point for the future of the subdiscipline of public archaeology.

If we argue that everyone should—and therefore, by implication, *can*—do public archaeology, we will (continue to?) create friction within the discipline and suffer a backlash from those who have no interest in actually *doing* archaeology and education. This is a wrong and false argument. Rather, we should be making all archaeology students aware of the need for public archaeology, providing them with a framework within which they can either specialize in this area or simply contribute and support without become heavily involved. This would also mean that archae-ologists specifically trained in public archaeology would be able to attain the same status and professional standing as their colleagues who specialize, for example, in midwestern archaeology or carbon-14 dating (see Bender and Wilkinson 1992). It means not only providing teaching at M.A. level as White argues (and which is already available at the University of Newcastle, U.K.), but also including basic compulsory courses in public archaeology in all first degree courses.

I am passionately committed to the development of public archaeology programs that address the needs of the full spectrum of society. I am conscious that such a development will and perhaps has already begun to have an effect on the nature of the discipline and how we study, and use, the past in the present. Less than a decade ago, I was privileged to be at one of the first meetings of the SAA's Public Education Committee at the 1991 conference in New Orleans. I can only marvel at what has been achieved in terms of public archaeology in North America since that meeting—much of which has been based on some of the long-term programs discussed in this book. However, I believe that public archaeology has had its honeymoon and must "come of age." This means the profession as a whole needs to address many of the issues raised in the rest of Part IV and needs to make some critical decisions about future methodologies and directions. The next six chapters in Part IV provide an excellent start for the debate that should precede such decisions.

Chapter Twenty-One

Politics, Publicity, and the Public
Urban Archaeology in the Public Eye

So you want to conduct an archaeological excavation in the city, involve students and the public, and get lots of publicity to boot? Here is a story from Baltimore, Maryland, that will help you deal with the politics of a bureaucracy, benefit from the inevitable publicity, and enhance public knowledge while still keeping your sanity.

The Beginning: Political Support

In Baltimore it all began with a newspaper article describing an exciting archaeology program in Annapolis, Maryland. Here, visitors were welcomed to a warehouse site and given a guided tour of the archaeological excavation. The mayor of Baltimore, William Donald Schaefer (perhaps best known for his promotional escapade in which he dove—clutching tightly to his rubber ducky—into the dolphin tank of the National Aquarium in Baltimore, having lost a bet on the completion date), was intrigued by the possibility of a similar project in Baltimore. His reasons were perhaps more pedestrian than those of the Annapolis folks. He viewed an archaeological excavation as an opportunity to promote a specific area of the city. So Baltimore hired its first city archaeologist and began the development of public archaeology in Baltimore.

Building on the success of other public archaeology programs and the interest of a local politician can both be extraordinarily useful to a start-up public program. A powerful political voice that senses the benefits of archaeology can be the driving force behind funding and logistical support. What do they get in return? The photo opportunities are an obvious answer, but along with that is the opportunity to provide quality-of-life benefits to students and constituents through public involvement opportunities and to feel, as the archaeologists do, that they are giving individuals a way to feel enfranchised with the past. Public education opportunities in archaeology can enhance community pride and boost the local economy through heritage tourism. Archaeology can contribute a unique sense of place, as well as a pride of a shared history, for a community. Each of these factors can be relied on to generate support from the political community for public archaeology programs. Considering the size of Baltimore and the extent of development over the last two decades within the city, very little archaeology had taken place. Perceived as a nuisance by the city and developers, archaeology was being viewed for the first time as a positive force.

Earlier in the year, a group of historic sites east of the Jones Falls had been linked by a self-guided walk called the Fallswalk. However, the Fallswalk had not gotten off on the right foot, probably because the surrounding area, while of historic interest, was bounded by low-income housing projects and severed from the main part of downtown by a very heavily traveled street. Clearly, the Fallswalk needed a shot in the arm, a new promotional angle. Perhaps a working archaeological excavation would draw people to the area as well as increase awareness of the historic sites, both below and above ground. Indeed, the planned construction of a major boulevard through the area had resulted in compliance-driven historic research and archaeological testing, demonstrating that remains of early Baltimore were intact below the surface.

A city-owned parking lot, where an early Baltimore brewery and later a casket company stood, was selected. Historical research told us that the brewery was built by a wealthy Philadelphian, Thomas Peters, who came to Baltimore in the 1780s. It was later owned by the third mayor of Baltimore, Edward Johnson, early in the nineteenth century and, best of all for the political purposes of the project, the flag that was the inspiration for the "Star Spangled Banner" was sewn together by Mary Pickersgill on the malt house floor in 1814. After the brewery ended its operation in the 1870s, the National Casket Company occupied the site until the 1960s. With urban renewal, the site became a city parking lot for fifty-six cars. As a microcosm of 200 years of Baltimore's industrial history, the selected site provided an opportunity to enfranchise the public with their past through archaeology. This would be accomplished through a combination of levels of involvement, from placard reading, to guided tours, to actual excavation experience through a student and public volunteer program.

The idea of using archaeology as a positive promotional tool is not usually the intent of the excavation. Even today, more than a decade into public archaeology, many professional archaeologists can be heard lamenting the time it takes to talk to the public or the press. They would much rather be left alone to dig in private. The public is almost universally curious about the past and their curiosity and interest can be seen in popular culture such as movies and advertisements. The challenge for archaeologists is to ensure that archaeology is not simply relegated to the role of tourism curiosity, but that important messages are conveyed to the public through interpretative programs. This is particularly important when dealing with students, as they need to understand their role in stewardship of archaeological resources now and carry that knowledge and sensitivity with them when they are adults.

Focus on the Public

Because the focus of the excavations in Baltimore would be the public, we tackled each part of the excavation planning from that point of view (Photo 21.1). A media consultant and a local university professor became integral parts of the public program. The archaeologists were trained to give tours and transfer their knowledge and enthusiasm to the public (Photo 21.2). Archaeologists and historians gave input into tour content and the formation of historical arguments for Baltimore. The project historian did additional research to find photographs, letters, and diaries that could be incorporated into the placards, brochures, and other publically oriented materials. This information formed the body of historic data from which the tour was developed. Specific historical facts were translated into arguments that, when linked to a feature or artifact, formed discreet parts of the tour.

As the program was developed, teaching became a major thrust—teaching not only visitors through tours but teaching volunteers and students on a tutorial basis. In order to realize this focus, a field school, consisting of students from local colleges and universities, was developed. They subsequently received credit from their home departments for their participation. It soon became obvious that a larger core of excavators was needed and a summer jobs corps program, sponsored by the mayor's office, provided eight Blue Chip-In students. These high-school and college students brought unique backgrounds and skills to the program (for example, a commercial art student and a mathematics major worked together to create wonderful maps and drawings). By the end of the summer, the Blue Chip-In workers became superb excavation technicians and, in turn, taught new volunteers.

Sharing multiple perspectives of history with the public and students is one of the most important roles of archaeological interpretation. And while archaeologists know the content, they are not generally experts in getting the message across to the public in a meaningful way. Training archaeologists to give tours enhances their ability to express themselves, and it has the added benefit of allowing each archaeologist the opportunity to reflect on their role in the excavation and interpretation of the past.

Photo 21.1. Volunteers at the Great Baltimore Brewery Dig were welcome during all regular excavation hours—Wednesday through Sunday, from 8 am to 4 pm. Dig hours thus accommodated the schedules of many different types of volunteers.

Photo 21.2. Tours of the excavation were conducted by archaeologists on a rotating basis, usually one morning or one afternoon per week. Here a group of visitors is listening to a tour of the Great Baltimore Brewery Dig while excavation takes place in the foreground.

Promotion and the Media

In Baltimore, as the beginning excavation date drew near, promotion became a concern. The public clearly needed to be told about this program. Since this excavation was to be Baltimore's first, it seemed appropriate to have an opening complete with the mayor, speeches, kids, balloons, root beer floats, and the media. This turned out to be the perfect way to capture the press and get the word out. A press release was issued and the lessons began immediately. One particularly nice reporter called and said he couldn't make it to the opening and could he have an interview, etc., beforehand. Being sympathetic and naive, I agreed. To my horror he did an exclusive the day before the opening, complete with pictures. Several, but not all, competing papers simply didn't cover the opening because of this. The ones who did come made the inevitable mistakes: wrong dates . . . misquotes . . . misinterpretations.

A public relations volunteer quickly stepped forward to help. She taught us to prepare written text and visual materials for the press and to give them good copy— written and verbal (Photo 21.3). Written press kits assured high-quality press coverage without the constant vigilance of the archaeologist talking to each reporter for hours. She taught us to stage good picture opportunities even if it meant not digging for a few minutes. We learned to hold the press's hand and make it very easy for them. It worked for us and kept them coming back. It also gave us control of what was said and written.

The word was sure to get out and it did. Throughout the excavation, the media, TV, radio, and newspapers focused a great deal of attention on "The Dig." The media coverage brought hundreds of volunteers whose hours of assistance translated into many thousands of dollars. And it brought thousands of visitors who learned about the importance of archaeology at "The Great Baltimore Brewery Dig."

Besides that, we printed and distributed brochures and flyers soliciting volunteers and inviting visitors to "The Dig" (Photo 21.4). "I DIG BALTIMORE" hats were ordered and distributed. The site was ringed by a 260-foot BALTIMORE ARCHAEOLOGY sign, and the entrance was surmounted by a sign: "The Great Baltimore Brewery Dig—Welcome." A billboard was erected over a major downtown street. Visitor information was sent to 1,400 travel agencies throughout the country.

The press can be your best friend if you take the time to understand how they work and what they need. Can you imagine having to learn enough about two or three completely unfamiliar subjects to write an intelligent article on each in one day under constant deadline pressures? The easier you make their job, the better the coverage. A written press kit is essential and will mean less time spent by the reporter trying to fill in the background data. This is translated into more column inches or air minutes to tell the story. Little tricks such as always using colored paper so the material stands out on a crowded desk, providing scanned images on disc for artifact illustrations and maps, and crafting solid quotes that can be dropped into an article are essential.

Photo 21.3. Publicity was an important factor at all excavations undertaken by the Baltimore Center for Urban Archaeology. Press kits were regularly delivered to television, radio, and print media, and the press often visited the excavation to get actual footage for the daily newscast or edition.

Photo 21.4. Special community days helped educate the neighbors about the latest excavation taking place in Baltimore. This is a hand-drawn flyer that we copied and delivered door to door to invite the local residents.

Donor Support and Volunteers

The value of the in-kind services provided by the City of Baltimore was most obvious during site preparation. Approximately $15,000 worth of heavy equipment for site preparation and testing was provided through the Department of Public Works—Bureau of Highways (DPW). Additionally, DPW provided shovels, paintbrushes, picks, wheelbarrows, whisk brooms, buckets, and so on. The surveying department of the city surveyed and gridded the site and made a site map. The Department of Recreation and Parks cleaned the area and provided benches.

While the various departments and resources of the city were available to the program at no cost, cash was needed to pay salaries. Grants from the local Humanities Council, two local foundations, and the National Trust for Historic Preservation supplemented the cash secured from the city. The cash budget for the project amounted to approximately $60,000, with contributed in-kind services worth $75,000.

Local companies were given the opportunity to contribute to the program. Several hardware stores gave Marshalltown trowels and a storage shed. A construction firm donated a typewriter and portable toilets. A public relations firm designed the flyer and brochure, and a radio station printed them. Even the U.S. Army was helpful. They provided four MASH tents to cover the excavation and excavators.

Public archaeology can bring support in the form of much needed money and services. A placard placed at the site entrance, which is updated with each new sponsor name, will generate more sponsorship. This list should also be part of the press kit. Tents loaned from the local Army National Guard, backhoe and grader time, and grant monies are all more easily secured when positive publicity is generated for the donor. No donation is too small or insignificant. Sodas from a local distributor on hot summer days; paper artifact bags; pencils and line levels, if purchased, will take real dollars from something else. Experience has shown that people genuinely want to help, they just need to be given the opportunity (Photo 21.5).

"The Great Baltimore Brewery Dig" site was open to the public while excavations were taking place. Wednesday through Sunday from 8 A.M. to 4 P.M., visitors were taken to the placard tent and then given a twelve- to fifteen-minute guided tour. This tour consisted of a series of arguments linking the archaeology and the past to the present. One such argument linked the high-status artifacts found in the privy to the availability of capital in early America and the development of banks and investment houses. The skyline of Baltimore, punctuated by the towers of commerce in the 1980s, products of the financial revolution that took place, was then woven into the argument.

Volunteers and students were given a guided tour, then asked to complete an information form (Photo 21.6). Data about previous archaeological experience in the form of fieldwork, classes, or simply a reading familiarity were requested. Each new volunteer was teamed with an experienced excavator. Early on, a core group of

Photo 21.5. We set up displays in many nontraditional venues such as shopping malls and elevators. This is a simple dirt-filled wooden box, containing a screen, equipment, and artifacts that we placed in a local school to encourage visits to our current excavation.

Photo 21.6. Dressed in their best, these local children were taught to be tour leaders at the excavation on a community day. They are standing in front of a typical sign placed at each excavation site to identify it for the visitor.

volunteers was formed. These were the folks that came faithfully each Thursday or Sunday, for example. Inevitably, their first question each week was: "What happened while I've been gone? Did you answer that question—or figure this out?"

Working with volunteers and students means changing your usual 9-to-5 schedule. Since most people are at work or in school during the week, keeping the excavation open on the weekends is an obvious tool for reaching the public. Regular volunteers who come each week can quickly be used to train and mentor new volunteers and students.

During "The Great Baltimore Brewery Dig," a volunteer or visitor would return to the site a week later with the answer to a question or the identity of an artifact. The daily radio updates also assisted in this process. "The Dig Update" aired at the same time each day over WCBM, a major Baltimore station. The live report included an artifact count and information on a newly discovered artifact or feature. Several particularly puzzling artifacts were described on the radio, and listeners came to the site or called with identification ideas. Once, after many phone calls and visits to museums in an attempt to identify an artifact, we placed its picture on the 6 P.M. television news and asked viewers to call the station if they know what it was. An elderly gentleman called to say that it was a cotton bale buckle and that his first job as a child had been to remove them from the cotton bales (see Box 21.1).

Box 21.1
The Legacy of Success

The media coverage of "The Dig" throughout the summer was astounding: five local TV news reports, a talk show, a national TV report, approximately thirty artifacts appearing in newspapers from Philadelphia to San Francisco, three magazine articles, and a radio show on National Public Radio's "All Things Considered."

Several thousand visitors and 302 volunteers became a part of the excavations by summer's end. And, by then, the archaeology at the "Great Baltimore Brewery Dig" had provided an excellent picture of industrial development in Baltimore.

The power of the media can be harnessed to help with research and to increase the support for and awareness of public archaeology worldwide. Numerous new public archaeology programs began following the success and publicity of the Baltimore program. Funding and support for Maryland's archaeology programs reached an all-time high following the success of Baltimore's pilot program and the positive publicity generated by the public programming.

After the Fieldwork

When the archaeology moved out of the field in September and into the laboratory, the volunteers moved with it. As during the field phase, lab volunteers scheduled specific hours or dropped in during open lab times outlined on the monthly schedule each was sent. These volunteers became the core for tour guides and excavators during future excavations.

Because the brewery excavation site would not be disturbed by development, it presented an opportunity to continue the public program in a permanent park setting. Perceived as an integral part of the Fallswalk through History, we convinced the city to abandon plans to return it to the parking lot function and, instead, work on a park design. A design charter was held in which urban planners, landscape architects, and outdoor museum specialists visited the site and formulated design ideas. The park integrates the exposed walls and features with interpretation markers. The theme of arguments, tying the archaeology to specific historical lessons, is continued and a visit is, in many ways, like the guided tour but without the archaeologist, perfect for school tours year-round.

It is vitally important to maintain the interest of the public even when the fieldwork is complete (Photo 21.7). Archaeologists know that fieldwork is only a very small portion of the archaeological process. The public needs to understand the entire process of archaeology. One way to do this is to maintain volunteer opportunities and publicity follow-ups. The camaraderie that is so much a part of fieldwork can be equally a part of laboratory research work with monthly volunteer lectures, field trips to other excavations and museum displays, and social events such as vessel-reconstruction bees. The media loves follow-ups to interesting stories and can place them on otherwise slow news days as filler (Photo 21.8). Keep their interest with an occasional phone call or letter update.

Program Longevity

The first home of the public archaeology program, named the Baltimore Center for Urban Archaeology (BCUA), was the office of the mayor. While this was a very fortuitous placement within the city system to get a program off and running, it was realized that a more permanent address was needed because if we stayed in the mayor's office we risked the program's longevity. When the administration changed (an inevitable happening in municipal government), the city archaeologists would be cleaned out with the rest of the personal staff of the current administration. Thus, choices for a permanent home for the public archaeology program ranged from city departments, such as planning, to local museums, such as the Museum of Industry. The Municipal Museum of Baltimore, the Peale Museum, one of the oldest museums in the country, was the final choice (Photo 21.9). This museum enjoyed private and city

Photo 21.7. Archaeology was seen as part of the larger tourism industry in Maryland. This poster, produced by the State Office of Tourism, was part of a heritage tourism initiative.

Photo 21.8. An "End of the Dig" party and press conference is a perfect way to launch the next phase of laboratory work or publicize the next excavation. It also gives the press a chance to "complete" the story that they earlier covered.

Photo 21.9. The perfect photo opportunity for politicians—complete with a pith helmet. This was a press conference with then Mayor William Donald Schaefer announcing the construction of a permanent museum home for the Baltimore Center for Urban Archaeology.

support and provided the BCUA with a recognizable name as well as stability within the city budget, as a funded line item. The support staff, collections, and library of the Peale Museum are very useful to the archaeologists. The Peale, in turn, benefits from an association with a highly visible public archaeology program.

At the same time that Baltimore began to develop the archaeology program, the mayor decided to create a Museum Zone, incorporating the Carroll Mansion (home of Charles Carroll of Carrollton, a signer of the Declaration of Independence) and several late eighteenth- and nineteenth-century residential structures. Located across the street from the brewery site, the BCUA museum includes a laboratory and museum and storage and office space. The new museum incorporates a hands-on excavation pit and the working laboratory as a part of the exhibit—teaching students and visitors first-hand, year-round, about Baltimore archaeology. Even with the construction and opening of this new structure, we never forget who helped us get to this point: the volunteers. All previous BCUA volunteers were invited to attend the opening. The invitation was an artifact bag that each could complete with "their" provenience information and in it place an item to be buried at the new museum. As our guests arrived at the opening, we recorded their donation in an "excavation register." Each became a part of what they loved—archaeology in Baltimore (Photo 21.10). All those "artifacts" remain buried under the courtyard of their city archaeology museum.

The most successful and long-lived of archaeology programs are those that become an integral part of the city, county, or state government (Photo 21.11). But the most important part of longevity for any public archaeology program is its ability to stay focused on the mission of educating and involving the public. The experience of the Baltimore Center for Urban Archaeology demonstrates that politics, publicity, and the public can create a synergy with archaeology. The result of this is success preserving, interpreting, and projecting the past to the present for students and the public.

Photo 21.10 Always taking the opportunity to educate, this flyer invitation to the "End of the Dig" party and press conference featured a conjectural drawing of wharf construction, information gathered during the course of the excavation.

Photo 21.11. A typical school group visits the excavation and is given a tour by an archaeologist. The public schools lacked money to pay for bus transportation, so we found a corporate sponsor to pay for the buses directly.

Chapter Twenty-Two

Crow Canyon Archaeological Center
*Why an Independent, Nonprofit Center
Makes Sense*

I have been asked to write on how and why we established Crow Canyon Archaeological Center in southwestern Colorado, and by what processes we operated the
center successfully, maintaining a high level of academic and financial stability
over the years. Further, what implications does the Crow Canyon approach have
for the evolution of institutions conducting archaeological education and research
in the future?

First, it's important to recognize that Crow Canyon was established with dual,
equally weighted purposes: The center was conceived, on the one hand, as a research
organization capable of a planned, regional-scale basic research program sustainable
for the long term, and on the other, as an organization intensely focused on broadening
and refining archaeology's educational reach into the American populace.

Speaking first of research, we must begin by recognizing a vast increase in the
numbers of institutions and individuals conducting some form of archaeological field
and laboratory work in the United States in recent decades. This has occurred at the
same time there has been major growth in anthropological and archaeological theory,
and this, in turn, has resulted in a substantial broadening of the research questions
archaeology believes it should and potentially can address.

Beginning in the 1950s and 1960s, archaeologists intensified their efforts to
reexamine fundamental truths about human behavior as viewed through time. Scholars
began to articulate new perspectives on major questions relating to cultural variability.

But at the same time, problem-oriented research efforts remained short term and small scale. Except for a few large but relatively short-lived federally funded multi-disciplinary projects or "showcase" salvage undertakings, the organizational complexity and longevity of archaeological research endeavors over the past forty years has increased very little. This fact is eloquently expressed in the nature of traditional research funding. Scholars in the United States undertake basic archaeological research largely with direct federal funding or private funding mandated by federal law. Funding is of two kinds: preservation or salvage contracts and basic research grants. Relatively recent federal laws require investigations to identify and, in some instances, salvage archaeological information before construction projects go forward. The vast majority of archaeological research underway in North America today is of this type. Significant, sharply defined space, time, and goal limitations are imposed on the archaeologists conducting this work.

Federal funding for basic research in archaeology comes from the National Science Foundation and the National Endowment for the Humanities. The budgets of these two agencies are and have always been quite limited. With intense federal downsizing pressures today, competition for these dollars is severe and growing more so all the time. Small grants are provided, each for a short period of time. Many important archaeological problems have evolved over the past three or four decades that cannot be solved with small, short-term funding, especially if continuation of that funding always remains uncertain and cannot be controlled (or sometimes even understood) by those doing the work.

The cornerstone of what became known in the 1960s as "the New Archaeology" is the interdisciplinary cooperation of scholars analyzing excavated remains of human societies, their environments, and the biological remnants of the people themselves, attempting to identify the causal relationships among the many important elements that comprise the human enterprise through the millennia. A growing number of archaeologists have come to believe that, by studying the remains of these prehistoric systems—society, environment, and human biology—and the interaction among and between them, important advances can be made in understanding the processes of cultural change.

To expand substantially its capacity to understand how culture functions, archaeology must accept the fact that the most brilliant scholar cannot begin to control the knowledge necessary to interpret the evidence of ancient human biology, the societies created by these people, and the environments to which both were adapted. This work requires the sustained, coordinated effort of researchers in many disciplines.

The independent, not-for-profit institution has become, for several interlocking reasons, the appropriate home for this kind of archaeological program. Why? First, *all* indirect cost monies derived from federal contracts and grants generated by the research and educational programs of the specialized archaeological institution go specifically to it and not to some larger agency, university, or museum's general fund.

Second, it is possible for leaders of the independent center to solicit gifts and grants without working at cross-purposes with the energetic university fund raisers and government agency budget creators who are committed to the well-established priorities of the parent organization. Third, it is possible to build a staff structure, create a field campus requiring substantial capital expenditures, devise an annual budget, establish new and sometimes idiosyncratic educational programs, all without parent institution review and approval—which may or may not be forthcoming depending on how they fit perceived institutional needs. Even some of the smaller organizing functions and roles within the complex archaeological research and educational program are not, understandably, familiar elements in traditional government, university, and museum staff structures: These fit more comfortably within an organization specifically established to accommodate them and their reasons for being. Finally, and most important, any institution that has a sharply defined focus can direct its energies, its resources, and its *public identity* entirely toward accomplishing its purposes. If well led and well managed (an entirely different matter), such an organization can expect to go farther, faster in achieving these specialized purposes than if it is imbedded in a highly diversified institution in which it occupies, and can only hope to occupy in the future, a relatively minor place.

Founding Crow Canyon Center

In 1982, the Crow Canyon Archaeological Center was created in the Four Corners area of southwestern Colorado with programs and goals very similar to those of the Kampsville-based Center for American Archaeology (C.A.A.), which I and several colleagues began building in the late 1960s. Initially, Crow Canyon was a western branch of the C.A.A.; in 1985, it became an independent Colorado not-for-profit institution. Crow Canyon's annual operating budget has been for the past ten years or more in the $3,000,000 to $3,600,000 range. Of this, less than 5% is governmental monies. The center has never had a contract archaeology program.

On the one hand, Crow Canyon was founded as an experiment in concentrating expertise and technology to conduct long-term research. Archaeological research in the Four Corners region of southwestern Colorado had reached the point where both new information and new questions about prehistoric life held promise for significant advances in understanding. This potential was enhanced by the fact that in recent decades, important advances had occurred in field and laboratory methods required to answer these questions: The challenge was to put together a program, staff, and research technology, rationalized by an appropriate research design, enabling scholars to employ the new methods in a sustained program.

This is the kind of research that conventional archaeological funding almost never allows. Crow Canyon's research budget has grown to become one of the largest of any institution in the United States today; depending on how you define "research," the center's budget for this purpose might be seen as ranging between $500,000 and $750,000 annually. These funds are focused on Crow Canyon's Four Corners research program. The staff operates on the basis of a five-year research design, which is annually reviewed and revised. The large, reliable research budget allows conduct of extensive field and laboratory studies; experiments whose benefits are long term are encouraged. Crow Canyon also funds coordinated research projects by outside scholars. Systems have been developed on the Cortez, Colorado, campus (new buildings specifically to support these activities were built in the 1980s) that enable the center's staff to prepare, edit, and publish, on paper or electronically, finished research. To better understand the relevance of Crow Canyon Center's educational mission, and why a private, independent nonprofit organization of this kind appears, at least to me, to be the most appropriate institutional context for building archaeological education in the U.S. today, we must look closely at the cultural milieu in which our discipline functions today.

The Cultural Milieu of Late Twentieth-Century American Archaeology

To begin with, let me assert frankly and unequivocally that it is highly unlikely that future archaeological education and research institutes in America will be governmental entities or institutions primarily sponsored by governmental monies. To understand why, we must step back and examine the general values, economics, and politics in which all of us in American archaeology have found ourselves in recent decades.

My overriding observation for the past thirty-five years is that archaeology occupies a marginal status in American life. Having spent more than three decades attempting to convince people that archaeology could be, and should be, important, I am struck that most individuals, regardless of education, view archaeology as interesting, even exciting, but of quite limited value.

This is understandable if we remember that archaeology has always been a very private enterprise in which a small band of scholars conducts its activities in the seclusion of a museum, university campus, government lab, or on a remote archaeological site. Even today, despite periodic public interest in high-profile, often preservation-oriented projects, archaeology remains a kind of romantic mythology peopled by small bands of intrepid professionals. Everyone wants to hear about it, see pictures of it, visit digs, and even send their daughters and sons to do it, but when faced with important dollar-allocating decisions, they turn to activities that touch them personally (such as the performing arts) or that are seen as having a direct impact on human well-being; included in the latter would be the education of the young, relief of human suffering (medical research and social services) and support of religious institutions viewed as critical to sustaining the fabric of life. How and why culture has taken the forms it has over thousands of years across the face of the earth is distant and obtuse.

Lamentably, archaeology's statements on human history are seen as sufficiently limited that decision makers today find it difficult to believe that knowledge of ancient societies carefully pieced together through archaeological research is likely to have an immediate or foreseeable impact on our lives. Scientific efforts (and related funding) are focused, rather, on research that has obvious significance for us (molecular biology, plant genetics, etc.).

Despite a growing sensitivity to and interest in Native American culture today, basic research into past pre-European cultures on this continent is not widely believed to be important for expanding our understanding of what most people think of as American culture. Our present culture is rooted in ever more swiftly evolving technologies that are vastly more complex than anything ancient Native Americans could have possibly imagined. The widely accepted corollary, whether correct or not, is that our culture, with all of its lumps and warts, is far superior to anything the Native Americans created anywhere at any time. Why, therefore, does it really matter if archaeology attempts to understand Indian history? It might be nice to know more about this history for a more balanced appreciation of this country's past, but to know it is not to know something that can significantly improve general well-being today or in the future. This conventional wisdom sees an understanding of the lifeways of the Native American as having no decisive relevance for us.

This widely held, if seldom spoken, belief is reflected in the fact that we still lack an in-depth human history for even a single region of North America that includes a genuinely authoritative account of the Asiatic American tenure. This is startling, since it was the descendants of Asiatic immigrants who exclusively occupied this continent for 95% of the total time human populations have dwelled here. Despite gestures toward an increasingly activist Native American community, this is quite acceptable to most people in this country, as reflected in the fact that, at least until very recently when we studied "American history" in the elementary grades and high school, we focused largely on the European experience over the past 500 years.

Therefore, U.S. archaeology, outside its application within the dramatically growing realm of historic preservation, fails to engender major support because of several deep-seated beliefs and public perceptions, as follows:

1. It is a romantic quest led by a small band of adventurers best left to themselves chasing long-lost remnants of history;
2. The vast majority of us hold a Eurocentric view of American history;
3. We believe in a strict utilitarianism in the expenditure of scientific research and philanthropic dollars; and
4. How can a technologically sophisticated America learn much of value from the history of simpler, preindustrial, preliterate Native American societies?

Certainly these views run counter to the democratizing tendencies of our times, but that does not change the fact that they are widely shared among today's decision-makers. This is principally why archaeology in the United States has never achieved, and in my opinion will not in the foreseeable future achieve, major status as an intellectual discipline.

It is hardly surprising, then, in the severe competition for dollars within government or traditional private institutions, that archaeology gets short shrift. If scholars in federal and state agencies, museum curators, or university professors decide to build a large, complex archaeological program, one that involves a substantial professional and support staff, considerable facilities, and large, continuing budgets, they are fighting a very powerful set of counterforces.

Having said this, let us examine the ideas underlying the creation of Crow Canyon Center, and observe how this institution has built itself by focusing squarely on the aforementioned values and prejudices of our society.

Crow Canyon and the Public

All archaeologists in this country are aware that, down through the years, the American public has had very little involvement in the archaeological research enterprise. Beginning with the Koster project in Illinois in 1970, the demands of the research program in which I was involved forced us to look for support beyond the traditional commitments of universities, museums, and government; we looked directly into the American populace itself.

For me at least, it's possible to identify the catalyst for this significant shift in viewpoint. In the spring of 1970, a veteran junior high-school teacher from Winnetka, Illinois, insisted that her seventh- and eighth-grade students would do a good job as Koster excavators . . . and they would be willing to pay a tuition fee to have this learning experience. Mrs. MacDougall's "I won't take 'No' for an answer" single-mindedness grew into more than twenty-five years of precollege student participation in the excavation at Koster and more than a dozen other prehistoric sites that comprise the Center for American Archaeology's Lower Illinois River valley research program.

Gradually the C.A.A., and later Crow Canyon Center, developed a variety of programs to involve the public in archaeology, both directly and indirectly. At first, an important motivation for this was the need to greatly expand the financial support for research. As time went on, the educational programs evolved their own independent missions. Today, the Illinois and Colorado Centers have broad, well-defined educational programs. In 1992, my last year as Crow Canyon president, the center served more than 4,000 people in its various educational programs. More than half of these were students, including elementary, junior and senior high school, as well as college undergraduates and graduate students. There were also large contingents of teachers and of adult lay persons, each in programs modeled to their special interest.

Crow Canyon involves many of these individuals in excavations as part of its overall research program. It also conducts a wide variety of campus-based seminars and workshops focused on Anasazi prehistory and on historic and contemporary Puebloan and Navajo culture. The center has a wide-ranging travel seminar program that brings together small groups of lay people with professional archaeologists visiting important sites in carefully designed itineraries, each covering hundreds of miles within the Southwest.

For elementary school students, the Crow Canyon staff has devised a curriculum involving excavation and study of simulated archaeological sites. The center also conducts an active program with Native American students; annually, several hundred Hopi, Zuni, Navajo, and Ute students are involved. Students come to our Colorado campus for workshops as short as two days and, in the case of university graduate students, for stays as long as six to eight months or more. The majority of participants are on campus from February through October each year. We can house, feed, and teach a maximum of 110 participants at one time.

The beauty of Crow Canyon is that it is not tied to traditional institutional roles. It can continue redefining itself without the strictures that museums, universities, governmental agencies, and private contract firms—the usual organizations within which archaeology is practiced today—have placed on them, either by mandate or by their long history. The center has the freedom to define for itself what roles it will perform in the life of contemporary America. We have found that there are important education and research roles that traditional institutions involved in archaeology touch tangentially or not at all. These include Crow Canyon's broad participatory excavation program; its programs in Native American cultures designed for southwestern Indian elementary school students; its archaeological and ethnographic travel seminars with their many facets; the campus workshops for adults; and most certainly, the in-depth self-sustaining Anasazi research program focused totally around the effort to answer important historical questions that may lie beyond the means of traditional archaeological research.

Crow Canyon's attractiveness to the public is attributable in part to a program mix that touches themes of major importance in the lives of Americans today, themes not effectively integrated into the activities of other academic or governmental institutions. For example, no organization in the Southwest has discovered more ways of relating Native American history and culture to today's predominantly non-Indian ("Anglo") population. A centerpiece of Crow Canyon's program is the effort to bring together two different Americas that traditionally have had negative or no relations with each other.

America's diverse cultural and ethnic segments can hold together, functioning as a working society, only insofar as understanding and mutual appreciation exists between them. We find ourselves living today in an America of growing ethnic blocks intent on building individual group identities while promoting their separate agendas.

In this world, Crow Canyon Center can be seen as a "bridging institution" dedicated to linking the majority of Americans with a wide range of southwestern Indian cultures. If America is to succeed in the twenty-first century, it will be as a multicultural, pluralistic society. As more of us come to learn the value and meaning of this idea, it becomes essential that there are active institutions preparing us for this. By conducting programs that cross traditional cultural boundaries, Crow Canyon is contributing significantly to this effort. The social environment of the Cortez campus itself eloquently speaks to this; here, students from affluent suburbs intermingle with inner-city minority students, with students from often depressed and depopulated rural areas, and with youngsters of the nineteen Pueblos, the Navajo, Ute, and other tribes that together comprise a large segment of the Native American population of the Southwest.

Increasing numbers of Americans are beginning to recognize that we live in a time when it is important to appreciate the character of Native American life so that thoughtful decisions can be made regarding urban America's relations with living Native American groups. Public attitudes, both within and outside the Native American community, will no longer allow these matters to be deferred. In this context, Crow Canyon's rapidly growing Native American program is creating important bridges between the cultures.

Still another reason that Crow Canyon's educational programs are of unusual value is that today's educators are increasingly conscious of the limitations of traditional classroom education for elementary and secondary school students. They have grown aware of the potential of achieving a higher level of student receptivity through experiential education that focuses on the interactive relationship between learner, the tools of learning, the teacher, and the subject matter. Crow Canyon's student excavation program and the many ancillary programs that have grown out of it, are examples of experiential education as its best.

When President Reagan's budget cutters swung into gear in 1980, their plan was to cut funding for much of the Federal initiative in historic preservation, including archaeology. They believed they would succeed in this effort because they recognized that most Americans had little or no knowledge of or commitment to the pre-European history of this country. Crow Canyon's educational programs may be seen as a small effort to alter this imbalance.

As Crow Canyon's educational program grew and diversified, it shifted from the simple idiom of "students helping archaeologists dig a site" and thereby learning about how field archaeology works, and in the process helping to fund the research enterprise (which, by design, had outgrown traditional funding sources), into a program that fulfills increasingly recognized educational purposes as well as broad societal needs. The educational program engenders much enthusiasm among philanthropic individuals and private fund agencies, and this accounts for much of the strong financial support enjoyed by Crow Canyon today. In fact Crow Canyon Center is not supportable at current levels, no matter what research, what grant writing, cultural resources management projects, or public relations efforts are undertaken, without the robust educational offerings, which are quite understandable and believable to those who are prepared to contribute financially.

In closing, let me examine what I hope are a few useful observations and ideas relating to the future development of independent, nonprofit archaeological centers.

Observations Affecting the Future Development of Independent Archaeological Centers

It is understandably difficult for those of us who have spent a lifetime in arch-aeology, often at considerable personal self-sacrifice and risk, to grasp the fundamental idea that the broader public may find what we do intriguing, but not very important. Certainly at least for financial decision makers, archaeology is not generally considered an enterprise to which significant budget allocations or gifts and grants should be made. However, this essay has argued that it is possible to define a series of perceived needs in American society today around which a group of privately supportable archaeological education programs can be built. That is what Crow Canyon Center has done over the past sixteen years. To the extent that the educational programs are carefully modeled to meet both the requirements of professional archaeological scholarship and education, and at the same time a growing, acutely felt public interest, they will be successful in recruiting both hands-on participants and financial support from individuals and organizations in the private sector.

Hard as it may be to believe, a much larger pool of support funds for archae-ology lies in the hands of private individuals, foundations, and corporations than exists in government agencies. It has always been our perception in archaeology that government is the major funding source, and we have come to accept this as holy writ. The experience of both the Center for American Archaeology in Illinois and Crow Canyon Center in Colorado speaks otherwise.

The reasons more archaeologists have not come to recognize this are not so difficult to understand when we reflect that most of us have no in-depth experience in the worlds of U.S. business and private philanthropy. Most of us have had very little contact with real money outside of research grants and CRM contracts, we really don't know who has it, or what they do with it and why. There is no reason we should have this knowledge. We didn't grow up wealthy and we have spent all or most of our adult life being educated in universities or working in archaeological organizations ranging from government agencies to private contract firms, uni-versities, and museums. We have lived and worked in a very narrow, specialized (and for the most part, enjoyable) realm.

For the past thirty years, I have straddled the specialized archaeological and the broader public worlds. My first observation from this experience is that it is a mistake to devote much effort in convincing traditional decision makers in government agencies and academic institutions to change their priorities; they won't do it. Further, *individuals* control huge financial resources in America today, far more than at any time in the past, here or elsewhere. Americans are by nature generous people. Many people with major resources want to do constructive things with some of their largesse. Our problem in archaeology is to convince them that what we are doing is worth their financial involvement. The kinds of programs in archaeological education that Kampsville and Crow Canyon have evolved into since 1970 have the ability to capture the attention of substantial numbers of wealthy individuals, not to mention foundations and businesses these individuals control or can influence.

In the preceding pages, I have enumerated the many reasons why it is easier to obtain private funding to meet archaeological research and education goals if the scholars and educators are working in a specialized, independent, nonprofit organization, rather than in a department or division of a large, broad public or private institution. The archaeologist is often handcuffed in a university, museum, or government agency by overall institutional priorities. From the private donor's viewpoint, archaeologists with interesting educational or research programs operating inside the larger, diverse organization are frequently perceived as less desirable recipients for private contributions.

There are a host of reasons for this. It is sometimes believed that the parent institution will siphon off a substantial portion of the gift earmarked for the archaeological program. Other donors think, usually erroneously, that the parent institution is wealthy or funded by taxpayers, and archaeologists employed by it don't really need their money. There are still other reasons, too numerous to mention here, that make an archaeological education or research program housed in a larger organization with diverse purposes poorly positioned to solicit and receive major private funding.

The following are a few of the most important considerations in building and sustaining an independent, nonprofit archaeological organization. First, there must be a leader, an individual who is perceived as understanding the mission of the organization, but at the same time capable of managing the institution's growth in an efficient and businesslike way.

This person need not be an archaeologist, but that certainly helps. The leader must be credible, both archaeologically and as an institution builder and manager. If this individual has a bigger-than-life persona, that helps. It is disastrous if the leader is an archaeologist who believes he or she can continue to personally conduct archaeological research while they build and manage the independent center. He or she must be sufficiently self-confident with their existing achievements in archaeological research and/or education to be comfortable in divorcing themselves from any effort to maintain a personal, first-hand involvement in research or teaching.

The leader's personal self-image must become that of an individual who is building an archaeological center. They can and should maintain overall strategic decision making in research and education, staying abreast of ongoing developments, but they must not visualize themselves as continuing their career as front-line academics. I do not believe that a leader of an emerging archaeological center can focus enough energy on the formidable tasks of building the organization if their persona is not concentrated on the role of institution-builder.

An additional factor in the effectiveness of the center's leader is the degree to which he or she has first-hand experience in the world of America's urban elite. The last thing I want to do is discourage one or more persons who aspire to launch an independent archaeological center, but like all subcultures, the urban elite has well-established principles for conducting their lives, including their philanthropy, and it is a distinct advantage if the center leader has personal familiarity and feels comfortable with these behaviors. If the leader doesn't understand them at the outset, it is imperative that they learn the values and modus operandi of the people they will be courting in hopes of involving them in the emerging center.

Because of its newness, a recently founded archaeological center does not have a long and widely held reputation that accounts for much of the major financial support enjoyed by universities, museums, and other private nonprofit institutions. Substituting for this is the personal image of the center's leader. If the leader is personally believable, with his or her goals seen as desirable and achievable, if his or her management and strategic planning skills are up to the task, and if the commitment to the new center is deep and unequivocal, then a potential donor may be prepared to make substantial financial and other commitments to the new institution.

This strong leader and his or her associates in the new center must identify a limited range of programs that will define the organization's mission. These must be carefully identified to be attractive from both the scholar and educator viewpoint, and from the viewpoint of the potential sources of private funding.

Here we find another frequent obstacle to building independent archaeological centers. Not every educational program or project an archaeologist's fertile mind can devise is marketable. And it is not always possible to execute successfully an educational program we can conceptualize, since we sometimes lack the knowledge or capital to carry it out adequately. Most of us in archaeology recoil at the idea that the marketability of an educational program should determine whether or not we initiate it. Our tendency is clearly (and rightfully) to do what we feel has educational merit, irrespective of its market potential. Alas, this is to live in fantasyland. Everything, including our much-cherished archaeological research goals, are subject to the values of the society in which we live. The National Science Foundation, we all know, will fund research it believes valuable by whatever standards and principles are currently in vogue in archaeological scholarship. So, too, is this the case in American society at large and in public education specifically.

It is therefore essential to define for the emerging archaeological center educational programs that have intrinsic merit but that are also attractive to elementary and secondary-school students, college undergraduates, teachers, adult lay persons, or whatever groups are perceived to be the target markets with the greatest potential.

The great quantities of money seemingly available for cultural resource management ("contract") archaeology today do not necessarily make the establishment of a contract program a particularly good idea if the purpose is to build an organization that will be primarily supported by private contributions and grants. Crow Canyon Center has never had a contract program, and this was probably the wisest decision we ever made. A contract program too often becomes "the tail that wags the dog" in the sense that its purposes will define and restrict the activities of the center and, at the same time, are not likely to be attractive to most sources of private funding.

Next to the strong, effective leader and a carefully defined marketable educational mission, the building of the independent archaeological center depends on its Board of Trustees. In a book I am presently writing, I devote three chapters to "the care and feeding" of the Board of Trustees. Building a strong, wealthy, generous, committed board is one of the leader's most important tasks, a task only exceeded by his or her ability to define and promulgate the organization's mission and promote its activities to those with the ability to support it.

Building an *effective* board is far more difficult and complex than is generally realized. Since the new archaeological organization is not a Harvard University with 350 years of reputation behind it, becoming a trustee of the XYZ Archaeology Center brings little prestige to the individual. Furthermore, in decisions about board membership, a widely held principle is that "big goes to big," "little goes to little." That is, big-scale philanthropists, people with major money and power, gravitate to the boards of widely recognized nonprofit institutions that seek them and to which they feel they can make a significant contribution. A newly founded archaeological center will find itself much more able to attract individuals with substantially less wealth, power, and board "savvy," and they have significantly less potential for making contributions to the center's financial well-being and to board decision making that affects the speed and direction of growth of the new center.

A major goal of the archaeology center leader should be to get a wealthy, powerful person to take the fledgling organization seriously, and therefore to devote not only significant money, but also considerable personal energy in helping the institution grow. My experience is that this is one of the very most difficult tasks to achieve. Speaking autobiographically, were it not for the deep involvement of Raymond T. Duncan, an independent Denver oil entrepreneur, it would have been impossible to launch and build Crow Canyon Center. During the crucial early phases of the center, Ray Duncan's start-up financial contributions, business savvy, and connections among the Colorado elite, made it possible for us to begin constructing the campus at Cortez, Colorado, while at the same time to begin building a strong Board of Trustees. Ray Duncan's personal reputation throughout Colorado provided me ready access to all of the private foundations that might have an interest in funding Crow Canyon. It was primarily his reputation that enabled us to present grant proposals to fourteen Colorado foundations and to receive substantial grants from every one. In the start-up years, our proposals were not turned down once, thanks in large measure to his reputation.

In building an independent archaeological center, one experiences momentum. Thus, the longer the building process goes on, the longer the programs function, the more the center is discussed in the media, the more willing individuals and foundations become to consider financial support. The young archaeological center begins to build on its own reputation. This has significant implications for the longer haul. As the independent center develops a reputation for success, in its research and educational activities, and in its businesslike way of operating, it builds confidence within the public sphere and this is expressed in larger and larger contributions and grants from those whose attention and increasing respect it has gained.

Crow Canyon has existed for seventeen years and is today capable of arguing that it has proven itself capable of performing quality research and education, thereby becoming the deserving recipient of major contributions. In the past twenty-five years, federal tax law has made it attractive for wealthy individuals to make large deferred gifts. These six or seven figure pledges can earn substantial financial savings for the donor immediately and in the long term. Once an independent archaeological center has earned a reputation for success, it can begin to explore large deferred gifts from those who have developed a personal identity with the organization. I must emphasize again how difficult it is for most of us to conceive of the amount of surplus dollars held by a surprisingly large number of Americans today. Crow Canyon received $2,300,000 from the estate of a modest, elderly person who showed few signs during their lifetime of being particularly affluent, yet this person had developed a deep proprietary interest in Crow Canyon Center, which they expressed in a very large deferred gift.

The preceding discussion leads us to a significant fact: For one or a few archaeologists to decide to begin building an independent archaeological research and education center they cannot expect success—and any hope of permanence—by devoting anything less than ten to fifteen years to the start-up operation. The problem is, of course, that one or a few individuals must make something equivalent to a total commitment of their career to building the institution without the assurance, perhaps even the likelihood, that they will succeed. This commitment is simply more than most individuals are willing to risk, and that fact is as a key limitation to those who might think of launching such an institution.

I want to make a few final remarks about building independent archaeological centers. It takes years to build an effective institution of this kind, and in turn takes enormous commitment by a few leaders. As the center grows, assuming its programs and financial support infrastructure have been planned and executed well, it will take on positive momentum that carries it forward to even greater achievement and deeper and broader financial support . . . institution building, like anything else in culture, has positive feedback loops.

But the key to this is the leadership. It must be committed to the long pull. This is risky, since the leaders must be willing to make a highly intensive, focused investment of energy now for potential success down the line. I think this fact more than any other, explains why the building of so few independent archaeological centers has been attempted in the United States in recent decades.

It is my impression that there has never been a better time in the almost fifty years that I have been involved with archaeology to launch and build independent archaeology centers. There are two reasons for this: (1) The incredible economic boom of the 1990s has vastly expanded the number of wealthy Americans, and (2) Never has interest in matters relating to the history and culture of the American Indian been higher than today. Over the past two decades, the populace of the United States, including decision makers has developed a much greater interest in and sensitivity to all matters relating to Native Americans. This interest translates into the most favorable environment I have seen for seeking private involvement in developing independent archaeological centers. The potential of these centers is immense, and I think we have only scratched the surface with Kampsville and Crow Canyon. Yet, their limited, but very real, success begins to reflect the possibilities.

This essay argues that, for those of us who still believe that archaeology can help us understand fundamental processes of culture change, and help us explain cultural variability, the independently funded archaeology center represents the best currently available means of concentrating the capital, technology, and expertise required to carry out the requisite longitudinal research. As for public education and archaeology, the independent center has the ability to fund far-reaching, continuing experimentation in this sector, a capacity far exceeding that of traditional educational institutions in this country today. The budget of the independent center can be closely focused on this educational mission, which is not usually the case in other organizations where archaeological education is conducted.

A well-operated, imaginative archaeological program with major hands-on participation by students and lay adults has today great potential for achieving private funding. The difficulty is that, even if one or more archaeologists are willing to make the personal investment to this kind of venture, their graduate school experience and their practical experience in the field, do not prepare them for the task. What I have learned over the past thirty years is not taught in any graduate school. Recently, both Yale and Harvard universities have made attempts to build graduate programs aimed at educating would-be nonprofit organization builders and managers. I hope they will institute one or more courses in archaeology center-building and management.

Chapter Twenty-Three
Teaching the Past in Museums

Archaeology education can take place in a variety of venues, but the single most common place where the public meets archaeology continues to be the museum. Museums are important for archaeology on a fundamental level because they house and exhibit archaeological artifact collections and because many archaeologists are employed or funded by museums. They are a place (often the only place) where the public comes into contact with the pots and projectiles that have been gathered during archaeological research. For much of the public, museums are archaeology.

The museum-going public has been growing, albeit more slowly recently than its doubling from the 1950s to the 1960s (Roberts 1997:65). While the usual museum visitor is an educated, middle-class person in his or her twenties (Zyskowski 1983:124), the future for museums lies in how it attracts and relates to young visitors, especially school groups. What the public will think about archaeology, about museums, and about continued public funding for these will be shaped by museum education programs for children and by community outreach (Duncan 1985:21).

For these reasons, archaeologists need to consider themselves to be part of the museum education team. They may be either museum educators themselves, or they may work in cooperation with the other education staff at museums. The archaeology educator developing programs for schools ought to have a clear understanding of how museums provide basic archaeology education to the general public, and especially to the literally millions of North American schoolchildren who visit them each year.

This chapter explores the issues of archaeology education in museum settings and presents a sample program for schoolchildren visiting a museum.

What Are Museums?

Museums are institutions for learning. Their focus may be history, science, nature, the arts, or some combination thereof. They may be large and government or business sponsored, or local, and volunteer operated. They may been seen as tourism sites (Boniface and Fowler 1993:102), as sites of "edutainment" (Soren 1990:iii), as academic guardians of "Great Objects of Great Value that represent Great Traditions" (Roberts 1997: 60), and as "repositories for the collection and study of documents and objects" (Walker 1997:33).

What they have in common and what defines museums (Martin Lewis, personal communication, 1985) are their functions, outlined by the acronym *ACRE*, namely:

Acquisition   the policies and processes for obtaining a collection
Conservation   the policies and processes for keeping stable, restoring, or protecting collections
Research   the policies and processes for understanding and interpreting the collections
Education   the policies and processes for sharing the museum's collections, expertise, and research

Of the four main museum functions, three relate to the internal museum workings. Only education technically requires consideration of the external world. Each function, however, affects how archaeology is represented. In fact, it is the impact of these functions in combination that have produced the image of archaeology that many people hold for a lifetime.

For instance, acquisition policies both dictate what museums collect and reflect what is considered worthy of being collected. Archaeology has, since its inception, been the main vehicle by which historical museums acquired their collections, so archaeology thereby became the *meaning* of those collections.

Conservation practices defined the public perception of archaeology by dictating the selection and method of exhibiting collections that would be displayed to, or accessed by, the public. To protect collections from breakage, light, humidity, or motion, only the more stable artifacts became part of permanent exhibits. Thus, to most people, archaeology came to be seen as groups of pottery and stone tools, guarded behind glass, removed from everyday life and protected from everyday people. It was, and is, remote.

Research established the authority of the museum and its reputation by virtue of its collection and conferred on the museum staff the power over interpretation of the artifacts. Archaeologists were authorities to a truth that they controlled. Educators changed the balance of power in the museum world, and with the change came different definitions of archaeology.

What Is Museum Education?

Education in museums is not a new concept. The original 1753 mandate of the British Museum was "not only for the Inspection and Entertainment of the learned and the curious, but for the general Use and Benefit of the Public" (British Museum 1997). In 1973, the American Association of Museums created its standing professional committee on education. What is new about education in museums is illustrated by the statement of Stone and Molyneaux (1994:17): "Most archaeologists want to teach archaeological skills and ideas; . . . whereas educationalists look for the means to stimulate the educational, rather than the archaeological development of children."

What is new about education in museums, then, is a focus on the visitor as participant, as learner rather than as recipient of a particular body of knowledge. Roberts sees this change as an empowerment issue, driven by educators over the objections of many curators because it transferred authority from the curators (including archaeologists) first to the educators, and "later, even to the visitor" (1997:45, 60, 73).

Once empowered, a museum visitor's own experiences become part of his or her comprehension of the collection. Educators use this understanding of "meaning-making" to develop exhibits or programs that enhance the visitor's involvement with the objects. The educator includes the needs of the visitor along with those of the museum (the "C" and "R" functions) when selecting and interpreting artifacts. The tools used to accomplish the newer approach to museum education include:

1. "market research" or visitor-tracking through exhibits, which lead to more engaging traffic flow patterns, light levels, labels, color and topic selection, graphics, and the use of varied and interactive technologies;
2. exhibits and programs that are seen as "communication systems" (Pearce 1990:159) based in communication theory studies and in which the visitor is an integral part;
3. entertainment, even to the degree of a call to use some of the techniques of Disney (Lumley 1994:66);
4. a cooperative approach that involves museum staff (curators, educators, designers) in a team and that seeks to work with other communities that participate in the museum (such as school boards, amateur and avocational societies, and ethnic societies); and
5. an understanding of education as a formal field of study, in particular as it relates the developmental stages of learners and the learning processes and the museum's collection.

Collection-Based Programming

It seems obvious that a museum would develop educational programming based on its own collection, but this has been a debated point (Herbert 1983:35). Some have questioned whether an educational mandate goes beyond the immediate museum collection to meeting the curriculum needs of the local community (i.e., suggesting that the museum ought to present an Inuit program, whether or not its collections contain any Inuit artifacts, because Inuit Life is taught in grade 4).

This debate about curriculum versus collection-based programming is underscored with educational program slogans such as that of David Hurst Thomas, cited by Crow Canyon staff, "It's not what you find; it's what you find out" (Ricky Lightfoot, personal communication:1997). Although this is an obvious truth to archaeologists on the one level, on another—and certainly in museums—it misses the point. Of course it's "what you find." Museums exist because of what was found; they proclaim it in each of their labeled, properly lit glass cases, and they attract the public because of it. Noel-Hume defined archaeology, too, in terms of what was found by calling it "material culture with dirt on it" (1978:21).

School groups are especially attracted to museums because of its objects. With the high costs of field trips and transportation, most teachers cannot get permission to leave the classroom unless they can obtain experiences for students that they can't provide in the classroom by themselves (i.e., to look at or touch [not talk about] "real" artifacts). To deny that archaeology in a museum setting is about "the object" is to be self-defeating, or at least, lonely.

Object-Based Learning

The issue, then, is the implications of an object-based focus for educational programming. First, programs should start with the collection, with an assessment of what it contains and its strengths. Next, the education staff should meet with community representatives (for example, teachers), to assess their needs and relate these to the collection. Museum educators then need to collaborate with other museum staff and to work in concert with the acquisition, conservation, and research functions of the institution. These steps could result in the following:

1. modifying acquisitions policies to develop collections that reflect local needs and the cultural diversity of the community;
2. deaccessioning duplicate artifacts from the collection for educational use and handling by the public;
3. creating reproductions of artifacts for public use (see Box 23.1);
4. researching and designing exhibitions that specifically address curricula;
5. incorporating conservation practices, such as wearing gloves for handling fragile artifacts, into educational programs;

Box 23.1
Is It Real Or Is It . . . ?

Reproduction artifacts can be perceived as "real" even when not authentic because of the context in which they are presented. Research has shown (Orvell in Roberts 1997:102) that museum visitors are satisfied with the reality of an experience, if it is presented with accuracy and integrity. This holds even when the visitors know that they are not experiencing the seventh century or wearing a genuine Roman toga. The backdrop of integrity provided by a museum's collection of authentic artifacts and the accuracy of museum research gives the aura of reality to the use of reproductions.

6. promoting archaeological stewardship, in contrast to the emphasis on obtaining artifacts that is highlighted by museum exhibits; and
7. providing space where educational programs can take place.

This last point implies calculating floor space per anticipated visitor, a designated area for coats, food, and supplies storage, sufficient washrooms to meet health code requirements, and adequately sized activity areas with running water and janitorial supplies. Child-sized furnishings (chairs, tables, coat racks, and toilets) are another consideration.

Museums such as Jorvik, at York, England, present the visitor with a simulated experience of that city's Viking past by combining the authentic and the real. Visitors ride a train back in time, traveling through part of a village peopled by costumed mannequins engaged in day-to-day activities. Facial features are even replicated using computer imaging from actual skulls found by archaeologists in the Viking-period cemetery (Karolyn Smardz, personal communication, 1997). The trip ends at the archaeological site that uncovered the evidence used to replicate the village, seemingly left just as it was when the archaeologists departed.

Interpretive centers (i.e., museums) at archaeological sites, historic sites, or heritage attractions such as at Wanuskiwin, L'Anse Aux Meadows, or Old Fort William, in Canada or in Williamsburg, Virginia, and many "living history" centers in the United States authenticate the reality presented by exhibiting excavated objects as proof. The object, therefore, remains central to the experience.

Museum programs will therefore be object centered. Museums are ideally suited to this approach because well-designed exhibits make connections for the visitor by displaying the objects in historical and often chronological context. This is an advantage museums have over archaeological sites in which the object's context is as an excavated artifact.

Educational Program Formats

A museum has several format options for educational programs. These may be dictated by practical considerations such as available floor space and staffing; by philosophical considerations about the nature of education, of archaeology, of history, and so forth, or by research about human learning processes and visitor preferences. Among these options are:

The Self-Guided Exhibit Tour

Visitors tour the museum with the aid of labels or brochures. This type of program can accommodate a large number of visitors in limited amounts of time for low costs. However, in this type of situation the public deals with the objects superficially. Visitors have been observed to spend only twenty to thirty seconds reading individual labels (Zyskowski 1983:123; Zorpette 1992:96). This format also imparts understanding at a superficial level, mostly in the form of facts and terminology. These are, in turn, labeled "knowledge" by educational psychologist Bloom, who defines "knowledge" as the lowest cognitive domain in his taxonomy of learning objectives (Bowd et al. 1982:301; Geraci, this volume [p. 95]).

Visitors feel alienated by museum labeling that is too detailed and academic. Conversely, visitors have been found to be alienated by too-brief labels, made with the intent of not unduly influencing the visitor's own interaction with the object (Zorpett 1992). When using this option, museums should consider the reading ability and first language of their visitors. Accessibility for younger, older, or challenged visitors may dictate Braille or large-print labels at wheel-chair or child height and/or audiotape cassette recordings of exhibit information.

The Guided Tour or Lecture

In this case, visitors' experiences with objects are augmented through the additional expertise of the docent or guide combined with an opportunity to ask questions and the enhanced experiential value of a personal relationship. Language and access issues are more readily addressed. The cognitive focus remains primarily knowledge, but can expand through discussion to include analysis, synthesis, and evaluation. While large numbers of visitors can still be accommodated, this format is less useful for groups of children. This is due to the limitations of their attention span, coupled with the greater impact of an active learning program on young students; research shows that children learn best by doing rather than by seeing or hearing (see Herbert 1983; Ellick, this volume).

To conduct a guided tour, a museum guide or archaeology educator should be trained not only in the history and interpretation of the collection but, equally important, in educational theory and interpersonal communication. Knowing a great deal about Blue-Willow–patterned or cord-wrapped ceramics does not necessarily make one a good archaeology educator, museum tour guide, docent, or interpreter.

The Discovery Program

In this format, visitors may be accompanied by either museum staff or by printed or taped information. Questions are provided to aid exploration by observing specific artifacts or collections. By answering the questions themselves over the course of their museum experience, visitors interact with the objects and learn to analyze the components of objects and exhibits. Sensory experiences enhance the sense of discovery. The interpretive centre at Sainte Marie-Among-The-Hurons in Midland, Ontario, Canada, includes walls covered in locally trapped furs and scents of the spices sought by explorers in its exhibits, while Jorvik, described above, uses essential oils to replicate smells of the barnyard, fish-drying racks, and even the Viking privy (Karolyn Smardz, personal communication 1998). Some museums, such as the Royal Ontario Museum (ROM) in Toronto, Ontario, Canada, have "Discovery Rooms" with deaccessioned collections used for exploration activities.

The Hands-On Program

This is the most demanding program format for a museum in terms of staffing, material, and preparation. It is therefore the most costly for visiting school groups. Hands-on programs offer the participant a personal understanding of the artifact's meaning through their interaction with it. The interaction may be as simple as holding an artifact or reproduction, or being dressed in a costume while in an exhibition gallery with a guide (Photos 23.1 and 23.2). More complex versions of this format could include:

1. detailed explorations of artifacts (by drawing them, taking rubbings of them, measuring them, smelling or tasting them);
2. making or using reproductions of artifacts (for example, pottery);
3. participation in structured (tell them what to do) educational activities that guide the visitor's interpretation (for example, give a student a bone awl and a steel needle to sew a leather garment. Then, ask students to comment on the effects of European contact on Native American lifeways vis-à-vis technology); and
4. participation in unstructured (don't tell them what to do) educational activities in which the visitor's experience with the object becomes its interpretation (for example, give students typical household items and ask them to improvise a scene from daily life of that culture. Then, discuss how the objects affected and reflected the lifeways of that culture in daily life).

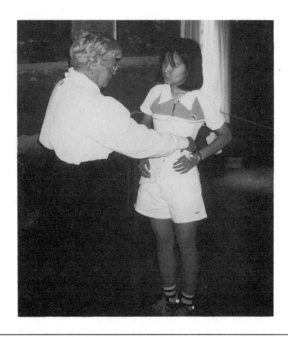

Photo 23.1. Student trying on a reproduction of a Victorian corset with the assistance of a museum guide.

Photo 23.2. Students using reproductions of nineteenth-century kitchen equipment.

The Responsibility of Museum Education

Whatever program format is used by museum educators, the goal is empowerment. Along with power comes the responsibility that museum educators have to ensure that all visitors are themselves empowered by contact with the object. As noted above, this responsibility can start with providing wheelchair access to exhibits and washrooms and displaying labels that are understandable. The responsibility goes beyond this level. It acknowledges the constructivist perspective that meaning is given by the visitor to an object from their own experience, as much as it is imparted by the museum. This is apparent when one hears a museum visitor exclaim, "My grandmother had one just like that!," followed by a flood of personal recollections.

The matter of responsibility to the visitor has been brought home in the public reaction to museum exhibits that deal with controversial subject matter. Notable in recent years have been the "Into the Heart of Africa" exhibit at the ROM, the "Enola Gay" exhibit at the Smithsonian Institution National Air and Space Museum (NASM), "The Peopling of London" exhibit at the Museum of London, in England, and the "Holocaust" exhibit at Beth Tzedec Temple, Toronto.

Each exhibit focused on objects in the museum's collection respectively: African artifacts brought to Canada by Christian missionaries and personal items of the missionaries; the airplane "Enola Gay," from which the first atomic bomb was dropped on Japan; artifacts illustrating the occupation of London, England; and artifacts from the Nazi concentration camps of World War II. Each exhibit was developed with academic rigor, historical accuracy, and current education and programming theory, yet the two former were met with storms of public controversy (Krauthammer 1995:68), and were closed. The latter two exhibits were considered successful. Why?

A key factor was that the ROM and NASM exhibits represented power over interpretation being maintained by museum staff, whereas the London and Beth Tzedec exhibits included the museum visitor in the interpretation process. Staff curators wrote the text for the ROM and NASM exhibits (see Canizzo 1989). Merriman's "Peopling of London" exhibit's development process involved hiring liaisons to meet with representatives of nineteen of the culturally diverse groups within the community (Coxall 1997:99). Beth Tzedec's exhibit reflected the stories and artifacts from the community itself.

Dismissing the need for inclusivity in museum education goes beyond the immediate effect of canceling exhibits to creating a legacy of distrust toward museums and marginalizing segments of a population. Native North Americans feel robbed by museums of their material culture; denied their voice in telling its story; and denied their cultural values, which placed "artifacts" in a living cultural context, rather than in a glass case (McMaster 1990:36). The Woodland Indian Cultural Centre on the Six Nations Reserve, in Brantford, Ontario, deliberately avoided naming itself a "museum" because of the discomfort within the community about such institutions (Tom Hill 1986:personal communication). Legislation in the United States (i.e., the Native American Graves Protection and Repatriation Act) addresses the issue of inclusion, but the museums themselves will bear the responsibility for restoring a relationship with the Native community. Postcolonial African countries are noted as beginning to consider the potential of museum education to regain identities that were hidden from them by museums that exhibited only the artifacts of the colonizers (Stone and Mackenzie 1990.) To succeed, museums need not only be inclusive in their programming, but responsive. Zorpette (1992:98) cites publicly funded curators who still question whether they "sometimes have to give the public what it wants." In answer: the Beth Tzedec exhibit contained an artifact that bore such emotional weight for the community that there was a request to remove it from the exhibit. It was removed. The curator at Beth Tzedec replied, by action, to the curators cited by Zorpette with a resounding "Yes."

Components of an Education Program

After having selected the artifacts for display; having wrestled with the responsibilities to the community; having consulted the contributors to the interpretive process; and having decided on the best program format, the museum educator finally faces the creation of a program. Programs for groups of school children require organization and the following components:

1. A previsit information package, sent to the visit coordinator (i.e., teacher), containing:
   - the cost-per-participant and payment options
   - directions to the museum
   - on-site facilities (washrooms, food services, cloakrooms)
   - accommodations for special needs students (such as wheelchair ramps)
   - duration of the program
   - recommended supervision ratio of adults to students
   - appropriate age for program participants
   - curriculum related to the program
   - an outline of program goals
   - an outline of program content
   - required materials to be brought (for example, pencils)
   - suggested previsit activities
   - suggested postvisit activities
   - the name and contact method (phone, e-mail) for educational staff
2. Program goals should be age appropriate, relevant to both curriculum and audience, and limited in number. A "three-item rule" is helpful. If, at the end of the program, participants can demonstrate understanding of three concepts to which they have been introduced, the program has been successful. To

learn more than three may be too demanding. The content of the "items" may vary with the sophistication of the audience, from "What is a stratum?" to "How did pipe designs demonstrate matrilineal kinship in Iroquoian society?"

3. Museum staff should give an introduction to both the facility and the program. It contains:
    * the name of the museum staff working with the group
    * the locations of: washrooms, telephones, cloakroom, food services, elevators, stairs, office where payment may be made
    * the time constraints of the visit
    * security and discipline expectations for the visitor (both students and adults)
    * the format and logistics of the program (including a gallery map)
    * an activity to focus the group's attention on the program content and help the group feel comfortable in its surroundings.

4. Program content should reflect the stated goals, and therefore also be specific or limited in focus. It should be presented in "bite-sized pieces" such as three fifteen-minute activities or discussions. Each should relate to one goal and be in the format of a mini-lesson, with its own introduction, application, and conclusion. By varying the pace of the activities, interest is better maintained.

Please note that the use of pencil and paper activity sheets should be undertaken with caution. Some students are too young for this format or may not have sufficient English skills to complete it comfortably. Others will focus their attention on completing a worksheet rather than on learning or on experiencing the collection. Worksheets can become litter, not lessons, especially if subjected to wind or rain during a museum visit.

5. A concluding activity should review the content covered during the program. This provides an opportunity for museum staff to evaluate the effectiveness of the program by gauging the level of understanding gained by visitors. A formal, written evaluation form should also be provided and a response requested of the group's supervisors—preferably before leaving the museum.

A brief program outline follows as an example (see Box 23.2).

Box 23.2
A Brief Program Outline

TITLE: Native American Technology

CURRICULUM RELATION: Grade 7 history unit: Native Peoples

GOALS: To complement Native Studies programs in elementary schools by establishing the relevance of the topic to modern life, addressing attitudes about Native cultures and peoples, and engaging visitors at the "Knowledge, Analysis, and Synthesis" levels of cognitive development.

OUTCOMES: The participant will:
- identify three examples of Native American technology
- explain the technological processes involved in producing artifacts exhibited
- evaluate cultural relevance in respect to technology

INTRODUCTION:
1. Museum staff will orient the school group to the museum.
2. Museum staff will ask the group for two lists of adjectives to describe Native American technology in the past, and contrast it with present day technology. Staff will record the lists for the group to see.
3. The participants will be divided into three groups and the logistics and activities of the program will be explained to each group.

PRESENTATION/APPLICATION: At three activity centers located near exhibits that contain examples of the artifacts to be studied, participants will use provided supplies to either duplicate the exhibited artifacts or to replicate how those items would have been used in the daily lives of the people that produced them, that is:
1. cordage
2. basketry
3. stone tools
Participants should rotate among the three centers at fifteen- to twenty-minute intervals, so all students experience each activity.

CONCLUSION: Participants should gather as a group to discuss:
- Have their perceptions of Native American technology changed?
- Would they revise the lists of adjectives created earlier? Why?
- What would they consider the main differences between Native American technologies of the past and present day technologies?
- Give examples from each activity center.

FOLLOW-UP ACTIVITY: Define "technology."

Conclusions

Education is a key function of museums. It is the one that is external to the museum in outlook and that links the public to the artifact. Because it is the collections that define a museum, and many of these are archaeologically obtained, museums ARE the face of archaeology for much of the public, especially school-aged children. How they perceive that face, the understanding they have of it, and the personal relationship they develop with it can affect the future of public or private funding for archaeological research or for museums themselves. It can affect how important the issue of stewardship of archaeological resources is to the public. It can affect how people see themselves in light of the knowledge of the past, and the kind of future they choose to build upon that knowledge. Archaeologists share with museologists the responsibilities and the rewards of bringing the past to the present.

RECOMMENDED READINGS

History News. American Association for State and Local History. Nashville, Tennessee.
    The AASLH produced numerous History Technical Leaflets; especially relevant is the 1971 26(3) volume. They are somewhat dated, but concisely present practical advice about many topics dealing with public programing in museums.

Hooper-Greenhill, Eilean, ed.
    1997   *Cultural Diversity.* Leicester University Press, Washington, D.C.
    An edited volume of twelve essays that examines interpretive, educational, and ethical considerations facing museums and other heritage agencies. This is one of several Leicester University Press publications on similar topics edited by Hooper-Greenhill.

Journal for Museum Education. Smithsonian Institution, Washington, D.C.
    This journal, in its various issues, explores subjects pertinent to museum education.

McMaster, Gerald
    1990   Problems of Representation. *Muse* 8(3):35–41.
    Muse is a Canadian journal for museum professionals and a forum for discussions such as the above, of museum-related issues and concerns, including education and interpretation.

Schlereth, Thomas
    1982   *Material Culture Studies in America.* AltaMira Press, Walnut Creek, California.
    Schlereth has authored numerous volumes exploring material culture studies in North America including this volume, which emphasizes historical analysis.

Chapter Twenty-Four

Teaching Archaeologists to Teach Archaeology

Teaching archaeology to the lay public in a nonacademic setting requires a philosophy, background training, and skills that are different than those with which most archaeologists are equipped in their academic careers. Knowing a subject well does not automatically enable one to teach it. The challenges of inspiring student archaeologists to work effectively with the public and of training them in the educational principles they will need are discussed in this chapter. For public education to be seen as a fundamental responsibility of being an archaeologist, the profession needs to invest in training students to meet this challenge. I present our experiences in one program of training archaeology students to do public education, and I offer ideas for incorporating such training into the university archaeology curriculum.

Background

How to do public archaeology and how to teach archaeology are not common emphases in most formal university programs that produce professional archaeologists. This is unfortunate; most archaeologists end up doing more public archaeology, including public education, than they would ever realize (Society for American Archaeology 1995b; Zeder 1997; Schuldenrein 1998). Today, every archaeologist must be prepared not only to deal with but also to embrace the public. Archaeologists must be teachers of archaeology and preservation as part of the everyday job in a professional career that will include interaction with Native Americans, children, taxpayers, news reporters, legislators, hobbyists, land developers, schoolteachers, art dealers, corporate decision makers, and public officials. And academic institutions have an ethical obligation to prepare their students to teach archaeology by giving them opportunities, theoretical background, and training in methods and techniques.

Two decades ago, the Anthropology Department at the University of South Florida radically shifted toward an emphasis in applied anthropology; for the graduate archaeology program this meant specializing in public archaeology. Originally defined as cultural resources management (CRM), the term "public archaeology" has evolved to mean much more (see Box 24.1). Included, and especially prominent today, is the focus on engagement of the lay public in archaeology. While there is no specific rigid course of study to become an educational archaeologist per se, working with the lay public is part of the general training for the M.A. in public archaeology. Similar training is becoming more available, more or less formally, and most often through departments that are known for applied anthropology, such as the Universities of Kentucky and Northern Arizona. As well, an appreciable number of students in public history M.A. and Ph.D. programs both in the United States and Canada are learning skills directly applicable to all forms of heritage education, including archaeology. Finally, the University of Newcastle in the United Kingdom has just initiated that nation's first public archaeology M.A.; it was designed by Dr. Peter Stone, executive director of the World Archaeological Congress, and was offered for the first time in the fall of 1999 with support from UNESCO.

As designed for the University of South Florida, the public archaeology component of the M.A.-level program includes the following foci, which are to be covered through a variety of readings, seminars, and activities over the course of the students' studies. The fundamental assumption underlying this training is that all archaeology is public archaeology, and that public archaeology is applied anthropology (White and Williams 1994; Sabloff 1996; Jameson 1997; White and Weisman In press).

Archaeology Education and Its Audience

No graduate archaeology program is complete without coursework and firsthand experience in public archaeology. Further, the archaeology student's theoretical foundation must include awareness of archaeology as social responsibility. Archaeological knowledge concerns the past of all humanity and also of specific peoples. The interpretation of the past affects and is affected by the politics and social situations of the present, and knowledge gained from archaeological research has value in many ways in the present.

Archaeology students need to carry these basics into their real-world jobs, with specific skills and abilities to do public archaeology. Especially, archaeologists entering the realm of the educator (teacher, park interpreter, exhibits designer) should

BOX 24.1
Public Archaeology Includes:

- historic preservation law, federal, state, and local, and the bureaucratic systems, the National Register of Historic Places and the concept of significance, legislative processes, including lobbying, legislative history, current government affairs
- both CRM and contract archaeology (which are very different things!)
- archaeological ethics
- anthropological understanding of Native American issues, and those of other cultural groups whose ancestral material culture and skeletal remains one might encounter and study in the process of doing archaeology
- writing for the public
- speaking to various public audiences, from schoolchildren to lawyers to Elderhostel groups
- archaeology in the communications media, from news reporting to portrayal in popular culture such as books and movies
- museology, exhibits preparation, and interpretation
- avocational archaeologists and associations, collectors' societies, looting vs. pothunting vs. amateur archaeology, including underwater
- antiquities laws, UNESCO Convention and other international agreements, and international cultural heritage management program, including divergence from law to practice, public attitudes in different countries
- general public understanding of the value of archaeology, of collecting and looting, especially as compared with other kinds of illegal activities
- putting on an archaeology day (or week or month) program
- writing/presenting popular summaries of specific research, even of thesis projects

be proficient in techniques and knowledge drawn from many and diverse specialties, from classroom teacher to public relations expert to anthropological theorist. As Ellick (this volume) points out, such a person may be the only archaeologist most people ever encounter; thus the message has to be related well. What follows is a description of some of the ways we have been teaching archaeology students how to teach archaeology as a part of the formal public archaeology internship requirement. In particular, I will present what we teach archaeology students about how to reach three specific audiences—the general public, schoolchildren, and teachers.

The General Public

The public is always there. Most research is supported by public funding or required by public law. Most of our knowledge of the locations and histories of archaeological sites comes from the local people. These days, as labor intensive as archaeology is, many field and lab projects could not be accomplished without lay volunteers. More and more archaeological sites are mined for artifacts by people seeking the fun (and increasing profit) of collecting something truly different. Wealthy and middle-class consumers alike, wanting new ways to spend money (ostentatiously or not), are finding ancient authentic art and craft items from all over the world to be the ultimate things to collect. The news media hunger for stories of discovery of ancient things bringing to light the human past and reflecting on the modern human condition. The greater audience for the archaeological product is the general public, which is fascinated with the romance of the past.

It is essential that the public and archaeology educator be trained to communicate archaeological concepts and information to people of all ages. Archaeologists encounter a typically positive reaction on mentioning to a new acquaintance what they study or do for a living. No encounter is too trivial, and the response to each question must achieve the maximum good: "Yes, we bring the human past to light, though these days we want to preserve more than dig"; or "Yes, it is a fascinating subject and there are some good new popular books (or a good lecture next week or a National Geographic program on tonight or a new museum exhibit this fall or a volunteer dig this summer) on the subject if you are really interested." Even the line that, "No, we do not study fossils but the things left by past people, such as stone tools, like evidence in a detective story," offers enlightenment.

The archaeology student must be well prepared to give an intelligent and useful answer. This is the basic beginning of all the training, knowing not only the material but the goals and politics of the profession well enough to explain them easily and informally. A second important principle is that archaeological knowledge can be related to any other field. This makes the teaching of archaeology relevant in contexts from history to technology to natural and physical sciences to the arts.

Techniques for Children in Schools

An underlying philosophy of the University of South Florida's program is that no student should be able to earn an archaeology degree without having had to speak in a classroom of elementary or secondary-school students. There now exist many tools to aid in this process (as described in this volume and elsewhere), from curriculum guides and lesson plans to children's archaeology books (Smith, this volume).

In addition to training students to give presentations to children of different ages and ability levels, and with many different learning styles (Johnson, Geraci, and

Wolynec, this volume), archaeology students must be taught to develop their own opportunities for reaching out to the public, and specifically to school children. Teachers are supportive of speakers with outside expertise, and many school systems have specific teach-in days or career days when professionals are asked to make presentations on what they do. Another avenue we suggest is volunteer speaker coordinating agencies; these seek experts requested by different schools and teachers. The University of Minnesota's Interdisciplinary Archaeology graduate program, for instance, maintains its own speakers' bureau to facilitate graduate students gaining experience in the classroom and in special interest group settings. And at South Florida, archaeology students are encouraged to get involved in museums or camps and to get involved in presenting children's or other public programs on Saturday mornings or during vacations. Instruction in how school contacts can be made, how classes, lesson plans, and field trips are designed and implemented, and how to assess the effectiveness and impact of any archaeology education program produced by students is crucial to ensuring that graduate students have the tools they need to teach archaeology effectively (McNutt, this volume).

Another issue that is dealt with in the context of teaching students to teach archaeology to a K–12 audience is resources and instructional media. While professionally produced curriculum materials, films, and computer games are available for purchase, many archaeological education tools are much simpler, consisting of actual or simulated artifacts or readily available household items. We're talking about the everyday life and environments of human beings at different times in the past, after all. Deer bone, clamshells, popcorn, and other native foods can be integrated into understanding natural environments, nutrition and health, or biological diversity and species loss through time. We use palmetto bark, clay, and bottle gourds from the grocery store and other easily available materials to show useful nonfood resources and to contrast with plastic and other nonbiodegradable modern materials. Examples of ancient writing can illuminate lessons in language arts classes, contrasting glyphs and alphabets or writing materials such as stylus and clay versus stone and chisel. Stone tools or potsherds and discussions of their manufacture, use, and deposition can be part of lessons in technology, physics, site formation processes and many other topics.

Besides materials already available for archaeological education, students at the University of South Florida learn to produce more locally relevant teaching kits to enhance their talks in the schools. The design and dissemination of these kits in various archaeological topics is a museological specialty; support for kit development in archaeology education programs can be sought from museums professionals and literature in that field. All audiences, especially children, love hands-on items. Better than items just for show-and-tell are artifacts that do something, such as atlatls, pump and bow drills, and other things that allow students to appreciate the skills of ancient peoples. Our students are taught that these are especially helpful for presentations to older children whose cognitive skills are tuned to active learning situations (Johnson, this volume). Archaeology students are often already developing these experimental studies in research and study contexts; doing them in a teaching context not only gives more experience, but also more research insights. After all, ancient technologies were often done around children or in the family context.

During their graduate work, archaeology education students must also be sensitized to the question of how to deal with controversial or potentially hurtful or confrontational matters that may arise when teaching archaeology. Race and ethnicity, religious issues, gender, treasure hunting, or environmental and historic preservation all present potential pitfalls for the neophyte archaeology educator. Students should be encouraged to seek guidance in developing presentations and learning materials that touch on such themes by becoming familiar with literature produced by professional educators in this regard (Moe, Connolly, Wolynec, this volume).

Especially in the realm of cultural diversity, public education in archaeology has enormous contributions to make. There are now many research projects investigating the material record of various historic ethnic, religious, and other groups in North America. Whatever the audience, some awareness of such sites and peoples should be brought into every school and public presentation. Teachers deal with these difficult issues every day; the archaeology educator will need to be very aware of the potential for conflict as well as the opportunity archaeology programming offers for ameliorating issues through the dissemination of anthropological and archaeological research results.

Archaeology students need to realize that methods and techniques necessary for public and educational archaeology may be new to their own field, but are well-established areas of expertise in other professional disciplines. Students need to learn to utilize professional literature in the fields of education, psychology, sociology, race relations, marketing, advertising, and communications in order to carry out their task of effectively bringing archaeology to children.

Schoolteachers

The Society for American Archaeology Public Education Committee, as well as similar committees in other professional organizations, have recently targeted classroom teachers as the single-most important audience for archaeological education. After all, each teacher can transmit to hundreds of schoolchildren over the course of his or her career the messages of heritage preservation, antilooting, the importance of archaeology as a means for discovering our human past, and many other concepts important to archaeology educators. So learning how best to work with, produce materials for use by, instruct, and learn from elementary and secondary-school teachers is a critical component of any archaeology education graduate training program.

Archaeology students usually meet schoolteachers when the teachers request information, materials, or speakers for their classes. It is possible to extend the relationship far beyond this brief meeting. For example, many state humanities councils offer summer workshops and other teacher training programs. In our experience, archaeology presentations can be related to many such workshop topics (examples for the Florida Humanities Council have included a morning of archaeology in weeklong workshops on "The History of Work" and "The Sea Around Us").

The National Endowment for the Humanities and other agencies sponsor workshops or short courses for teachers that the archaeology student can organize and write grant proposals to support. So, too, trips to local prehistoric mounds, historic sites, and the archaeology lab (where materials can be laid out for processing by the teachers themselves) are well-received highlights of such programs. Archaeology students must be encouraged to work with organizations of professional educators to provide workshops, talks and displays at national, regional and local teachers' conferences, and to publish in journals, electronic media and Internet Web sites aimed at elementary and secondary school teachers (Selig, this volume).

Greater interaction with schoolteachers can give the archaeology student an enhanced understanding of the needs of the classroom educator in today's schools, as well as local and regional curriculum priorities that offer an opportunity to the archaeologist to suggest places where heritage curriculum might be a suitable adjunct to required lesson plans. A familiarity with literature and other media for which schoolteachers are the audience is an important way for archaeology education students to gain access to information, techniques, and dissemination channels, as well. This course of practical instruction at the graduate level in public archaeology can take the process of reaching out to teachers beyond just planning and repeating a single talk, toward assisting in designing archaeology materials for the elementary or secondary-school curriculum.

Seizing the Day: Taking Archaeology to the Public

When an archaeologist is asked to do a presentation for schoolchildren, teachers, or special interest groups, most of us get out our slides, cut and paste a talk from a bunch of earlier articles and papers, and "dumb down" the language, originally designed to overwhelm our professional associates with our erudition, to a level we think might work for the lay public. There are many and various teaching methods that are more effective than the slide-aided lecture, however, especially with a subject as intrinsically interesting as archaeology. One of these is the Archaeology Day Program, the development and implementation of which is a feature of the graduate student's learning experience at the University of South Florida's Public Archaeology M.A. program (White and Williams 1994) (Photo 24.1).

Photo 24.1. Excited youngster is allowed to hold a prehistoric pot at University of South Florida's Archaeology Day program in northwest Florida.

An Archaeology Day is easy to organize in coordination with some local center, park, or school. Learning objectives must first be clearly defined by the archaeologist, and this is best done in consultation with educators. The required materials vary with the learning activity, location, time, money and expertise, but can be easy and inexpensive: perhaps a flintknapper to demonstrate tool making, a haystack to throw spears into, perhaps with an atlatl, a collection of slides and an upbeat and amusing talk to go with them, a well-designed and attractive handout, and some long tables for artifact and other displays. Publicity can be arranged by the students through local papers, radio stations, and photocopied flyers posted at local businesses; writing, sending out, and following up a press release are important parts of the learning experience for any would-be public archaeologist.

Our students' experience of such programming has been very positive; once area residents get into the spirit, various other activities can be added: firing pots in a pit kiln covered with brush, roasting or boiling whatever local wild resources one could eat, painting with natural pigments. Nearby indigenous peoples and other pertinent ethnic groups can be invited to give talks or make crafts for display or sale. The potential for adding activities is limitless. Clear educational objectives, creativity, and advance preparation are more important than elaborate materials and schedules. One of our best-received programs for schoolchildren consists of merely a talk in the lab showing artifacts and field equipment, then a trip outside to hurl simple spears of freshly cut, sharpened lengths of river cane.

Throughout their careers, archaeology education students will likely be involved in establishing and publicizing many such events; some states have expanded the official archaeology day or week to a whole month, which involves most archaeologists in the region in developing and mounting public programs. Our students are taught, though, that a daylong program need not be held only during the official month, as it is attractive any time and serves many crucial functions. Most important is public education; included in this is accountability for use of public funds and appreciation for the support of the area residents. Further, of enormous value to the archaeologist are the research data that can be collected, such as viewing, recording, and photographing local collections and knowledge of site locations. We come full circle as the public becomes involved in the data-collection process (Photo 24.2).

Photo 24.2. Graduate student at University of South Florida's research and public archaeology project in northwest Florida instructs young volunteers recovering artifacts and animal bone at a waterscreen at a Woodland period (A.D. 400–1000) campsite.

Public Education with Words and Communications Media

Working with various communications agencies and media is a fact of the archaeology educator's life. Earlier in this chapter, I mentioned that students in this subdiscipline require extensive training in communications skills to access the widest audience possible. The written word remains perhaps the most powerful tool of transmission to the largest audience, and students in the Public Archaeology M.A. program at the University of South Florida are encouraged to write for the public throughout the course of their program.

One need not lament the lack of ability in elocution to bring both exciting and accurate archaeology to the public (Fagan 1995). It is not difficult to write and speak simply; everyone started out doing it as a child. This is why it is an excellent idea for archaeology students to begin with schoolchildren, for whom "specialized resource procurement station" becomes "hunting camp," and "trajectory of lithic manufacture" becomes "the way they chipped stone tools." On the other hand, most kids (and lay adults) love to learn terms that are more accurate, such as projectile point, as well as the information that those are not arrowheads anyway since the bow and arrow was not introduced till later. Such tidbits (the sound bytes we are now so used to) often make them feel privy to the inside view of science. And we have yet to find a young audience that is not fascinated with the term and concept of a "coprolite," not to mention what can be learned from them these days, from diet to DNA information.

Graduate students often get into bad habits of writing overcomplicated, jargonistic, dense prose, usually because that is what they read and what they are expected to do by their professors. This is unfortunate for the whole profession, not just the public. We became archaeologists because it was fascinating, and now the articles put us to sleep. Comparison of a typical contract archaeology report and a current archaeological theory article frequently shows both to be equally boring. We need to show our students how to regain the magic and the mystery that attracted them to the field in the first place, and to use that skill to attract and educate the public.

Many universities offer support classes in good writing and public speaking. Getting students to go in pairs or groups to speak to schoolchildren is another helpful practice, as they can monitor each other. Archaeology students should be encouraged to keep repertoires of good lines and techniques to use and share as they get their degrees and go out into the workplace. And archaeology students, especially those going into interpretive and educational jobs, should be required to take formal education classes at their universities. They can get fundamental education concepts and techniques and better understand how to communicate with not only children but also their teachers by working with experts within the profession they are seeking to access.

Another way archaeology students learn public interpretation is through creating exhibits and displays, whether through a formal museology class, a cooperative program with a museum, a specific assignment in conjunction with a research or contract project, or a community institution's request. While museology and exhibits preparation classes may not be common at most universities, museums may welcome assistance with exhibits and other tasks. Student docents can learn not only collections research and curation systems that conserve artifacts for the public good, but also how to lead public tours. Whether in formal classes or during volunteer work, archaeology students can then also learn about assumptions behind interpretations presented in exhibits, whose voices and whose politics are being presented, and which segments of the public are being ignored or portrayed less positively.

It is easy and fun for archaeology students to stay abreast of the popular media's presentation of archaeology, but dealing with media attention in one's own work to assure it is beneficial to both the profession and the public requires special techniques. Some training in the methods and techniques developed for the fields of public and media relations is very important for any educational or public archaeologist. Writing press releases, developing media contact lists, and ensuring that what you are finding in your Middle Woodland site is not distorted by the media into a description of how King Arthur's Knights first settled the shores of Lake Erie requires considerable expertise, but it is a skill for which there is a lot of training and professional literature available.

Evaluation and Ethical Responsibility

All programs offered by archaeology education students, indeed, by any public archaeologist, should have a clear and well-developed method of evaluating its impact on the target audience. In graduate programs intending to train archaeologists to reach out to the public, it is crucial that the students understand the role of evaluation and apply its principals to ensure that the messages, concepts, and content of their programs are having the intended effect.

A serious gap in our knowledge and practice of public archaeology today is program evaluation. There is currently no verifiable understanding of the effect of public education in archaeology; is it saving sites or broadening an individual's intellect? Given the serious goals of public education and resource conservation, we need more than just anecdotal evidence of what works or does not work (McNutt, this volume).

Conclusions

Public and educational archaeology are relatively recently accepted subdisciplines of our profession. Both to inform the public and to effect real social and attitudinal change, archaeology students embarking on a career in this field require skills not found in traditional archaeology and anthropology syllabi. Until very recently, many of us were self-taught, with a smattering of knowledge gleaned from such diverse fields as educational psychology, journalism, museology, and communications tacked on to our expertise in our own particular archaeological specialty.

Fortunately, the development of programs such as the one described here, the new graduate program at the University of Newcastle, and the program planned for the University of Indiana at Bloomington are moving toward specialized curricula for graduate studies in educational and public archaeology.

Seeing the results of programs and policies will be helpful for inspiring archaeology students with a strong sense of their responsibilities. It needs to be clear that the public is not only essential to individual research, but also an ethically necessary component of good archaeology. For this reason, public archaeology should also be incorporated in some way into every graduate archaeology course, not to mention other graduate anthropology classes. As we move from knowledge to wisdom in the profession, we absolutely must realize the importance of going beyond even the most fascinating research and applying the lessons of the human past. The archaeological record's potential for offering insights and even solutions for modern problems, from global to local, needs to be described formally in the university classroom for the next generation, who are about to go out to meet those problems in their personal lives as they also do archaeology.

Training in educational archaeology is crucial, and not only for those who will become archaeology educators. The academic archaeology curriculum has been slow to include any public archaeology component (Bender and Smith 1998), but this is bound to change as we redefine the profession for the twenty-first century.

MARY L. KWAS ■

Chapter Twenty-Five

On Site and Open to the Public
Education at Archaeological Parks

There is nothing like the real thing to pique a child's interest. Visiting an archaeological site can bring students face to face with a palpable past, although few of the
sites lend themselves to class field trips. One often overlooked resource, however,
provides a unique opportunity for archaeological education. That resource is the
archaeological park.

Archaeological parks encompass both prehistoric and historic sites. Throughout
the Mississippi and Ohio River valleys and the southeastern United States, most
archaeological parks preserve Native American mounds and earthworks, such as
Cahokia in Illinois or Newark Earthworks in Ohio. In the west, ancient cliff dwellings
and pueblos, such as Mesa Verde, Colorado, are the focus of park developments.
North of the Canadian border, Head-Smashed-In-Buffalo-Jump bears witness to
prairie-dwellers' dependence on bison for food, while in Nova Scotia, Louisburg's
remarkable reconstruction brings to life the colonial French cod industry on the
eastern shore. Subjects of historic parks throughout the United States and Canada can
range from battlefields and forts to cemeteries and town sites.

Despite their diversity, archaeological parks share a combination of traits. These
include: being open to the public, often on a year-round basis, including weekends;
having some kind of site interpretation, from simple trail signs to museum exhibits;
and being set in the outdoors.

Archaeology educators should not overlook the many advantages of including
archaeological parks in their teaching or outreach programs, nor the possibility of
working in archaeological education as a staff member at an archaeological park. In

the following sections, I will discuss what archaeological parks are, the kinds of educational offerings typically available at archaeological parks, and factors to consider when designing programs around these special opportunities.

The Nature of Archaeological Parks

Very simply, an archaeological park is an archaeological site that has been preserved and opened to the public for visitation. Public development of an archaeological site immediately creates a conflict of purposes—that of preservation versus access. This conflict contributes to the complex nature of archaeological parks.

First and foremost, archaeological parks are archaeological sites. Their preservation and care are primary concerns. Any kind of development on an archaeological site creates an impact to the resource, both in the ground and visually. Therefore construction and placement of museum buildings, picnic shelters, trails, and even playground equipment must be carefully considered. Because sites in archaeological parks are protected, excavations may occur infrequently and are often limited in scope.

Second, because archaeological parks encompass large tracts of land, they are viewed as a type of park and are usually managed under state or provincial or federal park agencies. The outdoor spaces are ideal for holding events and festivals where large crowds can be accommodated. Hiking trails through woods and grassy areas offer other attractions for visitors. Management concerns range from mowing schedules to preventing or repairing erosion.

Third, archaeological parks also function as museums. Many have permanent and changing exhibits, maintain collections, and provide formal educational programs and a variety of special events (see Photo 25.1). Thus, the split personality of archaeological parks offers unique opportunities for educational programming, but also creates problems in management and utilization. For additional articles dealing with the nature of archaeological parks, see Kwas (1986a), Kwas and Mainfort (1996), Rolingson (1984), Svezia (1986), and Woodiel (1986).

Archaeological parks are inviting to the general public, in part, because they are perceived as tourist attractions. Individuals who would not attend more formal presentations on archaeology or visit traditional museums will bring children and out-of-town guests to an archaeological park. The parks' informal, nonthreatening settings attract a wide range of visitors who might not have any other opportunity to learn about archaeology (Photo 25.2).

This presents an interesting challenge to archaeologists engaged in education there. Programs and exhibits must be designed to meet visitors' needs for excitement and entertainment, yet must also meet educational goals. Creating a balance between what the public wants to see at an archaeological park and what the archaeological educator wants the public to learn is a worthwhile goal.

Photo 25.1. Children eagerly wait outside the entrance to the museum at Chucalissa, an archaeological park in Memphis, Tennessee. Thousands of area schoolchildren visit each spring and fall to enjoy guided tours and special events.

Photo 25.2. Youngsters wait their turn to try blowing a dart out of a cane blowgun in the village area at Chucalissa. Various traditional crafts and activities are demonstrated by staff and volunteers during a fall festival.

One other very important aspect of archaeological parks is that they are often open to the public year-round. Along with museums, archaeological parks provide public access to archaeology, not through excavations, but through exhibits, programs, and on-site staff. Education doesn't have to wait for "archaeology weeks" or other sponsored events to occur. Introductory audio-visual programs, permanent exhibits, and interpretive trail signs all give a basic level of education for the visitor. Staff is available to answer questions, visit schools, and interact with the public on a daily basis. This is, perhaps, the greatest strength of archaeological parks, and one not well recognized by professional archaeologists (see also Kwas 1994a, 1994b).

Education at Archaeological Parks

Archaeological parks are a wonderful educational resource for all ages that can be used by archaeological educators, both on-site and through other agencies, to provide meaningful programs. Children visit archaeological parks in a variety of ways, not just as school groups. They come with family groups and grandparents and as members of daycares, home schools, daycamps, and scout groups. These diverse audiences require a diversity of programs. Since many archaeological parks have staff members responsible for programming, I will discuss the typical kinds of educational offerings available at the parks and address concerns and recommendations for improving their quality. The content should also provide ideas for any archaeologists wishing to use archaeological parks in their education efforts.

Effective Exhibit Design

As mentioned above, one of the unique strengths of archaeological parks is their ability to reach the public in the absence of staff-intensive programs through such methods as exhibits and interpretive signs. Exhibits are available for the drop-in visitor as well as the structured group; they can be used independently or with a staff member as guide. Good exhibits can provide a broad informational background for the visitor, covering the particular site, area prehistory, and archaeological methods. Even better, daring exhibits can tackle difficult subjects in thought-provoking ways. Dealing with reburial issues, site destruction, pseudoscience, and other controversial topics may make the work of exhibit designers more difficult, but will provide a broader understanding of archaeology for the visitor.

Archaeologists may not be directly responsible for developing permanent exhibits at archaeological parks, but they are likely to have input when exhibits are redesigned or to be responsible for creating temporary exhibits or traveling displays. Many decades of experience have produced a solid resource literature in the museum field, and archaeological educators should look there for information needed. Two excellent sources are *Exhibits for the Small Museum*, by Arminta Neal (1976), and *Making Exhibit Labels*, by Beverly Serrell (1996), the latter of which offers guidance on content as well as design. Beyond exhibits, the literature of the museum field can provide insights and ideas to archaeological educators in areas of programming, visitor studies, evaluations, and interpretive methods, among other things. Archaeologists should make ready use of it. *Introduction to Museum Work*, by G. Ellis Burcaw (1997), is a good beginner's guide.

Self-Guided Archaeological Tours

Another often-used interpretive format is the self-guided tour, using a booklet keyed to stops along a trail or trail signs. Producing an effective tour guide requires understanding the audience. Text should be succinct, use image-rich words, and be free of jargon. Archaeological terms must be defined. Paragraphs should be short (three–five lines long) and there should be few of them. Text should be formatted for easy reading, using an adequate point size and breaking up grey text with bold subheads, bulleted lists, and interesting illustrations. Remember, people who are standing will not read long lines of text, so make your point clearly and keep it brief.

An important element in writing a tour guide is to focus on the most interesting aspect of each stop on the tour. Let your enthusiasm for the subject spill into your writing. If you have nothing interesting to say about a stop on the tour, then leave it off. The tour doesn't need to be an encyclopedia. Make the information memorable and make it human. Good interpretation goes beyond simply relaying facts. Good interpretation inspires and excites people, opening minds to new experiences and new ideas. Good archaeological interpretation helps living people relate to the lives of people from the past, and by doing so, understand our shared humanity.

Guided Tours

Guided tours operate on many of the same principles as self-guided tours. Keep in mind that it is difficult for people to stand in one place for extended periods; keep the group moving or, for longer presentations, sit down. Technical information is generally too difficult to cover on a walking tour and will quickly bore people; leave it for an interpretive display.

Interpretation Programs and Events

Introductory slides or videos are common at archaeological parks, and should also focus on interesting or unique features of the sites, within a broader context.

These shows should be kept short; people are eager to be viewing the exhibits or the site. Don't exceed fifteen minutes in length.

Programs at archaeological parks can be diverse; beside tours, they can encompass classes on Native American crafts or archaeology, festivals, demonstrations, and lectures. Programs may be designed to serve specific groups, such as elementary schools, home schools, daycares, daycamps, or Girl and Boy Scouts. At Toltec Mounds, Arkansas, programs are offered in American Sign Language. Each group has different needs and interests, and although programs may be similar, they are most effective when tailored to the group.

A daycare with preschool-age children, for example, will enjoy storytelling and the playing of musical instruments, but will get little out of a guided tour. Scout programs, now done at a number of archaeological parks, can be made to fit merit badge requirements; often the local scout council will cosponsor the activity. Programs exploring the methods of archaeology, community and local heritage research, and such diverse subject areas as language arts, science and geography, and environmental education (Frost, this volume) can be done with school classes. As Davis points out (this volume), these are particularly effective when they're designed to help teachers meet requirements under national, state, or provincial curriculum standards. Ensuring that new programs aimed at school groups meet curriculum standards will likely provide your park with a steady stream of field trips arranged by teachers because their curriculum needs are being met through participation in your park's programs.

Assistance with programs is available by using volunteers, demonstrators, and speakers. It falls on the archaeological educator, however, to select these assistants carefully. Not everyone willing to give a talk or demonstrate a skill is good with people. It is important to find individuals who can relay the excitement of a subject, not put people to sleep. For tips on skills needed to communicate effectively with the public, see Kwas (1995).

Assessment of Educational Programs

Finally, a good education program requires a method of evaluation. Too frequently this final step is overlooked, yet it is necessary for knowing how well programs are received and how effectively information is being relayed (McNutt, this volume). Although it is impossible to please all visitors, knowing the strengths and weaknesses of a program help to hone its quality. Sometimes, evaluations can even present major surprises. At one archaeological park in the southeastern United States, I organized a festival targeted to elementary schoolchildren. At the close of the festival the first year, we readily realized many of the design shortcomings; nonetheless, we sent a request for evaluations to the teachers who had attended. A response from one group of teachers took us completely by surprise. The group was critical of our program on southeastern Indians because it failed to meet their vision based on stereotypes of western Indians. However disappointing this evaluation was, it provided us with the knowledge to address that problem the following year.

An excellent manual on program development is Grant Sharpe's (1982) *Interpreting the Environment.* Although written for the interpretation of natural areas, the practical information is relevant to cultural interpretation. For more ideas on the kinds of programs offered at archaeological parks, see various articles in Kwas (1986b).

Making the Most of Field Trips

In an ideal world, classes would be small, teachers would be intellectually motivated, and students would be well mannered and thirsting for knowledge. Providing archaeological education programs in such an environment would be a piece of cake. In reality, educators at archaeological parks are frequently presented with large groups, distracted teachers, and rambunctious students. Making the best of the situation is a constant challenge for on-site staff. Other chapters in this book offer excellent ideas on designing educational programs, many of which can be adapted to archaeological parks. Instead, in the following section, I will deal with the mundane, but necessary, aspects of managing large school groups.

Visits from school classes make up a large portion of the overall visitation of archaeological parks, and such visits are critical to the assessment of a park's viability. Archaeological parks, like museums and zoos, are viewed by teachers as good places for field trips. When teachers take their classes on field trips, however, they are often limited by considerations beyond the educational experience. Buses have to be paid for and, thus, utilized efficiently. More than one place to visit may be scheduled in one day. School principals often require that if one class of a grade wants a field trip, then all the classes of the grade must go. For the educator at an archaeological park, this means that instead of being able to provide meaningful programs for a class of 15 to 30 students, one must deal with up to 200 children at a time, often within a limited time frame. There are various ways of managing large groups that can improve the experience of the visit, and this extends beyond what is offered educationally to mundane concerns of paperwork and bathroom breaks.

Whether managing large or small groups, potential problems can be reduced by adhering to a certain amount of paperwork. All group visits should require reservations followed by paper confirmations. A confirmation sheet should include the day and time of the planned visit as well as any basic information on park regulations or recommendations, such as how much time it will take for a class to use the restrooms or where picnic areas are located. To ensure the reservation form is read, keep it short and simple (no more that one page), and use visual aids, such as areas of bold text or simple illustrations as attention catchers. Be sure to request information about special challenges or medical requirements faced by any students, so that preparations can be made for meeting such potential needs as physical access, language comprehension, violent allergies, and hearing or visual difficulties (Wolynec, Smardz, this volume). Often, teachers are unaware that these challenges may limit a child's comprehension or enjoyment of a park experience. It is important to let teachers know that you are able to reroute or rearrange tours or programs to suit children with special needs, given appropriate advance warning.

Including pre- and postvisit materials in a confirmation packet will be appreciated by many teachers. Materials can include lesson plans, vocabulary lists, various activity sheets, background information on the site, and suggestions for further reading and study. Most parks operate on a very limited budget, and mailings of thick packets may be cost prohibitive. A good alternative to this is to maintain a park Web site, which can offer basic information on programs and site visits as well as a variety of information and activities that can be downloaded and used by teachers; be sure to include the Web address on the confirmation form. An added benefit to a Web site is that information about the archaeological park can even reach students and teachers who are unable to visit.

Once a group arrives at the park, aside from initial concerns as where to park buses, where to store bag lunches, and how to organize excited children, an archaeological educator's major challenge is how to deal with a too-large group in order to provide an effective educational experience for each participant. Much depends on the number of staff available to handle groups. Dividing large groups into smaller ones engaged in different but simultaneous activities is one solution. While one group is watching the introductory video, another may be participating in a guided tour, while a third enjoys an exhibit-hall activity or hands-on exercise.

Another solution used by a number of archaeological parks is to provide a several-day festival specifically for schoolchildren that offers many activities and can accommodate large numbers. These festivals can include Native American dances and storytelling, historical reenactments, demonstrations by crafts and technology specialists, and hands-on archaeological activities. Festivals are an effective way to reach many children, while meeting school demands and utilizing limited park resources and personnel (Photos 25.3 and 25.4).

An alternative approach, used at Cahokia, Illinois, is to require teachers to attend a previsit workshop to learn about the site and how to make use of the program offerings (Iseminger 1997:151). A similar program may work for other parks, also, but the acceptance of such a program will depend on the free time and motivation of individual teachers.

Reaching teachers requires a constant and ongoing effort to get the word out about a park's educational programs. As mentioned above, a Web site is one method. Another is to provide annual program brochures and updates. Often these can be distributed at no cost through a school system's internal mail network. Remember,

Photo 25.3. Choctaw dancers lead visitors in the snake dance on the plaza at Chucalissa during Native American Days, a festival targeted at elementary schoolchildren. Reconstructed Mississippian-period houses, seen in the background, add a suggestion of village life in the prehistoric past.

Photo 25.4. Chucalissa staff member and Choctaw Grady John demonstrate the making of pottery using the coil method to fascinated youngsters.

BOX 25.1
Program Samples from Archaeological Parks

Archaeological parks now offer a wide variety of programs for all age groups, and similar kinds of programs can be found at many of the parks. These include:
Craft classes and workshops:
- basket-making workshop, Wickliffe Mounds, Kentucky
- dreamcatcher workshop, Angel Mounds, Indiana
- coil-pottery workshop, Marksville, Louisiana
- Paleoindian spear factory, Mastodon Historic Site, Missouri
- archaeological methods workshop, Dickson Mounds, Illinois
- sandpainting and feathered-fan workshops, Toltec Mounds, Arkansas

Demonstrations, lectures, exhibits, and special programs:
- prehistoric lifeways demonstrations, Cahokia Mounds, Illinois
- exhibit of photographs on Hopi life, Anasazi Heritage Center, Colorado
- storytelling, SunWatch Archaeological Park, Ohio
- archeoastronomy lecture, Dickson Mounds, Illinois
- artifact identification day, Etowah Mounds, Georgia

Pow-Wows and Native American festivals:
- Summer Festival, Flint Ridge, Ohio
- Native American Festival, Moundville, Alabama
- Archeofest, Pinson Mounds, Tennessee
- Natchez Pow-Wow, Grand Village of the Natchez, Mississippi
- Native Harvest Festival, Cahokia Mounds, Illinois
- Native American Days, Chucalissa, Tennessee

Teachers' Resources:
- "People Who Came Before" curriculum guide, Hopewell Culture National Park, Ohio
- Archaeology Institute for Teachers, Elden Pueblo, Arizona
- teacher's activity guide and replica trunk, Aztec Ruins National Monument, Arizona
- teachers' workshop, Poverty Point, Louisiana

though, that teachers are deluged with paper; an attractive design can help them notice your brochure among many others. Use eye-catching colored paper; present your information clearly and succinctly, using bold fonts and bulleted lists to set off information; add simple illustrations for visual interest. Working with a school principal or the appropriate curriculum consultant may be useful in ensuring that the target audience of teachers is reached (MacDonald and Burtness, this volume).

Face-to-face contact with teachers is also important in getting the word out. It is useful to attend teachers' conferences and in-service sessions, both to get ideas of what teachers need and to promote your programs. Offering workshops at such sessions is an invaluable method for demonstrating how curriculum needs of professional educators can be addressed by participating in your park's programs (see Box 25.1). Lastly, try to find a motivated teacher in each part of the system to serve as a contact person; his or her information and knowledge about the school system can be invaluable.

Conclusion

Archaeological parks provide unique opportunities for public education. Through exhibits, tours, classes, and special events, information about archaeology and prehistory can be presented in an enjoyable and memorable way. Children, especially, benefit from a visit to an archaeological park, and through their visit, experience the past in a lively and engaging manner. Archaeological educators both on-staff and from other institutions can explore a wealth of educational ideas there. Perhaps better than elsewhere, archaeological parks provide the venue where past and present really meet.

RECOMMENDED READINGS

Burcaw, G. Ellis
    1997   *Introduction to Museum Work*, 3rd ed. AltaMira Press, Walnut Creek, California.
    A classic. An introduction to the methods and philosophies of the museum field.

Kwas, Mary L., ed.
    1986   *Archaeological Parks: Integrating Preservation, Interpretation, and Recreation*, Tennessee Department of Conservation, Division of Parks and Recreation, Nashville, Tennessee.
    A small early volume of collected papers on archaeological park management, with emphasis on public interpretation. Includes a paper on recommended readings from other fields.

Kwas, Mary L.
    1995   How to Communicate with the Public: Tips for Archaeologists Doing Public Education. *Tennessee Anthropologist* 20(1):74–78.
    Provides practical advice on putting together public talks, slides shows, and table-top exhibits to help capture and retain the interest of an audience.

Neal, Arminta
    1976   *Exhibits for the Small Museum: A Handbook*. American Association for State and Local History, Nashville, Tennessee.
    Guide to producing professional-looking but inexpensive exhibits.

Serrell, Beverly
1996 *Exhibit Labels*. AltaMira Press, Walnut Creek, California.
    This small but indispensible book gives tips on producing effective labels, from how to write informative, concise text to how to design labels that are readable and visually appealing.

Sharpe, Grant W.
1982 *Interpreting the Environment*, 2d ed. Wiley, New York.
    Although written for interpreters of parks and natural areas, the guidelines provided in this book are usable for archaeological and historical sites as well. A textbook for the beginner.

Chapter Twenty-Six

Archaeology Education Programs
A Long-Term Regional Approach

If you or your organization is thinking about beginning a public education program with a long-term emphasis and regional focus, then this chapter is designed to help you make the most of the steps that are ahead of you. It will outline the advantages and disadvantages of a long-term program, as well as program components and provide some practical suggestions as to how to begin. Since working specifically with schools, teachers, and precollegiate students means you will be interacting with a unique segment of the general population, separate sections explore various approaches and methods for introducing archaeological concepts to this dynamic group. An idealized situation is presented, along with ways to deal with the realities. Ideas are given on how you can prepare yourself and your program for success in working with precollegiate audiences.

Regional Archaeology Programs—the MVAC Approach

Mississippi Valley Archaeology Center (MVAC) is located on the campus of the University of Wisconsin-La Crosse, a city of approximately 60,000 in an otherwise rural part of the state. In 1997, MVAC celebrated its fifteenth anniversary as an organization. MVAC's mission incorporates both research and education. Efforts are regional in scope. In 1990, MVAC officially launched its Archaeology Education Program, which is designed to provide educational offerings to the public, precollegiate instructors and youth on a long-term basis.

Today, MVAC provides a variety of public offerings for all ages, which include: Archaeology Days, Artifact Identification Days, lectures, site tours, field schools, volunteer opportunities, and much more. The program also has numerous opportunities specifically designed for precollegiate instructors. These include: classes (undergraduate and graduate), field schools, workshops, newsletters, resources for classroom use, presentations, and more. Programs are also offered that bring archaeology programs to youth and families throughout the year. MVAC has made a commitment to give back to the community through education. In return, it is obvious to everyone involved with the program that efforts have resulted in a positive impact for the area's cultural resources (see Photo 26.1).

Photo 26.1. Staff who truly enjoy working with the public make events such as MVAC's public field schools and youth classes positive endeavors that actively involve people in discovering their past.

A description of MVAC's public education efforts is offered here for two reasons: (1) It represents an organization with successful long-term programs that are producing positive results, and (2) It encourages individuals and organizations that are either considering or are at the implementation stages of their own programs. In a relatively short time, through perseverance and many changes, MVAC has made positive strides in building a rapport with the public.

This chapter is a synthesis of concepts or ideas that have produced positive results, as well as factors that have been intrinsically part of the fabric of MVAC's growth and success. In many cases, the ideas presented here might appear to be nothing more than common sense. In MVAC's experience, theory, and practice, and through extensive consultation with other groups and organizations, it has been noted that even the most grandiose and noble endeavors might ensure their success through the generous application of some of these commonsense principals. Any successful program will be the result of finding ways to balance both financial and human resources effectively. I personally hope that this chapter helps you as you undertake your journey into combining archaeology with public education. Enjoy the challenge!

Advantages of a Long-Term Regional Program

There are definite advantages to the long-term regional approach to archaeology education. Most appealing to archaeologists is the positive impact that such a program has on cultural resources. As you, an archaeology educator, share your enthusiasm about your discoveries with the public, you will find that two very important effects occur naturally: (1) You will develop lasting relationships with collectors, land owners, contractors and politicians, and (2) Your group and your archaeological conservation program will enjoy increased community visibility; this in turn underscores the importance and need for preservation efforts. Both outcomes will aid in locating and pursuing sources of funding and open venues for the dissemination of information.

Giving back to the community by offering opportunities for public education is at the core of a positive relationship between archaeologists and the community. Archaeologists are aided in their preservation efforts because of popular support, and while the community learns more about the area in which they live, members become more involved in its past and its present.

The Down Side of a Long-Term Regional Program

There are definite challenges to implementing and maintaining a long-term regional approach to archaeology education. Time and money are the biggest challenges. Expenses can be formidable and difficult to fund. Many grants target specific populations, which may not be practical for your organization. Most granting agents and foundations are reluctant to offset operating and maintenance expenses for you or your organization; they will fund projects but not ongoing costs that you must meet to make the projects possible. Though individual philanthropists might enjoy a television special on the subject of archaeology, they might not be aware of your organization specifically or its work, or they might question its relevance compared to other "needy" endeavors (see Streuver, this volume).

Meaningful programs require considerable advance planning and an ongoing commitment, on you and your organization's behalf, to both the community and the programs you will be offering. Program staff members must be willing and able to appropriate considerable blocks of time to interact with the public and for program planning and implementation.

Suggested Components of a Long-Term Regional Program

Following are some components that will help ensure the success of a long-term regional program.

1. Continuity

In public programming, there is generally a lag between introduction and engagement. Most people must be exposed to something more than once, and usually from many sources, before they pursue more information or involve themselves in a cause or activity. Successful MVAC programs have been so because the public knows, or subconsciously perceives, that the organization has been around for some time, that its staff have been successful at what they do, and that the organization means to continue in the endeavor. Offering short-term, one-time events can be counter-productive. Consider how often one hears, "I heard about your organization from a friend who took your workshop. I decided that I wanted to do that, too, but it was never offered again!" Those who participate in your community-oriented programs are your best walking advertisements. Others, who were unable to participate in your offering this year, might have every good intention to attend a similar event in the future.

2. Visibility

Working in a region or community for a long time does not necessarily guarantee that there is a broad public awareness of your organization. Publicizing your efforts through a variety of media can go a long way in reaching larger populations. Even better, designate or hire a staff person specifically to deal with publicity and promotion. A public relations person knows how to establish effective relationships with contacts from the print and electronic media, and can completely dedicate their time to this activity. Waiting until your organization has planned "the event of the century" to get the media involved often results in disaster for your event and generally less-than-anticipated exposure level for your organization.

Continually pursuing opportunities to involve, educate, and build positive rapport with the media within your geographic area, on the other hand, provides you with ongoing visibility and a receptive relationship with journalists in your area. The significance of a major scientific find or your scheduled appearance of a noted guest speaker might be more readily received and accurately covered by reporters who know who you are and what you do.

Though seemingly insignificant to you, an announcement about someone on your staff attending a special conference, the relocation of your base of operations, or the receipt of a gift from a benefactor, all represent news to others. Releasing these bits of information to local media doesn't mean that they will necessarily be published or broadcast; however, in passing your name across their desks you begin to build an awareness among people who need to know about you . . . and care. When something significant ultimately occurs, your name and your organization are already known and recognized.

3. Meet the People

In most cases, there is no particular reason to assume that great numbers of people are aware of your organization and its work. By creating opportunities for you and your staff to interact with the local residents in a positive way, your organization can begin to build the framework for an ongoing community relationship. For instance, to increase exposure your organization might try an artifact identification event held at a local mall. You will certainly meet more people at an event of this type than you could ever possibly meet sitting in your office. You will meet people from a broad spectrum of interests, ranging from archaeology enthusiasts who have been trying it in their own backyards to ordinary people who are marginally interested in archaeology, and those who have obviously confused notions that blur archaeology and paleontology.

Perhaps, most importantly, you can attract those who don't have quite enough interest to search you out actively, but who will not hesitate to come over and look at the artifacts that you have on display. Your presence opens the door to a dialog, to an invitation to attend an event, to an offer to share, perhaps, artifacts that have been tucked in a grandparent's closet for years. Your new relationship might result in a new member for your organization and an enthusiast whose interest involves exactly what you do.

4. Offer a Variety of Levels of Involvement

Each year, season, or cycle offer a variety of activities that will involve people at all levels of interest. Offer basic activities that will encourage those people with only marginal interest to participate. Activities that require considerably more commitment of time or funds, such as a field school or laboratory experience, will satisfy others. Many who participate at one level will go on to become more involved if offerings are readily and practically available. A variety of programs enhances the possibility for continued interest in your organization and growth of its endeavors. There is a virtually limitless population that will always seem to be satisfied with activities at the introductory level, so these need to be continually available.

An argument against "bothering" with members of the public who are marginally interested in archaeology can be easily countered with:

- these people vote and can have a significant impact on cultural resources and funding issues;
- they have children who will be the custodians of our earth in a very short time and need your guidance in building a respect for cultural resource preservation and to become the archaeologists of tomorrow;
- they own land upon which you might find your next major discovery;
- they earn money, and how it is spent can consequently have an impact on your organization and its endeavors; and
- they live, work, and recreate in areas rich in cultural resources and take their attitudes, knowledge, and behavior with them wherever they go.

5. Provide Opportunities for a Variety of Audiences

You will work with people from all age groups and from a variety of interest groups and ability levels (Wolynec, this volume). Activities need to be designed to meet their age levels and special interests. People ranging from collectors, through land owners, contractors, politicians, teachers, youth, and college students can be offered uniquely different programs in archaeology that will encourage their support for heritage conservation, while giving them a learning experience that is both challenging and fun. A prepackaged and highly structured presentation or offering might meet the needs of one group superbly and be less than effective for another audience. By designing events that meet a specific group's needs, all will have a better experience that will ultimately encourage participants to continue their involvement.

6. Actively Involve the Public in the Program

A lecture or artifact show may be a good way to get someone involved in your program initially, but it will not keep most people coming back year after year. At some point, most people want to get their hands dirty and they long for the thrill of discovery; they want to touch a piece of the past, to sense the mystery and intrigue that is so much the perceived lure of archaeology. It seems logical that if those who are sincerely and genuinely interested at some level do not get an opportunity to act on their desire, they will ultimately look elsewhere, innocently try to record rock art, unwittingly dig on a family farm, or collect artifacts at a National Park. The energy spent actively telling members of the general public, "NO! NO! NO!" might be better spent devising and implementing ways for the public to feel that they are a part of what you as archaeologists are doing and, furthermore, that they too can make a significant contribution.

For some people, their expertise and enthusiasm can be best used on your organization's Board of Directors, for fund-raising drives, to give presentations, to assist with special events, or for tedious clerical responsibilities. Look for ways to not only involve members of your community in educational events but also provide ways for them to become involved in the furtherance of your organization and its mission.

By doing so, everyone benefits from a vast and diverse community pool of knowledge, enthusiasm, and expertise.

7. Public Education-Orientated Staff

Paramount to the success of a public education program is that the organization's staff enjoys what it is doing and is dedicated to work toward a cohesive education mission. Equally important is that these people love working with the general public. More than anything else, it is the sharing of the enthusiasm that archaeologists have for their work that really excites the public (see Photo 26.2).

Photo 26.2. Successful events reinforce staff members' commitment to dedicate the time and resources necessary to offer more public events year after year.

Not enough can be said to emphasize how beneficial it is for a project and an organization to have staff members who enjoy taking the time to share what they are doing and what they have learned with the public. Invariably, the sharing experience means that many of the same questions will have to be answered over and over again, year in and year out. It is important that they be answered with the same excitement and genuine enthusiasm with which they were answered the first time around. You may have said something or explained something a million times, but for most people it is the first time that they have come in contact with a professional archaeologist, a real scientist who they can relate to on a one-to-one basis.

8. Monitor the Growth and Effectiveness of Your Program

Programs and offerings should be continually monitored to make sure that efforts are meeting the needs of their intended audiences. It is wise to talk with people who attend events, not only about a particular event's content but also its structure and format. Encourage people to offer information by having them register for a free t-shirt in return for filling out a brief survey. Survey those who attend your events as well as those who don't. It's easy to get the notion that "everybody is interested in archaeology," when you only consider and deal with those who attend your organization's functions. It is wise to remember that there is a vastly larger number of people who stayed home or did something else! Ask people how they liked the events you offered. Ask for suggestions they might have for improvement and especially ask about other events they would like to attend and in what type of activities they would like to participate. People know what they want and, with a little encouragement, they will be glad to tell you what it is.

How to Begin a Long-Term, Regional Education Program

Below are a few pointers that will be helpful to you as you plan and implement a long-term regional program.

1. Be Realistic

Deciding what you and your organization can realistically accomplish and do well over an extended period of time (years) will help to keep dreams from becoming logistical nightmares. We all have grand ideas of what we want our public education program to do. In most cases, our highest aspirations for our ideas won't be experienced as realities overnight; it takes several years to build a program that meets the needs of archaeologists and the public with whom the organization works. Identify what and how many activities you can realistically accomplish with the staff and resources that you have at your disposal. The reality is that most tasks take more time and require more money than originally anticipated. Overextending yourself or your organization can lead to frustration and abandonment of otherwise premier programs. You can always add more to your offerings as staff, time, and money allow.

2. Identify the Bottom Line

Determining the bottom line of what you want to offer will not only help in planning long-range growth, but will also be important during periods when cutbacks become a reality. What are the basics that will happen every year no matter what? Basics like a newsletter, lectures, and an artifact identification day may be routine offerings, whereas an Archaeology Day may be an extra that you can only manage to bring together once every five years. Identifying the bottom line relates to continuity in that, in order for people to perceive themselves as part of a successful, ongoing program, they need to know what they can count on from your organization; what are the routine aspects of your program that they can recommend to their friends, relatives, and business associates? Plan and record those extras and improvements that you would like to include in your program as time and money allow. This can be both practical as well as a dream list. Having a plan becomes priceless when a potential benefactor says, "I'm not interested specifically in what you are currently doing or planning, but what could you do if I donated this or that?"

3. Begin Small

Although embarking on your new program should be done with enthusiasm, a prudent organization will keep in mind those goals and projects that can be realistically accomplished without overtaxing the available resources. Resources include the energy and time of an organization's staff as well as financial backing, physical equipment, and building space. Taking advantage of the assistance that other local organizations might provide, and using outside facilities in your community might mean the difference between having or not having a program. Your organization might be able to exchange an "Archaeology Video Night" for the venue to hold another offering or for a place to build an exhibit. Small steps, though seeming insignificant, will eventually lead to great strides.

4. Build Slowly

Being certain that you and your organization can deliver what you promise and then following through with a top-quality program will ultimately ensure a positive future for your program. There is a saying among theater people that it is better to have the performance of your life in a packed theater that seats only 20 than have the same performance before 20 people in an auditorium that seats 1,000. Take a bow for a performance that is well done and use the enthusiasm that is generated as an impetus for your next accomplishment. Along the way, opportunities will undoubtedly arise that will entice you to throw caution to the wind and be more adventurous and less cautious about your program's growth but, on the whole, growth is best accomplished by slow achievement and prudent investments of time and energy.

5. Maintain Continuity

Keep in mind that you are looking at the long term. Programs that start strong but lose their momentum tend to be frustrating and counterproductive for all who participate in them. For many archaeology is, or has been, a lifelong interest. Once a member of the general public makes a connection with you and your organization's programs, they will probably wish to maintain the relationship. It is hoped that you and your program will always be there to meet their needs.

6. Continually Monitor Your Audience

Market research is a skill that archaeology educators need to borrow from business and marketing experts. As you conduct your program, ask people informally or through a written survey what you can do to meet their needs. From their responses, it will be easier to determine exactly what things will mesh with your needs and objectives, and thereby plan accordingly.

7. Try New Things

Not being afraid to try something that you or others have never done before can sometimes lead to astonishing results. As your program continues to grow, you will need to come up with new ideas to keep people involved. Designing programs that fit your interests and resources might mean that offerings will change with changes in your staff, budget, or focus of research.

Visiting programs offered by other organizations, collecting literature on heritage education, attending teachers' in-service programs and conferences, borrowing from such disciplines as museum studies and environmental education and continually brainstorming with other staff and with teachers will all contribute to helping you and your colleagues bring fresh ideas and concepts to your program design. Remember to get permissions and give appropriate credit to those whose ideas and concepts are being integrated into your lesson planning, especially if you intend to publish in print or on the Web.

8. Form Partnerships with Teachers

Teachers are a great resource in a number of ways. When an organization works with teachers, it has an impact not only on the teacher but also on students, families, friends, and co-workers. Teachers will generally repeat successful programs and field trips over a period of years, which means that your organization, through the professional educator, will ultimately have an impact on vast numbers of young people.

As a group, teachers far outnumber archaeologists and have strong systems for networking, communicating and sharing their successes. Your success in sharing archaeology with teachers can have an affect that grows exponentially. With them, there is the potential to reach vast numbers of people with your education efforts.

Working with Precollegiate Teachers and Students

Since working with teachers is such a potentially productive endeavor, the following section is devoted to considerations in working with precollegiate instructors. Following is an Ideal Situation:

1. Teachers Would Be Trained in Archaeology

In an ideal world, teachers would have training in archaeology, including field and laboratory procedures as well as a knowledge of local pre-European cultures. This clear understanding of archaeology would be invaluable for teachers who choose to use the topic either specifically or as a thematic focus for teaching subjects across the curriculum.

2. Students Would Be Involved in
Archaeology Throughout the Year

Involving students in archaeology across the curriculum and on a year-round basis helps them to understand the integrated nature of archaeology, and its relevance on an ongoing basis. Students could then be involved in activities using archaeology as a thematic approach to learning math and science, as well as the humanities.

3. Long-Term Involvement: Seeds Planted
Would Grow to Maturity and Harvest

In the ideal precollegiate situation, an archaeologist would be involved with students starting in kindergarten, and would continue through twelfth grade. Concepts introduced in developmentally appropriate ways during the early stages of a student's education would form the foundation on which later enrichment could be progressively and successfully added. Students would be periodically reintroduced to a familiar realm of knowledge and information and subsequently encouraged and challenged to add to that knowledge or to pursue it in a different way. Ultimately, students would develop a rich sense of their human past, not only in their own regional geographic area but also on a global scale. This understanding would help foster understanding, respect, and tolerance of other cultures as well as an awareness of cultural resources and the need for their preservation.

Dealing with Reality

The chances that there is a school district that fits the previous scenario is most unlikely. This being the case, here are some ideas that will help you and your organization deal with what you will most likely experience:

1. Do Preliminary Research

Before accepting and embarking on a speaking or presentation engagement in a local classroom, some preliminary research will prepare you and your organization for what should be expected (Ellick, Lea this volume). Do your research: Ask the contact teacher numerous questions. How many students will be present? How much time is appropriated? What is the room layout? Are there tables or desks? Is the room square or a semi-circular auditorium? Can the room be darkened if necessary? Are there any students with special needs? What do the students already know about the subject? After you leave, will the material be discussed or enhanced?

The more questions you can have answered before your visit, the fewer surprises you will have to encounter when you arrive. And there are always surprises! Projectors break; classrooms are combined; fire alarms go off; students arrive later than expected, are anxious, or are completely disinterested.

2. Have Realistic Goals

Be realistic about the amount of material and activities that can be covered in the allotted time. As challenging and industrious as it might seem, it is impossible to condense a career's accumulation of knowledge into a one-hour presentation.

3. Make Lessons Developmentally Appropriate

Having a lot to say and delivering it with polish and enthusiasm is counter-productive if the message isn't organized and delivered in a way that corresponds to the developmental level of the audience (Johnson, this volume).

4. Work from the Familiar to the Unfamiliar

It may take some background work on your part, but look for ways to link the information that you wish to introduce to what students already know. Start from what the students know and proceed in small steps, moving toward the unfamiliar. People of all ages approach new information from a point of understanding with which they are already comfortable; they add information to their existing "database" gradually.

5. Use Questions

Learning to use questions as a way to lead students to seemingly obvious links of information can be frustrating and time consuming; however, students remember and understand concepts better if they are first challenged to draw on information they already possess to formulate an answer to a new question.

6. Limit Lecturing and Involve Students in
Interactive Activities

Limiting the time spent lecturing or talking to students and increasing their active involvement yields huge rewards for all concerned. Students learn more and remain on task longer if they are actively involved in learning. Instead of listening to a lecture, students are thrilled to analyze artifacts, participate in small group discussions, or become involved in any activity that requires that they do some thinking, not just listening.

7. Recognize Students' Egocentricity

Young people tend to think in egocentric ways, therefore your information needs to be relevant to them. You may have spent years on your research, and it may be fascinating to you and other archaeologists, but an effective presenter must ask himself or herself, "How does the material relate to the lives of the audience?" We are all more interested in things that directly affect us. Students are no different.

8. Make an Emotional Connection

Creating an emotional connection with the students will not only make the topic seem more relevant but will also engage them on another level. Consider whether students might be happy, angry, frustrated, or excited by the topics covered. As Connolly and Wolynec warn us (this volume), be careful regarding issues that touch on people's ethnic, religious, or political sensitivities. As archaeologists, the topic is people! How did they live? How were conflicts resolved? What social, political, or environmental pressures were placed on people? How did they respond or adapt? How did they express themselves intellectually, philosophically, artistically, musically, physically? Though the present social pendulum that we're experiencing in North America stresses an awareness of cultural diversity, human needs are—and have been—far more universal over time than students might realize. How would your students respond or feel in similar situations?

9. Work Within the Framework of
Students' Attention Span

Be aware of and work within the attention span of your audience. Young children have shorter attention spans than older students, so tailor your program accordingly. You may be asked to talk to a group of second graders for an hour, but to survive the experience it is probably more prudent to either request less time or divide the allotted time into several interactive tasks that are relevant and will engage the students for shorter periods.

10. Be Charismatic

Being naturally charismatic doesn't hurt, but if you're not and you know that you're not, be flamboyant. Energy and enthusiasm are two of the most powerful theatrics that can be brought to a classroom of students and can be the catalyst needed to create a rewarding experience for all concerned.

11. Know the Subject

This sounds like a given, as you have probably been studying your topic for a long time; it is your specialty. Think about your topic in a different way. Mentally, go back in time. Think about what you knew about your topic when you first became excited about the field, or when you were the same age as those in your audience. Your audience, in most cases, knows little or nothing about what you will present; remembering those bits of information that you gained early in your career will help you put together a presentation that will take your audience on a similar exciting journey. Step back from your topic and think about information as if it were building blocks. Use those simple blocks to lay a foundation, then add more blocks, systematically, to achieve your goal. An effective speaker first tells the audience specifically what he or she is going to talk about. The speaker then talks about that information and follows this with a summary to reinforce what has been said.

12. Consider Individual Differences

Within any group of students there is a broad spectrum of individual differences, including differences in learning styles and abilities, background experiences, and outlook. An effective presenter is mindful of these differences and considers different ways of presenting the same concept or idea (Wolynec; Geraci, this volume).

13. Remain Flexible

Remaining flexible and having back-up strategies can be invaluable assets to save a speaker's sanity and to help address any situation. Planning ahead always pays for itself. Usually, things will not go as planned, but you will be better able to deal with the unexpected if you have thought about it. Remain flexible! Be open to change! Think on your feet! Bring more ideas and materials to a presentation than you think you will need. Activities have a way of going faster or slower than anticipated. Audiovisual equipment breaks or is forgotten. Being prepared to deal with these situations and learning from your own experiences will be invaluable to you.

After reading the previous suggestions you might say to yourself, "Forget it! I'm not going to do that." In spite of all the surprises that can and do occur, working with young people can be extremely rewarding and exhilarating. Each mistake or unexpected turn of events is an opportunity to improve methods for your next presentation —if you are open minded enough to learn as much about yourself as you learn about the audiences seated before you.

Some people seem to have a natural gift for working with teachers and their students. Others find that with a little work and patience, they can achieve the necessary skills. If a person finds that, after repeated experiences, he or she really doesn't like working with young people, then it is probably for the best to discontinue the endeavor. Students are adept at sensing negative feelings and insecurity in a presenter. You're standing in front of them and have their full attention; that they can identify your weakest points within minutes is no surprise. If this is the case, it is wise to find someone else who sincerely enjoys the experience and possibly arrange for them to do presentations. Find another aspect of public education that fits your personality.

Preparing Yourself for Working with
Precollegiate Teachers and Students

You can enhance your precollegiate program capabilities by doing some preliminary work, including adding some research into formal pedagogical methodology, current curriculum priorities, and the appropriate ways to approach teachers, in particular, and the school district, in general.

1. Take Some Education Classes

The opportunity to work with precollegiate students can be greatly enhanced by taking a couple of education classes. Though it is an option that requires sincere commitment, it can provide the unique and priceless opportunity to meet both pre- and in-service teachers and to learn first-hand the things that they need to know to do their job effectively. Attending classes is an invaluable way to gain information on various teaching styles, student developmental levels, lesson planning, evaluation techniques, and much more.

Participating in a formal education program will help you better understand the needs of precollegiate teachers and their work environment. At the same time, it will help you refine your own teaching technique. If you don't have the time to take classes but have access to a university library, avail yourself of some of the fine textbooks on precollegiate education and some of the many education journals and magazines. It isn't necessary to memorize them from cover to cover, but browsing through publications such as these is bound to give you ideas, if not a new perspective.

2. Be Aware of Curriculum Standards

You need to be aware of the curriculum standards and requirements under which teachers are operating in your area (Davis, this volume). These change over time, so to attract and maintain your teacher audience, you must keep abreast of developments in curriculum requirements and foci in your area.

3. Attend Teacher Workshops

Before you decide to lead your own teacher workshop, participate in others that precollegiate teachers recommend. Attending such workshops is a great way to get a sense of the types of things that teachers seek out for use in their classrooms and, further, how to present ideas, concepts, and questions and how to display materials.

4. Talk to Teachers

Talking to teachers in your area can provide the best information regarding expectations and needs—what they want and how they will put it to use. Creating presentations, lesson plans, or prepackaged and formatted materials with the notion that teachers will accept them with open arms is usually a waste of time and money, besides being extremely frustrating. Teachers know exactly what they need, how to use what they have and which direction they will choose to take their students. School boards, school districts, state and provincial mandates, and parents have enough prepackaged notions about what should happen in classrooms. Conferring with teachers on a regular basis provides good insurance that what you propose or ultimately do will be readily accepted and appreciated (Wheat, this volume).

5. Visit a Classroom

Meet and work with teachers and students in the classroom. Watch others work with students to discover effective techniques to use. Interacting with children of your own is a tremendous help but the dynamics of a classroom are completely different. Build a relationship with a school and visit students at a variety of age levels.

Preparing Your Program for Working with Precollegiate Teachers

Following are some tips for building a "user friendly" teacher program. Similar to a business relationship, you are an archaeologist with a product and service to offer; teachers are your clients. Through careful planning and implementation of your program, you can provide your customers with a product that they'll want to routinely incorporate into their teaching repertoire.

1. Variety

Offer a variety of opportunities from basic to advanced and from short- to long-time commitments. Credit for clock hours spent furthering their own education or graduate/undergraduate credits can sometimes help teachers move up on their pay scale and provide them with an incentive to pursue archaeology as an area of study and personal interest.

2. Teacher-Friendly Format

Choose a format that works for teachers: class time, class length, season offered, and so forth. Talk to teachers to find out what works best for them. Teachers often budget blocks of their available time a year in advance!

3. Meet Teachers' Needs

You may have an agenda of things that you would like teachers to do, to learn, or to experience. Go to the end of the line! So does every other special-interest group in your community, not to mention requirements placed on teachers by their districts. Make your efforts congruent with and supportive of teachers' needs. Involve teachers in helping you to do this.

4. Fun

Teachers are among the most dedicated and hard-working people around. They put in long hours grading papers, preparing to teach new subject matter, filling out paperwork, and the list goes on. When they attend an archaeology event, it doesn't hurt to give them a chance to have some fun. It is possible to get information across to people who are having a good time. Teachers who enjoy an activity are more likely to recommend it to other teachers.

5. Continuity

Teachers need to know that you as a resource are going to be available in the future and that you will deliver what you promise. A teacher may not be able to fit a presentation into their schedule this year but might plan on including it the next. A teacher who cannot attend a class one summer will usually keep it in mind and plan accordingly if he or she is sure that the class will be offered every July, for example.

6. Support Teachers

Once teachers start to include archaeology in their classroom, they will need help; you are the one who can best meet their needs. Be available to answer questions. Provide a newsletter that contains content information, lists upcoming events, and recognizes teachers' efforts. Provide resources for classroom support and for teachers to preview. Be accessible for classroom presentations or field trips as requested.

Conclusions

Archaeology public education efforts can be extremely challenging and extremely rewarding. In establishing a long-term regional program, decide on a direction for your program and consider steps and resources that will be needed to accomplish your goals. If your program is to be successful, it should represent a comfortable blend of endeavors that will meet the needs of both you and your intended audience. Provide a quality program at a level that can be maintained. Build slowly and constantly reassess. Most of all, enjoy the experience!

PART V

Conclusions and Perspectives

The best and most effective archaeology education uses sound pedagogical principles, presents relevant and ethical archaeological information, and fits snugly with school curricula. *The Archaeology Education Handbook: Sharing the Past with Kids* is designed to assist archaeology educators with crafting and implementing programs that achieve these criteria. We, the editors, hope that it offers useful advice and practicalities for bringing exemplary heritage education to schoolchildren everywhere.

We have a number of other aspirations for this book as well. We want it to inspire archaeologists to get involved in the very meaningful and important task of sharing our profession's work with the public. If this book doesn't provoke debate, we've been too restrained, because there are very real and pressing issues in archaeology education that deserve scholarly discourse and research. It is our wish that *The Archaeology Education Handbook* will enable and encourage archaeologists to consider, as a matter of course, the educational potential of the projects and programs in which they are involved. And, if this volume soon is joined on the bookshelf by other books and journals on archaeology outreach and education, we will be most satisfied. Finally, we hope that this book will help to nurture archaeology education from the vigorous young sprout that it is today into a mature and vital aspect of North American archaeology.

Obviously the editors of a book like this are biased, but we think that an objective take on the future of archaeology education would present it as a growing enterprise. Since this is still a young endeavor, heritage professionals have the opportunity to shape its course thoughtfully and to influence its fit with its parent disciplines, archaeology and education. Several avenues of investigation are ripe for attention, and in closing this volume, we would like to identify the ones most apparent to us.

The Future of Archaeology Education

As readers have seen throughout this book, archaeology education has much to learn from pedagogy. One particularly relevant aspect of the education field is educational research; its methods and theories can be applied very fruitfully to several topics in archaeology education. Especially pressing is the need for archaeologists to gain an understanding of how children—and adults, for that matter—regard and assimilate concepts about the past and other cultures. When and in what manner are these concepts best presented? Evaluation is also a critical topic; are our efforts having the desired outcomes? What do children retain and how do they modify their attitudes and behaviors toward the archaeological record as a result of exposure to an archaeology education experience? What message is the public getting in the first place? Character (or values) education raises many questions for which we'd like answers. What are effective strategies (including such considerations as audience age, venue, and rural or urban settings) and reinforcements for encouraging reflective values formation in school children? How can dissonance between local or family values and stewardship be realistically addressed?

There's also work to do in reaching our intended audience in the education profession. Archaeological concepts and messages need to be linked more closely and explicitly with national and local curriculum standards. More teachers must know the educational benefits of teaching with archaeology. Archaeologists have to do more promotion and become actively involved with teacher education activities. Another question is whether the schoolhouse should remain the focus of most archaeology education efforts; can we connect more effectively and meaningfully with children through other media? It is important to remember that millions of children are not part of any formal educational system; they can be reached only through extra-schoolhouse strategies.

The contributors to this book have provided trustworthy guidance about reaching our intended audiences, but we must remember that a partnership with educators is a moveable feast. Their discipline is changing as rapidly as ours, if not more so. Different trends sweep through education continually. Many of these trends originate in academic and research settings, but education, being far less insulated than archaeology is, responds constantly and quickly to societal concerns and political pressures. This means that archaeology educators constantly must assess their interactions with educators so that instructional programs and materials remain relevant and useful. All of this is time consuming. Few archaeologists have time to conduct archaeology outreach and education of any kind, let alone to build relationships with educators and develop or test cutting-edge, tightly focused programs. Indeed, what archaeologist (or teacher) has enough time and support to do what they already must, let alone take on new responsibilities?

This volume has explored many ways to entice teachers into including archaeology in their classroom strategies, primarily by helping them meet educational requirements. But how do we entice more archaeologists to become involved and fit archaeology education into their work? How can we convince people in various heritage disciplines to stop preaching to the converted and reach out beyond gifted and talented suburban classrooms to connect with multicultural, disadvantaged, illiterate, and challenged students? How can we encourage the profession to recognize archaeology education as a responsibility and to develop accredited university courses and programs to prepare fledgling archaeologists?

We suggest that the profession of archaeology consider archaeology education as an investment, one for which the returns may take a while to materialize. Among the gains that we reasonably can expect to make are decreased looting and vandalism of archaeological sites and increased awareness and appreciation of the value of cultural diversity and heritage resources on the part of the future adult public. These are goals both noble and necessary for the vitality of archaeology in North America. The true return on the investment of archaeologists supporting education may well be a future public with a keen interest in the discipline. If we do our job right, people will have more than a dilettante's fancy; they will see what past cultures can offer to modern society and will endorse the benefits of archaeology for their own children's education.

A client public that insists on access to archaeologically derived knowledge means monetary support for more archaeology, either through public tax-based programs or through privately funded endeavors. Archaeologists working for school boards could become common. Institutions with the dual mission of research and education would not be unusual. Government-funded site mitigation would include public education and outreach components as a matter of course. A rising tide for archaeology education would raise all boats in the sea, so public support for archaeology in general would also grow. Once the public is educated about the values of archaeology, the findings of archaeological research would sustain their interest. Archaeology research and education become intrinsically linked, with outreach efforts being the public relations and marketing branch of the discipline.

We believe that this scenario is a very real possibility. Already, there can be no question that archaeology education has the support of professional archaeology organizations. Witness the active education committees, public education awards, educational materials, and statements of the candidates for office of the SAA and the SHA to gauge the significant changes over the last decade. However, these education and outreach efforts could evolve into another segregated subfield, rather than the integrative public face of the profession that, in our opinion, it should be. If our desired end is the sketch drawn above, then archaeology education requires a thoughtfully constructed fit with its archaeology parent.

A quick glance through the programs of the SAA and SHA annual meetings reveals the highly fragmented nature of our discipline. An ever-increasing plethora of subspecialties present real challenges to gaining a synthetic view of past cultures and how they changed. Archaeology education can serve as a counterforce to the negative consequences of specialization; it can be an integrating mechanism for the discipline. Our various publics are less interested in the subdisciplines into which archaeology continues to be divided than they are in what it all means. They want to know what archaeology can tell us about our human legacy, which is likely the quest that lured most archaeologists to choose the profession in the first place.

Archaeology education is at a crossroads; it can become either the discipline's weft or yet another warp thread. It can weave together the disparate foci of archaeology by coherently presenting information to the public, or it can look solely at issues and programs germane to the subspecialty of archaeology education. The dangers of the latter course have consequences for archaeology as a profession and for archaeology education. If archaeology educators become isolated from current research and findings, they lose their connection to what the public finds attractive and important about archaeological research. Moreover, the profession loses established conduits to its client public by not including archaeology education or its practitioners in its endeavors. Archaeology as a profession and archaeology education become impoverished and increasingly irrelevant. Why would the public want to pay for that?

If archaeology education is to mature into an integrative force within the discipline, we again must turn to other disciplines for assistance. Three others strike us as immediately applicable: marketing, communications (including public and media relations), and environmental education. Knowing how to select and transmit appropriate messages to target audiences is the essence of effective outreach. Marketing experts, who can turn the trade names for everyday products into worldwide household words, probably could teach archaeologists a thing or two about how to convince the public of the importance of archaeology and the stewardship of its resources.

Environmental education is a field with goals closely allied to our own; that is, instilling an ethic of appreciation for diminishing or threatened resources. In addition, it is a mature discipline, with professional organizations and journals, funded research, and widespread institutionalization in education systems. At the international level, cultural heritage conservation has been explicitly linked to the preservation of our natural world, as the UNESCO accord for World Heritage Sites demonstrates (Frost, this volume). The evolution of environmental education and the outcomes of approaches taken by that discipline offer valuable perspectives to archaeology educators striving for similar goals. Frost's contribution here provides grist for the mill and invites further discourse with practitioners of environmental education.

If our vision, or something like it, of the future of archaeology and public education comes to fruition, we can anticipate other effects on North American archaeology, not all of which may be welcomed by our colleagues. A public educated about the values of archaeological research and the importance of heritage resources may demand a measure of control over future directions in research, as well as increased lay participation. Certainly, the funding priorities of governmental agencies, and even private foundations, will be given more scrutiny; public archaeology will make all of us accountable to the people who ultimately pay our bills. We have referred to the public at times as archaeology's "client," but this isn't exactly accurate. To some extent, the job of a professional is to be a purist and pursue research questions that derive from extensive immersion in the field, not to be a for-hire scientist researching a less-educated public's whims. However, the public entrusts us with the conservation of the past through its support of heritage legislation and funding of archaeological work by public-sector agencies that sponsor research and preservation efforts. In this way, we serve as trustees on behalf of the general populace to conserve and interpret their prehistoric and historical heritage. Perhaps the balanced middle ground for archaeologists is to be more publicly accountable, explaining the reasons for and results of their research to the very people whose heritage it is they are researching.

Whatever future shape and role archaeology education is to have, the profession must address how to train the next generation of archaeologists so that they are prepared for their life's work. Archaeology education may be a specialty focus for some, but for most, their education should include guidance and examples of how to incorporate outreach into their everyday activities. Several universities now offer education and outreach programs at the graduate level; other schools offer individual courses, and many more include cross-listed programs in education and related fields as part of the course complement for M.A. or Ph.D. students. As the job market for public archaeologists increases, more universities will be attracted to the development of public archaeology courses to ensure the employability of their graduates.

Likewise, in many communities archaeological projects will be expected to include a public component. This already is the case in some areas where public archaeology programs have become the order of the day for public- and private-sector–operated projects. As the professional community becomes more accustomed to including a public education and participation element in their work, this trend can only increase. The professional societies have led the way already, and this book is a good example of the results that can occur when organizations like the SAA support and sponsor public archaeology and education efforts on behalf of their memberships.

The future of archaeology education rests with us today. We invite you to give thoughtful reflection to what you believe the desired future configuration of North American archaeology should be and how education and outreach fit into it.

A stimulus to such introspection is a review of the evolution of archaeology education thus far; after all, foresight is limited by hindsight. Martha Williams's personal retrospective on twenty-five years of involvement with archaeology education is the concluding chapter of the book. We hope that it, and *The Archaeology Education Handbook: Sharing the Past with Kids* as a whole, will provoke thought, debate and, most importantly, action.

As you include archaeology education in your professional life, remember to let your enthusiasm for what you do show. The most important teaching tool is a deep and abiding commitment to, and enjoyment of, your profession. This is more valuable than a practiced technique and careful preparation. While gaining skills and knowledge about effective teaching is critically important, don't forget that an audience picks up more from a presenter's attitude than it does from the words actually spoken. Recall an influential teacher in your own life. Chances are that you were drawn to learn more about a subject because the teacher communicated a strong interest and love for it, rather than because of a series of facts or workbook exercises.

Engaging in archaeology education can be personally rejuvenating and inspiring. Archaeology educators often find that the initial attraction and excitement that archaeology held for them is restored and even amplified by children's enthusiasm for what we do. A child's wonder reminds us of the real importance of our work—learning the stories of people in the past; exploring the history of humanity; and appreciating the value of our collective experiences over the millennia.

Chapter Twenty-Seven

Environmental Education
Perspectives for Archaeology

The purpose of this chapter is to examine the interrelationships of archaeology and environmental education. Many of the goals, methods, and challenges of archaeology and environmental education are similar: the preservation of vanishing resources; the development of an attitudinal change to encourage the public to value these resources; and participatory learning that allows people to make active and personal contributions to the conservation of these resources.

Can one learn from the other? The discussion will focus on sketching the evolution of environmental education, detailing the characteristics of various environmental education activities and programs, identifying the challenges of their inclusion and implementation in school curricula, and exploring the potential of coordination in a new framework for learning.

I. Evolution of Environmental Education

The formalization of environment in twentieth-century education has roots that go back to the beginnings of civilization. Aldo Leopold, whose essays on conservation in *A Sand County Almanac* have become environmental classics, was arguing for the preservation of the last remnants of wilderness when in 1949 he wrote:

> Wilderness is the raw material out of which man has hammered the artifact called civilization. Wilderness was never a homogeneous raw material. It was very diverse. These differences in the end-product are known as cultures. The rich diversity of the world's cultures reflects a corresponding diversity in the wilds that gave them birth. [Leopold 1966:264]

Although Leopold wrote from an environmental perspective, archaeologists might recognize the sentiments expressed here. Consider the concept of civilization as an arrangement of artifacts. As well, consider the connections between the diversities of environment and culture and that a reduction of environmental diversity may limit the choices that cultures can make. Just as the above statement was a plea to conserve the remnants of wilderness areas to show future generations the origins of their cultural inheritance, so, too, does the preservation of the remnants of cultural heritage strive to achieve a similar end. In fact, since artifacts are made of raw materials derived from the environment, the divide between human-produced and natural resources is much narrower than the separation of environmental and archaeological education might lead us to believe.

"Archaeology has the huge benefit of being able to place the impact of humanity's relationship with the environment into a long time framework" (Blockley 1998:11). Essentially, archaeology is the study of our human ancestors' relationship with the world in which they found themselves. Over the millennia, the archaeological record has evolved through patterns made by people's interactions with other living things and the environment as practical matters of survival and economic choice. History, the written record, further illuminates people's understanding of their place in the natural world by not only documenting practical needs and deeds of human cultures over time, but also by individual peoples' and entire societies' thoughts and beliefs.

> Conservation is a state of harmony between men and land. By land is meant all of the things on, over, or in the earth. Harmony with land is like harmony with a friend; you cannot cherish his right hand and cut off his left. . . . The land is one organism. . . . The outstanding scientific discovery of the twentieth century is not television, or radio, but rather the complexity of the land organism. Only those who know the most about it can appreciate how little is known about it. The last word in ignorance is the man who says of an animal or plant: "What good is it?" If the land mechanism as a whole is good, then every part is good, whether we understand it or not. If the biota, in the course of aeons, has built something we like but do not understand, then who but a fool would discard seemingly useless parts? To keep every cog and wheel is the first precaution of intelligent tinkering. [Leopold 1966:190]

During this century, environmental education has evolved from and developed with nature study, natural history, conservation, field studies, and outdoor and experiential education. Events of the latter half of the century have indicated the urgency and necessity of acquiring greater awareness, knowledge, and understanding of the environment so that individual and collective actions may be taken to sustain a viable home. I do not need to reiterate to the readers of this volume how seriously threatened cultural resources are.

One of the themes of this book is that archaeology education must lead to positive attitudinal change regarding the value of archeological resources. In terms of environmental education, a similar statement would read: Environmental education must lead to achievement of positive attitudinal change regarding the value of natural resources. The importance of these resources, from a global perspective, became more apparent when individuals began thinking about environmental problems and reflecting on the relationship between people and the environment. Books like Rachel Carson's *Silent Spring* in 1962 led to political and social changes that reflected preliminary attempts to reduce the impact of some of the more visible problems.

At the time Carson wrote, it was convenient to blame industry for the pollution of the air, the water, and the land, and considerable efforts were made in succeeding decades to develop laws and regulations to penalize the more obvious polluters. However, it soon became uncomfortably apparent that the circle of blame was much wider than originally cast—after all, the products of industry and commerce were purchased and thus supported by consumers who wanted to improve the materialistic quality of their lives in the short term, but they, in the long term, have *personally* contributed to the degradation of the environment and future quality of life.

The negativism pervaded for a long time. Attempts to make us feel better included the panacea of the 3Rs: reduce, reuse, and recycle. The first two were not really conducive to economic growth and have never been universally adopted. Recycling, on the other hand, did become accepted on a more widespread basis and became incorporated in many municipal and industrial waste management programs. The success of these programs with the public was mainly due to the fact that individuals could make personal and positive contributions to environmental conservation. But these actions, like other such solutions, are simplistic and really mask the need for a greater understanding of the underlying and fundamental relationships between the Earth and its inhabitants, which is where archaeology education comes in.

People take actions based on certain belief systems. Changing someone's belief structure is more difficult than simply adding knowledge. According to Gigliotti, the "underlying belief-value structure that most needs changing is the myth that people are separate from the environment—that we are somehow different from all other living things." Thus, each person has connection with and responsibility for their impact on the environment and its resources. Education, therefore, must make these connections clear, provide alternative actions that people can take to alleviate environmental problems and maintain resources, and "show logical connections between individual actions and solutions to environmental problems" (1990:10).

II. Environmental Activities and Programs

Education does not mean teaching people what they do not know. It means teaching them to behave as they do not behave. [Ruskin 1859]

Through formal schooling and informal venues of camping, recreation, park interpretation, and outdoor clubs, environmental education has taken on many forms.

In both the United States and Canada, the awareness and appreciation of the environment for a portion of the population have originated in experiencing the natural environment on an informal basis. For some others, especially indigenous peoples and those following other traditions, the relationship between people and the environment is an integral part of their spirituality and culture. For many others who do not have the spiritual, traditional, or reflective opportunities or backgrounds, environmental education is a new perspective.

Today, there are many different points of view on teaching and learning about environmental education. The following descriptions of activities and programs have been chosen to exemplify a range of opportunities in the field and to demonstrate important considerations for archaeology education. The descriptions are, by necessity, very brief in outline, and the reader is encouraged to seek more comprehensive resources in cited references, other literature, and from practitioners in the field.

In the following pages, I describe three well-received and widely known models for environmental education. Elements of each are directly applicable to the types of programs that would be effective for archaeological education purposes. Two of them, Project WILD and *Keepers of the Earth*, offer supplemental activities that are intended to be integrated (or "infused") into normal lesson planning inside the school curriculum. Earth Education, on the other hand, is a stand-alone program. While all three have been effective in advancing environmental knowledge, they struggle to various degrees with the development of positive environmental attitudes in their participants.

Project WILD

"Project WILD is an interdisciplinary, supplementary environmental and conservation education program for educators of kindergarten through high school age young people" (Western Regional Environmental Education Council 1990:i). In the introduction to the Activity Guide, Rudolph Schafer identifies two elements of society with key roles in shaping future environments: resource management and education. Members from these two elements were brought together in the early 1970s to form the Western Regional Environmental Education Council (WREEC). One of its earlier accomplishments is Project Learning Tree, also a supplementary and interdisciplinary program, that emphasized forest resources and our relationship with the natural world.

Project WILD aims "to motivate youngsters to take intelligent and constructive action to conserve wildlife and natural resources" (WREEC 1985:ix).

> What will our land be like in 20, 40 or 100 years from now? . . . We can be sure . . . that our environmental future is to a large degree in our hands. We have our technologies, and we are gaining in our ability to manipulate the physical environment and its resources—for better or for worse. The directions we take with our technologies are very much dependent upon the values we hold and the choices we make, individually and socially. [WREEC 1985:vii]

The conceptual framework is described in the appendices of the Activity Guide; each activity is designed to correspond to one or more points in the following:

1. Awareness and Appreciation of Wildlife
2. Human Values and Wildlife
3. Wildlife and Ecological Systems
4. Wildlife Conservation
5. Cultural and Social Interaction with Wildlife
6. Wildlife Issues and Trends: Alternatives and Consequences
7. Wildlife, Ecological Systems, and Responsible Human Actions

Activities are organized in a thematic and developmental order in chapters that follow the above titles and sequenced in such a way "to allow students to acquire knowledge, information, and skills to assist them in making informed and responsible decisions." It is left to the teacher to determine what activities are chosen to integrate into each subject in the curriculum. These activities may be used to teach required concepts and skills and, "at the same time [teach] about people, wildlife and the environment" (WREEC 1990:vii).

Keepers of the Earth

This is the first in a series of books by Michael J. Caduto and Joseph Bruchac "about living, learning and caring: a collection of carefully chosen North American Indian stories and hands-on activities that promote understanding and appreciation of, empathy for, and responsible action toward the Earth, including its people" (1988: xxiii). The purpose of each story is to engage children from ages five to twelve. It is a springboard designed to provoke curiosity and to facilitate discovery of their environments and the personal influences they have on their surroundings.

The activities "engage a child's whole self: emotions, senses, thoughts and actions" (Caduto and Bruchac 1988:xxiii). As you will see, the teaching program, sequence of lesson, and underlying concepts and philosophy behind *Keepers of the Earth* is fully congruent with meeting the goals and objectives of archaeology education, especially since it draws many of its approaches directly from cultural practices common to indigenous peoples in many parts of the world.

The book is divided into two parts. Part I offers suggestions on facilitating the use of stories and activities. In the teacher's guide (a separate publication), there is a discussion of the nature of Indian myths and the cultures from which these stories come. As well, educational philosophies and approaches are outlined. Part II has the stories and activities arranged under broad topical headings:

Creation
    Fire
        Earth
            Wind and Weather
                Water
                    Sky
                        Seasons
                            Plants and Animals
                                Life, Death, Spirit
                                    Unity of Earth

The authors also include a chapter on "Tips and Techniques for Bringing This Book to Life" (p. 15):

I. Telling Stories
    Seeing the Story   —read each story aloud to yourself several times
                            —let the story become a part of you
    The Setting of the Story—a quiet place
                            —people should sit in a circle
    Speaking the Story   —breathing from the diaphragm
                            —resonance, clarity, and pace
    Involving the Listeners—make eye contact with many individuals
                            —teach them singing, chanting, or movements
II. Conducting the Activities
    Plan Wisely and in Detail
    Choose and Adapt Activities for the Children's Levels
    Set the Stage
    Link the Activities in a Meaningful Way
    Put the Children into the Center of the Activity
    Teach by Example
    Use Firsthand Sensory Experiences Whenever Possible
    Use Creative Questions and Answers
    Emphasize Positive Feelings as Well as Knowledge
    Foster Aesthetic Appreciation
    Emphasize Group Work and Positive Social Interaction
    Foster Problem-Solving/Research Skills
    Use Long-Term Projects
    Include a Connection with Other Communities and Countries
    Include Moral Issues: Environmental and Social Ethics
    Face Problems and Controversy and Deal with Them Constructively
        and Positively
    Respect Spiritual and Religious Beliefs
    Respect the Privacy of Personal Beliefs and Feelings
    Discipline Compassionately and Decisively
    Keep a Sense of Humor, Joy, and Appreciation
    Be Yourself
    Provide a Culminating Activity or Experience

The above list of teaching suggestions provides sound advice for archaeology educators, too. Some of the activities are best done indoors, others outdoors. The authors include many helpful suggestions on how to plan and conduct excursions outdoors. *Keepers of the Earth* attempts to integrate two traditions: science and Indian myths. "The ecological lessons of science and North American Indian stories show us how to care for the Earth. Through their combined knowledge we can help children to discover their own roles in maintaining this fragile balance for themselves and all living things in the generations to come" (Caduto and Bruchac 1988:5).

Earth Education

The Institute for Earth Education had its origins in the efforts of several committed individuals who, in the mid-1970s, wanted to help people build a new sense of relationship with the Earth. Led by one of its founders, Steve Van Matre, it is a grassroots organization that depends on the energy and generous contributions of volunteers. Made up of an international network of individuals and member organizations, the institute's "primary work is to support the design, development and dissemination of specific educational programs that change people's view of their home, the planet earth, and the way they interact with it" (Van Matre 1990:310).

Unlike *Keepers of the Earth* and Project WILD, Earth Education is a comprehensive and coordinated program of study with a clear and explicit agenda— affecting attitudinal change toward environmental conservation. The cumulative and sequential nature of its program design provides an interesting model for instilling a stewardship ethic for archaeological resources. Model Earth Education programs that have already been developed and implemented include:

- Earth Caretakers (ages 10–11): a one-day trip away from school that initiates year-long learning and exploring;
- Earthkeepers (ages 10–11): a 2–3 day experience for preparing to use less energy and materials;
- Sunship Earth (ages 10–11): a week-long adventure in discovering seven key ecological principles; and
- Sunship III (ages 13–14): 2–3 day experience emphasizing the choices to be made about our impact on this planet.

Instructional materials, specialized equipment, and detailed "scripts" for instructors are provided for each program. These are comprehensive packages that have been piloted, reviewed, and revised. All the programs are designed to be experienced in a natural setting like that of an outdoor education center (see Box 27.1).

BOX 27.1
Ten Characteristics of an Earth Education Program

An earth education program:

1. Hooks and pulls the learners in with magical experiences that promise discovery and adventure (the hooker).
2. Proceeds in an organized way to a definite outcome that the learners can identify beforehand and rewards them when they reach it (the organizer).
3. Focuses on building good feelings for the earth and its life through lots of rich firsthand contact (the immerser).
4. Emphasizes major ecological understandings (at least four must be included: energy flow, cycling, interrelationships, change).
5. Gets the descriptions of natural processes and places into the concrete through tasks that are both "hands-on" and "minds-on."
6. Uses good learning techniques in building focused, sequential, cumulative experiences that start where the learners are mentally and end with lots of reinforcement for their new understandings.
7. Avoids labeling and quizzing approach in favor of the full participation that comes with more sharing and doing.
8. Provides immediate application of its messages in the natural world and later in the human community.
9. Pays attention to the details in every aspect of the learning situation.
10. Transfers the learning by completing the action back at school and home in specific lifestyle tasks designed for personal behavior change.

[Van Matre 1990:269–270].

As opposed to a collection of activities, an educational program, according to the institute, should be "a carefully crafted, focused series of sequential, cumulative learning experiences designed with specific outcomes in mind" (Van Matre 1990:16). Van Matre argues that "the environmental education mission has gone astray and is so broadly defined that almost anything could fit somewhere within it." And, he asserts: "Earth education is not environmental education. It is an alternative to it" (p. 47).

III. Inclusion in School Curricula:
The Challenges of Implementation

Does It Fit "The System"?

How do such activities or programs fit in the structure of a school's curriculum? Disinger states: "Like most curriculum reform movements initiated from outside the educational establishment, environmental education did not, and has not, established for itself, a pre-eminent, even accepted, position in schooling" (1985:5). He also recognized that schools are not designed or organized to deal with multiple subjects. In fact, schooling and professional practice both adhere to the "subject" approach to education (Borden 1985:3). Teacher education patterns, procedures for curriculum design, and academic rigor are all manifestations of this approach. Neither archaeology education nor environmental education fall neatly into one subject area.

In these circumstances, infusion of activities (such as Project WILD, *Keepers of the Earth*) would seem to work—individual activities are selected to complement a particular subject, and are not cumulative or sequential. Infusion, therefore, does not challenge traditional constructs. Teachers can also select activities that can be conducted in their regular classroom, in the gymnasium, or in the schoolyard.

Formal, sequential programs such as Earth Education, on the other hand, require considerably more organization, extra time and expense, and teacher participation, knowledge, and commitment. They are usually conducted in more natural settings away from traditional schools and are not so easily attributed to one subject or another —in fact, they are multidisciplinary or integrative. It takes a lot of dedication on the part of the teacher, students, parents, and volunteers to make these programs work.

From her investigations of the Earth Education program, Sunship Earth, involving Australian elementary students, Meg Keen found that the students participating in this program significantly increased their ecological knowledge but did not develop more positive environmental attitudes (Keen 1991:30–31). She attributed the latter finding to the short duration of the program at a residential center and to the lack of integration of the learning experience with the school curriculum. The importance of evaluation to ensure a program is meeting its objectives is clearly demonstrated in this example.

"The small amount of follow-up that was done concentrated on the ecological concepts, not on the development of positive environmental attitudes that the program intended to inculcate. Many of the teachers . . . did not feel comfortable teaching lessons specifically aimed at environmental attitudes" (Keen 1991:31). To make sure that learning experiences do not become isolated events, both archaeology and environmental educators must work with classroom teachers to develop "follow-through programs" that are based on the school's established curriculum and that allow for integration and personalization by the classroom teacher.

Outdoor Education Centers

Outdoor education centers may have a role to play. Essential to the success of some of these centers is the sharing of resources that are involved in cooperative living. Each person has a responsibility for maintaining the living environment and for having as little impact on that environment as possible. Living in close quarters can often produce conflict situations, which can only be resolved through tolerance and understanding—especially in multicultural situations. These centers allow young people to get closer, physically, intellectually, and spiritually to the natural world, using all the senses without the distractions of the largely "built'" world in which they normally live. Experiences are real and hands on, and experienced staff can facilitate these experiences. They are comfortable in this environment—this can be conveyed to others, especially those who have fears. They also have considerable knowledge, love, and appreciation of the natural world that can be shared.

Considering the challenges of implementing environmental education programs, outdoor centers are key to developing and promoting programs that are difficult to fit into traditional school settings. Regular classroom teachers do not have to set up these programs but become integral components through their participation in planning, conducting the outdoor program, and following through with supporting and assessing student outcomes back at the school and home. This applies both to heritage resources and education. "If ordinary people are given the opportunity to participate in the discovery and conservation of actual heritage remains, they will acquire a value for the past that no amount of preaching or promotion can accomplish" (Smardz 1995:15).

Some Considerations for Successful Implementation

The following sections address three questions that will affect the successful implementation of environmental materials in a school's curriculum:

1. How does the conceptual framework for environmental education relate to curriculum ?
2. Does it matter whether you infuse several activities or adopt a comprehensive program of learning?
3. What can and should be accomplished in teacher workshops?

1. Conceptual Framework

Project WILD has been criticized from both environmental and pedagogical perspectives. A former professor of mine vociferously admonished the project for its "management" perspective of wildlife and called it Project TAME—<u>T</u>oward <u>A</u> <u>M</u>anaged <u>E</u>nvironment. Project WILD is activity driven, although these activities are organized under headings of the conceptual framework that is hidden in the Appendices of the Guide. There must have been a great philosophical battle among the contributors to the development of the guide to result in the basic conceptual framework being relegated to the obscurity of the appendices rather than being up front as the basis for a program. Closer examination reveals that correlation of the activities and the conceptual framework is not easily accomplished, and there are many gaps. In effect, it seems that the conceptual framework was probably developed independently of the activities, most of which were not created to accomplish specific outcomes.

Earth Education programs, on the other hand, were developed by establishing the conceptual framework and then creating activities, experiences, and outcomes that were designed to achieve focused, sequential, and cumulative learning. It is therefore important to identify the parts in each subject of the school's curriculum that coincide with the conceptual framework of the environmental program.

2. Activities vs. Program

Project WILD is not a program, although it could be. It is left to the teacher to choose which activities, in what order, and for what end within a course of study. It seems a shame to lose the benefit of the expertise of the WILD developers in planning programs that would both meet the educational requirements of a course of study and provide a framework for learners to accomplish the goals of the project. *It is a meal without a menu.* From undocumented research, the authors of the Activity Guide indicate that the use of seven or more Project WILD activities with students during one school year will result in statistical significance in student learning. There is no identification of what activities were chosen, what learning occurred, or whether this "learning" had any impact on student values or responsible behavior.

Earth Education programs are developed according to a conceptual framework that fosters focused, sequential, and cumulative learning. The teacher chooses which program will be suitable for the level of the students and provides opportunities for the both teacher and students to fully participate. Acknowledging that long-term research has not yet be done to evaluate the effectiveness of earth education programs on people's values and behavior, Steve Van Matre postulates that "you will have a better chance of producing people who will live more lightly on the earth if you tell them that's your goal and begin helping them to do it" (1990:42).

Reflecting on the vulnerability of environmental education in the future, Doug Knapp (1998) asserts that "the field must look upon itself as a sequential learning process." Furthermore, "this process necessitates the decline of the activity guide mentality that has fostered a shallow view of environmental education and has helped promote biased activism rather than autonomous thinking" (Knapp 1998:4).

3. *Workshops*

Project WILD activities are supported by networks of educational and resource management leaders who conduct workshops for teachers. Dissemination of Project WILD materials is facilitated by these successful workshops, which not only introduce the activities but allow teachers to try them out. Their participation in several activities provides them with hands-on learning so that they better assimilate each activity's purpose, method of presentation, and potential outcomes. As well, they get a chance to critique the lessons with colleagues and, through discussion and reflection, develop strategies to infuse these activities in the curricula of their specific school programs.

Programs offered by the Institute of Earth Education require extensive participation by teachers in workshops to adequately personalize the material and become familiar with the scripted portions of each part of the program. Once again, active, hands-on learning is an integral part of these programs and discussions with workshop leaders, and participants are necessary and valuable for maintaining consistency and adherence to the conceptual framework. Personal reflection is a key part of the workshops and is an exemplar for student involvement in these programs.

Although there is a teacher's guide, the stories and activities of *Keepers of the Earth* could really use extensive workshops. Stories that are told need to be practiced to become "alive" for both the teller and the listeners. It takes a person with certain gifts to really tell a story. Time is needed to personalize the cultural backgrounds of each story—they come from many different traditions. The suggested activities need to be experienced by the story teller/teacher so that they become familiar. If these stories and activities are presented to complement an educational program, teachers would benefit from discussions with workshop leaders and colleagues.

New Frameworks for Learning

All of the above-discussed programs aim to develop questions in the minds of their audiences. How will we be judged 100, 1,000, or 10,000 years from now? How will the artifacts of our culture and society be interpreted to give an accurate rendering of the relationship that we have with our home, the Earth? Will the records show that we abandoned our cultural and natural resources with the belief that technology, the mechanisms and products of the human mind, would solve all of the present and future problems of our societies? Will we be measured by what we threw away rather than by what we cherished and created in viable and dynamic societies?

> Our children are our signature to the roster of history; our land is merely the place our money was made. There is as yet no social stigma in the possession of a gullied farm, a wrecked forest, or a polluted stream, provided the dividends suffice to send the youngsters to college. Whatever ails the land, the government

will fix it. . . . The problem, then, is how to bring about a striving for harmony with land among a people many of whom have forgotten there is any such thing as land, among whom education and culture have become almost synonymous with landlessness. This is the problem of conservation education. [Leopold 1966: 202, 210]

Leopold emphasized that striving was more important than achieving success because striving grows from within. Our economic and educational systems have guided people away from, rather than toward, an "intense consciousness of land" and a sense of our human place in the landscape. There is a growing distance, both physically and philosophically, between people, their heritage from the past, and the land that supports and nourishes them in the present. Education should include what has value, not only in an economic sense, but in a sense of the integrity, stability, and beauty of the land.

Archaeology education faces similar challenges, but its problems may be even more profound as many resources that are at risk are neither visible nor immediately familiar to most people. And, unlike environmental educators, archaeologists cannot even argue that living populations may be threatened by the destruction of one or the other heritage resource, as is the case with the fragile ecological network that supports life on our planet. Instead, you are asking students to help conserve below-ground or hidden remains of past cultures with whom they have no apparent intrinsic or emotional connection. You, the archaeology educator, have to build those links and establish those values before you can begin to transmit the stewardship message. This can be done either by developing independent activities that teach specific concepts and skills and that can be integrated into everyday teaching in the classroom (as *Keepers of the Earth* and Project WILD do for environmental education), or by establishing entire programs that would be taught sequentially (as with Earth Education).

In *Earth Education: A New Beginning*, Steve Van Matre describes a heritage interpretive site that was recreated to represent the lifestyles and times of the early 1600s in New England. Costumed interpreters would go about their chores as people would have done in that time period. Visitors to the site balked at some of the realistic portrayals of livestock slaughtering, for instance. A lifetime of purchasing plastic-wrapped meat meant that they were, in effect, "voyeurs on the killing of their own food." Van Matre comments:

Most people in our societies today have been so isolated for so long from the realities of life here that they simply do not grasp how their own lives are a part of the overall process of life on earth. We have to help them begin pulling away the disguises we have used here to mask the ecological processes that support us. [1990:134]

Others have commented that this Nature/Culture duality is detrimental to a complete understanding of earth systems. Colwell proposed changing these terms to *earth systems* rather than the separation that Nature (nonhuman) and Culture (human) conveys. He goes on to state:

> The subject matter of environmental education is neither nature nor culture but a single spectrum of interrelationships extending from predominantly non-human environments to predominantly human environments. Hence, the method of environmental education is neither scientific nor humanistic, but one that combines elements of both in an interdisciplinary fashion. [1997:8]

This is as good an argument for establishing an interrelationship between environmental and archaeological education models as one could wish.

Pike and Selby have developed the concept of *global education* as a method to learn about world systems and to promote better understanding of the multicultured aspects of earth. They advocate a systemic or holistic perspective when they assert that "human life is embedded in nature, humans are caught up in natural systems; to act as though this is not the case harms nature and ultimately endangers human survival" (1988:29). An underlying theme of global education is that, if we can better tolerate and appreciate one another, perhaps we can deal more effectively and compassionately with the rest of the natural world. If heritage resources are part of human culture, ought not heritage education be part of environmental, earth systems, or global education? Is not culture a manifestation of the impact of human actions on the environment?

Limits to Growth—Size Matters!

The United Nations explicitly links environmental and cultural heritage in its priorities for World Heritage Site conservation (see Box 27.2 and Box 27.3).

While this deals directly with stewardship, UNESCO has also established a series of conventions for environmental education per se. From a global perspective, UNESCO adopted the recommendations of the United Nations Conference on the Human Environment (Stockholm 1972) that were eventually formalized in the Belgrade Charter (1975). For many, the charter legitimized environmental education and its goals. Subsequent conferences at Tbilisi (1977), Moscow (1987), Rio de Janeiro (1992), and Thessaloniki (1997) have brought together representatives of United Nations organizations, governments, nongovernment organizations, experts, and other interested parties to develop strategies to implement worldwide environmental education programs.

From an evolutionary perspective, the more recent Thessaloniki Declaration may have sounded "the beginning of the end for [the term] environmental education" (Knapp 1998:2). This declaration suggests that "environmental education be referred to as education for environment and sustainability"(UNESCO-EPD 1997:2) and identified strategies to develop "action plans for formal education, mobilizing

BOX 27.2
UNESCO World Heritage Convention

The United Nations Educational, Scientific and Cultural Organization (UNESCO) seeks to encourage the identification, protection and preservation of cultural and natural heritage around the world considered to be of outstanding value to humanity. This is embodied in an international treaty called the Convention concerning the Protection of the World Cultural and Natural Heritage, adopted by UNESCO in 1972.

Cultural heritage refers to monuments, groups of buildings and sites with historical, aesthetic, archaeological, scientific, ethnological or anthropological value. Natural heritage refers to outstanding physical, biological and geological formations, habitats of threatened species of animals and plants and areas with scientific, conservation or aesthetic value. UNESCO's World Heritage mission is to:

- encourage countries to sign the 1972 Convention and to ensure the protection of their natural and cultural heritage;
- encourage States Parties to the Convention to nominate sites within their national territory for inclusion on the World Heritage List;
- encourage States Parties to set up reporting systems on the state of conservation of World Heritage sites;
- help States Parties safeguard World Heritage sites by providing technical assistance and professional training;
- provide emergency assistance for World Heritage sites in immediate danger;
- promote the presentation of cultural and natural heritage;
- encourage international cooperation in conservation of cultural and natural heritage.

Date of Issue: June 1996
http://www.unesco.org/whc/1mission.htm 19 October 1996
http://www.unesco.org/whc/nwhc/pages/doc/main.htm

BOX 27.3
The criteria for selection

To be included on the World Heritage List, sites must satisfy the selection criteria. These criteria are explained in the *Operational Guidelines* which, beside the text of the Convention, is the main working document on World Heritage. The criteria have been revised regularly by the Committee to match the evolution of the World Heritage concept itself. *Mixed sites* have both outstanding natural and cultural values. Since 1992 significant interactions between people and the natural environment have been recognized as *cultural landscapes.*

Cultural properties should:

i   represent a masterpiece of human creative genius, or

ii   exhibit an important interchange of human values over a span of time or within a cultural area of the world, on developments in architecture or technology, monumental arts, town planning or landscape design, or

iii   bear a unique or at least exceptional testimony to a cultural tradition or to a civilization which is living or has disappeared, or

iv   be an outstanding example of a type of building or architectural or technological ensemble, or landscape which illustrates a significant stage or significant stages in human history, or

v   be an outstanding example of a traditional human settlement or land-use which is representative of a culture or cultures, especially when it has become vulnerable under the impact of irreversible change, or

vi   be directly or tangibly associated with events or

Natural properties should:

i   be outstanding examples representing major stages of the earth's history, including the record of life, significant ongoing geological processes in the development of landforms, or significant geomorphic or physiographic features, or

ii   be outstanding examples representing significant ongoing ecological and biological processes in the evolution and development of terrestrial, fresh water, coastal and marine ecosystems and communities of plants and animals, or

iii   contain superlative natural phenomena or areas of exceptional natural beauty and aesthetic importance, or

iv   contain the most important and significant natural habitats for *in situ* conservation of biological diversity, including those containing threatened species of outstanding universal value from the point of view of science or conservation.

living traditions, with ideas or with beliefs, or with artistic and literary works of outstanding universal significance (a criterion used only in exceptional circumstances, or together with other criteria).

Equally important is the authenticity of the site and the way it is protected and managed.

The protection, management, and integrity of the site are also important considerations.

additional resources and investments into public education, and strengthening and reorienting teacher education" (Knapp 1998:2).

This new term reflects the realities of global politics and has the unfortunate outcome of once again separating human beings from their environment. If the signatories to the declaration had redefined environmental education as *education for a sustainable environment*, this separation would not be implied. But the isolation of the term, *sustainability*, suggests not environment, but economic systems and lifestyles.

It is very important that the nations of the world have come together to agree on so contentious and economically significant subjects as environmental and cultural conservation. If UNESCO can develop consensus at a global level, then archaeology educators can also achieve the same end at the community or school level. We need to transmit to our students that each one of us can make a difference, whether it be conserving our local environment or saving our community's heritage resources. Archaeology education, like environmental education, starts at the community level, and it takes a grassroot development to really make effective change.

Students of educational paradigms will recognize the following constructs in learning: *cognitive/affective/psychomotor*, or, *knowledge/attitudes/skills*. From Earth Education, consider *understanding/feeling/processing*. Now let us borrow the metaphor from Ruskin above and produce another construct: *head/heart/hands*. For both environmental and archaeology education, if we can get the head, the heart, and the hands working together, perhaps then we will achieve a widespread positive attitudinal change regarding the value of these resources.

Fine art is that in which the hand, the head, and the heart get together. [Ruskin 1990:310]

Chapter Twenty-Eight

Retrospective
Personal Thoughts on the
Maturation of Archaeological Education

Twenty-five years ago, the prospect of having to convey the concept of archaeology to a sea of thirty restless inquisitive eight year olds would have presented a daunting challenge, even to an experienced primary teacher, if indeed such a teacher would have attempted the task at all. The idea of doing the same would seldom, if ever, have occurred to most archaeologists of that era, unless perhaps they themselves were the parents of an energetic third grader.

I found myself facing just such a challenge several months ago. I emerged from that potential trial by fire unscathed and smiling, leaving behind both happy teachers and kids. That the two-hour session was a success was due in no small measure to the patience of a few forward-looking professional archaeologists; a twenty-seven–year teaching career; my long association with the Society for Historical Archaeology and my tenure as chair of its Public Education and Information Committee; and numerous colleagues in the fields of both education and archaeology. Many of them have contributed the articles that make up this book. This small retrospective is intended to pay tribute to those practitioners, and to describe the development of the movement to integrate archaeological concepts into precollegiate curricula.

Initial attempts to bring these concepts into nonuniversity settings began during the middle 1970s, a period in education characterized by tolerance for and encouragement of innovative, experiential-based learning modes; a search for ways to enrich and broaden standard secondary school curricula; the introduction of inquiry-based teaching methodologies; and, perhaps most importantly, generous school budgets.

At a meeting of the Society for Historical Archaeology in San Antonio in 1978, five secondary-school teachers from Texas, Virginia, Pennsylvania, and California discovered that they all had been buying into the current educational climate by introducing archaeological principles to their students and then taking those students out to excavate sites. All worked with degreed archaeologists or supportive academics like John Cotter of the University of Pennsylvania, or had formal archaeological training or field experience under professionals like Ivor Noel Hume, then the senior archaeologist at Colonial Williamsburg. Most important, all of them agreed that hands-on archaeology had become for them the most exciting venture that they had ever undertaken with their students.

At this point, precollegiate archaeology was new and untested, an extra-curricular enrichment program for which a formal curriculum had not yet gelled. During this formative period, the primary goal of excavation was to discover artifacts and expose features. The course of study and classroom strategies were geared almost exclusively to preparing students for field and laboratory work. Elements stressed included the principles of site organization; recognition of artifacts and features; the principles of stratigraphy; the techniques of data recording; and the fundamental techniques of artifact processing and inventory. Why excavations were undertaken (the research orientation of archaeology), site preservation, and the consequences of uneducated excavation were issues discussed with students almost as an afterthought. Rather than being presented with a research focus as the primary objective of the course, students were encouraged to interpret what they found only at the end of the exercise.

Archaeological programs of that period also unintentionally introduced the concept of community service, a somewhat novel notion at the time. Student excavators volunteered on National Park Service sites at Valley Forge and Gettysburg, Pennsylvania. In Philadelphia and City Point, Virginia, students assisted in rescue operations prior to construction of Interstate 95 through the oldest section of the city. Because, until 1978, Fairfax County's school program was the only archaeological investigative unit in northern Virginia, public agencies in the region frequently requested assistance in undertaking full-scale investigations of threatened sites, doing cultural resource surveys, and creating exhibits based on archaeological projects. After the county hired its first public archaeologist in 1978, summer school projects were selected to support identified county preservation goals, and a small cadre of students became year-round weekend volunteers.

By the early 1980s, the rapid expansion of elective programs in secondary school curricula around the country allowed the institution of a semester of for-credit, elective anthropology, of which archaeology became a major component. However, several price tags were attached to these efforts. Teaching archaeology and being one's own archaeologist was time consuming, as course instructors assumed the responsibility for completing site investigations and writing reports, in addition to maintaining their full teaching loads. During the school year, Saturdays often were spent completing field and lab work with a small band of dedicated students, while Sundays were reserved for putting together the requisite archaeological reports.

The times and experience, however, began to augur for changes in this somewhat single-minded approach to archaeological education. Educational philosophies began to retrench and to emphasize basic content and skills such as reading, writing, and research, rather than experiential learning. The number of non–Anglo-American students in school systems was increasing, but most archaeology programs left out the less academically oriented, the intellectually and economically disadvantaged, or minority students who could benefit from being involved in archaeological projects. The experience of writing reports led to the realization that archaeology was, in fact, an exercise in research, a skill that needed to be taught to all students, rather than just to the academically talented. Finally, formerly generous school budgets began to constrict, reducing funding for such frills as archaeology, either within the normal curriculum or as summer enrichment experiences. School administrators also were less willing to hire staff and adopt flexible scheduling to accommodate extra-classroom experiential learning modes.

As these factors restricted curricular options, interested teachers searched for ways to provide opportunities for archaeological fieldwork that would involve a wider range of students, incorporate all the skills inherent in major data recovery projects, downsize projects so that students could see the results and grasp the purpose of archaeological field work, and function within the time constraints of the normal school day. As teachers' understandings of archaeology broadened and deepened, they began to devise ways of bringing the site into the classroom. They adapted proven archaeologically based materials and teaching techniques to serve a broader segment of the student population, and identified links between archaeological concepts and the wider secondary curriculum.

Teachers discovered that the key to solving the dilemmas facing archaeological educators lay in using archaeological principles to teach research, inquiry, and logical thinking skills. By emphasizing material culture rather than archaeological techniques, and by stressing that material culture was a body of evidence that furthered understanding of ourselves and others, these teacher practitioners were able to integrate archaeological principles and materials into traditional curricular offerings and use archaeological studies as a basis for interdisciplinary projects. Most found that history and the social sciences offered the most opportune venues for using archaeological materials. For example, the basic mapping skills so critical to archaeology were fundamental elements of the geography curriculum, while preservation-based case studies could serve as springboards for discussing the operation of local government.

Moreover, with the cooperation of other faculty members, archaeological projects also could be integrated with other major fields of the precollegiate curriculum. Specialized analyses of ethnobotanical and faunal remains, soils, or lithics drew on methods and content from the biological and physical sciences. The types of record keeping required on a site or in the laboratory invited the application of drafting and design skills, including Computer Assisted Drafting programs. And the production of the necessary technical reports demanded precisely the logical writing skills that language arts instructors sought to inculcate in their students. Today, increasing numbers of strategies used to present archaeological concepts are designed to make many of these interdisciplinary connections.

None of these insights and transformations have been achieved unilaterally. Anthropological and archaeological studies that illuminated the nuances of modern material culture and rendered it worthy of scholarly examination have inspired creative approaches to presenting archaeological concepts. In anthropology, the Nacerima studies are particularly influential (Miner 1956), while Rathje's "Projet du Garbage" at the University of Arizona (Rathje and Murphy 1992) filled a similar niche for archaeology. These studies pointed the way for teachers to use their own and their students' material culture as a basis for planning and executing active archaeologically based programs.

Colleagues within the archaeology and teaching professions also have been equally important in furthering the cause of archaeology education. The opportunity to share collegially with another interested, supportive, and skilled teacher-archaeologist on a daily basis was critical during the initial years of curriculum development and experimentation. In 1986, thirteen like-minded members of the Society for Historical Archaeology (SHA) formed an interest group for archaeological education, a group that later was formally constituted as a standing committee of the society.

In 1990, similar efforts were launched by the Society for American Archaeology. The membership of these committees and their activities have grown exponentially, and they now provide a variety of curricular aids and strategies to foster precollegiate archaeological education. Since my own experience has been largely with the SHA, I speak from that perspective; the Society for American Archaeology's achievements in this area are reported by Ed Friedman in the Preface to this volume.

Over the years, the archaeology educators active in the SHA have assumed a leading role in advocating public programming in archaeology, particularly that aimed at precollegiate audiences. Through their efforts, the first international session on archaeological education was presented at the First Joint Archaeological Conference in Baltimore in 1989; each participant in that session contributed teaching strategies that provided the nucleus of one of the first precollegiate instructional manuals in archaeology. SHA sponsored one of the first professionally organized teacher workshops in archaeology education at its 1990 Meeting in Tucson, Arizona. Committee members also organized a ground-breaking exhibit of archaeologically related materials, an initiative that subsequently evolved into the core of the Society for American Archaeology's highly successful touring exhibit known as the Educational Resource Forum. The SHA has also worked with the SAA to foster intersociety cooperation through the Intersociety Working Group on Education, which today includes several U.S. and Canadian archaeological organizations.

As I entered that third-grade classroom recently, I drew on a twenty-five–year legacy of experience, advice, and lessons learned from publications, fellow professionals, and students alike; all continue to serve me well. And I continue to believe that archaeology, in all its various forms, is one of the most exciting vehicles by which a precollegiate teacher can challenge, motivate, inspire, and immerse all students in the excitement of learning.

References

Adams, C. E., and B. Gronemann
  1989   Garbage Can Archaeology. In *Archaeology in the Classroom: A Case Study from Arizona*, edited by A. E. Rogge and Patti Bell, insert. Technical Brief No. 4, Archaeological Assistance Program, National Park Service, U.S. Department of the Interior, Washington, D.C.

Allen, M. G., and R. L. Stevens
  1994   *Middle Grades Social Studies: Teaching and Learning for Active and Responsible Citizenship*. Allyn and Bacon, Boston

Ahler, J. G.
  1994   The Benefits of Multicultural Education for American Indian Schools: An Anthropological Perspective. In *The Presented Past: Heritage, Museums, and Education*, One World Archaeology Series, Vol. 25, edited by P. G. Stone and B. L. Molyneaux, pp. 453–459. Routledge, London.

American Association for the Advancement of Science
  1989   *Science For All Americans: A Project 2061 Report on Literacy Goals in Science, Mathematics, and Technology*. American Association for the Advancement of Science, Inc., Washington, D.C.

Anderson, C., P. Planel and P. Stone
  1996   *A Teacher's Handbook to Stonehenge*. English Heritage, London.

Archaeology
  1991   A Sampling of Creative Initiatives. In *Special Section: Archaeology in the Classroom. Archaeology* 44(1):40–43.

Arons, S.
  1995   Constitutional Implications of National Curriculum Standards. *Educational Forum* 58:4.

Astor, R. A.
1994   Children's Moral Reasoning about Family and Peer Violence: The Role of Provocation and Retribution. *Child Development* 65:1054–1067.

Baker, J., V. Cardennis, and S. Miller
1996   *Tabletop Archaeology: A Teacher's Guide.* Pennsylvania Archaeological Council for Pennsylvania Archaeology Month, October. Harrison City, Pennsylvania.

Banks, J. A.
1984   Teaching Strategies for Ethnic Studies. Allyn & Bacon, Boston.
1992   It's Up to Us. In *Teaching Tolerance*, pp. 20–23. Southern Law Poverty Center, Montgomery, Alabama.
1994   *Multiethnic Education: Theory and Practice*, 3rd ed. Allyn & Bacon, Boston.

Barton, J., and A. Collins, eds.
1997   *Portfolio Assessment: A Handbook for Educators.* Addison-Wesley, Menlo Park, California.

Bender, B.
1998   *Stonehenge: Making Space.* Berg, Oxford, England.

Bender, S. J., and G. S. Smith
1998   SAA's Workshop on Teaching Archaeology in the 21st Century: Promoting a National Dialogue on Curricula Reform. *SAA Bulletin* 16(5): 11–13.

Bender, S. J., and R. Wilkinson
1992   Public Education and the Academy. *Archaeology and Public Education* 3(1): 1–3.

Berk, L. E.
1994   Vygotsky's Theory: The Importance of Make-Believe Play. *Young Children* 50:30–39.
1996   *Infants, Children and Adolescents*, 2d ed. Allyn & Bacon, Boston.
1997   *Child Development*, 4th ed. Allyn & Bacon, Boston.

Birman, B. F., R. J. Kirshstein, D. A. Levin, N. Matheson, and M. Stephens
1997   *The Effectiveness of Using Technology in K-12 Education: A Preliminary Framework and Review.* U.S. Department of Education, Office of Educational Research and Improvement, Washington, D.C.

Black, S.
1996   The Character Conundrum. *The American School Board Journal*, December 1996:29–31.

Blanchard, C. E.
1991   Education and/or Entertainment: Archaeology and Prehistory in the Public Schools. *Archaeology and Public Education* 2(1): 1–3.

Blancke, S., and Cjigkitoonuppa J. P. Slow Turtle
1994   Traditional American Indian Education as a Palliative to Western Education. In *The Presented Past: Heritage, Museums, and Education*, One World Archaeology Series, Vol. 25, edited by P. G. Stone and B. L. Molyneaux, pp. 438–452. Routledge, London.

Blatt, M., and L. Kohlberg
1975   The Effects of Classroom Moral Discussion upon Children's Level of Moral Development. *Journal of Moral Education* 4:129–161.

Blockley, M.
1998   The Development of Environmental Education and Archeology in Education in the United Kingdom. Manuscript. On file, Ironbridge Institute, Birmingham, England.

Bloom, B. S., D. Krathwohl, and B. B. Masia
1956   *Taxonomy of Educational Objectives: Handbook 1, The Cognitive Domain.* David McKay, New York.

Bok, S.
1995   *Common Values.* University of Missouri Press, Columbia.

Boniface, P., and P. Fowler
1993   *Heritage Tourism in the Global Village.* Routledge, New York.

Boorstin, D. J., B. M. Kelly, and R. F. Boorstin
1992   *A History of the United States.* Prentice-Hall, Englewood Cliffs, New Jersey.

Borden, R. J.
1985   Technology, Education and the Human Ecology Perspective. *Journal of Environmental Education* 16(3): 1–5.

Borich, G.
1996   *Effective Teaching Methods.* Merrill/Prentice-Hall, Englewood Cliffs, New Jersey.

Bowd, A., D. McDougall, and C. Yewchuk
1982   *Educational Psychology.* Gage Publishing Limited, Toronto.

Boyd, S. M.
1996   Character Education, the U.S. Constitution, and the U.S. Supreme Court. *Update on Law-Related Education* 20(1): 23–25.

Bragaw, D.
1993   A Century of Secondary Social Studies: Looking Backward and Forward. In *Teaching Social Studies*, edited by V. S. Wilson, J. A. Little, and G. L. Wilson, pp. 45–64. Greenwood Press, Westport, Connecticut.

British Museum
1997   Education Service http://www.british-museum.ac.uk/edweb.htm.

Burcaw, G. E.
1975   *Introduction to Museum Work.* American Association for State and Local History, Nashville, Tennessee.

Butler, W. B., ed.
1992   *State Archaeological Education Programs.* Interagency Archaeological Services, Division of National Preservation Programs. Rocky Mountain Regional Office, National Park Service, Denver.

Bybee, R. W.
1997   *Achieving Scientific Literacy: From Purposes to Practices.* Heinemann, Portsmouth, New Hampshire.

Caduto, M. .J., and J. Bruchac
1988   *Keepers of the Earth.* Fulcrum, Golden, Colorado.

Cajete, G. A.
1994   *Look to the Mountain: An Ecology of Indigenous Education.* Kivaki Press, Durango, Colorado.

Canizzo, J.
1989   *Into the Heart of Africa.* Royal Ontario Museum, Toronto.

Carson, R.
1962   *Silent Spring.* Houghton Mifflin, New York.

Case, R.
1985   *Intellectual Development: Birth to Adulthood.* Academic Press, New York.

Character Education Partnership (CEP)
n.d.   *Character Education: Questions and Answers.* Character Education Partnership, Washington, D.C.

Charles, T., and M. B. Walden
1989   *Can You Dig It? A Classroom Guide to South Carolina Archaeology.* South Carolina Department of Education, Columbia, South Carolina.

Chiarulli B., and N. Hawkins
1998   Programs That Educate: Two Successful Archaeology Education Efforts Provide Models for Up-and-Coming Programs. *Archaeology and Public Education* 8(3): 6.

Christensen, B. L.
1995   Mississippi Valley Archaeology Center's Archaeology in Education Program. *Public Archaeology Review* 3(1 & 2): 4–8.

Cole, M., and S. R. Cole
1996   *The Development of Children,* 3rd ed. Freeman, New York.

Collier, M.
1975   Anthropology Curriculum Study Project: One Route for Pre-Collegiate Anthropology. In *Pre-Collegiate Anthropology: Trends and Materials,* edited by T. L. Dynneson, Anthropology Curriculum Project Publication No. 65–1. University of Georgia Press, Athens.

Colorado Department of Education
1997   Standards Based Education. Web Site: www.cde.state.us/#standards

Colwell, T.
1997   The Nature-Culture Distinction and the Future of Environmental Education. *Journal of Environmental Education* 28(4): 4–8.

Cooper, J. M.
1994   *Classroom Teaching Skills.* D. C. Heath, Lexington, Massachusetts.

Coxall, H.
1997   Speaking Other Voices. In *Cultural Diversity,* editedy by E. Hooper-Greenhill, pp. 99 ff. Leicester University Press, Washington, D.C.

Cross, C. T., and S. Joftus
1997   Commentary: Stumping   for   Standards. *Education   Week*   9   April. http://www.edweek.org/ew/1997/28cross.h16.

Damon, W.
1988   *The Moral Child.* Free Press, New York.

Davis, H. A.
1990   *Training and Using Volunteers in Archeology: A Case Study from Arkansas.* Archeological Assistance Program, Technical Brief No. 9. National Park Service, Washington, D.C.

Davis, Jr., R.P.S., Livingood, P. C., Ward, H. T., and Steponaitis, V. P., eds.
1998   Excavating Occanneechi Town, Archaeology of an Eighteenth-Century Indian Village in North Carolina, Chapel Hill, University of North Carolina Press. CD-ROM with eight-page booklet.

Dawdy, S. L.
1996a   From Plantation to Corporation: Public Archaeology at Orange Grove. Paper presented at the 1996 Annual Meeting of the Society for Historical Archaeology, Cincinnati.
1996b   Final Report for New Orleans Archaeology Planning Project. College of Urban and Public Affairs, University of New Orleans. Copies available from Louisiana Division of Archaeology, Baton Rouge.

Dean, A., S. Salend, and L. Taylor
1993   Multicultural Education: A Challenge for Special Educators. *Teaching Exceptional Children* 26:40–43.

DeCicco, G.
1988   A Public Relations Primer. *American Antiquity* 53:840–856.

Deloria, V., Jr.
1995   *Red Earth, White Lies: Native Americans and the Myth of Scientific Fact.* Scribner, New York.

Des Jean, T.
1990   Archaeological Teaching Equipment. *Grist* 34(4): 39.

Dewey, J.
1938   *Experience and Education.* Collier Books, New York.
1963   *Democracy and Education.* Macmillan, New York.

Disinger, J. F.
1985   Current Trends in Environmental Education. *Journal of Environmental Education* 17(2): 1–13

Dockterman, D. A.
1997   *Great Teaching in the One Computer Classroom.* Tom Snyder Productions, Watertown, Massachusetts.

Duncan, D.
1985   Keep Those Visitors Coming. In *Let's Get Organized,* p. 21. Ontario Historical Society, Toronto.

Dunn, R., and K. Dunn
1992   *Teaching Elementary Students through Their Individual Learning Styles: Practical Approaches for Grades 3–6.* Allyn & Bacon, Boston.
1993   *Teaching Secondary Students through Their Individual Learning Styles: Practical Approaches for Grades 7–12.* Allyn & Bacon, Boston

Durkheim, E.
1962   *Moral Education: A Study in the Theory and Application of the Sociology of Education.* Free Press, Glencoe, Illinois.

Echo-Hawk, R.
1993   Working Together: Exploring Ancient Worlds. *SAA Bulletin* 11(4): 5–6.
1997   Forging a New Ancient History for Native America. In *Native Americans and Archaeologists: Stepping Stones to Common Ground*, edited by N. Swidler, K. E. Dongoske, R. Anyon, and A. S. Downer, pp. 88–102. AltaMira Press, Walnut Creek, California.

Edel, M., and A. Edel
1968   *Anthropology and Ethics: A Quest for Moral Understanding.* The Press of Case Western Reserve University, Cleveland, Ohio.

Eisenberg, N.
1982   The Development of Reasoning Regarding Prosocial Behavior. In *The Development of Prosocial Behavior*, edited by N. Eisenberg, pp. 219–249. Academic Press, New York.

Ellick, C.
1991   Archeology Is More Than a Dig: Educating Children about the Past Saves Sites for the Future. In *Archeology and Education: The Classroom and Beyond*, edited by KC Smith and F. P. McManamon, pp. 27–31. Archeological Assistance Study, No. 2. National Park Service, Washington, D.C.

Emler, N.
1996   How Can We Decide Whether Moral Education Works? *Journal of Moral Education* 25(1): 117–126.

Erickson, P. A.
1990   Anthropology Teacher Training. In *Interim Report on Precollege Anthropology*, compiled by P. A. Erickson, pp. 3–15. Committee on Research, Task Force on Teaching Anthropology in Schools, American Anthropological Association, Washington, D.C.

Fagan, B. M.
1991   The Past as News. *CRM* 14(1): 17–19.
1993   The Arrogant Archaeologist. *Archaeology* 46(6): 14–16.
1995   Perhaps We May Hear Voices. In *Save the Past for the Future II: Report of the Working Conference*, pp. 25–30. Society for American Archaeology, Washington, D.C.

Feder, K. L.
1990   *Frauds, Myths, and Mysteries: Science and Pseudoscience in Archaeology.* Mayfield Publishing, Mountain View, California.

1999   *Frauds, Myths, and Mysteries: Science and Pseudoscience in Archaeology*, 3rd ed.
        Mayfield Publishing, Mountain View, California.

Fenton, E.
1991   Reflections on the New Social Studies. *The Social Studies* 82(3): 84–90.

Few, J., N. Hawkins, P. Hooge, C. MacDonald, KC Smith, and S. Smith
1995   *Teaching Archaeology: A Sampler for Grades 3 to 12.* Public Education
        Committee, Society for American Archaeology, Washington, D.C.

Finazzo, D. A.
1997   *All for the Children: Multicultural Essentials of Literature.* Delmar, Albany, New
        York.

Fink, K. D.
1997   The Utah Project: How One State Is Finding Success with Character Education.
        Character Educator, Character Education Partnership, Winter 1997:1, 6.

Fluehr-Lobban, C.
1998   Cultural Relativism and Universal Human Rights. *AnthroNotes: National Museum
        of Natural History Bulletin for Teachers* 20(2): 1–5, 16–18.

Gardner, H.
1993   *Multiple Intelligences: The Theory in Practice.* Basic Books, Harper Collins, New
        York..

Gardner, H., and T. Hatch
1989   Multiple Intelligences Go to School: Educational Implications of the Theory of
        Multiple Intelligences. *Educational Researcher* 18(8): 4–10.

Gathercole, P., and D. Lowenthal, eds.
1994   *The Politics of the Past.* Routledge, London.

Geography Education Standards Project
1994   *Geography for Life: National Geography Standards.* National Geographic
        Research and Exploration, Washington, D.C.

Giglotti, L. M.
1990   Environmental Education: What Went Wrong? What Can Be Done? *Journal of
        Environmental Education* 22(1): 9–12.

Golson, J.
1996   What Went Wrong with WAC-3 and an Attempt to Understand Why. *World
        Archaeological Congress Newsletter* 4:1.

Gonzales, C., and M. D. Roblyer
1996   Rhetoric and Reality—Technology's Role In Restructuring Education. *Learning
        and Leading with Technology* 24(3):11–15.

Grégoire R., R. Bracewell, and T. Laferrière
1996   The Contribution of New Technologies to Learning and Teaching in Elementary
        and Secondary Schools. On line.
        http://www.fse.ulaval.ca/fac/tact/fr/html/impactnt.html. 29 November 1997.

Gregorc, A.
1985   *Gregorc Style Delineator.* Gabriel Systems, Maynard, Massachusetts.

Gutmann, A.
1987   *Democratic Education.* Princeton University Press, Princeton, New Jersey.

Haas, J. D.
1976   *The Era of the New Social Studies.* Social Sciences Education Curriculum, Boulder, Colorado.

Hallahan, D., and J. Kauffman
1994   *Exceptional Children: An Introduction to Special Education.* Allyn & Bacon, Boston.

Hamburg, D. A.
1993   The Opportunities of Early Adolescence. *Teachers' College Press* 94:466–471.

Harrington, S.P.M.
1992   Bones and Bureaucrats: New York's Great Cemetery Imbroglio. *Archaeology* March/April:28–38.

Hawkins, N. W.
1991   *Classroom Archaeology: An Archaeological Activity Guide for Teachers,* rev. ed. Division of Archaeology, Office of Cultural Development, Department of Culture, Recreation and Tourism, State of Louisiana, Baton Rouge.
1996   Instruction or Destruction: Archaeologists Make a Difference. Paper presented at the 61st Annual Society for American Archaeology Meeting, New Orleans, Louisiana.
1998   To Dig or Not to Dig? *Archaeology and Public Education* 8(3): 10–11.

Heath, M. A.
1997   Successfully Integrating the Public into Research: Crow Canyon Archaeological Center. In *Presenting Archaeology to the Public: Digging for Truths,* edited by J. H. Jameson, Jr., pp. 65–72. AltaMira Press, Walnut Creek, California.

Herbert, M.
1983   Museums and Schools. *Journal of Education* 7(4): 34–38.

Herman, J. L., M. Gearhart, and P. R. Aschbacher
1996   Portfolios for Classroom Assessment: Design and Implementation Issues. In *Writing Portfolios in the Classroom,* edited by R. Calfee and P. Perfumo, pp. 25–59. Lawrence Erlbaum Associates, Mahwah, New Jersey.

Herscher, E., and F. P. McManamon
1995   Public Education and Outreach: The Obligation to Educate. In *Ethics in American Archaeology: Challenges for the 1990s,* edited by M. J. Lynott and A. Wylie, pp. 42–44. Society for American Archaeology, Washington, D.C.

Hodder, I., M. Shanks, A. Alexandri, V. Buchli, J. Carman, J. Last, and G. Lucas, eds.
1995   *Interpreting Archaeology.* Routledge, London.

Hoffman, M. L.
1988   Moral development. In *Developmental Psychology: An Advanced Textbook,* 2d ed., edited by M. H. Bornstein and M. E. Lamb, pp. 497–548. Lawrence Erlbaum Associates, Hillsdale, New Jersey.

Hoffman, T.L.
1991   Stewards of the Past: Preserving Arizona's Archaeological Resources through Positive Public Involvement. In *Protecting the Past*, edited by G. C . Smith and J. E. Ehrenhard, pp. 253–259. CRC Press, Boca Raton, Florida

Holm, K. A,, and P. J. Higgins, eds.
1985   *Archeology and Education: A Successful Combination for Precollegiate Students.* Anthropology Curriculum Project, University of Georgia, Athens.

Iseminger, W. R.
1997   Public Archaeology at Cahokia. In *Presenting Archaeology to the Public: Digging for Truths*, edited by J. H. Jameson, Jr., pp. 147–155. AltaMira Press, Walnut Creek, California.

Jameson, J. H., Jr.
1997   Editor. *Presenting Archaeology to the Public: Digging for Truths.* AltaMira Press, Walnut Creek, California.
2000   Public Interpretation, Education, and Outreach: The Growing Predominance in American Archaeology. In *Cultural Resource Management in Contemporary Society: Perspectives on Managing and Presenting the Past*, One World Archaeology Series, Number 33, edited by F. P. McManamon and A. Hatton, pp. 288–299. Routledge, London and New York.

Judge, C.
1988   Archaeology and Grade School Children. *South Carolina Antiquities* 20(1&2): 49–58.

Kamii, M.
1996   *Through Lines: Evolving Standards and Assessment. Fieldwork: An Expeditionary Learning Outward Bound Reader*, Vol. 2. Kendall/Hunt Publishing Company, Dubuque, Iowa.

Kaupp, P. A.
1997   Kennewick Man: A Teacher for All Ages. *AnthroNotes: National Museum of Natural History Bulletin for Teachers* 19(3): 7–8, 19.

Kearsley, G., B. Hunter, and M. Furlong
1992   *We Teach with Technology: New Visions for Education.* Franklin, Beedle & Associates, Wilsonville, Oregon.

Keefe, J. W.
1987   *Learning Style: Theory and Practice.* National Association of Secondary School Principals, Reston, Virginia.

Keen, M.
1991   The Effect of the Sunship Earth Program on Knowledge and Attitude Development. *Journal of Environmental Education* 28(2): 12–14.

Keene, A. S.
1993   Stories We Tell: Gatherer-Hunters as Ideology. In *Ela 'Qua: Essays in Honor of Richard B. Woodbury*, edited by D. S. Krass, R. Brooke Thomas, and J. W. Cole, pp. 61–74. Research Report 28, Department of Anthropology, University of Massachusetts, Amherst.

Kidder, R. M.
1994   *Shared Values for a Troubled World: Conversations with Men and Women of Conscience.* Jossey-Bass, San Francisco.

Kilpatrick, W. K.
1992   *Why Johnny Can't Tell Right from Wrong.* Simon & Schuster, New York.

Kluckhohn, C.
1955   Ethical Relativity: Sic Et Non. *Journal of Philosophy* 52(23): 663–677.

Knapp, D.
1998   The Thessaloniki Declaration—The Beginning of the End for Environmental Education? *Environmental Educator* 28(2): 12–14.

Knoll, P. C., ed.
1990   *Listing of Education in Archeological Programs: The LEAP Clearinghouse. 1987–1989 Summary Report.* U.S. Department of the Interior, National Park Service, Archeological Assistance Division, Washington, D.C.
1992   *Listing of Education in Archeological Programs: The LEAP Clearinghouse. 1990–1991 Summary Report.* U.S. Department of the Interior, National Park Service, Archeological Assistance Division, Washington, D.C.

Kohlberg, L.
1976   Moral Stages and Moralization: The Cognitive-Developmental Approach. In *Moral Development and Behavior: Theory, Research, and Social Issues,* edited by T. Lickona, pp. 31–53. Holt, Rinehart & Winston, New York.
1978   Revisions in the Theory and Practice of Moral Development. In *New Directions for Child Development: Moral Development,* edited by William Damon, pp. 83–87. Jossey-Bass, San Francisco.
1984   *Essays on Moral Development,* Vol. 2. The Psychology of Moral Development. Harper & Row, San Francisco.

Kraft, R., and M. Sakof, eds.
n.d.   *The Theory of Experiential Education,* 2d ed. Association for Experiential Education, Boulder, Colorado.

Krass, D. S.
1994   Making the Grade: Evaluating Archaeology Education Programs. Symposium presented at the 59th Annual Meeting of the Society for American Archaeology, Anaheim, California.
1995   Public High School Teachers and Archaeology: Exploring the Field. Unpublished Ph.D. dissertation, Department of Anthropology, University of Massachusetts, Amherst, and University Microfilms, Ann Arbor, Michigan.

Krauthammer, C.
1995   History Hijacked. *Time* 13 February:68.

Kruger, A. C.
1992   The Effect of Peer and Adult-Child Transactive Discussions on Moral Reasoning. *Merrill-Palmer Quarterly* 38:191–211.

Kuhn, D.
1992 Cognitive Development. In *Developmental Psychology: An Advanced Textbook*, 3rd ed., edited by M. H. Bornstein and M. E. Lamb, pp. 211–272. Lawrence Erlbaum Associates, Hillsdale, New Jersey.

Kuhn, D., J. Langer, L. Kohlberg, and N. Haan
1977 The Development of Formal Operations in Logical and Moral Judgement. *Genetic Psychology Monographs* 95:97–188.

Kwas, M. L.
1986a Archaeological Parks: A Horse of a Different Color. In *Archaeological Parks: Integrating Preservation, Interpretation, and Recreation*, edited by M. Kwas, pp. 1–9. Tennessee Department of Conservation, Division of Parks and Recreation, Nashville.
1986b Editor. *Archaeological Parks: Integrating Preservation, Interpretation, and Recreation.* Tennessee Department of Conservation, Division of Parks and Recreation, Nashville.
1994a Archaeological Parks: Year-Round Centers for Public Education. *Public Archaeology Review* 2(3): 10–12.
1994b Public Education at Archaeological Parks. *SAA Bulletin* 12(2): 18.
1995 How to Communicate with the Public: Tips for Archaeologists Doing Public Education. *Tennessee Anthropologist* 20(1): 74–78. (Also reprinted in abbreviated version in Archaeology and Public Education 5[4]:18.)

Kwas, M. L., and R. C. Mainfort, Jr.
1996 From Ancient Site to Tourist Attraction and Beyond: Archeological Parks in the Delta. *Common Ground* 1(1): 34–38.

Lal, B. B.
1976–77
Indian Archaeology: A Review. New Delhi, Archaeological Survey of India.

Lane, C.
n.d. The Role of Technology in the Systemic Reform of Education and Training. FarWest Laboratory, San Francisco. On-line. http://www.fwl.org/edtech/reformtechpart1.html. 26 November 1997.

Lavin, M. B.
1996 So, You're Still Not Sure About Archaeology and Eighth Graders? *Archaeology and Public Education* 6(2): 4–5, 14.

Lazear, D. G.
1992 *Teaching for Multiple Intelligences.* Phi Delta Kappa, Bloomingdale, Illinois.

Lee, R. F.
1970 *The Antiquities Act of 1906.* National Park Service, Washington, D.C.

Lehman, D. R., and R. E. Nisbett
1990 A Longitudinal Study of the Effects of Undergraduate Training on Reasoning. *Developmental Psychology* 26:952–960.

Leming, J. S.
   1981   Curricular Effectiveness in Moral/Values Education: A Review of Research. *Journal of Moral Education* 10(3): 147–164.
   1993   Synthesis of Research: In Search of Effective Character Education. *Educational Leadership* 51(3): 63–71.

Leone, M. P., P. B. Potter, Jr., and P. A. Shackel
   1987   Toward a Critical Archaeology. *Current Anthropology* 28(3): 283–302.

Leone, M. P. and R. W. Preucel
   1992   Archaeology in a Democratic Society: A Critical Theory Perspective. In *Quandaries and Quests: Visions of Archaeology's Future*, edited by L. Wandsnider. Centers for Archaeological Investigations, occasional paper No. 20, pp. 115–135. Southern Illinois University, Carbondale.

Leopold, A.
   1966   *A Sand County Almanac, With Essays on Conservation from Round River.* Oxford University Press, Oxford.

Lerner, S.
   1991   Saving Sites: Preservation and Education. In *Protecting the Past*, edited by G. S. Smith and J. E. Ehrenhard, pp. 103–108. CRC Press, Boca Raton, Florida.

Lerner, S., and T. L. Hoffman
   2000   Bringing Archaeology to the Public: Programs in the Southwestern United States. In *Cultural Resource Management in Contemporary Society: Perspectives on Managing and Presenting the Past*, One World Archaeology Series, Number 33, edited by F. P. McManamon and A. Hatton. Routledge, pp 231–246. London and New York.

Lewis, B.
   1991   *The Kid's Guide to Social Action.* Free Spirit Publishers, Minneapolis.

Lewis. C. S.
   1996   *The Abolition of Man.* Simon & Schuster, New York.

Lickona, T.
   1991   *Educating for Character: How Our Schools Can Teach Respect and Responsibility.* Bantam Books, New York.

Lipe, W. D.
   1974   A Conservation Model for Archaeology. *The Kiva* 39(1–2): 213–243.

Lounsbury, J. H., ed.
   1992   *Connecting the Curriculum Through Interdisciplinary Instruction.* National Middle School Association, Columbus, Ohio.

Lumley, R.
   1994   The Debate on Heritage Reviewed. In *Towards the Museum of the Future*, edited by R. Miles and L. Zavala, pp. 57–70. Routledge, New York.

Lynott, M. J., and A. Wylie
   1995a   Stewardship: The Central Principle of Archaeological Ethics. In *Ethics in American Archaeology: Challenges for the 1990s*, edited by M. J. Lynott and A. Wylie, pp. 28–32. Society for American Archaeology, Washington, D.C.

1995b   Editors. *Ethics in American Archaeology: Challenges for the 1990s*. Society for
         American Archaeology, Washington, D.C.

MacDonald, C.
1995   Historical Archaeology Meshes Learning Experiences for Kids. *Archaeology and
         Public Education* 6(1): 5.

MacKinney, L. H.
1994   That Sense of Adventure: Front-End Interviews about Archaeology and Indiana
         Jones with Visitors to the California Academy of Sciences. Ms. On file, California
         Academy of Sciences.

Martin, D. J.
1997   *Elementary Science Methods: A Constructivist Approach*. Delmar Publishers,
         Albany, New York.

Martorella, P. H.
1996   *Teaching Social Studies in Middle and Secondary Schools*. Merrill/Prentice-Hall,
         Englewood Cliffs, New Jersey.

Master Teacher, Inc., The
1998   *Lesson Plans for Character Education, Elementary Edition*. The Master Teacher,
         Inc., Manhattan, Kansas.

Matthews, B. E., and C. K. Riley
1995   *Teaching and Evaluating Outdoor Ethics Education Programs*. National Wildlife
         Federation, Vienna, Virginia.

McCarthy, B.
1987   *The 4MAT System*. Teaching To Learning Styles. Excell, Barrington, Illinois.

McManamon, F. P.
1991   The Many Publics for Archaeology. *American Antiquity* 56(1): 121–130.
1994   Presenting Archaeology to the Public in the USA. In *The Presented Past: Heritage,
         Museums, and Education*, edited by P. G. Stone and B. L. Molyneaux, pp. 61–81.
         Routledge, London and New York.
1996   The Antiquities Act—Setting Basic Preservation Policies. *CRM* 19(7): 18–23.
1998   Public Archaeology: A Professional Obligation. *Archaeology and Public Education*
         8(3): 3, 13.

McManamon, F. P., and A. Hatton, eds.
1999   *Cultural Resource Management in Contemporary Society: Perspectives on
         Managing and Presenting the Past*, One World Archaeology Series, Number 33.
         Routledge, London and New York.

McMaster, G.
1990   Problems of Representation. *Muse* 8(3): 35–41.

McNutt, N.
1992 [1988]
         Project Archaeology: Saving Traditions: Archaeology for the Classroom, 2d ed.
         Sopris West Inc., Longmont, Colorado.
1993a   Passages: A Timeline of Southeast Alaska. USDA, Forest Service. Copies available
         from Tongass National Forest, P.O. Box 309, Petersburg, AK 99833.

1993b   Action Archeology: Tracing Our Past. USDA Forest Service. Copies available from Tongass National Forest, P.O. Box 309, Petersburg, AK 99833.

Means, B.
1994   Introduction: Using Technology to Advance Educational Goals. In *Technology and Education Reform: The Reality Behind the Promise*, edited by B. Means, pp. 1–22. Jossey-Bass, San Francisco.

Means, B., J. Blando, K. Olson, T. Middleton, C. C. Morocco, A. R. Remz, and J. Zorfass
1994   Using Technology to Support Education Reform. U.S. Department of Education, Office of Educational Research and Improvement. On-line. http://gopher.ed.gov/pubs/EdReformStudies/TechReforms/index.html.

Messenger, P. M.
1994   The Future of the Past: SAA Maps a Long-Term Strategy. *Archaeology and Public Education* 5(2): 1, 3, 11.
1995   Public Education and Outreach. In *Ethics in American Archaeology: Challenges for the 1990s*, edited by M. J. Lynott and A. Wylie, pp. 68–70. Society for American Archaeology, Washington, D.C.

Messenger, P. M., and W. W. Enloe
1991   The Archaeologist as Global Educator. In *Protecting the Past*, edited by G. S. Smith and J. E. Ehrenhard. CRC Press, Boca Raton, Florida.

Metcalf, F.
1992   Knife River: Early Village Life on the Plains. A "Teaching with Historic Places." Supplement. *Social Education* 56(5): 312 ff.

Milanich, J. T.
1991   Archaeology in the Sunshine: Grass Roots Education through the Media and Public Involvement. In *Protecting the Past*, edited by G. S. Smith and J. E. Ehrenhard, pp. 109–116. CRC Press, Boca Raton, Florida.

Miller, P. H.
1993   Theories of Developmental Psychology. Freeman & Co., New York.

Miller-Lachmann, L., and L. S. Taylor
1995   *Schools for All: Educating Children in a Diverse Society*. Delmar, Albany, New York.

Miner, H.
1956   Body Ritual of the Nacirema. *American Anthropologist* 58(3): 180–182.

Mitchell, B. M., and R. E. Salsbury
1996   *Multicultural Education: An International Guide to Research, Policies, and Programs*. Greenwood Press, Westport, Connecticut.

Mitchum, B. A., and J. Giblin
1995   Archaeology in Action: Interpreting Archaeology for Elementary School Students. *Public Archaeology Review* 3(1&2): 4–8.

Moe, J. M.
1996   *Project Archaeology Primer: Establishing a State or Regional Program*. Bureau of Land Management, Anasazi Heritage Center, Dolores, Colorado.

2000   America's Archaeological Heritage: Protection through Education. In *Cultural Resource Management in Contemporary Society: Perspectives in Managing and Presenting the Past*, One World Archaeology, Number 33., edited by F. P. McManamon and A. Hatton, pp. 276–287. Routledge, London and New York.

In press Project Archaeology: Putting the Intrigue of the Past in Public Education. Public Benefits of Archaeology Conference.

Moe, J. M., and K. A. Letts
1998   Education: Can It Make a Difference? *Common Ground: Archaeology and Ethnography in the Public Interest* 3(1): 24–29.

Molyneaux, B. L.
1994   The Represented Past. In *The Presented Past: Heritage, Museums and Education*, One World Archaeology Series, Vol. 25, edited by P. G. Stone and B. L. Molyneaux , pp. 1–13. Routledge, London.

Nash, G. B., C. Crabtree, and R. E. Dunn
1997   *History On Trial: Culture Wars and the Teaching of the Past*. Knopf, New York.

Nash, R. J.
1997   *Answering the "Virtuecrats": A Moral Conversation on Moral Education*. Teachers College Press, Columbia University, New York.

National Center for History in the Schools
1996   *National Standards for History*. National Center for History in the Schools, Los Angeles.

National Commission on Excellence in Education
1983   *A Nation at Risk: The Imperative for Educational Reform*. U.S. Department of Education, Washington, D.C.

National Research Council
1995   *National Science Education Standards*. National Academy Press, Washington, D.C.

Neal, A.
1976   *Exhibits for the Small Museum: A Handbook*. American Association for State and Local History, Nashville, Tennessee.

Nieto, S.
1992   *Affirming Diversity: The Sociopolitical Context of Multicultural Education*. Longman, New York.

Nobles C. H.
1992   *Adventures in Classroom Archaeology*. Louisiana Division of Archaeology, Baton Rouge.

Noblit, G. W., and V. O. Dempsey
1996   *The Social Construction of Virtue: The Moral Life of Schools*. State University of New York Press, Albany.

Noel-Hume, I.
1978   Material Culture with Dirt on It. In *Material Culture and the Study of American Life*, edited by I. Quimby, pp. 21–40. W.W. Norton, New York.

Nucci, L. P.
    1989   Challenging Conventional Wisdom about Morality: The Domain Approach. In
            Moral Development and Character Education: A Dialogue, edited by L. P. Nucci,
            pp. 183–203. McCutchan Publishing, Berkeley, California.

Nusbaum, J. L.
    1929   *Annual Report of Jesse L. Nusbaum, Department Archaeologist and Superintendent
            of Mesa Verde National Park to the Secretary of the Interior, 1929.* U.S.
            Government Printing Office, Washington, D.C.

O'Brien, W. , and T. Cullen, eds.
    1996   *Archaeology in the Classroom: A Resource Guide for Teachers and Parents.*
            Archaeological Institute of America. Kendall/Hunt Publishing Co., Dubuque, Iowa.

Orlich, D. C., R. J. Harder, R. C. Callahan, D. P. Kauchak, and H. W. Gibson
    1994   *Teaching Strategies: A Guide to Better Instruction.* D. C. Heath, Lexington,
            Massachusetts.

Patton, M. Q.
    1990   *Qualitative Evaluation and Research Methods.* Sage Publications, Newbury Park,
            California.

Pearce, S.
    1990   *Archaeological Curatorship.* Leicester University Press, New York.

Peñalva, M.L.S.
    1994   *Sources for Archaeology Education in New York City.* Geoarchaeology Research
            Associates, Riverdale, New York.

Peters, K. S., E. A. Comer, and R. Kelly
    1987   *Captivating the Public through the Media While Digging the Past.* Technical
            Series, No. 1. Baltimore Center for Urban Archaeology, Baltimore, Maryland.

Piaget, J.
    1964   Development and Learning. In *Readings on the Development of Children*, 2d ed.,
            edited by M. Gauvain and M. Cole, pp.19–28. Freeman and Co., New York.

Pierangelo, R., and R. Jacoby
    1996   *Parents' Complete Special Education Guide: Tips, Techniques and Materials for
            Helping Your Child Succeed in School and Life.* The Center for Applied Research
            in Education, West Nyack, New York.

Pike, G., and D. Selby
    1988   *Global Teacher, Global Learner.* Hodder & Stoughton, Toronto.

Postman, N.
    1995   *The End of Education: Redefining the Value of School.* Knopf, New York.

Potter, P. B., Jr.
    1994   *Public Archaeology in Annapolis: A Critical Approach to History in Maryland's
            Ancient City.* Smithsonian Institution Press, Washington, D.C.

Praetzellis, A., and M. Praetzellis, eds.
    1998   Archaeologists as Storytellers. *Historical Archaeology* 32(1), special edition.
            Society for Historic Archaeology, Washington D.C.

President's Committee of Advisors on Science and Technology
1997   *Report to the President on the Use of Technology to Strengthen K–12 Education in the United States*. Panel on Educational Technology, U.S. Department of Education, Washington, D.C.

Price, D., and G. Gebauer
1996   *Adventures in Fugawiland!: A Computer Simulation in Archaeology*. Mayfield Publishing, Mountain View, California.

Rao, N.
1994   Interpreting Silences: Symbol and History in the Case of Ram Janmabhoomi/ Babri Masjid. In *Social Construction of the Past*, edited by G. C. Bond and A. Gilliam, pp. 154–163. Routledge, London.

Rathje, W. , and C. Murphy
1992   *Rubbish*. Harper Perennial Press, New York.

Raths, L. E., M. Harmin, and S. B. Simon
1966   *Values and Teaching: Working with Values in the Classroom*. Charles E. Merrill Publishing, Columbus, Ohio.

Ravitch, D.
1995   *National Standards in American Education*. The Brookings Institution, Washington, D.C.

Redfield, R.
1973   The Universally Human and the Culturally Variable. In *Ethical Relativism*, edited by John Ladd, pp. 129–143. University Press of America, Lanham, Maryland.

Reissman, R.
1994   *The Evolving Multicultural Classroom*. Association for Supervision and Curriculum Development, Alexandria, Virginia.

Rice, M. J.
1995   Precollege Anthropology/Archaeology. In *Teaching Social Studies*, edited by V. S. Wilson, J. A. Little, and G. L. Wilson, pp. 201–226. Greenwood Press, Westport, Connecticut.

Rice, P.
1990   Anthropology Curricula. In *Interim Report on Precollege Anthropology*, compiled by P. A. Erickson, pp. 31–36. Committee on Research, Task Force on Teaching Anthropology in Schools, American Anthropological Association, Washington, D.C.

Rief, S. F.
1993   *How to Reach and Teach ADD/ADHD Children: Practical Techniques, Strategies, and Interventions for Helping Children with Attention Problems and Hyperactivity*. The Center for Applied Research in Education, West Nyack, New York.

Roberts, L. C.
1997   *From Knowledge to Narrative*. Smithsonian Institution Press, Washington, D.C.

Roerden, L. P.
1997   *Net Lessons: Web-Based Projects for Your Classroom*. Songline Studios, Sebastopol, California.

Rogge, A. E., and P. Bell
1989   *Archeology in the Classroom: A Case Study from Arizona.* Technical Brief No. 4, Archaeological Assistance Program, National Park Service, U.S. Department of the Interior, Washington, D.C.

Rogoff, B.
1993   Children's Guided Participation and Participatory Appropriation in Sociocultural Activity. In *Development in Contexts: Acting and Thinking in Specific Environments*, edited by R. H.Wosniak and K. W. Fischer, pp. 121–153. Lawrence Erlbaum Associates, Hillsdale, New Jersey.

Rolingson, M. A.
1984   Archaeology and Prehistory in Public Parks, Southeastern North America. *Midcontinental Journal of Archaeology* 9(2): 155–171.

Rowland, F. S.
1993   President's Lecture: The Need for Scientific Communication with the Public. *Science* 260:1571–1576.

Ruskin, J.
1859   *The Two Paths: Being Lectures on Art and Its Application to Decoration and Manufacture.* J. Wiley, New York.
1990   Quote. In *Earth Education: A New Beginning*, by Steve Van Matre, p. 310. Institute for Earth Education, Greenville, West Virginia.

Rusnak, T.
1998   *An Integrated Approach to Character Education.* Corwin Press, Thousand Oaks, California.

Ryan, K., and K. E. Bohlin
1999   *Building Character in Schools: Practical Ways to Bring Moral Instruction to Life.* Jossey-Bass, San Francisco.

Sabelli, N. H., and L. K. Barrett
1993   Learning and Technology in the Future. National Science Foundation Workshop. October 4–6, 1993. National Science Foundation, Directorate for Education and Human Resources, Washington, D.C.

Sabloff, J.
1996   The Past and Future of American Archaeology. Distinguished Lecture, presented at the American Anthropological Association annual meeting, San Francisco.

Sadker, M., and D. Sadker
1994   Failing at Fairness, How America's Schools Cheat Girls. Scribners & Sons, New York.

Said, E.
1978   *Orientalism.* Vintage Books, New York.

Salmon, M.
1997   Ethical Considerations in Anthropology and Archaeology, or Relativism and Justice for All. *Journal of Anthropological Research* 53:47–63.

Santrock, J. W.
1997 *Children*, 5th ed. Brown & Benchmark, Madison, Wisconsin.

Schirmer, J.
1988 The Dilemma of Cultural Diversity and Equivalency in Universal Human Rights Standards. In *Cultural Survival Report 24: Human Rights and Anthropology*, edited by T. E. Downing and G. Kushner. Cultural Survival, Cambridge, Massachusetts.

Schuldenrein, J.
1998 Changing Career Paths and the Training of Professional Archaeologists: Observations from the Barnard College Forum. Society for American Archaeology Bulletin 16 (1): 31–33.

Schur, S., S. Lewis, K. LaMorte, and K. Shewey
1996 *Signaling Student Success: Thematic Learning Stations and Integrated Units for Middle Level Classrooms*. National Middle School Association, Columbus, Ohio.

Scott, D. D., and M. A. Connor
1986 Post-Mortem at the Little Big Horn. *Natural History* June:46–54.

Selig, R. O.
1989 Anthropology in Public Schools: Why Should We Care? *Anthropology Newsletter* (February 1989): 28.
1991 Teacher Training Programs in Anthropology: The Multiplier Effect in the Classroom. In *Archaeology and Education: The Classroom and Beyond*, edited by KC Smith and F. P. McManamon, pp. 3–7. Archeological Assistance Study, No. 2, National Park Service, Washington, D.C.
1995 Teacher Training in One Wyoming Community: An Argument for Anthropologists' Involvement in American Schools. *Wyoming Contributions to Anthropology* 4:15–23.
1997 The Challenge of Exclusion: Anthropology, Teachers and Schools. In *The Teaching of Anthropology: Problems, Issues, and Decisions*, edited by C. P. Kottak, J. J. White, R. H. Furlow, and P. C. Rice, pp. 299–307. Mayfield, Mountain View, California.

Selig, R.O., and P. J. Higgins, eds.
1986 Practicing Anthropology in Pre-College Education. Special double issue of *Practicing Anthropology* 8(3–4).

Selig, R. O., and J. Lanouette
1983 A New Approach to Teacher Training. *Museum News* 61(6): 44–48.

Selig, R. O., and M. R. London, eds.
1998 *Anthropology Explored: The Best of Smithsonian AnthroNotes*. Smithsonian Institution Press, Washington, D.C.

Sengstack, J.
1997 Easier, Cheaper Recordable CDs Finally Break the Mold. On-line. 13 January. www.pcworl.com/hardware/cd-rom_drives/articles/Jun97/1506p068

Serrell, B.
1983   *Making Exhibit Labels: A Step-by-Step Guide.* American Association for State and Local History, Nashville, Tennessee.

Shanks, M.
1992   *Experiencing the Past: On the Character of Archaeology.* Routledge, London.

Shanks, M., and C. Tilley
1987   *Re-Constructing Archaeology: Theory and Practice.* Routledge, London.

Sharpe, G. W.
1982   *Interpreting the Environment,* 2d ed. John Wiley and Sons, New York.

Short, G. S., and C. Burke
1991   *Creating Curriculum: Teachers and Students as a Community of Learners.* Heinemann, Portsmouth, New Hampshire.

Shrimali, K. M.
1998   Ayodhya Archaeology: From Imbroglio to Resolution. Paper presented at the World Archaeological Congress Inter-Congress on the Destruction and Restoration of Cultural Property, Brac, Croatia.

Shurban
1989   Archaeology Is More than a Dig. In *Fighting Indiana Jones in Arizona. Proceedings of the 1988 American Society for Conservation,* edited by A. E. Rogge, pp. 75–79. Portales, New Mexico.

Siegler, R. S.
1991   *Children's Thinking,* 2d ed. Prentice-Hall, Englewood Cliffs, New Jersey.

Simon, S. B., L. W. Howe, and H. Kirschenbaum
1972   *Values Clarification: A Handbook of Practical Strategies for Teachers and Students.* Hart Publishing, New York.

Sitton, T., G. L. Mehaffy, and O. L. Davis, Jr.
1983   *Oral History: A Guide for Teachers and Others.* University of Texas Press, Austin.

Skinner, S. A.
1997   The Boy Scouts Are Calling. *Society for American Archaeology Bulletin* 15(4): 17.

Skinner, S. A., D. A. Poirier, D. L. Krofina, and P. Wheat
1998   Be Prepared: The Archaeology Merit Badge Is Here. *Common Ground: Archaeology and Ethnology in the Public Interest* 3(1): 38–41.

Skolnik, R., and R. G. Kanning
1994   Multimedia Technology. In *Multimedia and Learning: A School Leader's Guide,* edited by A. W. Ward, pp. 3–20. National School Boards Association, Alexandria, Virginia.

Smardz, K.
1990   Archaeology in the Toronto School System: The Archaeological Resource Centre. In *The Excluded Past: Archaeology in Education,* edited by P. Stone and R. MacKenzie, pp. 293–307. Unwin Hyman, London.
1991   Teaching People to Touch the Past: Archaeology in the Toronto School System. In *Protecting the Past,* edited by G. S. Smith and J. E. Ehrenhard, pp.135–148. CRC Press, Boca Raton, Florida.

1995   Archaeology and Multiculturalism. *Archaeology and Public Education* 5(3): 1–3, 15.
1997   The Past Through Tomorrow: Interpreting Toronto's Heritage to a Multicultural Public. In *Presenting Archaeology to the Public: Digging for Truths*, edited by J. H. Jameson, Jr., pp. 101–113. AltaMira Press, Walnut Creek, California.

Smetana, J. G.
1981   Preschool Children's Conception of Moral and Social Rules. *Child Development* 52: 1333–1336.
1985   Preschool Children's Conceptions of Transgressions: Effects of Varying Moral and Conventional Domain-Related Attributes. *Developmental Psychology* 21:18–29.
1989   Toddlers' Social Interactions in the Context of Moral and Conventional Transgressions in the Home. *Developmental Psychology* 25:499–508.

Smith, B. D.
1993   A New Goal for Academia. *Archeology and Public Education* 3(3): 1.

Smith, D. D., and R. Luckasson
1992   *Introduction to Special Education: Teaching in an Age of Challenge*. Allyn & Bacon, Boston.

Smith, G. S., and J. E. Ehrenhard
1991   *Protecting the Past*. CRC Press, Boca Raton, Florida.

Smith, KC
1990   *Pathways to the Past. Educator's Guide to Resources in Archaeology*. Museum of Florida History, Tallahassee, Florida.
1991a   *Classroom Sources for Archaeology Education*, rev. ed. 1997. Society for American Archaeology. Washington, D.C.
1991b   At Last a Meeting of the Minds. *Archaeology* 50(1): 36–46, 80.
1991c   By Land Or by Sea: Archeology Programs for Youths at the Museum of Florida History. In *Archeology and Education: The Classroom and Beyond*, edited by KC Smith and F. P. McManamon, pp. 13–17. Archeological Assistance Study, No. 2. National Park Service, Washington D.C.
1995   Picture This: Using Photographs to Study the Past. *Archaeology and Public Education* 6(1): 6–8.
1998   One Era Ends, Another Begins. *Archeology and Public Education* 8(3): 2, 15.

Smith, KC, and F. P. McManamon, eds.
1991   *Archaeology and Education: The Classroom and Beyond*. Archeological Assistance Study, No. 2, National Park Service, Washington, D.C.

Smith, S. J., J. M. Moe, K. A. Letts, and D. M. Paterson
1996   *Intrigue of the Past: A Teacher's Activity Guide for Fourth Through Seventh Grades*, reprint. Bureau of Land Management, Anasazi Heritage Center, Dolores, Colorado.

Smithsonian Institution
1990–1997
        Teaching Anthropology Modules. Smithsonian Institution, Washington, D.C.

Social Science Education Consortium, Inc.
1996   *Teaching the Social Sciences and History in Secondary Schools: A Methods Book.* Wadsworth Publishing, Belmont, California.

Society for American Archaeology (SAA)
1995a   *Guidelines for the Evaluation of Archaeology Education Materials.* Prepared by the Precollegiate Education Subcommittee, Public Education Committee, Society for American Archaeology, Washington, D.C.
1995b   *Save the Past for the Future II: Report of the Working Conference, Breckenridge, Colorado, Sept. 19–22, 1994.* Society for American Archaeology, Washington, D.C.
1999   *Exploring Public Attitudes about Archeology: A Proposal by the National Park Service and the Society for American Archaeology.* Society for American Archaeology, Executive Office, Washington, D.C.

Soren, B.
1990   Curriculum-Making and the Museum Mosaic. Unpublished thesis, Department of Museum Studies, University of Toronto.

Sroufe, L. A., R. G. Cooper, and G. B. DeHart
1996   *Child Development: Its Nature and Course,* 3rd ed. McGraw-Hill, New York.

Stone, P.G.
1994   The Re-Display of the Alexander Keiller Museum, Avebury and the National Curriculum in England. In *The Presented Past: Heritage, Museums, and Education,* One World Archaeology Series, Vol. 25, edited by P. G. Stone and B. L. Molyneaux, pp. 1–13. Routledge, London.

Stone, P.G., and R. Mackenzie, eds.
1990   *The Excluded Past: Archaeology and Education.* One World Archaeology Series, Vol. 17. Routledge, London.
1997   Presenting the Past: A Framework for Discussion. In *Presenting Archaeology to the Public: Digging for Truths,* edited by J. H. Jameson, Jr., pp. 23–34. AltaMira Press, Walnut Creek, California.

Stone, P. G., and B. L. Molyneaux, eds.
1994   *The Presented Past: Heritage, Museums and Education.* One World Archaeology Series, Vol. 25. Routledge, London.

Stuart, G. E., and F. P. McManamon
1996   *Archaeology and You.* Society for American Archaeology, Washington, D.C.

Svezia, E.
1986   Cahokia Mounds: A New Strategy for Management. In *Archaeological Parks: Integrating Preservation, Interpretation, and Recreation,* edited by M. Kwas, pp. 43–48. Tennessee Department of Conservation, Division of Parks and Recreation, Nashville.

Takanishi, R.
1993   Changing Views of Adolescence in Contemporary Society. *Teachers College Record* 94:459–465.

Taylor, S.
1991   *Try It! Improving Exhibits Through Formative Evaluation.* Association of Science and Technology Centers, Washington, D.C.

Thomas, R. M.
1996   *Comparing Theories of Child Development,* 4th ed. Brooks/Cole, Pacific Grove, California.

Tiedt, P. L., and I. M. Tiedt
1995   *Multicultural Teaching: A Handbook of Activities, Information, and Resources,* 4th ed. Allyn & Bacon, Boston.

Turiel, E., J. G. Smetana, and M. Killen
1991   Social contexts in social cognitive development. In *Handbook of Moral Behavior and Development,* Vol. 2, edited by W. M. Kurtines and J. L. Gewirtz, pp. 307–332. Lawrence Erlbaum Associates, Hillsdale, New Jersey.

Ucko, P. J.
1987   *Academic Freedom and Apartheid.* Duckworth, London.

UNESCO
1997   Declaration of Thessaloniki. UNESCO Publication NO. EPD–97/CONF.401/ CLD.2. Paris, France.

U.S. Department of Education
1997a   National Education Goals 2000. Web site: www.ed.gov/pubs/Teachers Guide/natgoals.html
1997b   *Parents' Guide to the Internet.* Washington, D.C.
1998   *Partnerships in Character Education.* Washington, D.C.

Van Matre, S.
1990   *Earth Education: A New Beginning. Institute for Earth Education,* Greenville, West Virginia.

Viadero, D.
1996   Culture Clash. *Education Week* 10 April, p. 39.

Vygotsky, L. S.
1978   *Mind in Society: The Development of Higher Mental Processes.* Harvard University Press, Cambridge, Massachusetts.

Walker, S.
1997   Black Cultural Museums in Britain: What Questions Do They Answer? In *Cultural Diversity,* edited by Eileen Hooper-Greenhill, pp. 32–49. Leicester University Press, Washington, D.C.

Western Regional Environmental Education Council (WREEC)
1985   Project WILD: Elementary Activity Guide. Project Wild, Boulder, Colorado.
1990   Project WILD: Activity Guide. Project Wild, Boulder, Colorado.

Wheat, P., and C. Colón
1997   *Games That Enrich Archaeological Studies.* Society for American Archaeology. Washington, D.C.

Wheat, P., and B. Whorton
    1990   *Clues from the Past: A Resource Book on Archeology.* Hendrick-Long Publishing Co., Dallas.

White, N. M., and B. Weisman
    In press Graduate Education in Public Archaeology. Proceedings of the 1995 Chacmool Conference, Public or Perish: Archaeology into the Next Millennium. University of Calgary.

White, N. M., and J. R. Williams
    1994   Public Archaeology in Florida, USA: A Review and Case Study. In *The Presented Past: Heritage, Museums and Education*, One World Archaeology Series, Vol. 25, edited by P. Stone and B. Molyneaux, pp. 82–94. Routledge, London.

White, P.
    1996   *Civic Virtues and Public Schooling: Educating Citizens for a Democratic Society.* Teachers College Press, Columbia University, New York.

Whitney, P.
    1998   *The Psychology of Language.* Houghton Mifflin, Boston.

Wiley, L. S.
    1998   *Comprehensive Character Building Classroom: A Handbook for Teachers.* Longwood Communications, DeBary, Florida.

Willey, G. R., and J. A. Sabloff
    1980   *A History of American Archaeology*, 2d ed. W. H. Freeman, San Francisco.

Williams, J. A.
    1989   *Illinois Archaeological Resource Materials with Annotated Bibliography for Teachers.* Illinois Historic Preservation Agency. Springfield.

Williams, S.
    1988   Some Fantastic Messages from the Past. *Archaeology* 41(5): 62–70.
    1991   *Fantastic Archaeology: The Wild Side of North American Prehistory.* University of Pennsylvania Press, Philadelphia.

Williamson, D.
    1991   A Simulated Archaeological Dig for High School. *Teaching Anthropology Newsletter* 18:8–9.

Wolf, E.
    1982   *Europe and the People without History.* University of California Press, Berkeley.

Wolynec, R. B.
    1996   Teaching Children about Archaeology Should Not Be a Trivial Pursuit! Paper presented at the 61st annual meetings of the Society for American Archaeology, New Orleans.

Woodiel, D.
    1986   Archaeological Parks in Louisiana: Interpretation and Management. In *Archaeological Parks: Integrating Preservation, Interpretation, and Recreation*, edited by M. Kwas, pp. 49–53. Tennessee Department of Conservation, Division of Parks and Recreation, Nashville.

Wynne, E. A., and K. Ryan
 1997 *Reclaiming Our Schools: Teaching Character, Academics, and Discipline.*
       Prentice-Hall, Upper Saddle River, New Jersey.

Zeder, M. A.
 1997 *The American Archaeologist.* A Profile. AltaMira Press, Walnut Creek, California.

Zimmerman, L. J., S. Dasovich, M. Engstrom, and L. E. Bradley
 1994 Listening to the Teachers: Warnings about the Use of Archaeological Agendas in
       Classrooms in the United States. In *The Presented Past: Heritage, Museums, and
       Education*, One World Archaeology Series, Vol. 25, edited by P. G. Stone and B.
       L. Molyneaux, pp. 359–374. Routledge, London.

Zorpette, G.
 1992 What Do Museum Visitors Want? *Art News* 91(10): 94–98.

Zyskowski, G.
 1983 A Review of Literature on the Evaluation of Museum Programs. *Curator* 26(2):
       121–128.

About the Authors

ELLEN DAILEY BEDELL has a Ph.D. in Egyptology from Brandeis University, where she wrote her dissertation on criminal law in the Ramesside period. She also studied archaeology and has worked on archaeological sites in the Middle East, North America, and Central America. Ellen has been teaching for the past six years at The Ellis School, an independent college preparatory school in Pittsburgh, Pennsylvania, where she developed a program in anthropology. She is presently involved in teaching a series of workshops to train other educators to teach archaeology, and recently received an NEH fellowship to participate in a program on teaching archaeology sponsored by the Archaeological Institute of America at Boston University.

ROBERT H. BRUNSWIG, JR. (Ph.D., University of Colorado) is associate professor of anthropology at the University of Northern Colorado. His primary academic interests are research archaeology and archaeology education. His research experience spans nearly three decades, and he has conducted field projects in the Arabian Peninsula, southern Asia and Europe, and the western United States. He has been director of UNC's South Platte Archaeological Project since 1992 and recently initiated a research study of highland-lowland cultural adaptations of Late Ice Age populations in southern France and the southern Rocky Mountains. Throughout his academic career, Bob has been involved in undergraduate and graduate teacher training by teaching archaeology-focused teacher education courses and workshops and by integrating in-service teachers in his various field projects.

PAULA BURTNESS has been an elementary and middle school teacher in Minnesota, Wisconsin, and Oregon, and has served as a consultant, developer, and presenter of incorporating on-line learning projects in the classroom. Her long-time interest in archaeology began with childhood visits to the Grand Mound in northern Minnesota. She has a particular interest in meeting the needs of high-ability students within regular classroom setting. Paula is currently the specialist for talented and gifted children for Beaverton public schools, Beaverton, Oregon.

BEVERLY MITCHUM CHIARULLI has a Ph.D. in anthropology/archaeology from Southern Methodist University, Dallas, Texas, where her dissertation research was on lithic artifacts from Cerros, Belize. She was the director of the Workshop for Educators in Maya Civilization and Tropical Forest Ecology held in Belize in July 1997 and has been the coordinator for Project Archaeology: Pennsylvania since 1996. She is on the planning board for Pennsylvania Archaeology Month, is a founding member of SAA's Public Education Committee, and has for several years served as Network Coordinator for all of North America. She is associate director of Archaeological Services and assistant professor of anthropology at Indiana University of Pennsylvania

BONNIE L. CHRISTENSEN is the director of Public Education for Mississippi Valley Archaeology Center (MVAC) at the University of Wisconsin-La Crosse. She is a Wisconsin-certified precollegiate instructor and has been involved in precollegiate education for the past twenty-five years. As a staff member of MVAC, she has participated in all phases of laboratory and field work. She is an associate member of the UW-La Crosse graduate faculty and teaches classes on archaeology for precollegiate instructors. She serves on the SAA's Public Education Committee and Formal Education Subcommittee and has served on the State Historical Society of Wisconsin's Office of School Services Advisory Committee. Bonnie has written several articles on archaeology education for archaeological and educational journals and has edited a double issue of *Public Archaeology Review.*

JOËLLE CLARK is an archaeologist and educator at Northern Arizona University, Flagstaff. She has designed and taught informal science curricula and professional development programs with teachers, archaeologists, and students of all ages. She is currently on the executive committee of the Arizona Archaeological Council and was chair of its Archaeology for Educators Committee. She is chair of the Society for American Archaeology Public Education Committee Electronic Communications Subcommittee.

ELIZABETH ANDERSON COMER, principal of EAC/A (a cultural resources consulting firm specializing in archaeology and public interpretation), is an archaeologist, cultural resource manager, and tourism expert. She was the first Baltimore City archaeologist and director of the Baltimore Center for Urban Archaeology, developing a public archaeology program that is recognized worldwide. For eight years, she served in various positions for the State of Maryland's Office of Tourism Development. She teaches at the University of Maryland College Park in the Historic Preservation Program and is the UNESCO Chief technical adviser for public archaeology programs in the Asian region.

MARJORIE CONNOLLY has a B.A. in anthropology and an M.A. in education. She has conducted archaeological fieldwork and educational programs and has collected oral histories in Alaska and the Southwest. Marjorie is currently assistant director of education and Native American Activities Coordinator at Crow Canyon Archaeological Center.

M. ELAINE DAVIS received her Ph.D. from the University of North Carolina at Chapel Hill in social foundations of education, with a minor in anthropology. She has fourteen years of experience as a classroom teacher and has been active in archaeology education for the last eight years, designing and conducting programs for teachers and elementary school students. Her research interests center around issues of constructivisim in social education; she is now involved in studies of how children construct the past and conceptualize culture. Elaine is director of education at Crow Canyon Archaeological Center in Cortez, Colorado.

CAROL J. ELLICK has a B.A. in anthropology and an M.A. in education. She has been active in the development of public archaeological programs since 1987. Carol joined Statistical Research, Inc. in 1989, and has been director of the Public Programs Division since its inception in 1994. She is an active member of the Society for American Archaeology Public Education Committee; past chair of the Arizona Archaeological Council, Archaeology for Educators Committee; and currently president of the Arizona Archaeological Council.

ED FRIEDMAN (Ph.D., Washington State University, 1976) has been with the Department of the Interior for nineteen years, and has served as federal preservation officer for sixteen of those years. He has worked for the U.S. Geological Survey, the Minerals Management Service, and the Bureau of Reclamation. Affectionately known as "Public Ed," Friedman was founding chair of the SAA's Public Education Committee, and between 1990 and 1997 worked hard to establish what has become the largest and one of the most productive committees within that organization. Ed has received many awards for his excellent service to archaeology and education. Some of these include: Presidential Recognition Award (SAA, 1998); Department of the Interior Superior Service Award (1996); Bureau of Reclamation Exceptional Performance Award (1991–1995); Bureau of Reclamation Resource Management Award (1994); Society for American Archaeology Presidential Recognition Award (1994); Colorado Archaeological Society Exceptional and Sustained Award (1993);

Colorado Historical Society Stephen H. Hart Award (1992); and Colorado Archae-ological Society Advancement of Archaeology Award (1990).

NORMAN R. FROST has been an outdoor environmental education teacher at the Boyne River Natural Science School near Shelburne, Ontario, Canada, for the past twenty years, and is now coordinator in Outdoor Education for the Toronto District School Board. As director of the Council of Outdoor Educators of Ontario, Norm advises the provincial government on the integration of environmental education into a new subject area, "Interdisciplinary Studies." He is past president of the Ontario Recrea-tional Canoeing Association, an executive of the Niagara Escarpment Biosphere Reserve Studies project that involves students in the UNESCO environmental monitoring protocol, TreeWatch, and an advocate of sustainable living systems, particularly the use of solar aquatic technologies for the treatment of waste water.

VICTOR W. GERACI taught social studies in grades K–12 for over twenty years and presently is assistant professor of history at Central Connecticut State University. He received his Ph.D. in history in 1997 from the University of California at Santa Barbara, where he also served as a lecturer, student teacher supervisor, and academic coordinator in the Graduate School of Education. As a public historian, Victor actively pursues multidisciplinary projects with his students that bring local and regional history to secondary teachers and their students.

NANCY J. HAWKINS received her B.S. from Southern Methodist University, Dallas, Texas, and an M.A. from Colorado State University, Fort Collins, both in anthro-pology. She is an archaeologist for the Louisiana Division of Archaeology and has served as outreach coordinator there since 1981. In that capacity, she has developed exhibits, prepared audiovisual materials, written and edited booklets, organized Louisiana Archaeology Week, developed archaeology materials for teachers, and led teachers' workshops. She also coordinates the regional and state archaeology programs, which enhance identification, preservation, and public interpretation of Louisiana's archaeological sites.

EMILY JOHNSON received her B.S. in education from the University of Wisconsin-Stevens Point, her M.Ed. from the University of Minnesota in Early Childhood Education, and her Ph.D. from the University of Wisconsin-Madison in Child and Family Studies. Her research interests include parent-child relationships and children and adolescents. She has taught at the preschool and elementary school levels and at Ohio State University. Emily is assistant professor in the Department of Psychology at the University of Wisconsin-La Crosse where she teaches many of the human development courses.

DOROTHY SCHLOTTHAUER KRASS served as manager of public education programs for the Society for American Archaeology from 1995 to 1999, and has been a member of SAA's Public Education Committee since 1990. She was the director of education and outreach for University of Massachusetts Archaeological Services from 1990 to 1994, and is currently chair of the Committee on Teaching Anthropology of the General Anthropology Division of the American Anthropological Association, and SAA's state archaeology education coordinator for Washington, D.C. Her anthropological research has centered on hunters and gatherers in Scandinavia during the Mesolithic, Native Peoples in New England since the sixteenth century, and high-school teachers and their understanding of archaeology. Dorothy received her Ph.D. in anthropology from the University of Massachusetts, Amherst, in 1995.

ALANA KUPERSTEIN is currently museum editor for internship programs at the Museum of Jewish Heritage—A Living Memorial to the Holocaust, New York City, where she coordinates programs that engage students of all ages in studies of the Holocaust, Jewish culture, and museum education. After completing her undergraduate studies at Duke University (Cultural Anthropology and French), Alana pursued her Master's degree at George Washington University (Anthropology and Museum Studies). In addition to being a teaching assistant for the Anthropology Department, Alana iterned and did independent research with Ruth Selig at the National Museum of Natural History and the National Anthropological Archives of the Smithsonian Institution as part of her program at GW. Her contributions to this text are a direct result of this research.

MARY L. KWAS (M.A., University of Wisconsin-Milwaukee) is an education specialist/ archaeologist with the Arkansas Archeological Survey in Fayetteville. She has served as site manager of Pinson Mounds State Archaeological Area and as curator of education at the C.H. Nash Museum-Chucalissa, both archaeological parks in Tennessee.

JOANNE LEA holds degrees in both archaeology and education, has served in administrative positions in museum education and interpretation, and also works in the field of professional education. A member of the SAA Public Education Committee, Joanne serves on committees for several archaeological and teaching associations in Canada. As an educational archaeology consultant, she has developed curricula and workshops for several projects, including the national curriculum for the Canadian Archaeological Association.

CATHY MACDONALD was educated at St. Michael's College, the University of Toronto, and at the Ontario Institute for Studies in Education. She earned her M.A. with a thesis on the integration of archaeology into regular school curricula. Currently, she is head of the Social Sciences Department at Fr. Leo J. Austin Catholic Secondary School in Whitby, Ontario, Canada. A founding member of the Public Education Subcommittee, Cathy received an SAA award for her work as education station coordinator for *Archaeology and Public Education*.

FRANCIS P. MCMANAMON (Ph.D., University of New York at Binghamton, 1984) is the chief archaeologist of the National Park Service. He also serves as departmental consulting archaeologist, carrying out responsibilities assigned by several statutes to the Secretary of the Interior. Frank oversees the Archeology and Ethnography Program of the NPS National Center for Cultural Resource Stewardship and Partnerships in Washington, D.C. He has been involved in archaeological investigations in northeastern North America, western Europe, and Micronesia. His areas of professional expertise include: eastern and northeastern North American prehistory, public archaeology and cultural resource management, archaeological education and outreach, and archaeological methods and techniques.

NAN MCNUTT received her B.A. in anthropology and M.Ed. in science curriculum and instruction from the University of Washington. As a teacher of students from the elementary school level through the university level, she nurtures discovery and appreciation of one's own culture as well as others. She is the author of several books on archaeology and Northwest Coast Indians for children and adults). Nan works in close conjunction with Indian educators and artists of Alaska and the Northwest coast, archaeologists and anthropologists, and classroom teachers to produce materials that reflect authenticity of culture and experience. She has also worked with a number of museums, including ten years at the Pacific Science Center.

JEANNE MOE is an archaeologist and educator for the Bureau of Land Management (BLM) in Salt Lake City, Utah. She serves as the National Project Archaeology Coordinator for BLM's Heritage Education Program.

K. ANNE PYBURN has a B.A. from Reed and an M.A. and Ph.D. from Arizona University. She is an associate professor at Indiana University. Anne was director of the Center for Archaeology in the Public Interest (1995–98) and has been director of the Chau Hiix Archaeological Project, Belize from 1989 to the present. She does research on the evolution of social complexity, focusing on reconstruction of ancient Maya communities and settlement in the context of the political economy of modern Belize.

RUTH OSTERWEIS SELIG, anthropologist/administrator/educator, is currently special assistant to the director, National Museum of Natural History, and editor of

AnthroNotes in the Department of Anthropology there. Since completing her formal education in history (Wellesley), social science education (Harvard), and anthropology (George Washington University), and after ten years of teaching history and anthropology in Boston and Washington, D.C., public and private schools, Selig co-directed and directed NSF- and NEH- funded anthropology teacher training programs in Washington, D.C., and Laramie, Wyoming. While holding a number of senior administrative positions at the Smithsonian, she has continued to publish on anthropology and education, co-edit the Smithsonian publication *AnthroNotes, Museum of Natural History Publication for Educators*; and, most recently, with M. R. London, edited *Anthropology Explored: The Best of Smithsonian AnthroNotes* (Smithsonian Institution Press, 1998).

KAROLYN SMARDZ is currently doing her doctorate at the University of Waterloo on the history of race and slavery. She has devoted her career to public and educational archaeology, most often working on historic sites. In 1985, she and her colleague, Peter Hamalainen, founded the Archaeological Resource Centre in Toronto, and she later developed public programs for the Institute for Minnesota Archaeology. Internationally noted as a public heritage consultant, speaker, and writer, Karolyn is especially concerned with the role archaeology education can play in developing intercultural tolerance and understanding in today's global village. She conducts research in underground railroad history.

KC SMITH is a program supervisor with the Museum of Florida History in Tallahassee, and is responsible for the development of educational materials and programs dealing with history, archaeology, and folklife. A participant on shipwreck projects since 1973, she specializes in precollegiate resources that pertain to maritime history and underwater archaeology. She coedits the PEC newsletter, *Archaeology and Public Education,* and chairs the PEC Education Resource Forum Subcommittee.

SHELLEY J. SMITH has a B.A. from Pennsylvania State University and an M.A. from Washington State University, both in anthropology. She is chief of the Environmental and Planning Branch in the Bureau of Land Management, Utah State office. Shelley directed the development of the Intrigue of the Past Archaeology Education program and has written numerous articles and papers on archaeology and environmental education She is vice-chair of the SAA's Public Education Committee.

PETER STONE is internationally known as a leader in archaeology and education. After teaching history in secondary school and working as an archaeologist, he completed his Ph.D. on the teaching of the past in English primary education, with special reference to prehistory. He managed the Archaeology and Education Project at the University of Southampton for three years before joining English Heritage, where he worked for the next ten years—mainly within the Education Service. He now lectures in heritage education and presentations at the University of Newcastle, U.K. He is the chief executive officer of the World Archaeological Congress. He has published widely on heritage education and interpretation.

STUART STRUEVER is former professor of archaeology at Northwestern University and past president of the Society for American Archaeology. He is the founder of the Center for American Archaeology at Kampsville, Illinois. There he launched his first experiential education program with junior and senior high school students in 1970 in association with the excavation of Koster and other prehistoric sites. Dr. Struever founded Crow Canyon Archaeological Center in southwestern Colorado in 1982, where some 3,500 students and lay adults participate in archaeological education programs each year.

CEIL LEEPER STURDEVANT has a B.S. in Art Education and Elementary Education from Westminister College and an M.Ed. from the University of Pittsburgh. In collaboration with Ellen Bedell, she has presented papers and workshops at the National Council for the Social Studies and the Society for American Archaeology on simulated excavations, the National Conference for Education on the Ceramic Art on the combination of art and archaeology in simulated excavations, and the Maya Weekend sponsored by the University Museum in Philadelphia. She is a noted ceramic sculptor and art teacher at the Ellis School in Pittsburgh, Pennsylvania.

PATRICIA (PAM) WHEAT received her B.A. and M.A. from the University of Texas-Austin, and has taught history to students from kindergarten through college. She has worked in a variety of senior capacities, combining her skills in archaeology and professional education. Pam served as president of the Houston Council for Social Studies, as president of the Texas Archeological Society in 1991–92, and as chair of the Heritage Education Committee for the Greater Houston Preservation Alliance. She is also a long-term member of the SAA Public Education Committee. Her publications include many articles as well as a book entitled *Clues from the Past: A Resource Book on Archeology* (Hendrick-Long Publishing Co., Dallas, 1990.). She has curated several exhibits, including Houston Underground, Dig It, and Archeology in Texas. Wheat was director of education at Crow Canyon Archaeological Center in Cortez, Colorado, before joining the Texas Historical Commission, and now is director of education for the Houston Museum of Natural Science.

NANCY MARIE WHITE received a Ph.D. from Case Western Reserve University and is an associate professor of anthropology at the University of South Florida in Tampa, where she teaches in the Public Archaeology graduate program. Her professional interests include New World prehistory, gender studies in archaeology, and public archaeology. Currently, she conducts a field research program investigating the prehistory of northwest Florida's Apalachicola River Valley.

MARTHA WILLIAMS holds advanced degrees in education (M.Ed. 1965, University of Pennsylvania) and in applied history (M.A. 1987, George Mason University). She has been a secondary school social studies classroom teacher for twenty-seven years and also organized and managed fifteen summer seminars in historical archaeology for high school students in the Fairfax County (Virginia) public schools. A principal organizer of the Public Education Committee for the Society for Historical Archaeology, Martha Williams continues to plan and implement public outreach activities in her position as project manager and historical archaeologist with R. Christopher Goodwin & Associates, Inc.

RENATA B. WOLYNEC (Ph.D., Northwestern University, 1977) is professor of anthropology at Edinboro University of Pennsylvania, where she has been on the faculty since 1973. She has been active on national, state, and local levels in the development of archaeology education opportunities; has directed the Fort LeBoeuf Museum since 1982; and has been chair and co-chair of the Pennsylvania Archaeological Council Education Committee since 1991. As a member of the SAA Public Relations committee, she was responsible for the initial stages of development of a public information referral network for the SAA.

Subject Index

The following typographical conventions are used in the index: *f* denotes figures; *p* denotes photographs; *t* denotes tables.

role in teaching moral reasoning, 259–260
role in teaching values, 254, 275
see also Crow Canyon
public archaeology excavation (sample)
    donor support for, 294
    maintaining long-term interest in, 297–300
    promoting, 292–293*p*, 294, 295*p*
    site selection, 289
    use of the media to promote, 292–293*p*, 296, 298*p*
    volunteers in, 290–291*p*, 292, 294, 29*p*, 296, 297
public archaeology graduate students
    importance of writing skills for, 337
    interacting with schoolteachers, 333–334
    museum training, 337–338
    teaching techniques for schoolchildren, 331–333, 336*p*
    teaching techniques for the general public, 331
Public Education Committee (PEC) (SAA), 13–16, 156, 165–166, 167, 287

Reasoning
    abstract, 88, 89
    empirico-inductive, 88
    hypothetical-deductive, 88
    moral, 78–79, 251–252, 259–260
Redford, Robert, 254
regional archaeology programs, long-term
    advantages of, 354
    building, 359–362
    challenges to, 354
    components of, suggested, 355–359
reliability, 196
religion, and archaeology, 270–271
research, archaeological, 302
    funding, 302–303, 309–310, 311
Roberts, L. C., 317
role models, 255
Ruskin, J., 393

SfAA, *see* Society for American Archaeology
SACC, *see* Society for Anthropology in Community Colleges, The
safety, student, 47, 109, 242, 243, 244
Sakof, M., 269
sample
    simulated excavation site report, 230*f*
samples
    activity sheet, 127
    archaeological park programs, 350

archaeology lessons (K-12), 82–83
artifact card, 126
artifact identification form, 229*f*
basic concepts for presentations, 187–188
educational technology in archaeology education, 176–178
excavation in context of archaeological process, 188–189
lesson plan, 124–125
moral dilemma and archaeology, 259–260
museum education program outline, 326
museum visitor survey, 199
plan for education assessment, 195–203
presentation for special-needs children, 109–110
presentations, 189–190
simulated excavation student job descriptions, 224*f*
simulated excavation site form, 226*f*
simulated student site report, 230*f*
student job descriptions, 224*f*
student simulated excavation, 220–230
teaching archaeology with educational technology, 176–177*t*
using Gardner's seven intelligences, 99–100
scaffolding, 75, 85, 186
Schaefer, William Donald, 288, 299*p*
school districts, U.S., 44
science, 276
    fit with archaeology, 119, 120, 124–125, 275, 396–397
    standards and archaeology, 62, 67–69, 147
    use of archaeology to teach values in, 258–259
Science Teachers' Association of Ontario, The, 155, 160
scripts, 77–78
Selby, D., 390
Selman, Robert, 80
sensorimotor child, 73–74
shared understanding, *see* intersubjectivity
Silent Spring, The, 379
site designation, Smithsonian code for, 225
site management teams, U.S., 44
skills, 122
Smithsonian Institution, 157–158, 163
    code for site designation, 225
Social Education, 154
social studies
    fit with archaeology, 22, 119, 124–125, 154
    standards, and archaeology, 61
    as venue for character education, 61

Washington Post, 134
Web sites
  American Anthropological Association, 162
  Anthropology Explored: The Best of Smithsonian AnthroNotes, 163
  Archaeological Institute of America, 161
  British Columbia Teachers' Association, 160
  Canadian Archaeological Association, 162
  Centre for the Study of Curriculum and Instruction, The, 159
  Cobblestone: The History Magazine for Young People, 161
  Developing Educational Standards, 63
  Faces: The Magazine About People, 161
  Head-Smashed-In-Buffalo-Jump, 163
  Mississippi Valley Archaeology Center, 161
  museums, 163
  National Council for the Social Studies (NCSS), 14
  National Education Association, 154
  National Science Teachers' Association, 159
  Project Archaeology, 150
  Social Sciences Department, The Ellis School, 161
  Social Studies, The, 160
  Society for American Archaeology, 13
  Society for Historical Archaeology, 161
  Strategic Plan, of PEC, 14
  Teachers' Packet in Anthropology, 163
  Teaching Professor, The, 160
  UNESCO, 391
  World Heritage, 391
Western Beaver School District simulated excavation, 220–221
Western Regional Environmental Education Council (WREEC), 380
White, Nancy, 280, 285–286
White, Patricia, 256
women's history, 55
wokshops, used to teach archaeology to educators, 146–147, 149
World Heritage Convention (UNESCO), 391
World Heritage List, inclusion criteria, 392–393
World Heritage Sites, 157, 374, 390
World Wide Web, 180
World Wide Web browser, 180
WREEC, *see* Western Regional Environmental Education Council
WWW, 180

Zone of proximal development, 75–76, 85, 86
Zorpette, G., 324

Author Index